Environmental Communication
and the Public Sphere

For Julia
And others working for an environmentally
just and sustainable world

Environmental Communication
and the Public Sphere

Robert Cox
University of North Carolina at Chapel Hill

SAGE Publications
Thousand Oaks ▪ London ▪ New Delhi

For information:

Sage Publications, Inc.
2455 Teller Road
Thousand Oaks, California 91320
E-mail: order@sagepub.com

Sage Publications Ltd
1 Oliver's Yard
55 City Road
London EC1Y 1SP
United Kingdom

Sage Publications India Pvt. Ltd.
B-42, Panchsheel Enclave
Post Box 4109
New Delhi 110 017 India

Printed in the United States of America

Library of Congress Cataloging-in-Publication Data

Cox, Robert.
Environmental communication and the public sphere / Robert Cox.
    p. cm.
Includes bibliographical references and index.
ISBN 0-7619-3049-3 (cloth) — ISBN 0-7619-3050-7 (pbk.)
    1. Communication in the environmental sciences—Textbooks.
2. Mass media and the environment—Textbooks. I. Title
GE25.C69 2006
333.72′01′4—dc22   2005024700

This book is printed on acid-free paper.

06   07   08   09   10   9   8   7   6   5   4   3   2   1

Acquisitions Editor:	Todd R. Armstrong
Editorial Assistant:	Deya Saoud
Production Editor:	Astrid Virding
Copy Editor:	April Wells-Hayes
Typesetter:	C&M Digitals (P) Ltd.
Proofreader:	Katherine Pollock
Indexer:	Julie Grayson
Cover Designer:	Janet Foulger

Contents

Acknowledgments

Environmental communication draws from many fields, and a book claiming to introduce this area could not have been written without the help of numerous individuals. The idea for the book came initially from Todd Armstrong, my editor at Sage Publications, without whose vision and encouragement this project would never have been completed. And along the way, my friend Robert Newman's sense of urgency about the fate of our world remained a source of inspiration.

I am especially appreciative of colleagues who took the time to comment extensively on earlier drafts and whose counsel aided me more than I can express here. In particular, I want to thank Steve DePoe and Phaedra Pezzullo, who again and again provided assistance and suggestions throughout the writing of this book. I also am indebted to Kevin DeLuca, Dennis Jaehne, Tarla Rai Peterson, Steve Schwarze, and Sue Senecah for their invaluable help in many sections of the book. I am indebted to Paul Mohai for his helpful advice on environmental journalism and opinion research. In addition, I thank the Institute for the Arts and Humanities at the University of North Carolina for its generous provision of a Chapman Fellowship, which enabled me to take a leave of absence from my teaching duties at an early phase in this project.

The following reviewers are greatly acknowledged: Terence Check, St. John's University; Helen M. Correll, Metropolitan State University; Kevin DeLuca, University of Georgia; Steve Depoe, University of Cincinnati; Adrian Ivakhiv, University of Vermont; Dennis Jaehne, San Jose State University; Jennifer A. Peeples, Utah State University; Tarla Rai Peterson, University of Utah; Phaedra Pezzullo, Indiana University; Steve Schwarze, University of Montana; Susan L. Senecah, The State University of New York College of Environmental Science and Forestry; and Christina Zarcadoolas, Brown University.

Many other colleagues in the academy and the U.S. environmental movement responded to pleas for help, provided materials, and gently pointed out omissions and errors in earlier drafts. In particular, I thank Bill Balthrop, my chair at the University of North Carolina at Chapel Hill, for support enabling me to complete this project. My appreciation also goes to Marcus Peterson, Jonathan Riehl, Eric Schulzke, Caitlin Wills Toker, Gregg Walker, and Steve Wing, as well my colleagues at the Sierra Club who have been gracious as always in their help. In particular, my thanks to colleagues there go to John Barry, Andy Bessler, Bob Bingaman, Kim Haddow, Bruce Hamilton, Joan Hamilton, Cindy King, Lawson Legate, Michael McCloskey, Steve Mills, Carl Pope, and Debbie Sease. I benefited as well from the thoughtful suggestions and help of many students in my environmental communication classes and the Ecology Curriculum at UNC, including Charles Anderson, Shelly Bibb, James Carsten, Jenna Cramer, Gabriel Cumming, Ginny Franks, Andrew George, David Havlick, Ian Kibbe, Diana Knott, Elizabeth Markovits, Barbara Miller, Carla Norwood, Mary O'Connor, Elizabeth Selig, Elizabeth Veazey, Brooke Wheeler, and many others whom I surely have overlooked. Special thanks go to Adrian Van Dellen, Ned Stone, Peggie Griffin, Brenda Ivey, and Natalie Foster for allowing us to use their photos on the cover. At Sage Publications, my thanks go to Deya Saoud for her generous help as senior editorial assistant throughout the writing process, and also to Astrid Virding's skillful work as project editor, and to April Wells-Hayes, whose discerning eye as copy editor saved me from many stumbles in the text. Although I have benefited from the suggestions and help of many, I am clearly responsible for any errors that have found their way into the text.

I have drawn also on my own and co-authored work in a couple of cases. In particular, I am indebted to Phaedra Pezzullo of Indiana University for permission to cite material in Chapter 8 from our unpublished paper, "Re-Articulating 'Environment': Rhetorical Invention, Subaltern Counterpublics, and the Movement for Environmental Justice" (2001). Also in Chapter 8, portions of the St. James Parish case study and analysis of the indecorous voice are drawn from a paper I presented at the Fifth Biennial Conference on Communication and Environment (Cox, 2001).

Finally, it is surely an understatement to say that this project would never have seen the light of day without the counsel and encouragement of my partner and colleague, Julia Wood, to whom I dedicate this book.

Introduction

Speaking for the
Environment—For Ourselves

A book on environmental *communication?* With news reports of global warming, toxic chemical spills, and the destruction of tropical rain forests, why should you read a textbook about communication? Wouldn't it make more sense to read about how we can prevent environmental disasters from happening in the first place?

Legendary environmentalist David Brower, whom nature writer John McPhee (1971) called the "Archdruid," once told me, "We're fiddling while the earth burns. We need to *act!*" At the time—1995—I had taken a leave of absence from the University of North Carolina at Chapel Hill to serve as president of the Sierra Club, one of the largest environmental organizations in the United States. During lunch at one of David's favorite cafés in San Francisco, I asked him, "What should the Sierra Club be doing at a time when the U.S. Congress is trying to reverse years of environmental law?" As usual, David was ready with ideas, but he also replied quietly, "Explain to the American public what's happening. *Talk* to them."

David's advice returned me to my research as a communication scholar who studies social movements and the dynamics of social change in the United States. In fact, history remembers David Brower himself as a pioneer in communicating to public audiences about human threats to wild places. As one of the most innovative leaders of the modern environmental movement, David took out bold, full-page ads in the *New York Times* and the *Los Angeles Times* that successfully rallied the public to stop the construction of two proposed dams in the Grand Canyon. He introduced exhibit-format books of stunning nature photography, such as *In Wildness Is the Preservation of the World* (Porter, 1964), and captured the wild beauty of Glen Canyon on film, documenting this once-wild canyon in southern Utah (now dammed and flooded). He never separated his sense of urgency about a problem from the need to communicate urgently to others. Indeed, David's genius was to realize that somebody must speak for nature and rally others to add their own voices on behalf of threatened forests, wild rivers, and the wildlife they sustain.

Communication and Nature's Meaning

David Brower was a powerful advocate for the environment. But not everyone sees herself or himself as an environmental advocate or an environmental communication professional such as journalist, filmmaker, lobbyist, or science educator. Some of you may be reading this book simply to learn more about environmental issues. Yet, it is impossible to separate our knowledge about environmental issues from communication itself. As environmental communication scholars James Cantrill and Christine Oravec (1996) make clear, the "environment we experience and affect is largely a product of how we come to talk about the world" (p. 2). That is, *the way we communicate with one another about the environment powerfully affects how we perceive both it and ourselves and, therefore, how we define our relationship with the natural world.*

Each of us is already enmeshed in many environments: a house or apartment, a workplace, a favorite camping site in a national forest, a congested daily commute to campus. And all of us probably have searched for the words to describe our experience of such places: "I feel peaceful when I'm walking along the bay," or "I worry about my kids peeling paint off the walls in my old apartment building," or (often) "There's too much smoke in this bar!" For his part, Harvard University scientist E. O. Wilson (2002) uses the language of biology to describe the environment as "a membrane of organisms wrapped around Earth so thin it cannot be seen edgewise from a space shuttle, yet so internally complex that most species composing it remain undiscovered" (p. 3). On the other hand, a second-generation logger in the Pacific Northwest may see old-growth forests not through the metaphor of a membrane but as a source of employment. Both scientist and logger may look at the same environment but see it quite differently and thus hold different opinions about the need to protect a fragile habitat or to develop its resources.

The images and information we receive from friends, popular films, the news media, and books play a powerful role in influencing not only how we perceive the environment but also what actions we take. A riveting example occurred several years ago, when an undercover video taken aboard a foreign fishing trawler showed dolphins trapped in nets as deckhands dragged large catches of tuna aboard. The images of dolphins struggling and dying on the decks of these trawlers led to a popular outcry for labels certifying "dolphin safe" on cans of tuna sold in the United States. In another case, after September 11, 2001, President George W. Bush used patriotic vocabulary calling for "energy independence" in the United States to build support for oil drilling on public wild lands in Western states. And at the start of a modern ecology era, biologist Rachel Carson (1962) aroused national concern over chemical poisoning of the environment in her best-selling book *Silent Spring*.

Deciding what action society should take toward the natural world is not automatically given to us. On the one hand, nature is far from silent—indeed, it can be rather noisy. The world of animals includes rich networks of intraspecies communication, and, as I'll describe in Chapter 2, visual arts such as painting and photography open worlds of information and insight about nature to those paying attention. Yet, in one important sense, the natural world is silent. Not dolphins nor caribou nor future generations speak to humans directly of their concerns. Although the images of dolphins thrashing on the deck of a fishing trawler certainly communicate, we encounter these images through the labor of others—filmmakers, reporters, environmental activists—who focus our attention in dramatic ways. Indeed, it is scientists, EPA officials, environmental advocates, business lobbyists, and ordinary citizens who debate the meaning of environmental questions. For example, can the United States meet its energy needs through greater conservation, or must it drill for oil in the Arctic National Wildlife Refuge? Is it safe for the U.S. Army to burn stores of chemical weapons near schools and residential neighborhoods? Is it our role as humans to subdue the earth, to use its resources wisely, or to respect the values of nature in their own right? In engaging such questions, we rely on speech, symbols, art, persuasion, and debate to imagine, describe, dispute, and celebrate our multiple relations with the natural world.

That's one reason I wrote this book: I believe that communication about the environment matters. It matters in the naming of the conditions that we take to be problems, but it also matters in the ways we interact with our communities, our workplaces, and the natural world. And it matters ultimately in the choices we make about the policies business and government adopt toward the environment. This book, therefore, focuses on the role of communication—from advocacy campaigns and news programs to citizen testimony at public hearings—in helping us negotiate the relationship

Figure 1   A dead dolphin bearing the scars of a final struggle in large
fishing nets

(© Greenpeace / Steve Morgan)

between ourselves and the thin "membrane of organisms" that makes up
our environment. As environmental communication scholar James Cantrill
(1993) has reminded us, "If we wish to assist those who advocate environmental policy, we must attend to the myriad ways in which people make
sense out of environmental discourse itself" (p. 68).

The purpose of *Environmental Communication and the Public Sphere* is
threefold: (1) to increase your insight into how communication shapes our
perceptions of environmental issues; (2) to acquaint you with some of the
media and public forums that are used for environmental communication,
along with the communication practices of ordinary citizens, scientists, corporate lobbyists, and others who seek to influence decisions about nature
and the human environment; and (3) to enable you to join in conversations
and debates that are already taking place both locally and globally that may
affect the environments where you yourself live, study, work, and play.

Speaking for the Environment—For Ourselves[1]

At first glance, there appears to be little need for persuasion and debate
about environmental issues. Since the first Earth Day in 1970, U.S. opinion

polls have reported that the public is concerned about environmental problems and strongly supports environmental values. On the 30th anniversary of Earth Day, a Gallup poll found that 83 percent of Americans "readily agreed with the broadest goals of the environmental movement" (Guber, 2003, p. 3).

Such support for environmental values is not surprising. Marine sciences professor Willett Kempton, along with anthropologists James S. Boster, and Jennifer A. Hartley (1996) found that "most Americans share a common set of environmental beliefs and values" (p. 211). They found that even radically divergent groups in U.S. society shared more agreement than one might expect. For example, workers who had been laid off from lumber sawmills in the Pacific Northwest and members of the radical environmental group Earth First! agreed on a range of questions about what they valued. More than two-thirds of respondents from the two groups agreed with such statements as

- "We have to protect the environment for our children and for our grandchildren, even if it means reducing our standard of living today.
- We have a moral duty to leave the earth in as good or better shape than we found it. . . .
- The reason politicians break their promises to the people to clean up our environment is the power of industry lobbyists." (pp. 204–205)

Although the public's concern for the environment is significant, considerable differences exist among individuals over how society should solve environmental problems. A good example is global warming. A poll conducted by the World Wildlife Fund found that 74 percent of the public felt that the problem of warming of the earth's atmosphere was either "somewhat serious" or "extremely serious." Differences were revealed, however, when people were asked what actions the United States should take to reduce the major cause of global warming: "Do you think we should rely mainly on strict regulations to limit emissions of carbon dioxide, or do you think we should rely mainly on incentives that cause the free market to discourage carbon dioxide pollution?" Respondents were split almost evenly between those who favored government regulation (37%), those who supported free market options (32%), and those who felt they lacked enough information to choose (30%) (Guber, 2003, pp. 30–31).

The complexity of issues such as global warming makes the finding of a public consensus difficult. And as the different voices of scientists, the Business Roundtable (a corporate lobbying group), and environmental groups such as Greenpeace and the Sierra Club enter the public debate, widely divergent viewpoints compete for our support.

There exists, then, a dilemma. Although nature is silent, others—politicians, business leaders, environmentalists, the media—claim the right to speak for nature, or for their interests in the use and value of natural resources. Hence, the dilemma: If nature cannot speak, who has the right to speak on nature's behalf? Who should define the interests of society in relation to the natural world? Is it right, for example, to drill for oil in fragile wilderness areas? Should it be the businesses that pollute or the taxpayers who bear the cost of cleaning up abandoned toxic waste sites? Who should decide what restrictions should be placed on logging in the national forests—the U.S. Forest Service, timber-dependent communities, or the broader public? These questions illustrate the rhetorical nature of environmental communication. Only in a society that allows public debate can the public mediate among the differing voices and ways of understanding the environment–society relationship. That is one of my purposes in writing this book: I believe that you, I, and everyone we know have a pivotal role in speaking about these larger environmental issues.

Background and Perspective of the Author

After inviting you to join in conversations about the environment, perhaps it's time I described myself and my own involvement in the field. In recent years, I have been involved in a leadership role in the environmental movement while also teaching as a communication professor at the University of North Carolina at Chapel Hill. From 1994 to 1996, and again from 2000 to 2001, I served as president of the national Sierra Club, based in San Francisco. I continue to serve on its board of directors and am also an adviser to its media and public communication campaigns.

However, my interest in the environment arose long before I had heard of the Sierra Club. As a boy growing up in the Appalachian region of southern West Virginia, I fell in love with the wild beauty of the mountains near my home and the graceful flow of the Greenbrier River. However, as I grew older, I saw coal mining's devastating effects on the natural landscape and on the streams and water supplies of local communities. The awful curse of black lung disease also placed hardship on coal miners and their families. Later, in graduate school in Pittsburgh, I saw the health effects of air pollution from steel mills, and I began to realize how intimately people and their environments are bound together. Human beings and nature do not stand apart from each other.

As a professor at the University of North Carolina at Chapel Hill, I began to volunteer with environmental groups. Although I was motivated initially by my personal experiences, I soon became aware of the essential role of communication in the work of these organizations as they sought to educate public audiences and policymakers. I would also spend most of my time as president of the Sierra Club communicating with the public in some form: briefing newspaper editorial boards, testifying before Congress, speaking at public rallies, organizing in communities, talking with reporters, and helping to design elements of advocacy campaigns.

As a result of these experiences and also as a result of my own research and teaching in environmental communication, I've become more firmly persuaded of several things:

1. Individuals and communities have a stronger chance to safeguard the environmental health and quality of their local environments if they understand some of the dynamics of and opportunities for communication about their concerns.

2. Neither environmental issues nor public agencies need to remain mysterious, remote, complex, or impenetrable. The environmental movement, legal action, and the media have helped to demystify governmental procedures and to open the doors and computer files of government bureaucracies to greater public access and participation in environmental decisions.

3. As a consequence, individuals have opportunities to participate in meaningful ways in public debates about our relationship with our environment. That is why I wrote *Environmental Communication and the Public Sphere*.

One other thing: Largely because of my work in the U.S. environmental movement, I cannot avoid a personal perspective on many of the issues discussed in this book, nor do I wish to. In this sense, I am clearly biased in favor of environmental values and certain approaches to environmental protection. I will, however, do three things as I develop the topics in this book. First, when I introduce views or positions, I'll try to acknowledge any bias or personal experience that I might have. Second, I'll explain how I arrived at my perspective, based on my experience and my knowledge or research.

Finally, I'll include a brief "Another Viewpoint" in some chapters to alert you to important disagreements or debates. For example, because I believe that states and the federal government have an important role to play in protecting the environment, I'll also refer you to sources that favor a private-sector or market approach. (See "Another Viewpoint: Green Conservatism" as an example.) My aim is not to set up false dichotomies but to introduce a multiplicity of perspectives. I'll also refer you to sources and URLs that challenge my own stance to allow you to learn about other views.

Another Viewpoint: Green Conservatism

In proposing what he calls a "conservative" approach to protecting the environment, communication scholar John Bliese (2001) calls for the prudent use of the free market instead of government regulations:

> In sum, the proper role for conservatives is to use the market where it would work to protect the environment, as opposed to the liberals' penchant for command-and-control regulation, and to restrain the market where it would degrade the environment, as opposed to the libertarians' penchant for sacrificing anything that cannot be turned to profit. . . . By making use of market-based mechanisms, tempered by the basic virtues of piety and prudence, conservatives could have the best policies for a much cleaner environment, a more efficient system with equitable assignment of costs ('the polluter pays'), sustainable use of natural resources, and a much better quality of life for ourselves and for countless generations to come.

SOURCE: John R.E. Bliese, *The Greening of Conservative America* (Boulder, CO: Westview, 2001), p. 261.

For a major environmental organization that favors the use of market approaches in protecting the environment, check out the group Environmental Defense at www.environmentaldefense.org.

Distinctive Features of the Book

As its title suggests, the framework for *Environmental Communication and the Public Sphere* is organized around two core concepts:

- The importance of human communication in shaping our perceptions of the environment and our relationships with it
- The role of the public sphere in mediating or negotiating among the different voices seeking to influence decisions and the environment

I'll use the idea of the **public sphere** throughout this book to refer to the realm of influence that is created when individuals engage others in communication—through conversation, argument, debate, and questions—about subjects of shared concern or topics that affect a wider community.

Nor is communication limited to words: Visual and nonverbal symbolic actions such as sit-ins, Greenpeace banners, and a two-year-long tree sit by the young Earth First! volunteer Julia "Butterfly" Hill[2] have prompted discussion, debate, and questioning of environmental policy as readily as editorials, speeches, and TV newscasts.

Along with the focus on human communication and the public sphere, this book includes several distinctive features:

1. A survey of the legal rights of ordinary citizens—and practical ways in which they can participate publicly—in influencing the decisions of governmental agencies that affect the environment

2. Attention to new media (Internet) as well as other important but less-studied forms of environmental communication such as citizen lawsuits, collaborative partnerships, corporate green marketing, and the advocacy campaigns of environmental groups

3. A focus on theories of media effects of news and advertising about the environment

4. Inclusion of the voices of scientists, journalists, and business lobbyists, as well as voices from the grassroots movement for environmental justice

5. Discussion of post-9/11 challenges to the public's access to information and participation in environmental decision making on the basis of national security

6. Use of personal experiences and cases studies in the U.S. environmental movement to illustrate key points about advocacy campaigns, the media, and barriers to community involvement in environmental decisions

7. Emphasis on opportunities to apply your knowledge of the principles of environmental communication on your campus or in your community. You'll find "Act Locally!" exercises in most chapters.

New Terrain/New Questions

I recognize that you probably bring a range of views and assumptions to the subject of the environment and to the study of environmental communication. Some of you may be a little suspicious of environmentalists, perhaps thinking they're somewhat strange (as in the popular image of "tree huggers"). Others of you may hope to work in the environmental field in the future or consider yourselves environmental activists. Many of you—perhaps the majority—may not label yourself environmentalists at all but nevertheless support recycling, clean air, and preserving more green space on your campus. And I suspect that some of you may have questions about your ability to affect any of the big problems, such as global warming, the loss of tropical rain forests, or the safety of genetically modified organisms (GMOs) in our food chain.

In this book, I start at the beginning. I do not assume any special knowledge on your part about environmental science or politics. Nor do I assume that you know about particular theories of communication. For example, I use **boldface** type when I introduce and define an important term. I also include a list of these key terms at the end of each chapter. In some cases, an "FYI" feature provides background information to familiarize you with theories or issues raised in a chapter.

In turn, I hope you'll be open to exploring what might be a new perspective: the role of human communication in shaping how we understand and respond to environmental problems. One goal of this book is to suggest new possibilities for you in joining the ongoing conversations about environmental problems, as well as ways to be more effective in voicing your own concerns and effecting change.

I also hope you'll seriously reflect on material that may challenge your own assumptions or views, not only about environmentalists but also about the roles of science, the news media, television programming, corporations, and environmental groups in constructing our views of nature and the environment. For example, a common misconception is that people who espouse environmental values are an elite group, that they want to "turn back the clock" to an earlier, romanticized past (Hays, 2000, p. 23). Yet, there is little support for such views. As we'll see, some of the most environmentally engaged citizens of recent years have been residents of low-income, at-risk communities that are plagued by polluting industries, incinerators, and toxic waste landfills.

In my own work, I've found that debates about environmental concerns have emerged as a kind of crucible for a participatory, democratic culture in the United States. As environmental goals broaden beyond wilderness and wildlife to include urban concerns about pollution and the quality of the places where people live and work, more and more people of diverse backgrounds—university faculty, students, neighborhood activists, scientists, residents of low-income communities, and affluent suburbanites—are increasingly working together to protect the health of their communities as well as the natural world.

Similarly, I want to challenge those of you who may be in environmental organizations or who hope to work in the environmental arena later. Too often, many of us who have been active in this field (and I include myself) assume that most environmental problems are self-evident and that others share our views. A central thesis of this book, however, is that what constitutes a "problem" is itself rhetorically constructed and often fiercely contested by others. For example, a grazing allotment for cattle in the arid West may be seen as ecological degradation by some and as a property right by others, particularly ranchers. This doesn't mean there is no truth in such cases or that it's all relative. As political scientist Deborah Guber (2003) explains, it does mean that if they want to "motivate and mobilize latent support among average Americans, environmentalists need to become more proficient at communicating with the public by first understanding the root of its concerns" (p. 9).

Conclusion

The study of environmental communication invites us to explore new paths and unfamiliar terrain. In some cases, those paths lead to local town hall meetings as citizens voice their concerns over pollution. Other paths will take you inside the advocacy campaign of a Southwest indigenous tribe that sought to protect its sacred lands, or into the 1991 summit of African American, Latino/a, and Native American leaders protesting environmental racism in their communities. Still other paths invite you to request information under the Freedom of Information Act or to call a radio talk show to voice concerns about too many orange or red alerts on bad air days.

In traveling these new paths, we'll look especially for the ways in which language, symbols, discourse, and ideology shape our perceptions of nature and our own relationship with the environment. By becoming aware of some of the dynamics of human communication in constructing our response to environmental problems, we are able to join in public conversations about not only the fate of the earth in the abstract, but the fate of the places where we live, work, and enjoy everyday life.

KEY TERMS

Environmental communication: A study of the ways in which we communicate about the environment, the effects of this communication on our perceptions of both the environment and ourselves, and therefore on our relationship with the natural world. For a formal definition of *environmental communication*, see Chapter 1.

Public sphere: The realm of influence created when individuals engage others in communication—through conversation, argument, debate, questions, and nonverbal acts—about subjects of shared concern or topics that affect a wider community.

DISCUSSION QUESTIONS

1. What comes to mind when you hear the term *environmentalist*? How do friends, family, media, or others use this term? Do you consider yourself to be an environmentalist or an environmental advocate? What do you mean by these terms?

2. Can nature speak? Or is the natural world silent? Can you understand, appreciate, or relate to the natural world without language?

3. Is it necessary for humans to speak for the natural world in order to protect endangered habitats or species? Without communication, what happens to nature?

4. What are some of the urgent environmental problems in your community? In the United States? Around the globe? What changes do you believe you, society, or governmental institutions need to make to protect the natural and human environments?

5. Have you ever spoken publicly about the environment at a town meeting, called in to a radio talk show, participated in an Earth Day event? How did you feel about this experience? What was its impact on you and on others?

REFERENCES

Alston, D. (1990). *We speak for ourselves: Social justice, race, and environment.* Washington, DC: Panos Institute.

Bliese, J. R. E. (2001). *The greening of conservative America.* Boulder, CO: Westview.

Cantrill, J. G. (1993). Communication and our environment: Categorizing research in environmental advocacy. *Journal of Applied Communication Research, 21,* 66–95.

Cantrill, J. G., & Oravec, C. L. (1996). Introduction. In J. G. Cantrill & C. L. Oravec (Eds.), *The symbolic earth: Discourse and our creation of the environment* (pp. 1–8). Lexington: University of Kentucky Press.

Carson, R. (1962). *Silent spring.* Boston: Houghton Mifflin.

Guber, D. L. (2003). *The grassroots of a green revolution: Polling America on the environment.* Cambridge: MIT Press.

Hays, S. P. (2000). *A history of environmental politics since 1945.* Pittsburgh: University of Pittsburgh Press.

Kempton, W., Boster, J. S., & Hartley, J. A. (1996). *Environmental values in American culture.* Cambridge: MIT Press.

McPhee, J. (1971). *Encounters with the archdruid.* New York: Farrar, Straus & Giroux.

Porter, E. (1967, 1974). *In wildness is the preservation of the world*. New York: Sierra Club/Ballantine.

Wilson, E. O. (2002). *The future of life*. New York. Alfred A. Knopf.

NOTES

1. The late civil rights and environmental author and activist Dana Alston (1990) spoke eloquently of the need for people of color to "speak for ourselves" about environmental problems facing communities of color. The phrase has been taken up by others to ensure that their voices will be heard as part of a democratic debate about the environment.

2. Environmental activist Julia "Butterfly" Hill lived for two years on a 200-foot-tall ancient redwood tree named Luna in northern California to protest logging in old-growth redwood forests. Hill's dramatic act involved not only her material act of sitting in Luna but also cell phone calls, messages lowered to others, and e-mail and Web conferencing from her wireless laptop. Her words and action were covered by media throughout the world and sparked discussion and debate in classrooms, cafes, music venues, and the halls of Congress. For more information, see www.circleoflife.org.

PART I

Conceptual Perspectives

1

The Study of Environmental Communication

J ust before sitting down to write this morning, I had a cup of coffee and read the morning newspaper. Its pages were filled with stories related to the environment: Salmon runs are declining on the Columbia and Snake Rivers in Oregon and Washington; university officials in North Carolina evacuated dormitories after discovering mold in the air that could make students sick; oil companies hope to drill in Alaska's Arctic National Wildlife Refuge; and the Environmental Protection Agency's Office of Inspector General reports, "EPA Misled Public on 9/11 Pollution." According to this unsettling story, after the World Trade Center collapsed, the EPA was preparing to warn New York City residents that the air quality at Ground Zero might be too polluted for residents to return to their apartments, but that warning was overruled by the White House (Garrett, 2003, p. A1).

Similar stories about the environment surround us daily. They appear when we tune into the Nature Channel, CNN, or the satirical series *The Simpsons*. We see such stories when we open the *New York Times* or the local newspaper. We find them when we visit websites such as *Environment News Network* (www.enn.com) or *Rachel's Environment & Health News* (www.rachel.org), two popular environmental news websites. Radio talk shows and programs across the country air commentaries about environmental concerns of the day. While National Public Radio's "Living on Earth" reports on efforts to preserve the environment, conservative commentator Rush Limbaugh criticizes environmental "wackos." Media also feature a wide range of environmental topics: hydrogen-powered cars, the effects of genetically altered agriculture on butterflies, proposals to bring back the controversial pesticide DDT to help eradicate mosquitoes carrying the deadly West Nile virus—and the list goes on.

Twenty-five years ago, when I first began my study of environmental communication, the news carried few stories like these. Few courses about the environment existed on campuses. Today, environmental studies programs have become extremely popular; environmental studies is one of the fastest-growing majors for students (Crawford-Brown, 2005, p. B15). The environment is also one of the most important areas of research and employment in this century. And courses in environmental communication are becoming popular on many campuses.

This chapter describes environmental communication as a new, multi-disciplinary field of study. As a growing number of people realize that our understanding of nature and our behavior toward the environment depend not only on ecological sciences but also on public debate, media representations, websites, and even ordinary conversation, courses and research are emerging devoted specifically to environmental communication.

The first section of this chapter defines the term *environmental communication* and identifies the seven principal areas of study in this emerging field. The second section introduces the three themes that constitute the framework of this book: (1) human communication is a form of symbolic action; (2) our beliefs, attitudes, and behaviors relating to nature and environmental problems are mediated or influenced by communication; and (3) the public sphere (or spheres) emerges as a discursive space for communication about the environment. Finally, the third section describes the diverse voices that speak publicly about the environment and whose communication practices we'll study in this book—the voices of local citizens, scientists, public officials, news media, Internet wire services, environmental groups, and corporations.

After reading this chapter, you should understand what environmental communication includes, and you should recognize the range of voices and communication practices through which environmental groups, ordinary citizens, and opponents of environmentalism discuss important questions about the environment. As a result, I hope that you not only will become a more critical consumer of environmental communication but that you also will discover opportunities to add your own voice to this conversation already in progress.

Environmental Communication as an Area of Study

Along with the growth of environmental studies, courses devoted specifically to the role of human communication in environmental affairs also have emerged. These courses study environmental news media, methods of public participation in environmental decisions, the use of environmental rhetoric, risk communication, environmental conflict resolution, advocacy campaigns, "green" marketing, and images of nature in popular culture.

On a practical level, the study of environmental communication prepares you to enter many professional fields. Law firms, governmental agencies, businesses, public relations firms, and nonprofit environmental groups increasingly employ consultants and practitioners in environmental communication. Skills in environmental communication have become vital to a growing number of public and private organizations, from the Society of Environmental Journalists (www.sej.org) to the Environmental Protection Agency.

On a more conceptual level, the study of environmental communication contributes to theories about human communication itself. For example, its focus on the roles of speech, art, symbols, and so forth in defining the human–nature relationship is perhaps the clearest example of the thesis that human communication mediates or negotiates our relations to, and understanding of, the world beyond our minds. Relatedly, the study of environmental communication reminds us of the very material consequences of our communication choices. For example, citizens' comments in public hearings on an air quality permit, or an advocacy campaign to close a hospital waste incinerator—and countless other modes of communication about environmental concerns—contribute to actions that protect, harm, nurture, sustain, alter, or otherwise change aspects of our material world.

Origins of the Field

The study of environmental communication grew out of the work of scholars who used the tools of rhetorical criticism to study conflicts over natural resources, including wilderness, forests, farmlands, and endangered species. Such scholars studied the rhetoric of campaigns to preserve California's Yosemite Valley in the 19th and early 20th centuries (Oravec, 1981, 1984), warnings of an irreparable loss ("Extinction is forever!") by ecologists who sought to mobilize public support for endangered species (Cox, 1982), and the dust bowl rhetoric of conservationists who tried to change ecologically destructive farming practices during the Depression (Peterson, 1986). Other scholars began to study the rhetoric of radical environmental groups such as Earth First! (Lange, 1990; Short, 1991) as well as conflicts over the spotted owl and old-growth forests of the Pacific Northwest (Lange, 1993; Moore, 1993).

At the same time, the field of environmental communication began to widen to include the roles of science, media, and industry in responding to threats to human health and safety. Early studies investigated issues such as industry's use of public relations and mass-circulation magazines to construct an "ecological" image (Brown & Crable, 1973; Greenberg, Sandman, Sachsman, & Salamone, 1989; Grunig, 1989); the nuclear power industry's response to dramatic accidents at Three Mile Island and Chernobyl (Farrell & Goodnight, 1981; Luke, 1987); and risk communication in conveying the dangers of recombinant DNA experiments (Waddell, 1990). Scholars in the fields of journalism and mass communication began a systematic study of the influence of media depictions of the environment on public attitudes (Anderson, 1997; Shanahan & McComas, 1999, pp. 26–27). In fact, the study of environmental media has grown so rapidly that many now consider it a distinct subfield.

More recently, scholars have expanded their research into nontraditional subjects, media, and forms of environmental communication. Recent topics include "toxic tours" conducted by members of poor and minority communities, who invite news reporters to witness their struggles against chemical pollution in their region (Pezzullo, 2003); collaboration and consensus-based approaches in managing environmental disputes (Daniels & Walker, 2001); and the use of image events by radical environmental groups to convey their protests through the media (DeLuca, 1999; DeLuca & Peeples, 2002). For example, the images of Greenpeace's use of inflatable Zodiac boats to interfere with the harpooning of whales in the Pacific Ocean captured worldwide interest. Finally, scholars in political science, sociology, and public health have begun to document the communication barriers some citizens face in persuading the government to clean up chemical problems in their communities (Reich, 1991; Williams & Matheny, 1995), whereas others have tried to describe what a "green" or "environmental" public sphere would look like (Torgerson, 1999).

The sheer range of subjects makes defining environmental communication difficult. For example, Stephen DePoe (1997) defined the field as the study of the "relationships between our talk and our experiences of our natural surroundings" (p. 368). Yet, DePoe cautioned that environmental communication is more than simply "talk" about the environment. Before I give a more precise definition, I'll briefly illustrate the range of study in this emerging field by introducing the seven major areas of teaching and research that constitute environmental communication.

Areas of Study in Environmental Communication

Although the study of environmental communication covers a wide range of topics, most research and public and professional practice fall into seven areas. We'll explore these areas more deeply in later chapters. For now, I'll identify the kind of concerns that environmental communication scholars currently are pursuing.

1. *Environmental rhetoric and discourse.* Rhetorical studies of the communication of environmental writers and campaigns emerged as an early focus of the new field. This is also one of the broadest areas of study; it includes the rhetoric of environmental groups, nature writing, business PR campaigns, environmental media, and websites. Generally, a **rhetorical focus** includes two sub-areas: (a) a study of the sources and modes of persuasion that individuals and groups use to communicate about the environment; and (b) a study of critical rhetorics, or communication that questions or challenges the discursive framing of the relationship between nature and society.

In the first sub-area, rhetorical scholars have studied the range of persuasion influencing our beliefs, attitudes, and behaviors toward nature or the environment. For example, they have described the persuasion used by wilderness preservation advocates who evoke a "sublime" appreciation of nature (Oravec, 1981), metaphors of space and time in the disputes over biodiversity (Zagacki, 1999), and the role of an alternative "ethical voice" in the writings of scientists who warn of ecological dangers (Killingsworth & Palmer, 1992). Others have identified psychological and social factors that contribute to an *environmental self,* a construct that helps to explain why some individuals are, and others are not, persuaded by environmental messages (Cantrill, 1993). Finally, scholars such as Donald Carbaugh (1992, 1996) have stressed the roles of different cultures in shaping their members' understanding and appreciation of nature, community, and place. As we'll see in a case study of an environmental advocacy campaign in Chapter 7, cultural dimensions of communication help define the sense of place that is experienced and given voice by different communities.

In the second sub-area, scholars studying critical rhetorics examine the role of communication in questioning or challenging society's values and assumptions about nature and our relationships to the environment. Scholars have studied such topics as the questioning of the ideology of "progress" by radical activists with Earth First! (Cooper, 1996); eco-feminists' critiques of discourses that encourage attitudes of dominance and exploitation of the earth (Bullis, 1992); and the way in which early photographs of the American West nurtured an image of a pristine nature that erased the living presence of Native Americans (DeLuca & Demo, 2000). We'll discuss such rhetorical foci for the study of environmental communication in Chapters 2 and 7.

2. *Media and environmental journalism.* In many ways, the study of environmental media has become its own subfield. It focuses on the ways in which

the news, the Internet, advertising, commercial programs, and alternative media portray nature and environmental concerns, as well as the effects of such media programming on public attitudes. Traditional subjects include the agenda-setting role of the news media—its ability to influence which issues audiences think about—and media framing of stories that evoke certain perceptions and values rather than others. For example, Shanahan and McComas (1999) studied the media's framing of stories about global climate change, from the 1980s until the early 1990s. They discovered a pendulum swing, particularly in news coverage, where "in five short years, global warming's 'imminent disaster' had become the cranky forecast of socialist-environmental 'wackos'" (p. 162).

More recent studies in environmental media look at topics such as the shaping of readers' and viewers' perceptions of nature by mainstream magazine and television programming (Meisner, in press); the uses of investigative reporting to expose environmental problems such as asbestos sickness (Schwarze, 2003); and the rise of alternative media in reporting environmental news or events. These latter studies analyze the roles of independent media (e.g., www.indymedia.org), anarchist websites (Owens & Palmer, 2003), and street carnivals used by the anti-globalization movement at meetings of the World Trade Organization (Leclair, 1993). Chapter 5 explores the role of environmental media in more depth.

3. *Public participation in environmental decision making.* Some scholars have begun to work directly with government agencies such as the U.S. Forest Service to study the opportunities for—and barriers to—the participation of ordinary citizens, environmentalists, industry, and scientists in an agency's decision making (Depoe, Delicath, & Aepli, 2004). Their work includes the study of citizens' comments on national forest management plans (Walker, 2004), innovative models for using citizens' recommendations on water quality in the Great Lakes (Waddell, 1996), public access to information about sources of pollution in local communities (Beierle & Cayford, 2002), and barriers to citizens' testimony at a public hearing for a chemical plant in Louisiana's notorious "Cancer Alley" (Cox, 1999).

Other important questions have focused on the public's right to know about environmental information that is held by the government and private industry. For example, does public disclosure of information about the environmental performance of local industries affect factories that pollute a community's air or water? Possibly. Mark Stephan (2002) found that public disclosure of a factory's chemical releases or its violation of air or water permits may trigger a "shock and shame" response, whereby a shocked public demands that the "shamed" factory clean up its pollution (pp. 190,

194). We'll explore the public's right to know and other avenues of public participation in Chapter 3.

4. *Advocacy campaigns.* A less-studied but nonetheless important area of environmental communication is the advocacy campaigns waged by many environmental groups. Advocacy campaigns rely on communication to persuade key decision makers to act on certain objectives—from campaigns that mobilize the public to protect a wilderness area, halt a waste dump, or raise the fuel efficiency on cars and SUVs, to corporate accountability campaigns to persuade businesses to abide by strict environmental standards (for example, convincing building-supply stores to buy lumber that comes only from sustainable forests).

Scholars have used a range of approaches in the study of campaigns. For example, in his history of the idea of "wilderness," Roderick Nash (2001) describes the successful campaign for the Alaska National Interest Lands Conservation Act of 1980, which protected 104 million acres of natural areas throughout Alaska as wilderness, national parks, or wildlife refuges. Although Nash credits the public pressure brought by the Alaska Coalition—"the largest and most powerful citizen conservation organization in American history" (p. 299)—for the act's passage, he gives no attention to the communication strategies that accompanied this campaign. On the other hand, rhetorical scholar Christine Oravec (1984) argued that the different rhetorical definitions of the public interest in the controversy over the Hetch Hetchy Valley in northern California in the early 20th century explain the failure of preservationists to halt the damming of the river flowing through this wild valley. Another rhetorical scholar, Jonathan Lange (1993), observed that, ironically, forest protection groups used communication strategies similar to the logging industry's in their public information campaign to protect old-growth forests in the Pacific Northwest.

During my term as president of the Sierra Club, I saw the reliance of major environmental organizations on advocacy campaigns. What I saw and learned convinced me that we need to examine the role of campaign communication in environmental policy more closely. Therefore, I'll look more closely at advocacy campaigns in Chapter 7.

5. *Environmental collaboration and conflict resolution.* Dissatisfaction with adversarial forms of public participation and methods of settling environmental disputes has led practitioners and scholars alike to explore alternative models of resolving environmental conflicts. The search for alternatives often draws inspiration from the success of local communities that have discovered ways to bring disputing parties together. For instance, the Applegate Partnership in southwestern Oregon and northern California is

one of earliest models involving **stakeholders,** the parties who are most affected, in making decisions (Rolle, 2002). In this case, local communities, environmentalists, business leaders, and state representatives cooperated in deciding how to manage the watershed and public lands of this region.

At the center of these modes of conflict resolution is the ideal of **collaboration,** a mode of communication that invites stakeholders to engage in problem-solving discussion rather than advocacy and debate. Such collaboration is characterized as "constructive, open, civil communication, generally as dialogue; a focus on the future; an emphasis on learning; and some degree of power sharing and leveling of the playing field" (Walker, 2004, p. 123). Steven Daniels and Gregg Walker's (2001) groundbreaking research on collaboration in environmental conflicts is presented in their book, *Working through Environmental Conflict: The Collaborative Learning Approach.* For example, they describe use of a collaborative learning approach by the U.S. Forest Service that involved members of the public in developing plans for fire recovery in the Wenatchee National Forest and in drafting a management plan for the Oregon Dunes National Recreation Area (pp. 205–261). Chapter 4 describes the use of collaboration in managing environmental conflicts.

6. *Risk communication.* Should the EPA regulate the amount of the toxic chemical dioxide in sewage sludge that is used as fertilizer for agricultural crops? Does the outbreak of mad cow disease in cattle on one farm pose an unacceptable risk for people who eat beef regularly? These questions arise out of recent cases that illustrate a growing and independent area of research in both public health and environmental communication.

The study of risk communication includes three areas:

1. Traditionally, scholars have evaluated the effectiveness of particular communication strategies for conveying information about health risks to potentially affected populations, such as the residents of cities with air pollution (Johnson, 2003).

2. Since the late 1980s, scholars also have begun to look at the impact of cultural understandings of risk on the public's judgment of the acceptability of a risk (Plough & Krimsky, 1987). For example, risk communication scholar Jennifer Hamilton (2003) found that sensitivity to cultural—as opposed to technical—understandings of risk influenced whether the residents living near the polluted Fernald nuclear weapons facility in Ohio accepted or rejected certain methods of cleanup at the site.

3. Finally, scholars have begun to question the narrow technical definitions of risk and have started to call for more democratic methods to involve affected communities in evaluating risk (Fiorino, 1989; Fischer, 2000).

For our purposes, we will look at the ways in which the acceptability of a risk may depend as much on how risk is defined and who is being asked to bear the risk as it does on research findings from toxicology or epidemiology. We'll examine issues relating to risk communication in Chapter 6.

7. *Representations of nature in popular culture and green marketing.* The use of images of nature in popular music, television shows, photography, and commercial advertising is hardly new or surprising. What is new is the questioning of how such images of nature shape popular culture or influence the general public's attitudes toward nature. Scholars in cultural studies as well as environmental communication have begun to map some of the ways in which images of nature in popular media actually sustain values of dominance and exploitation of the natural world rather than values of reduced consumption or preservation of wild lands.

Recent studies have examined such diverse topics as the corporate marketing of nature in theme parks such as Sea World in San Diego (Davis, 1997), capitalist narratives in the well-known board game in *Monopoly™: The National Parks Edition* (Opel, 2002), the role of Hollywood movies in perpetuating the myths of agrarian life (Retzinger, 2002), and the diverse portrayals of nature on the popular Weather Channel (Meister, 2001). Some scholars also have shown an interest in what Canadian social theorist Toby Smith (1998) called the "myth of green consumerism." Smith argues that this myth is invoked whenever corporate advertising encourages consumers to feel they are preserving nature by buying "green" products, such as cosmetics at the Body Shop. In subsequent chapters, we'll describe some of the ways in which nature is portrayed in visual arts such as photography (Chapter 2), news and entertainment (Chapter 5), and corporate marketing (Chapter 10).

A Definition of Environmental Communication

With such a diverse range of topics, the field can appear at first glance to be confusing. If we define *environmental communication* as simply "talk," or the transmission of information about the wide universe of environmental topics—whether it's acid rain or grizzly bear habitat—our definition will be as varied as the topics for discussion.

A clearer definition takes into account the distinctive roles of language, art, photographs, street protests, and even scientific reports as forms of **symbolic action**. The term comes from Kenneth Burke (1966), a 20th-century rhetorical theorist. In his book *Language as Symbolic Action,* Burke stated that even the most unemotional language is necessarily persuasive. This is so because our language and other symbolic acts *do* something as well as say something.

The view of communication as a form of symbolic action might be clearer if we contrast it with an earlier view, the **Shannon–Weaver model of communication**. Shortly after World War Two, Claude Shannon and Warren Weaver (1949) proposed a linear model that defined human communication as simply the transmission of information from a source to a receiver. There was little effort in this model to account for meaning or for the ways in which communication acts on, or shapes, our awareness. Unlike the Shannon–Weaver model, symbolic action assumes that language and symbols do more than transmit information: *they actively shape our understanding, create meaning, and orient us to a wider world.* Burke went so far as to claim that "much that we take as observations about 'reality' may be but the spinning out of possibilities implicit in our particular choice of terms" (p. 46). For example, when lobbyists from the oil industry used terms such as "new technology," "cautious," and "tiny footprint" to describe the impact of oil drilling on land in the Arctic National Wildlife Refuge, they constructed a reality that invited others to view such oil drilling as compatible with the fragile tundra and wildlife there.

If we focus on symbolic action instead of taking a transmission view of human communication, then we can offer a richer definition. In this book, I use **environmental communication** to mean *the pragmatic and constitutive vehicle for our understanding of the environment as well as our relationships to the natural world; it is the symbolic medium that we use in constructing environmental problems and negotiating society's different responses to them.* Defined as a type of symbolic action, then, environmental communication serves two different functions:

1. *Environmental communication is* **pragmatic**. It educates, alerts, persuades, mobilizes, and helps us to solve environmental problems. It is this instrumental sense of communication that probably occurs to us initially: communication-in-action. It is a vehicle for problem solving and debate and is often part of public education campaigns. For example, a pragmatic function of environmental communication occurs when car manufacturers buy an ad in the *Washington Post* opposing higher miles-per-gallon fuel standards, or when an environmental group rallies support for protecting a wilderness area.

2. *Environmental communication is* **constitutive**. On a subtler level, environmental communication also helps to constitute, or compose, representations of nature and environmental problems themselves as subjects for our understanding. By shaping our perceptions of nature, environmental communication may invite us to perceive forests and rivers as threatening or as bountiful, to regard natural resources as for exploitation or as vital life support systems, as something to conquer or as something to cherish. For example, a campaign to protect wilderness may use instrumental means for planning a

press conference, but at the same time, the words in the press statement may tap into cultural constructions of a pristine or unspoiled nature. (In Chapter 2, we'll look closely at the role of communication in shaping perceptions of a pristine American West in 19th-century art, photographs, and literature).

Such communication also assists us in defining certain circumstances as problems; as in the definition of a certain amount of the chemical mercury that accumulates in fish as harmful to pregnant women. It also associates particular values in the public's mind with these problems—health, a legacy of clean air and water for our children, a resource for new medicine, and so forth. In doing so, this constitutive shaping of our perceptions also invites pragmatic communication as we educate, organize, and rally the public to act on these problems and values.

Our understanding of environmental communication as a pragmatic and constitutive vehicle that takes place particularly in the public spaces of our national life serves as the framework for the chapters in this book. The book builds on the three core principles mentioned at the beginning of the chapter:

- Human communication is a form of symbolic action.
- Our beliefs, attitudes, and behaviors relating to nature and environmental problems are mediated by communication.
- The public sphere emerges as a discursive space for communication about the environment.

These principles obviously overlap (see Figure 1.1). As I've noted, our communication (as symbolic action) actively shapes our perceptions when we see the natural world through myriad symbols, words, images, or narratives. And when we communicate publicly with others, we share these understandings and invite reactions to our views. For example, in the 1990s, when environmentalists sought to protect millions of acres in the California desert as wildlife sanctuaries and national parks, opponents argued that the desert was barren. Yet, the resulting public discussion and debate introduced new information and perspectives about this fragile area, its wildlife, and archeological and ecological values. As a result, in 1994 Congress enacted the California Desert Protection Act, setting aside nearly 8 million of the state's 25 million acres of desert as national parks and other natural areas.

As we and others discuss, question, and debate this information and these differing viewpoints as well as our own experiences, we might reinforce our judgments or perhaps gain new understanding of a problem. In other words, as we engage others, our communication *mediates*, or shapes, our own and others' perceptions, beliefs, and behavior toward the environment.

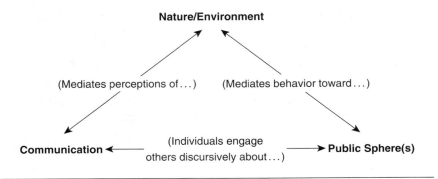

Figure 1.1   Nature, communication, and the public sphere

Nature, Communication, and the Public Sphere

Let's return to the three basic themes that organize the chapters in this book: (1) communication is a form of symbolic action; (2) our beliefs, attitudes, and behaviors relating to nature and environmental problems are mediated by communication; and (3) the public sphere emerges as a discursive space for communication about the environment. I'll introduce and illustrate these themes briefly here and then draw on them in each of the remaining chapters.

Human Communication as Symbolic Action

Earlier, I defined environmental communication as a form of symbolic action. Our language and other symbolic acts *do something*. They create meaning and actively structure our conscious orientation to the world. Speeches, film, photographs, art, folklore, and other forms of human symbolic behavior act upon us. They invite us to view the world this way rather than that way; to affirm these values, not those. Our stories and words warn us, but they also invite us to celebrate.

At the end of 1995, former secretary of the interior Bruce Babbitt delivered a speech that celebrated the return of wolves to Yellowstone National Park. Earlier that year, he had carried the first American gray wolf into the transition area in the national park where she would later mate with other wolves also being returned. After setting her down, Babbitt recalled, "I looked . . . into the green eyes of this magnificent creature, within this spectacular landscape, and was profoundly moved by the elevating nature of America's conservation laws: laws with the power to make creation whole" (para. 3).

Babbitt's purpose in speaking that day was to support the beleaguered Endangered Species Act, which was under attack in the Congress at the time. In recalling the biblical story of the Flood and Noah's ark from his childhood, Babbitt evoked a powerful narrative for valuing wolves and other endangered species. In retelling this ancient story to his listeners at Yellowstone, he invited them to embrace a similar ethic in the present day:

> And when the waters receded, and the dove flew off to dry land, God set all the creatures free, commanding them to multiply upon the earth.
>
> Then, in the words of the covenant with Noah, "when the rainbow appears in the clouds, I will see it and remember the everlasting covenant between me and all living things on earth."
>
> Thus we are instructed that this everlasting covenant was made to protect the whole of creation . . . We are living between the flood and the rainbow: between the threats to creation on the one side and God's covenant to protect life on the other. (Babbitt, 1995, paras. 34–36, 56)

Because communication provides us with a means of sense making about the world, it orients us toward events, experiences, people, wildlife, and choices that we encounter there. And because different individuals (and generations) affirm, define, or value nature in different ways, we find our voices to be part of a conversation about which definition or meaning of nature is the best or the most useful. Secretary Babbitt invoked an ancient story of survival to invite the American public to appreciate anew the Endangered Species Act. So, too, our own communication mediates or helps us to make sense of the different narratives, ideologies, and appeals that people use to define what they believe is right, feasible, ethical, or just "common sense."

Human communication therefore is symbolic *action* because we draw upon language and other symbols to construct a framework for understanding and valuing and to bring the wider world to others' attention. We'll explore this aspect of communication more closely in Chapter 2.

Symbolic Action Mediates Our Perceptions of "Nature"

It may seem odd to place "nature" in quotation marks. The natural world certainly exists. Forests are logged or left standing; a red-tailed hawk just now flew into the tree near my office window; streams may be polluted or clean; and large glaciers in Antarctica definitely are caving into the ocean. So, what's going on? As one of my students skeptically asked me, "What does *communication* have to do with nature or the study of environmental problems?" My answer to her question takes us into the heart of this book.

Simply put, whatever else "nature" and "the environment" may be, they are also words and therefore *ideas*. And ideas have consequences. For instance, is "wilderness" a place of primeval beauty or a territory that is dark, dangerous, and alien to humans? Early settlers in New England saw North American forests as forbidding and dangerous. Michael Wigglesworth, a Puritan writer, described the region as "a waste and howling wilderness, / Where none inhabited / But hellish fiends, and brutish men / That Devils worshiped" (quoted in Nash, 2001, p. 36). Indeed, writers, scientists, business leaders, citizens, poets, and conservationists have fought for centuries over whether forests should be logged, rivers dammed, air quality regulated, and endangered species protected.

Consider again wolves. Once ranging in every region in North America, by the 19th and early 20th centuries the wolf had become a symbol of "monstrous cruelty and incredible cunning" (Fischer, 1995, pp. 10). Although ancient folklore nurtured fear and hatred of wolves, hostility toward them sharpened as farms, towns, and industries spread into the West. Historian Richard Bartlett (1985) noted that the punitive labels assigned to wolves in this era reached "pathological proportions" (p. 329). In 1914, Congress appropriated funds to eradicate wolves in the West. Fisher writes that within 12 years wolves had essentially disappeared from their historic habitat in wild places like Yellowstone National Park (p. 22).

Not everyone saw wolves in this light. The wildlife ecologist Aldo Leopold (1966/1949) described seeing a wolf die as he was hunting deer in the Southwest in the 1920s. He and his companions had spotted what they took to be a doe fording a turbulent river. When she reached the shore and shook her tail, they realized that she was a wolf. Suddenly, a half-dozen wolf pups sprang from the willows to greet her "in a welcoming mêlée of wagging tails and playful maulings" (p. 138). Leopold describes what happened next.

> In those days we had never heard of passing up a chance to kill a wolf. In a second we were pumping lead into the pack, but with more excitement than accuracy. . . . When our rifles were empty, the old wolf was down, and a pup was dragging a leg into impassable slide-rocks. We reached the old wolf in time to watch a fierce green fire dying in her eyes. I realized then, and have known ever since, that there was something new to me in those eyes—something known only to her and to the mountain. I was young then, and full of trigger itch; I thought that because fewer wolves meant more deer, that no wolves would mean a hunters' paradise. But after seeing the green fire die, I sensed that neither the wolf nor the mountain agreed with such a view. (pp. 138–139)

I suspect that others in your class will have differing views of wolves and wilderness as you discuss these concerns. My point is simply that, although

Figure 1.2   The gray wolf is being reintroduced to areas such as Yellowstone
National Park

(© Greenpeace / Daniel Beltra)

nature inspires different responses in us, nature is ethically and politically
silent. Ultimately, it is we who invest its seasons and species with meaning,
significance, and value. Similarly, some problems become problems only
when someone identifies a threat to important values we hold. Indeed, decisions to preserve habitat for endangered species or impose regulations on
factories emitting air pollution seldom result from scientific study alone.
Instead, a choice to take action arises from a crucible of debate and (often)
public controversy. Even as Aldo Leopold, after seeing "something new" in
the old wolf's dying eyes, felt a need to write about its meaning for him, so
too are we led into the realm of human communication in our study of
nature and environmental problems.

The Public Sphere as Discursive Space

A third theme central to this book is the idea of the public sphere or, more accurately, public spheres. Earlier, in the Introduction, we defined the **public sphere** as the realm of influence that is created when individuals engage others in communication—through conversation, argument, debate, or questioning—about subjects of shared concern or topics that affect a wider community. The public comes into being both in our everyday conversations and in our more formal interactions with others where we sustain talk about the environment or other topics. And, as I pointed out, the public sphere is not just words: Visual and nonverbal symbolic actions, such as sit-ins, banners, photography, film, and Earth First! tree sits, also have prompted discussion, debate, and questioning of environmental policy as readily as editorials, speeches, and TV newscasts.

The German social theorist Jürgen Habermas (1974) offered a similar definition when he observed that "a portion of the public sphere comes into being in every conversation in which private individuals assemble to form a public body" (p. 49). As we engage others in conservation, questioning, or debate, we translate our private concerns into public matters and thus create spheres of influence, which affect how we and others view the environment and our relation to it. Such translations of private concerns into public matters occur in a range of forums and practices that give rise to something akin to an environmental public sphere—from a talk at a local ecology club to scientists' testimony before a congressional committee. In public hearings, newspaper editorials, Web alerts, speeches at rallies, street festivals, and countless other occasions in which we engage others in conservation, debate, or other forms of symbolic actions, the public sphere emerges as a potential sphere of influence.

But private concerns are not always translated into public action, and technical information about environmental subjects sometimes remains within scientific journals or specialized conferences. Therefore, it is important to note that at least two other spheres of influence exist parallel to the public sphere. Communication scholar Thomas Goodnight (1982) has called these the *personal* and the *technical* spheres. For example, two strangers arguing at an airport bar is a relatively private affair, whereas the technical findings of biology that influenced Rachael Carson's (1962) discussion of DDT in *Silent Spring* were originally limited to technical journals. Yet Carson's book presented this scientific information in a context that engaged the attention—and debate—of millions of readers and scores of public officials. In so doing, it gave rise to a sphere of influence that occurs when personal or technical concerns are translated into matters of public interest.

Goodnight cautioned that, in contemporary society, information needed for judgments about the environment and other technical subjects may cause both private and public conversations to defer to scientific or technical authority. The danger in such situations obviously is that *the public sphere can decline*. It can lose its relevance as a sphere of influence that exists in a democracy to mediate among differing viewpoints and interests. Goodnight himself feared that "the public sphere is being steadily eroded by the elevation of the personal and technical groundings of argument" (p. 223). In Chapter 9, I'll examine the tension that exists between one technical sphere— environmental science—and arguments in the public sphere over environmental regulation of industry.

Because the idea of the public sphere is easily misunderstood, I also want to address briefly three common misconceptions about it here. These are the beliefs that the public sphere is (1) only an official site or forum for government decision making, (2) a monolithic or ideal collection of all citizens, and (3) a form of "rational" or technical communication. Each of these ideas is a misunderstanding of the public sphere.

First, the public sphere is not only, or even primarily, an official space. Although there are forums and state-sponsored spaces, such as public hearings that invite citizens to communicate about the environment, these official sites do not exhaust the public sphere. In fact, discussion and debate about environmental concerns more often occur outside government meeting rooms and courts. The early 5th-century Greeks called these meeting spaces of everyday life *agoras*, the public squares or marketplaces where citizens gathered during the day to sell farm products, tools, clothes, and other items and also to exchange ideas about the life of their community. At the dawn of one of the first experiments in democracy, Greek citizens believed they needed certain essential skills to voice their concerns publicly and influence the judgment of others, skills they called the art of rhetoric. (I will return to this background in Chapter 2.)

Second, the public sphere is neither monolithic nor a uniform assemblage of all citizens in the abstract. As the realm of influence that is created when individuals engage others discursively, a public sphere assumes more concrete forms: calls to a local talk radio show, letters-to-the-editor, blog sites, news conferences, local meetings where residents question public health officials about possible risks to their health from contaminated well water. As Habermas noted, some form of the public sphere comes into existence whenever individuals question, converse, debate, collaborate, mourn, or celebrate with others about subjects of shared concern. Indeed, some have argued that environmental groups now have the ability to create an "alternative

public realm" for environmental communication through their own publications and other ways of reaching supporters and journalists (Downing,
1988). In doing so, they articulate for themselves a space within society
in which "their own discourse can be privileged and their own knowledge
pursued" (p. 45).

Third, the definition of the public sphere as a space for popular or democratic communication is meant to counter the idea that communication in
the public sphere is a kind of elite conversation or specialized or "rational"
form of communication. Such a view of the public sphere unfairly and inac-
curately ignores the diverse voices and communication styles that characterize a robust, participatory democracy. In fact, in this book I'll introduce
the voices of ordinary citizens and the special challenges they face in gaining a hearing about matters of environmental and personal survival in their
communities.

Mapping the Terrain: Voices and Visions

The landscape of environmental politics and public affairs can be as diverse,
serious, controversial, colorful, and complex as an Amazonian rain forest or
the Galapagos Islands' ecology. The callers on talk radio who berate Earth
Liberation Front activists for setting SUVs afire differ dramatically from the
residents who complain of contaminated well water at a meeting in their
community center. These groups, in turn, seem a world apart from scientists
at the National Press Club who warned of a dangerous collapse of ocean
marine life. Whether at press conferences, in community centers, on Internet
listservs, or outside the fenced barriers of a World Bank meeting, individuals and groups speaking about the environment appear today in diverse sites
and public spaces.

In this final section, I'll introduce six of the major points of view, or "voices"
(Myerson & Rydin, 1991) of environmental communication in the public
sphere, along with some of the features that distinguish these viewpoints:

- citizens and community groups
- environmental groups
- scientists and scientific discourse
- corporations and business lobbyists
- anti-environmentalist groups
- media and environmental journalism

Citizens and Community Groups

Community residents who question and complain to town officials or organize their neighbors to take action are one of the most common and effective sources of environmental change. Some citizens are motivated by urban sprawl or development projects that destroy homes as well as local green spaces, the surviving natural areas in cities and towns. For others who may live near a refinery, hazardous waste incinerator, or chemical plant, noxious fumes or pollution may motivate them to organize resistance to that industry's lax air quality permit.

In 1978, Lois Gibbs, resident of the working-class community of Love Canal in Niagara Falls, New York, and mother of two small children, grew concerned when her five-year-old son, Michael, complained of rashes and headaches after playing in the nearby elementary school yard. Gibbs had just read a newspaper report that Hooker Chemical Company, a subsidiary of Occidental Petroleum, had buried dangerous chemicals on land it later sold to the local school board. The report raised suspicions on the part of Gibbs and her neighbors, many of whom had noticed odors and oily substances surfacing in their yards and on the school's playground (Center for Health, Environment, and Justice, 2003, para. 1).

As Gibbs talked with her neighbors, she discovered that other children had health problems similar to Michael's. She also learned that miscarriages, birth defects, and cancer had occurred at higher-than-normal rates among these children's parents and others in Love Canal. After her requests for help were denied by local and state health officials, Gibbs began to go from door to door organizing parents and gathering signatures on a petition to close the school. When school officials refused to close the school, Gibbs and others formed the Love Canal Home Owners Association to demand help from the New York State Department of Health and the governor of New York.

Despite an initial denial of the problem by state officials, Lois Gibbs and her neighbors persisted. They organized media coverage, carried symbolic coffins to the state capital, marched on Mother's Day, and pressed health officials to take their concerns seriously. Then, on August 2, 1978, New York's Department of Health issued an order recommending that the school be closed and cautioning that pregnant women and children under the age of 2 needed to be evacuated from the area closest to the school (Center for Health, Environment, and Justice, 2003, para. 2). In 1982, the citizens succeeded in persuading the federal government to relocate the residents of Love Canal who wanted to leave. Finally, the U.S. Justice Department prosecuted

Hooker Chemical Company and imposed large fines on it (Shabecoff, 1993, pp. 234–235).

FYI: Love Canal: The Start of a Movement

For more information on the story of Love Canal, New York, and the origins of a grassroots anti-toxics movement in the United States, see "Love Canal: The Start of a Movement" at the website of the Center for Health, Environment, and Justice, www.chej.org/movement.htm. For a firsthand account of the Love Canal controversy by Lois Marie Gibbs, see her two books, *Love Canal: My Story* (Albany: State University of New York Press, 1982) and *Love Canal: The Story Continues* (Stony Creek, CT: New Society, 1998).

Love Canal ultimately became a symbol, in the nation's consciousness, of abandoned toxic sites and fueled a citizens' anti-toxics movement in the United States. Due largely to the publicity created by Gibbs and her neighbors, in 1980 Congress initiated the **Superfund** program, which authorizes the Environmental Protection Agency to clean up toxic sites and hold the responsible parties accountable for their share of the costs. Lois Gibbs herself set up the Citizens Clearing House for Hazardous Waste—now called the Center for Health, Environment, and Justice (www.chej.org)—in 1981 to share with other communities the lessons of her struggle in Love Canal.

Lois Gibbs's story is not unique. In rural towns in Louisiana, in innercity neighborhoods in Los Angeles, on Native American reservations in New Mexico, and in communities throughout the country, citizens and community groups have launched campaigns to clean up polluting plants, protect green space, and halt mining operations on sacred tribal lands. As we'll learn in later chapters, local activists and residents face the challenges of finding a voice and securing the communication resources to express their concerns and to persuade others to join with them to demand accountability of public officials. Chapter 3 describes some legal guarantees of the public's right to know about polluting companies, as well as opportunities to participate in federal and state decision making about environmental matters. On the other hand, in other chapters we'll examine communities that often are targeted as "sacrifice zones" for hazardous facilities and whose residents face subtle and not-so-subtle barriers to being heard. For example, in Chapter 8, we'll look more closely at the movement for environmental justice in many communities of color, in workplaces, and on Native American reservations.

Environmental Groups

U.S. environmental groups are one frequently encountered source of communication about the environment, as are the growing number of international conservation organizations. This diverse movement comprises a wide array of groups and networks, each with its own focus and mode of communication. They range from thousands of grassroots and community groups to regional and national environmental organizations such as the Natural Resources Defense Council, the Sierra Club, the Audubon Society, and the National Wildlife Federation, and international groups such as Greenpeace, Friends of the Earth, Conservation International, and the World Wide Fund for Nature.

These groups address a diversity of issues and often differ significantly in their modes of advocacy. For example, the Wilderness Society and the Sierra Club focus on the protection of public lands through public advocacy campaigns and lobbying of the U.S. Congress. On the other hand, the Nature Conservancy and hundreds of local land conservancy groups protect rare and endangered habitat on private lands by actually purchasing the properties. Still other groups, such as Greenpeace and Rainforest Action Network, have turned to image events (DeLuca, 1999) to shine the spotlight of media attention on concerns as diverse as illegal whaling and the destruction of tropical rain forests. (For information on U.S. and international environmental groups, see Brulle, 2000; Dunlap & Mertig, 1992; Sale, 1993; Shabecoff, 2003; Shaiko, 1999; and Taylor, 1995.)

Some regional and national groups actually are networks of hundreds of local organizations. For example, the Center for Health, Environment, and Justice (started by Lois Gibbs) shares information with local groups that are struggling with hazardous facilities in their communities. Other regional networks, such as the Dogwood Alliance (southern United States), the Southern Utah Wilderness Alliance, and the National Forest Protection Alliance, help hundreds of wilderness and forest protection groups plan campaign strategy, from media events to legal challenges to national forest management plans. For example, the Clean Water Network coordinates the work of more than 1,000 local groups on water issues—such as soil erosion from logging that harms trout streams, and mountaintop removal, in which coal companies in West Virginia, Kentucky, and Tennessee blast the tops of mountains to expose coal seams, pushing the excess earth over the sides and clogging the streams in valleys below.

Act Locally!

Identify a representative from a local environmental group to inter-view for your class. Such a person can be helpful in describing some of the differences among the thousands of local and national groups that are concerned about the environment.

Ask this person to speak about these things:

- The nature of the organization: Is it local, regional, or an affiliate of a national environmental group? What is its mission? Is it member based?
- The forms of communication used by this group to pursue its mission: Public education? Political advocacy? Lobbying? Door-to-door can-vassing? Newspaper, radio, or television ads? The effectiveness of this group's environmental communication: What is an example of its effectiveness? What does its representative see as the biggest barrier to success?

Nationally, there has been an attempt to bring many of the advocacy groups together in what is called the Green Group. Originally called the Group of Ten during the Reagan Administration in the 1980s, the Green Group is an occasional meeting of executive directors of national environmental groups who consult informally. It consists of roughly 30 groups who share an inter-est in shaping environmental policy. These include such diverse groups as American Rivers, Defenders of Wildlife, Rails to Trails, the National Parks Conservation Association, the Public Interest Research Group (PIRG), the Sierra Club, Greenpeace, and the National Tribal Environmental Council.

Scientists and Scientific Discourse

The widening hole in Earth's ozone layer over Antarctica first was publi-cized in 1985 when scientists discovered that the chlorofluorocarbons (CFCs) used in air conditioning, aerosols, refrigerators, and other products were breaking down the protective ozone shield. The ozone layer filters harmful ultraviolet rays that damage crops and forests, cause skin cancer and other human diseases, and can damage the corneas of mammals, includ-ing humans. In 1987, the United States and 23 other nations signed the **Montreal Protocol**, an international treaty requiring signatory nations to phase out the production of CFCs.

As in the case of the ozone layer, scientific reports have led to important investigations of—and debate about—problems affecting human health and Earth's biodiversity. From asthma in children caused by air pollution to the spreading desertification in sub-Saharan Africa, scientific research and the alerts of scientists have contributed substantially to public awareness and to debate about environmental policy.

However, the link between scientific research and public policy is not always direct. Scientific findings in such areas as genetically modified organisms, HIV-AIDS research, or the use of stem cells in research, to name a few, often are not immediately accepted, because they challenge long-held beliefs or convictions. As we'll see in Chapter 9, the results of environmental science are sometimes disputed or ignored, its findings distorted by public officials, radio talk-show hosts, and environmental skeptics. For example, the respected journal *Science* described the campaign by political partisans to discredit the work of atmospheric scientists on ozone depletion (Taubes, 1993). Stanford University biologists Paul and Anne Ehrlich (1996) became so alarmed at the misuses of science by talk-show commentators and anti-environmentalist groups that they warned of a trend toward "anti-science—a twisting of empirical science—to bolster a predetermined worldview and to support a political agenda" (pp. 11–12).

Finally, we will examine the question of whether environmental scientists have an ethical duty to speak publicly to warn of impending dangers, or whether their place is more appropriately in their laboratories, away from public controversy. These questions have been vigorously debated in editorial pages and journal articles in the fields of ecology and conservation biology. We will look more closely at the discourse of science in Chapter 9.

Corporations and Business Lobbyists

Environmental historian Samuel Hays (2000) reports that, as the new environmental sciences began to document the environmental and health risks from industrial products, the affected businesses challenged the science "at every step, questioning both the methods and research designs that were used and the conclusions that were drawn" (p. 222). As part of this opposition, industries organized trade associations to defend their practices and to lobby against environmental regulations.

Organized, corporate opposition to environmental protection measures appears to be based on two things: (1) resentment of restrictions on traditional uses of land, and (2) threats to the economic interests of newer industries such as petrochemicals and electronics. The first basis of opposition comes from the extractive or resource industries. These include the logging,

ranching, farming, and mining industries, in which many owners and workers believe that their traditional ways of life are restricted by new environmental standards. For example, many in these industries resent rules that
limit the amount of logging in national forests or restrict arsenic drainage
from mines, and some ranchers object to rules that require buffer strips to
protect streams and riparian areas where cattle graze.

The second basis of environmental opposition comes from such 20th- and
21st-century industries as petrochemicals, computers, transportation, automobile manufacturing, and energy. Worried by the threat of tighter limits on air
and water discharges from factories and refineries, many corporations have
formed trade associations such as the Business Round Table, the Chemical
Manufacturers Association, and the Global Climate Coalition to lobby the
U.S. Congress on behalf of their industries (Hays, 2000). For example, the
Business Round Table devotes considerable resources to lobbying and to issuing press releases and position papers on a range of environmental issues. It
also claims to support positions that "embrace sustainability as defined by economic vitality and growth, [and] superior environmental performance" (See
Business Round Table at www.brtable.org). On the other hand, many trade
associations have opposed environmental policies, including higher standards
for fuel efficiency in cars and trucks, reauthorization of the Superfund law for
cleaning up toxic waste sites, and the U.S. Senate's ratification of the Kyoto
Treaty on global warming. We'll explore the role of business opposition to
certain forms of environmental protection in Chapter 10.

Anti-Environmentalist Groups

Although it may be difficult to conceive of groups that are opposed to
protection of the environment *per se* (clean air, healthy forests, safe drinking
water, etc.), some believe that a *green backlash* against government regulations that protect environmental values has been growing in recent years. In
part, this backlash is fueled by the perception that environmentalism harms
economic growth and jobs. In her study of the bases of opposition to environmental rules, Jennifer Switzer (1997) also identified an ideological challenge from individuals who feel marginalized or overlooked by government
regulators. This sense of marginalization is felt particularly by some who live
near public lands such as national parks and wilderness areas and who
believe themselves limited in their use of these lands.

One early expression of this resentment was the **Sagebrush Rebellion** of the
late 1970s and 1980s, an effort by traditional land users to take control of federal land and natural resources in the West. Environmental journalist Philip
Shabecoff (2003) reported that, "the [cattle] stockmen, miners, and other range

users, long accustomed to treating the public lands as a private fiefdom, reacted angrily to what they perceived as a threat to their rights and their livelihood" (p. 155). In response, these sagebrush rebels "evoked states' rights, the free market, and rugged cowboy individualism to assert their right to use the land for grazing, to mine coal and other materials, and to drill for oil. . . . They attacked, sometimes physically, and vilified federal land managers and sought to discredit conservationists as un-American left-wingers" (p. 155).

Today, offshoots of the Sagebrush Rebellion call themselves **Wise Use** groups, or property rights groups. These groups organize individuals who resent restrictions on the use of their property for such purposes as protection of wetlands or habitat for endangered species. They include groups as diverse as the Oregon Lands Coalition (a pro-logging group), the National Wetlands Coalition (opposed to wetlands preservation), the Blue Ribbon Coalition (whose aim is to organize motorized recreationalists and other resource users to oppose wilderness designations), and Wise Use advocate Ron Arnold's Center for the Defense of Free Enterprise (opposed to environmental regulations generally). Arnold, a controversial figure in the anti-environmentalist movement, once told a reporter, "Our goal is to destroy environmentalism once and for all" (Rawe & Field, 1992, in Helvarg, 2004, p. 7.)

FYI: Anti-Environmentalist Groups

To learn more about the history of the opposition to environmentalism in the United States and the backlash against it, see David Helvarg's *The War Against the Greens: The "Wise-Use" Movement, the New Right, and the Browning of America* (Rev. ed., 2004), and Jacqueline Switzer's *Green Backlash: The History and Politics of Environmental Opposition in the U.S.* (1997).

For an example of the Wise Use movement's opposition to environmental regulations, read Ron Arnold's and Alan Gottlieb's *Trashing the Economy: How Runaway Environmentalism Is Wrecking America* (2nd ed., Merril Press, Bellevue, WA, 1998). Websites for Ron Arnold's Center for the Defense of Free Enterprise and other major Wise Use and property rights groups are as follows:

- Center for the Defense of Free Enterprise: www.cdfe.org
- Alliance for America: www.allianceforamerica.org
- Blue Ribbon Coalition: www.sharetrails.org/index.cfm?page=12

Media and Environmental Journalism

It would be difficult to overstate the impact of television, radio, print, and Internet news on environmental politics. News media act not only as voices in their coverage of issues and events but as conduits for other voices that seek to influence public attitudes. These voices range from scientists and corporations to radical environmentalists. The news media also are a constitutive force through their **agenda-setting** role. The term *agenda setting* refers to the effect of media on the public's perception of the salience or importance of issues. As early as 1963, journalism scholar Bernard Cohen (1963) explained that the news media filter or select issues for readers' or viewers' attention and set the public's agenda, telling people not what to think but what to think *about*. For example, the public's concern over the deaths of sea otters, shore birds, and salmon soared after television coverage of the 11 million gallons of crude oil that spilled from the *Exxon Valdez* supertanker in Alaska's Prince William Sound in 1989.

Act Locally!

Choose a television news show, newspaper, or website to watch or read for the next week. Try to notice the agenda-setting role in the selection of stories and topics that are reported in each newspaper article, Web post, or television broadcast. Ask yourself these questions:

What was called to your attention? How often? How prominently was a story displayed? Was it the lead story or headline news? Was it accompanied by photos or film? Whose voices or viewpoints were included? Whose were excluded? Overall, did the media's filtering of stories affect your thinking about the environment? Were you more aware of certain topics? Did your views change? What did you think should have been reported but was not covered that week?

Although the *Exxon Valdez* story focused on a single, dramatic event that fulfilled criteria for newsworthiness, most environmental topics, even quite serious ones, are less dramatic. As a result, media often have discretion in choosing what events or information to cover and also how to frame or package a news story. Indeed, the many voices and viewpoints in the media illustrate a wide range of approaches to environmental concerns, from conservative websites like that of the Cooler Heads Coalition, a group that claims to dispel myths of global warming (www.globalwarming.org), to a scientific news story in the *New York Times*, "Scientists Predict Widespread Extinction by Global Warming" (Gorman, 2004, p. A4). In Chapter 5, we'll examine such issues as agenda setting, media frames, and the media's criteria for newsworthiness of environmental news stories.

Conclusion

This chapter introduced the emerging field of environmental communication by illustrating the diversity of areas that scholars study, from advocacy campaigns and environmental conflict resolution to the images of nature in popular culture and corporate green marketing. The study of environmental communication inquires into the dynamics of human communication—speech, art, symbols, street performances, media, and campaigns—that shape our understandings of nature and environmental problems. It also studies the occasions on which ordinary citizens, environmental groups, journalists, scientists, corporations, and others seek to influence decisions affecting the environment.

Although there is a considerable range of areas in the study of environmental communication, two basic functions underlie much of our talk about nature and environmental problems: (1) a pragmatic function, in which we educate, alert, mobilize, and persuade others, and (2) a constitutive function, in which language and other symbols themselves help to shape our perceptions about reality and the nature of environmental problems. These two functions are included in the basic definition of *environmental communication* as the pragmatic and constitutive vehicle for our understanding of the environment as well as our relationships to the natural world; it is the symbolic medium that we use in constructing environmental problems and in negotiating society's different responses to them.

Drawing on this definition of environmental communication, I've said that this book will be organized around three basic themes: (1) human communication is a form of symbolic action, (2) our beliefs, attitudes, and behaviors relating to nature and environmental problems are mediated or influenced by communication, and (3) the public sphere emerges as a discursive space for communication about the environment. It is within these wider conversations and forums that citizens, environmental groups, media, scientists, and corporate lobbyists seek to influence others about environmental issues.

Now that you have learned what environmental communication is and how widely it is practiced, I hope you'll feel inspired to join (or to renew your commitment to) the public conversations already in progress about the environment. Also, I hope that you'll discover your own voice and develop personal efficacy in speaking on behalf of the natural world and your own communities.

KEY TERMS

Agenda setting: The alleged ability of media to affect the public's perception of the salience or importance of issues; in other words, news reporting may not succeed in telling people what to think, but it succeeds in telling them what to think *about.*

Agora: In ancient Greece, the public square or marketplace where citizens gathered during the day to sell produce and other products and to exchange ideas about their community.

Collaboration: A mode of communication that invites stakeholders to engage in problem-solving discussion rather than advocacy and debate.

Constitutive: A characteristic of environmental communication whereby representations of nature and environmental problems are composed as subjects for our understanding.

Environmental communication: The pragmatic and constitutive vehicle for our understanding of the environment as well as our relationships to the natural world; the symbolic medium that we use in constructing environmental problems and in negotiating society's different responses to them.

Montreal Protocol: An international treaty requiring the United States and 23 other signatory nations to phase out the production of chlorofluorocarbons (CFCs).

Pragmatic: Instrumental; a characteristic of environmental communication whereby it educates, alerts, persuades, mobilizes, and helps us to solve environmental problems.

Public sphere: A realm of influence that is created when individuals engage others in communication—through conversation, argument, debate, or questioning—about subjects of shared concern or topics that affect a wider community.

Rhetorical focus: (a) The study of the sources and modes of persuasion that individuals and groups use to communicate about the environment. (b) The study of critical rhetorics, or communication that questions or challenges the discursive framing of the nature–society relationship itself.

Sagebrush Rebellion: An effort in the late 1970s and 1980s by traditional land users to take control of federal land and natural resources in the West.

Shannon–Weaver model of communication: A linear model that defined human communication as the transmission of information from a source to a receiver.

Stakeholder: The party most affected by a decision.

Superfund: A federal law authorizing the Environmental Protection Agency to clean up toxic sites and hold the responsible parties accountable for the costs.

Symbolic action: The property of language and other acts to *do something* as well as literally to say something. Even the least emotional language is necessarily persuasive.

Wise Use groups: Groups that organize individuals who oppose restrictions on the use of their own (private) property for purposes such as protection of wetlands or habitat for endangered species. Also called property rights groups.

DISCUSSION QUESTIONS

1. Which of the seven areas of environmental communication most interest you? Why?

2. Think about the different sources—television, radio, websites, lectures, friends—from which you receive information about the environment. How do the information and viewpoints you receive from these sources personally affect your views of the natural world or environmental problems?

3. The rhetorical theorist Kenneth Burke wrote, "Much that we take as observations about 'reality' may be but the spinning out of possibilities implicit in our particular choice of terms"? What does he mean by this claim? Do you agree with him?

4. Are wolves intrinsically cruel? After looking into the eyes of a dying wolf, Aldo Leopold wrote, "There was something new to me in those eyes–something known only to her and to the mountain." What did he mean? What was Leopold's purpose in writing about wolves and his own knowledge of the natural world?

5. Does the public sphere exist? Where? Where do you find yourself discussing concerns about the environment? Do your views change as a result of this interaction with others?

6. In our society, whose voices are heard most often about environmental issues? Do you believe that ordinary citizens like yourself are likely to be heard by government officials or policymakers when they make decisions about environmental topics?

REFERENCES

Anderson, A. (1997). *Media, culture, and the environment.* New Brunswick, NJ: Rutgers University Press.

Arnold, R., & Gottlieb, A. (1998). *Trashing the economy: How runaway environmentalism is wrecking America* (2nd ed.). Bellevue, WA: Merril Press.

Babbitt, Bruce. (1995, December 13). Between the flood and the rainbow. Speech. Retrieved April 20, 2001, from www.fs.fed.us/eco/eco-watch/ew951218.htm

Bartlett, R. A. (1985). *Yellowstone: A wilderness besieged.* Tucson: University of Arizona Press.

Beierle, T. C., & Cayford, J. (2002). *Democracy in practice: Public participation in environmental decisions.* Washington, DC: Resources for the Future.

Brown, W. R., & Crable, R. E. (1973). Industry, mass magazines, and the ecology issue. *Quarterly Journal of Speech, 59,* 259–272.

Brulle, R. J. (2000). *Agency, democracy, and nature: The U.S. environmental movement from a critical theory perspective.* Cambridge: MIT Press.

Bullis, C. (1992). Retalking environmental discourses from feminist perspectives: The radical potential of ecofeminism. In C. L. Oravec & J. G. Cantrill (Eds.), *The Conference on the Discourse of Environmental Advocacy* (pp. 346–359). Salt Lake City: University of Utah Humanities Center.

Burke, K. (1966). *Language as symbolic action.* Berkeley: University of California Press.

Cantrill, J. G. (1993). Communication and our environment: Categorizing research in environmental advocacy. *Journal of Applied Communication Research, 21,* 66–95.

Carbaugh, D. (1992). "The Mountain" and "The Project": Dueling depictions of a natural environment. In C. L. Oravec & J. G. Cantrill (Eds.), *The Conference on the Discourse of Environmental Advocacy* (pp. 165–182). Salt Lake City: University of Utah Humanities Center.

Carbaugh, D. (1996). Naturalizing communication and culture. In J. G. Cantrill & C. L. Oravec (Eds.), *The symbolic earth: Discourse and our creation of the environment* (pp. 38–57). Lexington: University of Kentucky Press.

Carson, R. (1962). *Silent spring.* Boston: Houghton Mifflin.

Center for Health, Environment, and Justice. (2003). Love Canal: The start of a movement. Retrieved January 7, 2004, from www.chej.org/movement.htm

Cohen, B. C. (1963). *The press and foreign policy.* Princeton: Princeton University Press.

Cooper, M. M. (1996). Environmental rhetoric in an age of hegemony: Earth First! and the Nature Conservancy. In C. G. Herndl & S. C. Brown (Eds.), *Green culture: Environmental rhetoric in contemporary America.* Madison: University of Wisconsin Press.

Cox, J. R. (1982). The die is cast: Topical and ontological dimensions of the *locus* of the irreparable. *Quarterly Journal of Speech, 6,* 227–239.

Cox, J. R. (1999). Reclaiming the "indecorous" voice: Public participation by low-income communities in environmental decision making. In C. B. Short & D. Hardy-Short (Eds.), *Proceedings of the Fifth Biennial Conference on Communication and Environment.* Flagstaff: Northern Arizona University School of Communication, pp. 21–31.

Crawford-Brown, D. (2005, May 20). Forging a place for environmental studies. *Chronicle of Higher Education,* p. B15.

Daniels, S. E., & Walker, G. B. (2001). *Working through environmental conflict: The collaborative learning approach*. Westport, CT: Praeger.

Davis, S. G. (1997). *Spectacular nature: Corporate culture and the Sea World experience*. Berkeley: University of California Press.

DeLuca, K. M. (1999). *Image politics: The new rhetoric of environmental activism*. New York: Guilford Press.

DeLuca, K., & Demo, A. T. (2000). Imaging nature: Watkins, Yosemite, and the birth of environmentalism. *Critical Studies in Mass Communication, 17,* 241–260.

DeLuca, K. M., & Peeples, J. (2002). From public sphere to public screen: Democracy, activism, and the "violence" of Seattle. *Critical Studies in Media Communication, 19,* 125–151.

DePoe, S. (1997). Environmental studies in mass communication. *Critical Studies in Mass Communication, 14,* 368–372.

Depoe, S. P., Delicath, J. W., & Aepli, M. F. (Eds.). (2004). *Communication and public participation in environmental decision making*. Albany: State University of New York Press.

Downing, J. (1988). The alternative public realm: The organization of the 1980s anti-nuclear press in West Germany and Britain. *Media, Culture, and Society, 28,* 38–50.

Dunlap, R. E., & Mertig, E. G. (1992). *American environmentalism: The U.S. environmental movement, 1970–1990*. Philadelphia: Taylor & Francis.

Ehrlich, P. R., & Ehrlich, A. H. (1996). *Betrayal of science and reason: How anti-environmental rhetoric threatens our future*. Washington, DC: Island Press.

Farrell, T. B., & Goodnight, G. T. (1981). Accidental rhetoric: The root metaphors of Three Mile Island. *Quarterly Journal of Speech, 48,* 271–300.

Fiorino, D. J. (1989). Technical and democratic values in risk analysis. *Risk Analysis, 9,* 293–299.

Fischer, F. (2000). *Citizens, experts, and the environment: The politics of local knowledge*. Durham, NC: Duke University Press.

Fischer, H. (1995). *Wolf wars*. Helena, MT: Falcon Press.

Garrett, L. (2003, August 23). EPA misled public on 9/11 pollution: White House ordered false assurances on air quality, report says. *San Francisco Chronicle,* pp. A1, A4.

Gibbs, L. M. (1982). *Love Canal: My story*. Albany: SUNY Press.

Gibbs, L. M. (1998). *Love Canal: The story continues*. Stony Creek, CT: New Society.

Goodnight, T. G. (1982). The personal, technical, and public spheres of argument: A speculative inquiry into the art of public deliberation. *Journal of the American Forensic Association, 18,* 214–227.

Gorman, J. (2004, January 8). Scientists predict widespread extinction by global warming. *New York Times,* p. A4.

Greenberg, M. R., Sandman, P. M., Sachsman, D. B., & Salamone, K. L. (1989). Network television news coverage of environmental risk. *Risk Analysis, 9,* 119–126.

Grunig, L. (Ed.). (1989). *Environmental activism revisited: The changing nature of communication through organizational public relations, special interest groups, and the mass media.* Troy, OH: North American Association for Environmental Education.

Guber, D. L. (2003). *The grassroots of a green revolution: Polling America on the environment.* Cambridge: MIT Press.

Habermas, J. (1974). The public sphere: An encyclopedia article (1964). *New German Critique 1*(3), 49–55.

Hamilton, J. D. (2003). Exploring technical and cultural appeals in strategic risk communication: The Fernald radium case. *Risk Analysis, 23,* 291–302.

Hays, S. P. (2000). *A history of environmental politics since 1945.* Pittsburgh: University of Pittsburgh Press.

Helvarg, D. (2004). *The war against the greens: The "wise-use" movement, the new right, and the browning of America.* Boulder, CO: Johnson Books.

Herndl, C. G., & Brown, S. C. (Eds.). (1996). *Green culture: Environmental rhetoric in contemporary America.* Madison: University of Wisconsin Press.

Johnson, B. R. (2003). Communicating air quality information: Experimental evaluation of alternative formats. *Risk Analysis, 23,* 91–103.

Kempton, W., Boster, J. S., & Hartley, J. A. (1996). *Environmental values in American culture.* Cambridge: MIT Press.

Killingsworth, J. M., & Palmer, J. S. (1992). *Ecospeak: Rhetoric and environmental politics in America.* Carbondale: Southern Illinois University Press.

Lange, J. (1990). Refusal to compromise: The case of Earth First! *Western Journal of Speech Communication, 54,* 473–494.

Lange, J. I. (1993). The logic of competing information campaigns: Conflict over old growth and the spotted owl. *Communication Monographs, 60,* 239–257.

Leclair, L. (1993). Carnivals against capital: Rooted in resistance. In A. Opel & D. Pompper (Eds.), *Representing resistance: Media, civil disobedience, and the global justice movement* (pp. 3–15). Westport, CT: Praeger.

Leopold, A. (1966). *A Sand County almanac.* New York: Ballantine Books. (Original work published 1949 by Oxford University Press.)

Luke, T. W. (1987). Chernobyl: The packaging of transnational ecological disaster. *Critical Studies in Mass Communication, 4,* 351–375.

Markowitz, G., & Rosner, D. (2002). *Deceit and denial: The deadly politics of industrial pollution.* Berkeley: University of California Press.

Meisner, M. (in press). Knowing nature through the media: An examination of mainstream print and television representations of the non-human world. In G. B. Walker & W. J. Kinsella (Eds.), *Proceedings of the Seventh Biennial Conference on Communication and the Environment.* Corvallis: Oregon State University Department of Speech Communication.

Meister, M. (2001). Meteorology and the rhetoric of nature's cultural display. *Quarterly Journal of Speech, 87,* 415–428.

Meister M., & Japp, P. M. (Eds). (2002). *Enviropop: Studies in environmental rhetoric and popular culture.* Westport, CT: Praeger.

Moore, M. P. (1993). Constructing irreconcilable conflict: The function of synecdoche in the spotted owl controversy. *Communication Monographs, 60,* 258–274.

Myerson, G., & Rydin, Y. (1991). *The language of environment: A new rhetoric.* London: University College London Press.

Nash, R. (2001). *Wilderness and the American mind* (4th ed.). New Haven: Yale University Press.

Opel, A. (2002). *Monopoly™: The National Parks Edition:* Reading neo-liberal simulacra. In M. Meister & P. M. Japp (Eds.), *Enviropop: Studies in environmental rhetoric and popular culture* (pp. 31–44). Westport, CT: Praeger.

Opel, A., & Pompper, D. (2003). (Eds.). *Representing resistance: Media, civil disobedience, and the global justice movement.* Westport, CT: Praeger.

Oravec, C. (1981). John Muir, Yosemite, and the sublime response: A study of the rhetoric of preservationism. *Quarterly Journal of Speech, 67,* 245–258.

Oravec, C. (1984). Conservationism vs. preservationism: The "public interest" in the Hetch Hetchy controversy. *Quarterly Journal of Speech, 70,* 339–361.

Owens, L., & Palmer, L. K. (2003). Making the news: Anarchist counter-public relations on the World Wide Web. *Critical Studies in Media Communication, 20,* 335–361.

Peterson, T. R. (1986). The will to conservation: A Burkeian analysis of dust bowl rhetoric and American farming motives. *Southern Speech Communication Journal, 52,* 1–21.

Pezzullo, P. C. (2003). Touring "Cancer Alley," Louisiana: Performances of community and memory for environmental justice. *Text and Performance Quarterly, 23,* 226–252.

Plough, A., & Krimsky, S. (1987). The emergence of risk communication studies: Social and political context. *Science, Technology, & Human Values, 12,* 4–10.

Rawe, A. L., & Field, R. (1992, Fall). Interview with a "wise guy." *Common Ground of Puget Sound,* 1.

Reich, M. R. (1991). *Toxic politics: Responding to chemical disasters.* Ithaca, NY: Cornell University Press.

Retzinger, J. P. (2002). Cultivating the agrarian myth in Hollywood films. In M. Meister & P. M. Japp (Eds.), *Enviropop: Studies in environmental rhetoric and popular culture* (pp. 45–62). Westport, CT: Praeger.

Rolle, S. (2002). Measures of progress for collaboration: Case study of the Applegate Partnership. Retrieved May 22, 2003, from www.fs.fed.us/pnw/pubs/gtr565.pdf

Sale, K. (1993). *The green revolution: The American environmental movement 1962–1992.* New York: Hill & Wang.

Schlesinger, W. H. (2003, May 18). Academics have right to speak out. *Raleigh News and Observer,* p. A23.

Schwarze, S. (2003) Juxtaposition in environmental health rhetoric: Exposing asbestos contamination in Libby, Montana. *Rhetoric & Public Affairs, 6,* 313–335.

Shabecoff, P. (1993). *A fierce green fire: The American environmental movement.* New York: Hill & Wang.

Shabecoff, P. (2000). *Earth rising: American environmentalism in the 21st century.* Washington, DC: Island Press.

Shabecoff, P. (2003). *A fierce green fire: The American environmental movement* (Rev. ed.). Washington, DC: Island Press.

Shaiko, R. G. (1999). *Voices and echoes for the environment: Public interest representation in the 1990s and beyond.* New York: Columbia University Press.

Shanahan, J., & McComas, K. (1999). *Nature stories: Depictions of the environment and their effects.* Cresskill, NJ: Hampton Press.

Shannon, C., & Weaver, W. (1949). *The mathematical theory of communication.* Urbana: University of Illinois Press.

Short, B. (1991). Earth First! and the rhetoric of moral confrontation. *Communication Studies, 42,* 172–188.

Smith, T. M. (1998). *The myth of green marketing: Tending our goats at the edge of the apocalypse.* Toronto: University of Toronto Press.

Stephan, M. (2002). Environmental information disclosure programs: They work, but why? *Social Science Quarterly, 83*(1): 190–205.

Switzer, J. V. (1997). *Green backlash: The history and politics of environmental opposition in the U.S.* Boulder, CO: Lynne Rienner.

Taubes, G. (1993). The ozone backlash. *Science, 260,* 1580–1583.

Taylor, B. R. (Ed.). (1995). *Ecological resistance movements: The global emergence of radical and popular environmentalism.* Albany: State University of New York Press.

Torgerson, D. (1999). *The promise of green politics: Environmentalism and the public sphere.* Durham, NC: Duke University Press.

Waddell, C. (1990). The role of pathos in the decision-making process: A study in the rhetoric of science policy. *Quarterly Journal of Speech, 76,* 381–401.

Waddell, C. (1996). Saving the great lakes: Public participation in environmental policy. In C. G. Herndl & S. C. Brown (Eds.), *Green culture: Environmental rhetoric in contemporary America* (pp. 141–165). Madison: University of Wisconsin Press.

Walker, G. B. (2004). The roadless area initiative as national policy: Is public participation an oxymoron? In S. P. Depoe, J. W. Delicath, & M-F. A. Elsenbeer (Eds.), *Communication and public participation in environmental decision making* (pp. 113–135). Albany: State University of New York Press.

Williams, B. A., & Matheny, A. R. (1995). *Democracy, dialogue, and environmental disputes: The contested languages of social regulation.* New Haven: Yale University Press.

Zagacki, K. (1999). Spatial and temporal images in the biodiversity dispute. *Quarterly Journal of Speech, 85,* 417–435.

2

Rhetorically Shaping the Environment

What could they see but a hideous & desolate wilderness, full of wild beasts & wild men?

—William Bradford, *Of Plymouth Plantation,* 1620–1647

Here I can be the voice and face of this tree, and for the whole forest that can't speak for itself.

—Julia "Butterfly" Hill (n.d., para. 2)
sitting in Luna, a 1,000-year-old redwood tree

Writing of settlers' hardships at Plymouth in 1620, William Bradford described the landscape beyond the colony as a "hideous and desolate wilderness." With that phrase, he began what environmental historian Roderick Nash (2001) called a "tradition of repugnance" for nature (p. 24). His account of the New England forests also would be the start of a long-running controversy over how to define and shape the meaning of the relationship between human society and the environment.

In 1999, Julia "Butterfly" Hill voiced quite a different view of humans' relationship with the environment while she lived for two years high in the branches of an ancient redwood tree (named Luna) to prevent loggers from cutting it down. (For more information, see www.circleoflife.org.) Bradford's fears and Hill's desire illustrate two different views of nature, each of which

Figure 2.1   Julia "Butterfly" Hill and Luna
(Photo: Doug Wolens)

has evoked wide-ranging passion, debate, imagination, and angst. Nash (2001) observed in his classic study, *Wilderness and the American Mind,* that the term *wilderness* "is so heavily freighted with meaning of a personal, symbolic, and changing kind as to resist easy definition" (p. 1).

The diverse meanings of *wilderness* as well as the term *environment* remind us that these are powerful and changing ideas the meanings of which have consequences for our behavior toward them. For example, the designation of old-growth forests as wilderness under the 1964 Wilderness Act has had the effect of removing land from the timber base and restricting commercial development on it. And the charge of environmental racism applied to the dense concentration of hazardous factories and landfills in minority neighborhoods has led to a new scrutiny of society's placement of toxic wastes. Because differing views of the environment have serious economic, health, and social consequences, many people throughout the history of the United States have "battled mightily and often" over the best ways to define humans' relation to the natural world (Warren, 2003, p. 1).

From a communication perspective, the history of human behavior toward the natural world is one of competing voices and interests struggling in various public spheres to define, shape, redefine, and challenge prevailing social and political attitudes about the environment. What the term *environment* symbolizes at any particular time depends upon the specific communications of these differing interests. This chapter briefly traces this history and introduces the perspective of rhetorical theory we'll use to describe the ongoing attempts by environmentalists, businesspeople, scientists, journalists, and ordinary citizens to shape our relationships with the natural world.

The first section of this chapter traces the development of the environmental movement in the United States, to provide historical background. We'll also look at four major moments in U.S. history, points at which individuals, environmental groups, and media transformed societal attitudes about the environment.

The second section introduces a rhetorical perspective for the study of environmental communication. A *rhetorical perspective* focuses on purposeful and consequential efforts to influence society's attitudes and behaviors through communication, which includes public debate, protests, news stories, advertising, and other modes of symbolic action. The third section of this chapter extends the scope of rhetoric to include visual media such as photographs, art, and film. Just as speeches, reports, or testimony at public hearings can persuade others, so, too, can nonverbal images affect attitudes and behavior toward nature.

The Environmental Movement in the United States

During the last three decades of the 20th century, the environmental movement altered American consciousness and behavior as profoundly as any movement since the antislavery movement of the 19th century (Sale, 1993). Yet the roots of this achievement lay in centuries-old efforts to transform the relationship between the environment and society by challenging society's discourses about human dominion and the conquest of nature.

Important to transforming prevailing beliefs are **antagonisms.** In everyday language, *antagonism* means "conflict" or "disagreement." Here, I'm using the term in a more specialized way to denote the recognition of the *limit* of an idea, a widely shared viewpoint, or ideology that allows an opposing idea or belief system to be voiced (Laclau and Mouffe, 1985). A limit is recognized when questioning or criticism reveals a prevailing view to be inadequate or unresponsive to new demands. Recognizing the limit creates an opening for alternative voices and ideas to redefine what is appropriate or just—in this case, the relationship between the environment and society. In the history of the U.S. environmental movement, four major antagonisms define recognitions of ideological limits, at which point new voices and interests challenged the prevailing views of society:

1. Preservation and conservation of nature versus exploitation of it

2. Human health versus business and manufacturing activity

3. Environmental justice versus a vision of nature as a place apart from the places where people live, work, learn, and play

4. Protection of the global commons and communities versus economic globalization

One important note about histories of the U.S. environmental movement: Traditional accounts describe the 19th century as an era that focused on protection of wilderness, and the post-1960s as a period of awakening to concerns about human health. As Gottlieb (1993b) observed, the problem with this historical divide in recounting the movement is "who is left out and what it fails to explain" (p. 1). Although I'll follow this standard account to some extent, I'll also try to bring in "who is left out," figures such as Alice Hamilton (1943), who urged a concern for the "dangerous trades" of urban environments as early as the 1920s. Also, in describing the post-1960s period, I'll highlight minority citizens' demands for environmental justice, as well as new concerns for the environment under unrestrained economic globalization.

Preservation and Conservation
Versus the Exploitation of Nature

The first serious questioning of the exploitation of the nation's remaining wild areas began in the late 18th century. This was in sharp contrast to a centuries-old tradition of loathing wilderness and seeking to subdue wild nature. Puritans such as Michael Wigglesworth (1662) had described the dark forests as "a waste and howling wilderness" (p. 83, quoted in Nash, 2001, p. 36). And in his classic essay "The Historical Roots of Our Ecological Crisis," historian Lynn White, Jr. (1967) noted that Europeans and, later, early American settlers[1] inherited a specific religious injunction to "subdue" nature—a belief that it was "God's will that man [sic] exploit nature for his proper ends" (p. 1205).

Nevertheless, by the late 18th century the questioning of this tradition of repugnance for wild nature had begun. In art, literature, and on the lecture circuits, voices began to challenge the view of nature as alien or exploitable. Nash identifies three major sources of these challenges: (1) Romantic ideals in art and literature, (2) a search for national identity, and (3) transcendentalist ideals in writings of Henry David Thoreau and others.

The first source of resistance to aversion toward wilderness came through the influence of Romantic and primitivist ideals in art and literature. Nash (2001) writes that 18th- and early 19th-century English nature poets and aestheticians such as William Gilpin "inspired a rhetorical style for articulating

[an] appreciation of uncivilized nature" (p. 46). These writers and poets, along with Edmund Burke, Jean-Jacques Rousseau, and other, earlier writers, fostered in American art and literature an ideal of sublimity in wild nature. The **sublime** was an aesthetic category that associated God's influence with the feelings of awe and exultation that some experienced in the presence of wilderness. "Combined with the primitivistic idealization of a life closer to nature, these ideas fed the Romantic movement which had far-reaching implications for wilderness" (Nash, 2001, p. 44).

A second challenge to the tradition of repugnance toward wilderness was the young nation's quest for a sense of national identity. Believing that America could not match Europe's history and soaring cathedrals, advocates of a uniquely American identity sought to champion the distinctive characteristics of the American landscape. "Nationalists argued that far from being a liability, wilderness was actually an American asset" (Nash, 2001, p. 67). Writers such as James Fenimore Cooper and artists of the Hudson River school such as Thomas Cole celebrated the wonders of the American wilderness by defining a national style in fiction, poetry, and painting. In his 1835 "Essay on American Scenery," Cole argued that the new nation did not need to feel inferior to "civilized Europe," for "American scenery . . . has features, and glorious ones, unknown to Europe. The most distinctive, and perhaps the most impressive, characteristic of American scenery is its wildness" (quoted in Nash, 2001, pp. 80–81).

Finally, the 19th-century emergence of **transcendentalism** as a major philosophical perspective proved to be an important impetus for the reevalution of wild nature. "The core of [t]ranscendentalism was the belief that a correspondence or parallelism existed between the higher realm of spiritual truth and the lower one of material objects. . . . Natural objects assumed importance because, if rightly seen, they reflected universal spiritual truth" (Nash, 2001, p. 85). Among those who drew upon transcendentalist beliefs to challenge older discourses about wilderness was the writer and philosopher Henry David Thoreau. For Thoreau (1862/1893), wilderness was more valuable than urban areas because it more closely embodied the truth of this transcendental realm. He argued that, "in Wildness is the preservation of the World," and that there exists "a subtle magnetism in Nature, which, if we unconsciously yield to it, will direct us aright" (pp. 251, 265; see also Cox, 1980). By the late 19th century, Thoreau's writings had influenced others to preserve remnants of the vanishing American wilderness.

John Muir and the Wilderness Preservation Movement

By the 1880s, key figures in California and elsewhere had begun to argue explicitly for the preservation of wilderness areas.[2] Arising out of these efforts were campaigns to protect coastal forests and spectacular regions of natural scenery such as Yosemite Valley in the Sierra Nevada Mountains. **Preservationism** sought to ban commercial use of these areas, to preserve wild forests and other natural areas for appreciation, study, and outdoor recreation. This movement also would be one of the two major forces of the early 20th century, along with *conservationism,* to challenge the rapacious exploitation of wild nature. (We'll turn to this second challenge shortly.)

One of the leaders of the preservation movement was the Scottish immigrant John Muir, whose literary essays in the 1870s and 1880s did much to arouse national sentiment for preserving Yosemite Valley. Communication scholar Christine Oravec (1981) has observed that Muir's essays evoked a **sublime response** from his readers through his description of the rugged mountains and valleys of the Sierra Nevada. This response on the part of readers was characterized by (1) an immediate awareness of a sublime object (such as Yosemite Valley), (2) a sense of overwhelming personal insignificance and awe in the object's presence, and (3) ultimately a feeling of spiritual exaltation (p. 248). Typical of this style was Muir's depiction of the 2,425-foot Yosemite Falls, the world's fifth highest: "Gray cliffs, wet black rock, the white hill of ice, trees, . . . and the surging, roaring torrents escaping down the gorge in front, glorifying all, and proclaiming the triumph of Peace and eternal Harmony" (Oravec, 1981, p. 249). Muir's influence and the support of others such as Robert Underwood Johnson, editor of the literary magazine *Century,* led to a national campaign to preserve Yosemite Valley. By 1890, these efforts had resulted in the creation of Yosemite National Park by Congress, "the first successful proposal for preservation of natural scenery to gain widespread national attention and support" from the public (p. 256).

Similarly, aggressive logging in the 1880s of giant redwood trees along California's coast fueled further interest in the preservation movement. Laura White and the California Federation of Women's Clubs were among those who led successful campaigns to protect redwood groves in the late 19th century (Merchant, 2002). As a result of these early campaigns, groups dedicated to wilderness and wildlife preservation began to appear: John Muir's Sierra Club (1892), the Audubon Society (1905), the Save the Redwoods League (1918), the National Parks and Conservation Association (1919), the Wilderness Society (1935), and the National Wildlife Federation (1936). In the 20th century, these groups launched other preservation campaigns that challenged exploitation of these wild lands. (For a history of this period, see Merchant, 2002, and Warren, 2003.)

Conservation and the Efficient
Use of Natural Resources

Muir's ethic of preservation soon clashed with a competing vision that sought to manage America's forests and other natural resources for efficient and sustainable use. Influenced by the philosophy of **utilitarianism,** the idea of "the greatest good for the greatest number," some in the early 20th century began to promote a new conservation ethic. Associated principally with Gifford Pinchot, President Theodore Roosevelt's chief of the Division of Forestry (now the U.S. Forest Service), the term **conservation** meant "the wise and efficient use of natural resources" (Merchant, 2002, p. 128). For example, in managing public forest lands as a source of timber, Pinchot instituted a sustained yield policy, according to which logged timberlands were to be reforested after cutting, to ensure future timber supplies (Hays, 1987; Merchant, 2002; for more about Pinchot, see Miller, 2004.)

The tension between Muir's ethic of preservation and Pinchot's conservation approach came to a head in the fierce controversy over the building of a dam in Hetch Hetchy Valley in Yosemite National Park. In 1901, The City of San Francisco's proposal to dam the river running through this valley as a source for its water sparked a multi-year dispute over the purpose of the new park. At the heart of the controversy were two differing views of the public interest (Oravec, 1984). As an ideal, the **public interest** is a symbolic marker of legitimacy for actions taken in the name of the nation's people or the common good. (We'll return to the idea of symbolic legitimacy later in the chapter.)

The tension between the aesthetic and practical values of Hetch Hetchy Valley would continue to incite debate long after the dam was approved in 1913 (Oravec, 1984). Although in the following decades Pinchot's conservation approach strongly influenced the management of natural resources by agencies such as the Forest Service and the Bureau of Land Management (BLM), preservationists, too, won significant victories. (Appendix A summarizes these achievements.) One major accomplishment of preservationists was the National Parks Act of 1916, which established a national system of parks that continues to expand today. Other designations of parks, wildlife refuges, and wild and scenic rivers would follow throughout the 20th century. Perhaps the preservationists' most significant victory was the 1964 Wilderness Act. The Wilderness Act authorizes Congress to set aside wild areas in national forests, national parks, and other strictly managed public lands to preserve such areas' "primeval character and influence" (Warren, 2003, p. 243).

The tension between preservation and conservation continues to be central in current debates about U.S. environmental policies. For example, during the last 20 years some—but not all—environmental groups have called for an end to all commercial logging, mining, and grazing on U.S. public lands. Others believe that better forest management practices are sufficient. Meanwhile, timber workers and forest activists in the Pacific Northwest continue to battle each other over the amount of logging allowed in old-growth forests. (For another viewpoint, see "The Trouble with Wilderness.")

Another Viewpoint: "The Trouble With Wilderness"

The idea of wilderness has been challenged in recent years from a viewpoint other than Pinchot's conservation ethic. Historian William Cronon (1996) has argued that wilderness "is quite profoundly a human creation" (p. 69) that diverts attention from the places nearby, where people live and work. Cronon argued,

> The trouble with wilderness is that it . . . represents the false hope of an escape from responsibility, the illusion that we can somehow wipe clean the slate of our past and return to the tabula rasa that supposedly existed before we began to leave our marks on the world. . . . This, then, is the central paradox: [W]ilderness embodies a dualistic vision in which the human is entirely outside the natural. If we allow ourselves to believe that nature, to be true, must also be wild, then our very presence in nature represents its fall. The place where we are is the place where nature is not. (pp. 80–81)

Interestingly, Cronon is arguing not for the elimination of wild areas but for a questioning of the idea embraced in some understandings of the term *wilderness* as a place beyond human presence.

Partly as a result of the perceived failure of mainstream groups to preserve more wild lands, by the early 1980s a split had developed in the movement. Disillusioned wilderness activists formed the radical group Earth First! to engage in **direct action,** physical acts of protests such as road blockades, sit-ins, and **tree spiking.**[3] Other groups, such as the Earth Liberation Front, have turned to arson and property damage in a controversial move to protect endangered species and to protest society's material consumption. Still other groups have voiced a more critical rhetoric, questioning many of society's core values in the name of "deep ecology" and "eco-feminism." Overall, the contemporary movement consists of a broad and diverse range of both voices and strategies for the protection of wild nature.

Public Health and the Human Environment

By the 1960s, along with the continued interest in wilderness and forest issues, a second antagonism arrived, which focused on the effects of environmental pollutants on human health. At a time when environmental standards for air and water pollution were weak or nonexistent, more and more citizens began to question the effects of unregulated business and manufacturing activities. Their concerns included pollution by factories and refineries, abandoned toxic waste sites, exposure to pesticides used on agricultural crops, and radioactive fallout from above-ground nuclear testing.

Traditional accounts of the U.S. environmental movement credit biologist and writer Rachel Carson for voicing the first public challenge to business practices that affect the natural environment and human health. In her eloquent book *Silent Spring,* Carson (1962) wrote, "we are adding a . . . new kind of havoc—the direct killing of birds, mammals, fishes, and indeed, practically every form of wildlife by chemical insecticides indiscriminately sprayed on the land" (p. 83). Fearful of the consequences for human health from insecticides like DDT, she warned that modern agribusiness had "armed itself with the most modern and terrible weapons, and that in turning them against the insects it has also turned them against the earth" (p. 262). (For more information on the significance of Carson's *Silent Spring,* see Craig Waddell's anthology, *And No Birds Sing* [2000]).

Environmental writer Kirkpatrick Sale (1993) remarked that, with Rachel Carson's "angry and uncompromising words, it can be said that the modern environmental movement began" (p. 3). Although *Silent Spring* did prefigure a popular movement that prompted new environmental protections, earlier voices from the 1880s through the 1920s had warned of dangers to human health from poor sanitation and occupational exposures to lead and other chemicals. Trade unions, "sanitarians," reformers from Jane Addams's Hull House in Chicago, and public health advocates had warned of hazards to both workplace and urban life: "contaminated water supplies, inadequate waste and sewage collection disposal, poor ventilation and polluted and smoke-filled air, [and] overcrowded neighborhoods and tenements" (Gottlieb (1993a, p. 55).

Urban environmental historian Robert Gottlieb (1993a) has called attention particularly to the influence of Dr. Alice Hamilton, "a powerful environmental advocate in an era when the term had yet to be invented" (p. 51), who worked in the 1920s to reform the "dangerous trades" of urban work-places. With the publication of *Industrial Poisons in the United States* (1925) and her work with the Women's Health Bureau, Hamilton became "the country's most powerful and effective voice for exploring the environmental consequences of industrial activity," including the impacts of occupational hazards on women and minorities in the workplace (Gottlieb, 1993a, p. 51).

Still, until the 1962 publication of *Silent Spring*, there was no such thing as an environmental movement in the United States in the sense of a "concerted, populous, vocal, influential, active" force (Sale, 1993, p. 6). However, by the late 1960s news coverage of contaminated food, heavy air pollution in many cities, nuclear fallout, oil spills off the coast of Santa Barbara, California, and the Cuyahoga River near Cleveland, Ohio, which burst into flames when its polluted surface was ignited, had fueled a public outcry for greater protection of the environment. One result was the **National Environmental Policy Act** (NEPA), signed into law by President Nixon on January 1, 1970. This would become the cornerstone of modern environmental law. The act requires every federal agency to prepare an environmental impact statement for any project that would affect the environment. At the end of 1970, by executive order President Nixon also created the Environmental Protection Agency (commonly known as the EPA) to implement and oversee the enforcement of new environmental laws such as the Clean Air Act and the Clean Water Act (1970).

By the first Earth Day on April 22, 1970, students, public health workers, new activist groups, and urban workers had coalesced into a recognizable movement to champion environmental controls on industry and governmental activities. Drawing some 20 million people and involving protests, teach-ins, and festivals at schools, colleges, and universities throughout the country, the inaugural Earth Day was one of the largest demonstrations in American history. Its events involved "every strata of American society" (Flippen, 2003, p. 272). At the same time, new groups arose to address the relationship between human health and the environment. Among the earliest were the Environmental Defense Fund (1967), Environmental Action (1970), and the Natural Resources Defense Council (1970). Finally, the growing popularity of the "ecology movement"—the term used in the 1970s for the environmental movement—led lawmakers to enact new legislation to strengthen protections for air and water quality and to regulate production and disposal of toxic chemicals. (These accomplishments are summarized in Appendix B. For more information on the U.S. environmental movement generally, see "Suggested Readings" at the end of this chapter.)

Whereas the ecology movement championed human health and environmental quality against industrial pollution and underregulated commerce, much of the initial focus of the new environmental groups was at the federal

Figure 2.2   Large banner at an Earth Day Demonstration, c. 1970
(copyright Getty Images: Earth Day 1970 #3208016)

level (enacting new laws). However, by the end of the 1970s, the challenge to industrial pollution became manifest at a local level as communities became increasingly worried by the chemical contamination of their air, drinking water, soil, and school grounds. For example, the small, upstate New York community of Love Canal became a symbol of the nation's widening consciousness of the hazards of chemicals in their economy. (See the brief description of the Love Canal case in Chapter 1.) Ordinary citizens felt themselves surrounded by what Hays (1987) termed "the toxic sea around us" (p. 171) and began to organize in hundreds of community-based groups to demand cleanup of their neighborhoods and stricter accountability of corporate polluters.

Prompted by the toxic waste scandals at Love Canal and other places such as Times Beach, Missouri, Congress passed the **Superfund** law of 1980, which authorized the Environmental Protection Agency to clean up toxic sites and take action against the responsible parties. Local citizens also took advantage of new federal laws such as the Clean Water Act to participate in local decision-making venues, such as state agencies' issuance of air and water permits for businesses. (We will describe these new guarantees for public participation more fully in Chapter 3.)

Environmental Justice: "Where We Live, Work, Play, and Learn"

Even as the environmental movement widened its concerns in the 1960s to include health and environmental quality along with wilderness preservation, there remained a language of the environment that provided "disjointed and at times contradictory" accounts of humans' place in nature and assumed a "long-standing separation of the social from the ecological" (Gottlieb, 2002, p. 5). However, by the 1980s new activists from minority and low-income communities had begun to challenge the view of nature as "a place apart" from the environments where people lived and worked, disclosing a third antagonism in prevailing views of the environment.

Re-Articulating the Meaning of Environment

Despite some earlier efforts to bring environmentalists, labor, and civil rights and religious leaders together to explore common interests in the 1960s and 1970s[4], national environmental groups largely failed to recognize the problems of urban residents and minority communities. For example, sociologist Giovanna Di Chiro (1996) reported that in the mid-1980s residents in south central Los Angeles who were trying to stop a solid waste incinerator from being located in their neighborhood discovered that "these issues were not deemed adequately 'environmental' by local environmental groups such as the Sierra Club or the Environmental Defense Fund" (p. 299). Activists in communities of color were particularly vocal in criticizing mainstream environmental groups for being "reluctant to address issues of equity and social justice, within the context of the environment" (Alston, 1990, p. 23).

By the 1980s, residents and activists in some low-income neighborhoods and communities of color had started to take matters into their own hands. In a historically significant move, they proposed to rearticulate the word *environment* to mean the places "where we live, where we work, where we play, and where we learn" (Lee, 1996, p. 6). A key moment in the launching of this new movement occurred in 1982 with the protests by residents of the largely African American community of Warren County, North Carolina. Local residents and leaders of national civil rights groups tried to halt the state's plans to locate a toxic waste landfill in this rural community by sitting in roads to block 6,000 trucks carrying PCB (polychlorinated biphenol)-contaminated soil.[5] More than 500 protesters were arrested in what sociologists Robert Bullard and Beverly Hendrix Wright (1987) called "the first national attempt by blacks to link environmental issues (hazardous waste and pollution) to the mainstream civil rights agenda" (p. 32). (For more on the significance of this event as a "story of origin" in the movement, see Pezzullo, 2001.)

With similar struggles in other parts of the nation and reports of the heavy concentration of hazardous facilities in minority neighborhoods (Lee, 1993; Cole & Foster, 2001), some charged that these communities suffered from a form of environmental racism. Residents and critics alike began to speak of being poisoned and "dumped upon," and of certain communities targeted as "sacrifice zones" (Schueler, 1992, p. 45). Importantly for these critics, the term *environmental racism* meant not only threats to their health or livelihood from hazardous waste landfills, incinerators, agricultural pesticides, sweatshops, and polluting factories, but also the disproportionate burden that these practices placed on people of color and the workers and residents of low-income communities.

Defining Environmental Justice

Emerging from these struggles was a pluralistic vision of environmental justice. For most activists, this term connected the safety and quality of the environments where people lived, worked, played, and learned with concerns for social and economic justice. Residents and movement activists insisted that *environmental justice* referred to the basic right of all people to be free of poisons and other hazards. At its core, environmental justice also was a vision of the democratic inclusion of people and communities in the decisions that affected their health and well-being. Many people criticized decision-making processes that failed to provide meaningful participation "for those most burdened by environmental decisions"; they called for greater collaboration among government officials, experts, and the affected communities (Cole & Foster, 2001, p. 16).

The demand for environmental justice received significant publicity in 1991, when delegates from local communities, along with national leaders of civil rights, religious, and environmental groups, convened in Washington, D.C., for the First People of Color Environmental Leadership Summit. For the first time, the different strands of the emerging movement for environmental justice came together to challenge mainstream definitions of environmentalism. The delegates to the summit also adopted a powerful set of 16

"Principles of Environmental Justice" that enumerated a series of rights, including "the fundamental right to political, economic, cultural, and environmental self-determination of all peoples" (*Proceedings,* 1991, p. viii). (For a copy of the "Principles of Environmental Justice," see http://saepej.igc.org/Principles.html.)

In 1994, the movement achieved an important political goal when President Clinton issued an executive order directing each federal agency to "make achieving environmental justice part of its mission by identifying and addressing . . . disproportionately high and adverse human health or environmental effects of its programs, policies, and activities on minority populations and low-income populations in the United States" (Clinton, 1994, p. 7629). (The order remains in effect as of this writing.) Nevertheless, the movement continues to face real-world, on-the-ground challenges to building sustainable and healthy communities. Beyond the disproportionate burden of hazards on communities is the movement's insistence on the democratic inclusion of peoples and communities in the decisions affecting their lives, a vision that is still largely unrealized. (We'll describe the origins of this movement and its rhetorical effort to redefine environmentalism as environmental justice in more detail in Chapter 8.)

Global Environmentalism

Over the last two decades, an enthusiastic and diverse movement has been growing in countries throughout the world to protect environments in local communities and the global commons—oceans, climate, and biodiversity. This movement arises from a variety of sources: activism by local villagers; management of wildlife sanctuaries by international conservation groups such as Conservation International and the World Wide Fund for Nature; publicity and political efforts by Greenpeace and Friends of the Earth; and large protests by labor unions, farmers, anarchists, and indigenous peoples at meetings of the World Trade Organization in Seattle, Prague, and Cancun. Together, diverse peoples and organizations are forming a global environmental movement that is characterized by such actions as these:

> In Washington, D.C., a group of well-tailored public-interest lawyers and scientists . . . sit[s] down with State department officials to discuss the U.S. negotiating position on a global warming treaty. In the hills of Uttar Pradesh in India desperately poor villagers wrap their arms around trees to protect them from the logger's ax. . . . In Botswana, members of the Kalahari Conservation Society fight to block diversions of the Okavango River, which supports one of the great remaining wildlife habitats in Africa, from being diverted for use by a diamond mine. . . . (Shabecoff, 1996, pp. 60–61)

These and thousands of other actions reflect diverse agendas, and they rely on different tactics and methods of communication. This sometimes makes it difficult to recognize these actions as a single or unified movement. Nevertheless, struggles for environmental quality internationally are fueled by three different sources of grievance:

1. At the local level, increasing environmental deterioration has threatened livelihoods and traditional patterns of life. This includes examples such as the erosion of farmland in Asia and in many parts of Africa, foreign exports of trees from village forests in Mexico and India that deplete fuel and foods for these communities, and industrial pollution of urban areas in Eastern Europe and Russia. In addition, large increases in human population are straining natural habitat as well as farmland and water sources that are needed to sustain healthy communities.

2. Globally, industrial nations' pollution and high energy use have begun to damage the earth's commons through increased pollution of oceans, destruction of the earth's protective ozone layer, and gradual warming of the earth's climate.

3. New, international free-trade arrangements, such as the North American Free Trade Agreement (NAFTA) and the World Trade Organization, contain legal language that potentially undermines participating countries' ability to protect citizens' health, workers' safety, and the environment.

Additionally, a major stimulus in the spread of environmentalism came in the 1992 United Nations Conference on Environment and Development (informally called the **Earth Summit**) in Rio de Janeiro, Brazil. Representatives from nations at the Earth Summit reaffirmed an earlier Declaration of the United Nations Conference on the Human Environment, adopted at Stockholm in 1972, and pledged to work "towards international agreements which respect the interests of all and protect the integrity of the global environmental and developmental system." The **Rio Declaration** had considerable influence in spreading concern for environmental values internationally. (For the full text of the Rio Declaration, see www.unep.org/Documents/Default.asp?Document ID=78&ArticleID=1163.)

Resistance by local communities and the campaigns of international groups suggest that a fourth antagonism is emerging: a desire to protect the global commons and the earth's communities from the abuses of globalization. Globalization has been defined in varying ways, but here I use the term to denote liberalized rules for corporate investments abroad, movement of manufacturing—and its pollution—to poorer nations, and multinational trade agreements that threaten to undermine local rules for workers' safety, health, and environmental protections in many nations. Indeed, environmental and human rights critics charge that NAFTA and other trade agreements have "created [a] new language for challengers to use against environmental restrictions" (Andrews, 1999, p. 343; see also Esty, 1994, pp. 48–50; and Cox, in press).

Environmental progress also has been made in a number of international agreements. Among these are bans on trade in endangered species and new restrictions on "toxic traders," firms that sell hazardous waste materials to other nations. Recent attempts also have been made to establish standards for reducing chemical pollutants that affect Earth's climate and ozone layer. (Appendix C summarizes some of these agreements.)

As we've seen in the development of these four antagonisms, the concepts of nature and the environment are highly contingent. That is, they are subject to redefinition as new voices and interests contest prevailing understandings of our environments. The core of these challenges is a distinctly *rhetorical* process of human influence, questioning, and persuasion, and it is this perspective that we will explore in the following section.

A Rhetorical Perspective on the Environment

As we've just seen, few words have acquired the same symbolic currency as *environment*. (Closely related may be *ecology* and *nature*.) Literary scholars Carl G. Herndl and Stuart C. Brown (1996) note that the richness of this term has nurtured "not one environmental discourse but many" (p. 4). From its origin in wilderness preservation campaigns in the 19th century to calls for environmental justice in the 20th century, the environmental movement in the United States has drawn on a rich variety of languages and symbols to shape public perceptions of nature. *Environment* now signifies a wide range of concerns, from wilderness, air and water pollution, and toxic wastes to urban sprawl, global climate change, and the quality of life where people live, work, play, and learn.

Perhaps due to the diversity of meanings for the word *environment*, some communication scholars have begun to examine the key role of language and other symbols in the discursive framing and contestation of environmental concerns. For example, Herndl and Brown (1996) argue somewhat provocatively that the term *environment* is "a concept and an associated set of cultural values that we have constructed through the way we use language. *In a very real sense, there is no objective environment in the phenomenal world, no environment separate from the words we use to represent it*" (p. 3; emphasis added). This is not to suggest that there is no material world "out there."

Of course there is. But it is through differing symbolic modes that we understand and engage this world, infuse it with significance, and act toward it.

If the environment is something that we know partly through language and other symbols, then different linguistic and symbolic choices construct diverse meanings for the worlds we know. As a result, some scholars adopt a rhetorical perspective to study the different ways in which journalists, scientists, corporations, environmentalists, and citizens attempt to influence our perceptions and behavior toward the environment. A **rhetorical perspective** focuses on purposeful and consequential efforts to influence society's attitudes and ways of behaving through communication, which includes public debate, protests, news stories, advertising, and other modes of symbolic action (Campbell & Huxman, 2003).

In this section, I'll introduce the concepts of rhetoric and its pragmatic and constitutive roles. I'll also describe discourse and symbolic legitimacy boundaries—the other main ideas composing the rhetorical perspective that we'll use in this book.

The Art of Rhetoric

The study of rhetoric traces its origins to classical Greek philosopher-teachers such as Isocrates (436–338 B.C.E.) and Aristotle (384–322 B.C.E.), who taught the arts of citizenship to political leaders in democratic city-states such as Athens. The practice in these city-states was for citizens to speak publicly in law courts and the political assembly, where each citizen represented his own interests. (In Athens and other cities, civic speech was limited principally to male, property-owning citizens.) As a result, competency in public speaking, debate, and persuasion was vital for conducting civic business—war and peace, taxes, construction of public monuments, property claims, and so forth.

It was during this period that Aristotle summarized the teachings in the art of civic speaking when he defined **rhetoric** as "the faculty [power] of discovering in the particular case what are the available means of persuasion" (Cooper, 1960, p. 7). This art of rhetoric rested not simply on skillful delivery but on the ability to discover the resources for persuasion that were available in a specific situation. Aristotle's focus on the speaker's ability draws our attention to one of the early definitions of rhetoric as a purposeful (instrumental) choice among the available means of persuasion that a speaker uses in order to accomplish some effect or outcome.

In Chapter 1, we defined *environmental communication* in part as the pragmatic and constitutive vehicle for our understanding of the environment as well as our relationships to the natural world. As I just noted, rhetoric traditionally has been viewed primarily as *pragmatic* or instrumental activity that enables individuals to choose from the available means of persuasion to effect a desired outcome. Let me briefly illustrate this pragmatic role and then suggest a second function in which rhetoric may also be viewed as a constitutive vehicle.

Rhetoric as a Pragmatic Vehicle

An example of rhetoric's pragmatic role in influencing environmental policy is the newspaper advertisement that appeared in the June 9, 1966, editions of the *New York Times,* the *Washington Post,* the *Los Angeles Times,* and the *San Francisco Chronicle.* The full-page ad was an important means of persuasion in a Sierra Club campaign opposing plans by the U.S. Bureau of Reclamation to build dams inside the Grand Canyon to provide electricity for industries in the Southwest. In what was at the time the "best known campaign for [preservation] in newspaper history" (Turner, 1991, p. 172), the ad and letters it prompted to Congress and the president succeeded in blocking the construction of the dams.

The Sierra Club's executive director, David Brower, actually had two different versions of the June 9th ad. In the first version, Brower wrote a factual letter to the secretary of the interior, Stewart Udall, arguing against the dams. In the second version, Sierra Club media consultant Jerry Mander composed a splashier script. Its headline announced, "Now Only You Can Save Grand Canyon From Being Flooded . . . For Profit" (*New York Times,* 1966, p. 35). (See Figure 2.3.) This ad included a mock photo of a flooded Grand Canyon and details of the plan, and it concluded with the emotional core of the Club's rhetorical strategy: "Remember, with all the complexities of Washington politics . . . and the ins and outs of committees and procedures, there is only one simple, incredible issue here: This time it's the Grand Canyon they want to flood. *The Grand Canyon*" (Zakin, 1993, p. 165).

Brower convinced each newspaper to split its press runs so that he could determine which version worked better—his open letter to Secretary Udall or Mander's harder-hitting version (Zakin, 1993). Writer and editor Tom Turner (1991) reported, "Mander's outdrew Brower's by about three to two, as measured by the coupons soliciting donations to the Club that were clipped and returned to Club headquarters" (p. 171). More importantly, the Mander version produced a firestorm of media coverage and political reaction. "Response to the ad was so overwhelming that the ad itself became news" (Zakin, 1993, p. 165), and it prompted a heavy-handed response from President Lyndon B. Johnson's administration. On June 10th, the day after the ad ran, the Internal Revenue Service threatened the Sierra Club's tax-exempt status. Turner chronicles what happened next: "The press got the

Figure 2.3   Advertising for a Canyon, *New York Times*, June 9, 1966

story and blistered the IRS. Freedom of [s]peech became an issue along with conservation. As Brower said later, 'People who didn't know whether or not they loved the Grand Canyon knew whether they loved the IRS'" (p. 172). The Sierra Club's membership soared. The following year, the Bureau withdrew its proposal for the two dams in the Grand Canyon.

The Sierra Club's Grand Canyon ad illustrates rhetoric's pragmatic or instrumental role, but it also illustrates the power of symbolic actions to affect events beyond the specific intent of an author or speaker. On one hand, the ad succeeded by adapting the best means of persuasion to achieve its goal. But *the ad itself triggered other rhetorical resources*—the action by the IRS and the subsequent media coverage and public outrage. This resulting, symbolic drama between a powerful and disliked government agency (the IRS) and a nature club had effects beyond Mander's intent. In other words, rhetorical agency also may include the capacity of language and other symbolic forms to affect perceptions and behavior beyond an author's or speaker's intent.

Rhetoric as a Constitutive Force

Although traditional definitions of rhetoric emphasize its instrumental or pragmatic role, recent definitions have broadened rhetoric's scope by noting its *constitutive* function as well. This is the capacity of symbolic action to affect or constitute our perceptions of reality itself. For example, rhetorical scholars have pointed out that rhetoric often constitutes a sense of collective identity when politicians address U.S. citizens as "Americans" or simply as "the people" (McGee, 1975).

The literary theorist Kenneth Burke makes a similar point about language in describing the use of **terministic screens,** the way in which our language orients us to see certain things, some aspects of the world and not others. Burke (1966) proposed that, "if any given terminology is a *reflection* of reality[,] by its very nature as a terminology it must be a *selection* of reality; and to this extent it must function also as a *deflection* of reality" (p. 45). That is, our symbolic or terministic screens powerfully shape or mediate our experiences—what is selected for notice, what is deflected from notice, and therefore how we understand our world. As a result, whenever we speak or write, we actively participate in constituting our world.

A striking illustration of rhetoric's constitutive role comes from a recent dispute between environmentalists and the U.S. Department of Commerce over the meaning of "dolphin safe," which appears on the labels on cans of tuna fish. Since 1990, the government has prohibited companies from using "dolphin safe" to label tuna caught by fishing fleets that chase and encircle dolphins in order to catch tuna. The reason is that dolphins often swim above schools of tuna and are snared in the fleets' encircling nets when the tuna is hauled on board. However, in 2002 the Commerce Department ruled that trapping dolphins while using encirclement nets to catch tuna does not significantly harm dolphin populations. As a result of this ruling, exporters of tuna to the United States could use the label "dolphin safe" even though they fished with controversial nets, as long as their fleets employed observers on board to certify that they saw no dolphins killed (M., 2003).

In response to the new rule, Earth Island Institute, Defenders of Wildlife, and other environmental groups filed a lawsuit to prevent the use of "dolphin safe" labels on tuna caught with encirclement nets. They argued that, even with observers, these nets "deplete dolphin populations by separating calves from mothers and causing stress-related deaths" (M., 2003, p. 3). Meanwhile, tuna companies like Star Kist realized that it would be "a PR nightmare to anger legions of dolphin-loving school kids armed with lunch-pails" by using the relaxed standards. Therefore, many of these companies pledged to adhere to the older, stricter rules for use of the "dolphin safe" label (p. 3).

The point is that, in this and other environmental disputes, the public becomes concerned as a result of the selective presentation of terms and information that *name* or constitute the issues at hand. German sociologist Klaus Eder (1996) explains that often it is "the methods of communicating [about] environmental conditions and ideas, and not the state of deterioration itself, which explain . . . the emergence of a public discourse on the environment" (p. 209).

Act Locally!

"Dolphin Safe" Labels: How Safe Are Dolphins?

Do cans of tuna fish in your local grocery stores still carry the "dolphin safe" label? What does this label mean today? Does the label mean that fewer dolphins die as a result of fishing methods used to catch tuna?

In 2004, a U.S. District Court judge issued a preliminary injunction that kept the strict "dolphin safe" standard in place until the court can hear a lawsuit on the issue brought by environmental groups. As I write this book, that case (*Earth Island Institute v. U.S. Commerce Secretary Donald Evans*) is still pending.

What is the most recent court ruling in this case, and what does "dolphin safe" mean today? Start by checking the websites of two of the leading plaintiffs in the case, Earth Island Institute (www.earthisland .org/news/news.cfm) and Defenders of Wildlife (www.defenders.org/ wildlife/new/dolphins.html).

Rhetoric's constitutive role is particularly important in communication that names a state of affairs as an environmental problem. Political scientist Deborah Stone (2002) explains that: "Problems . . . are not given, out there in the world waiting for smart analysts to come along and define them correctly. They are created in the minds of citizens by other citizens, leaders, organizations, and government agencies" (p. 156). Rhetoric's constitutive force comes into play in this ability to characterize a set of facts or a condition in the world one way rather than another and therefore to name it as a problem or not. It is for precisely this reason that questions of "how and why certain environmental issues become identified as 'problems,' including contestation of such claims as problematic," are such an important part of environmental communication itself (Tindall, 1995, p. 49; emphasis added).

Dominant and Insurgent Discourses

Earlier, I referred to a dominant discourse that viewed wild nature as a commodity to be used. The idea of discourse is a very important concept in contemporary communication theory. It asserts that persuasive effects are present in sources of communication that are broader than any single speech or utterance. Instead, a **discourse** is an overall *pattern* of speaking, writing, or other symbolic action that results from multiple sources. It functions to "circulate a coherent set of meanings about an important topic" (Fiske, 1987, p. 14). Such meanings often influence our understanding of how the world works or should work. For example, Gifford Pinchot's conservation discourse in the early 20th century helped to justify utilitarian uses of nature such as logging, and John Muir's discourse of preservation served to justify a ban on all commercial activities in wilderness areas. We also saw that, in the late 20th century, activists calling for environmental justice criticized the prevailing discourse of environmentalism that overlooked the places where people lived, worked, played, and learned. Each of these discourses arose from multiple sources—speeches, essays, and other symbolic acts—that articulated a coherent view of nature and our relationships to the environment.

When a discourse gains a broad or taken-for-granted status in a culture (for example, "growth is good for the economy") or when its meanings help to legitimize certain policies or practices, it can be said to be a **dominant discourse**. Often, these discourses are invisible, in the sense that they express naturalized or taken-for-granted assumptions and values about how the world is or should be organized. Perhaps the best example of a dominant environmental discourse is what biologists Dennis Pirages and Paul Ehrlich (1974) called the **Dominant Social Paradigm** (DSP). Although they use the term *paradigm*, communication scholars would note that the DSP is a *discursive* tradition that has sustained attitudes of human dominance over nature. As expressed in literature, art, political speeches, advertising, photography, and so forth, the DSP affirms society's "belief in abundance and progress, our devotion to growth and prosperity, our faith in science and technology, and our commitment to a laissez-faire economy, limited government planning and private property rights" (quoted in Dunlap & Van Liere,

1978, p. 10). In everyday terms, the DSP is recognized in references to free markets as the source of prosperity and the wise use of natural resources to build a strong economy and so forth.

Other discourses may question society's dominant discourses and their assumptions. These alternative ways of speaking, writing, or portraying nature in art, music, and photographs illustrate **insurgent discourses.** These are modes of representation that challenge society's taken-for-granted assumptions and offer alternatives to prevailing discourses. In some ages, insurgent discourses are muted or absent, whereas in other periods they may be boisterous and wide-spread. In our own time, insurgent discourses have infiltrated mainstream media in popular films such as *Erin Brockovich* (2000), alternative news and opinion journals such as *Earth Island Journal* (www.earthisland.org/eijournal/journal .cfm), on the websites of groups such as Common Dreams (www.common-dreams.org), Truthout (www.truthout.org), and Women's Voices for the Earth (www.womenandenvironment.org), and through multi-media networks for news such as the Independent Media Center (www.indymedia.org), a network of more than 110 centers in 35 countries (Kidd, 2003, p. 224).

Some point to an insurgent discourse emerging in popularity after Earth Day, 1970, called the **New Environmental Paradigm** (NEP). The NEP empha-sizes beliefs and values such as "the inevitability of 'limits to growth,' . . . the importance of preserving the 'balance of nature,' and the need to reject the anthropocentric notion that nature exists solely for human use" (Dunlap & Van Liere, 1978, p. 10; see also Dunlap, Van Liere, Mertig, & Jones, 2000). Other examples of insurgent discourses have appeared in writings such as Paul Ehrlich's (1968) *The Population Bomb*, Rachel Carson's (1962) *Silent Spring,* and Murray Bookchin's (1990) *Remaking Society: Pathways to a Green Future.* These authors appropriated an **apocalyptic narrative** literary style to warn of impending and severe ecological crises. Literary critics Jimmie Killingsworth and Jacqueline Palmer (1996) explained that, "in depicting the end of the world as a result of the overweening desire to control nature, [these authors] have discovered a rhetorical means of contesting their opponents' claims for the idea of progress with its ascendant narratives of human victory over nature" (p. 21). Similarly, supporters of deep ecology such as Christopher Manes (1990) have criticized society's "culture of extinction" and its pursuit of "short-term affluence at the cost of impoverishing the environment," a pathway that risks "the specter of ecological collapse" (p. 24).

As dominant discourses coalesce around specific policies and institutions, they form symbolic boundaries that help to legitimate these policies. These *symbolic legitimacy boundaries* serve to safeguard specific policies and prac-tices, and the authority of certain groups and institutions. I'll describe this final concept next.

Symbolic Legitimacy Boundaries

Throughout this book, we will focus on public debate, media reports, and other forms of communication that seek to shape perceptions and policies about the environment. In an important sense, the function of such communication is to help establish—or challenge—the **legitimacy** of actions affecting the environment. Legitimacy is generally defined as the right to exercise authority. Yet. such a right is not granted naturally. Instead, recognition of legitimacy depends upon a specifically *rhetorical* process. Communication scholar Robert Francesconi (1982) defines this rhetorical basis of legitimacy as "an ongoing process of reason-giving . . . which forms the basis of the right to exercise authority as well as the willingness [of audiences] to defer to authority" (p. 49). Importantly, legitimacy may be *claimed* by a person or group, but it is *granted by others*–voters, a group's members, or other constituencies. Francesconi explained that rhetoric performs "a vital socio-political function by bridging the gap between legitimacy as *claimed* by those who would exercise authority and legitimacy as *believed* by those who would obey it" (p. 50).

One of the most persuasive ways to earn legitimacy is to link a policy or idea with certain values. Sociologist Talcott Parsons (1958) defined the legitimation (granting of legitimacy) as "the appraisal of [an] action in terms of shared or common values" (p. 201). For example, proposals to protect old-growth forests may be seen as more or less legitimate, depending upon public perception of the values that are at stake: Is the nation experiencing a shortage of timber supply, or is it facing a loss of biodiversity? Detailed knowledge of how a proposal works, while obviously important, may be only part of the story of its legitimacy.

One of the most rhetorically powerful claims to legitimacy in American political culture is that something is just **common sense**. The term is imprecise, but it generally refers to what people assume to be the views of "everybody"—what is generally agreed to be true. When politicians or others invoke common sense to advocate the use of natural resources to spur economic growth, they also implicitly draw on the discourse of the Dominant Social Paradigm, noted earlier.

The claim to be talking from common sense has become a source of legitimacy in recent debates over Western wildfires and ways to safeguard nearby homes and communities from these fires. For example, the George W. Bush administration called its proposal to thin Western forests (that is, to selectively log trees) to prevent wildfires the Healthy Forests Initiative. Rolling out his proposal, President Bush told a crowd in Portland, Oregon:

> We need to make our forests healthy by using some *common sense*. . . . We've got to understand that it makes sense to clear brush. We've got to make

sense—it makes sense to encourage people to make sure that the forests not only are healthy from disease, but are healthy from fire. . . . This is just *common sense.*" (White House, 2002, emphasis added.)

The President sought rhetorically to justify his proposal for selective logging of the forests—described as clearing brush—in terms of values that his listeners presumably shared about the caution or care they take around their own homes, summed up as common sense.

Because legitimacy is rhetorically constituted, it is also open to question and challenge. An appeal to common sense is usually an effective means of gaining legitimacy, since it purports merely to describe things "as they really are." However, part of its power is that it also may mask other meanings or alternatives. For example, environmental groups challenged the common sense of logging old-growth trees—part of the President's plan—as well as brush, thus beginning a public debate over the legitimacy of the President's Healthy Forests plan.

Political scientist Charles Schulzke (2000) observes that the outcome of arguments between parties over legitimacy turns only partly on facts. Equally important are **symbolic legitimacy boundaries**. Schulzke defines these as the symbolic associations that politicians, business, and the public attach to a proposal, policy, or person. Symbolic legitimacy boundaries define a particular policy, idea, or institution as reasonable, appropriate, or acceptable. They also help to establish a presumption of normalcy that comes from being in the political center. For example, Paul Ehrlich (2002), the Bing Professor of Population Studies at Stanford University, attempted to locate environmental concerns *inside* the symbolic boundaries of science and reason when he declared, "There is little dispute within the knowledgeable scientific community today about the global ecological situation" (p. 31).

On the other hand, the symbolic associations that make up a legitimacy boundary also name what or who is unreasonable, unwise, or unacceptable. For example, when conservative radio commentator Rush Limbaugh called environmentalists "wackos" and "dunderheaded alarmists and prophets of doom" in his best-selling book *The Way Things Ought to Be* (1992, pp. 155–157), he was portraying those who worried about such matters as the ozone layer as *outside* the symbolic boundaries of common sense. As a consequence, symbolic legitimacy boundaries tell us "what or who is included or excluded in a category," says Stone (2002). They "define people in and out of a conflict or place them on different sides" (p. 34).

As with legitimacy itself, symbolic legitimacy boundaries are not granted automatically but are constituted in the rhetorical struggle that makes up public debate and controversy in our modern-day *agora,* or public sphere. Stone (2002) says that, in these struggles to create public support, "symbols, stories, metaphors, and labels are all weapons in the armamentarium (to use a metaphor). . . . By conveying images of good and bad, right and wrong, suffering and relief, these devices are instruments in the struggle over public policy" (p. 156). (In Chapter 9, we will examine the rhetorical struggle over an important symbolic legitimacy boundary in environmental policy—the public's respect for scientific knowledge.)

Visual Rhetorics: Portraying Nature

As I noted earlier in this chapter, rhetoric is not limited to speech or writing. Visual representations of the environment have been prominent in shaping Americans' perceptions at least since the early 18th and 19th centuries, in oil paintings and photographs of the American West. Since then, visual portrayals of nature have ranged from popular Hollywood films such as *The Day After Tomorrow* (2004) and television ads of SUVs driving in forests, to image events of Greenpeace activists placing themselves between whalers' harpoons and whales (DeLuca, 1999).

Recently, rhetorical scholars have begun to look closely at the rhetorical significance of visual symbols in culture generally. For example, Robert Hariman and John Louis Lucaites (2002) argue that the famous photograph of five marines and navy soldiers raising the American flag on Iwo Jima in 1945 is symbolically powerful and illustrates the fact that visual media are "particularly good at activating aesthetic norms that can shape audience acceptance of political beliefs and historical narratives" (p. 366). Other scholars have looked at the importance of visual symbols in post–cold-war images of nuclear devastation and waste (Taylor, 2003); the Vietnam War photograph of a young girl running down a road, screaming in pain from napalm (Hariman & Lucaites, 2003); and the cultural significance of monuments and popular films such as *Saving Private Ryan* that remember World War II (Biesecker, 2002). Hence, I believe it's important to end our discussion of a rhetorical perspective by describing the function of **visual rhetorics** of the environment, that is, the role that visual images and representations of nature play in influencing public attitudes toward the environment.

Refiguring Wilderness in Art and Photographs

Earlier, we saw that 18th- and 19th-century artists such as Thomas Cole, Albert Bierstadt, and the Hudson River school painters were a significant source of the public's awareness of the American West. Equally important were the artists and photographers who followed military expeditions and surveyors into Western territories. Rhetorical critics Kevin DeLuca and Anne Demo (2000) have argued that landscape photographers such as Carleton Watkins, Charles Weed, and William Henry Jackson were among the first to portray the West to many people who lived in eastern cities and towns. Photographs of Yosemite Valley, Yellowstone, the Rocky Mountains, and the Grand Canyon not only popularized these sites but, as they became broadly available in the media, "were factors in building public support for preserving the areas" (p. 245).

With such popularization, however, came an embedded orientation and an ideological disposition toward nature and human relationships with the land. On the one hand, the paintings of the Hudson River school aided in consti-tuting natural areas as pristine and as objects of the sublime. Yet, rhetorical scholars Gregory Clark, Michael Halloran, and Allison Woodford (1996) have argued that such portrayals of wilderness depicted nature as separate from human culture; the viewpoint of paintings distanced the human observer by viewing the landscape from above, or in control of nature. They concluded that, although expressing a reverence for the land, such depictions functioned "rhetorically to fuel a process of conquest" (p. 274).

More recently, DeLuca and Demo (2000) have argued that what was left out of landscape photographs of the West may be as important as what was included. They gave the example of early photos of Yosemite Valley taken in the 1860s by the photographer Carleton Watkins. DeLuca and Demo wrote that, when Watkins portrayed Yosemite Valley as wilderness devoid of human signs, he also helped to construct a national myth of pristine nature that was harmful. In a critique of the implicit rhetoric of such scenes, they argued that the "ability of whites to rhapsodize about Yosemite as paradise, the original Garden of Eden, depended on the forced removal and forgetting of the indige-nous inhabitants of the area for the past 3,500 years" (p. 254). Writer Rebecca Solnit (1992) has pointed out, "The West wasn't empty, it was emptied— literally by expeditions like the Mariposa Battalion [which killed and/or relo-cated the native inhabitants of Yosemite Valley in the 1850s], and figuratively by the sublime images of a virgin paradise created by so many painters, poets, and photographers" (p. 56, quoted in DeLuca & Demo, p. 256).

Whether or not one agrees with DeLuca's and Demo's claim about the impact of Watkins's photos, it is important to note that these and other images often played pivotal roles in shaping perceptions of natural areas, endangered species, and (with recent visual awareness of the impacts of pol-lution and toxic waste) peoples and human communities. As DeLuca and Demo (2000) argue, these visual portrayals often are "enmeshed in a turbu-lent stream of multiple and conflictual discourses that shape what these images mean in particular contexts"; indeed, in many ways such pictures *constitute* "the context in which a politics takes place—they are creating a reality" (p. 242).

A striking example of the capacity of photos to construct a context in which politics take place occurred in 2003 during a Congressional debate about the opening of the Arctic National Wildlife Refuge to oil drilling.

Photography and Controversy
Over the Arctic National Wildlife Refuge

In October 2000, a 33-year-old physicist named Subhankar Banerjee, a native of Calcutta, India, cashed his savings and left his job at the Boeing Company in Seattle, Washington, to begin a two-year project to photograph the seasons and the biodiversity of Alaska's Arctic National Wildlife Refuge. His project, which took him on a 4,000-mile journey by foot, kayak, and snowmobile through the wildlife refuge in winter as well as summer, culminated in a collection of stunning photographs that were published in his book *Arctic National Wildlife Refuge: Seasons of Life and Land* (2003). (For a sample of the photographs and description of Banerjee's project, see www .wwbphoto.com.)

Banerjee hoped that his book of photographs would educate the public about threats to the future of Alaska's remote refuge. The Smithsonian Museum in Washington, D.C., had scheduled a major exhibition of Banerjee's photos for spring 2003. However, the young scientist-photographer suddenly found his photos and the Smithsonian exhibit caught in the midst of a political controversy. During a March 18, 2003, debate in the U.S. Senate about oil drilling in the Arctic National Wildlife Refuge, Senator Barbara Boxer of California urged every senator to visit Banerjee's exhibit at the Smithsonian "before calling the refuge a frozen wasteland" (Egan, 2003, p. A20). The vote to open the refuge to oil drilling later failed by four votes—52 to 48. (As I write, another effort is being made in 2005 to open the refuge to oil drilling.)

Although Banerjee's photos were certainly not the only influence on the Senate's vote, the controversy over the photos caused a political firestorm and helped to create a context for debate over the refuge itself. Washington Post writer Timothy Egan (2003) reported that Banerjee had been told by the Smithsonian that "the museum had been pressured to cancel or sharply revise the exhibit" (p. A20). Documents from the museum give an idea of the changes. Egan reported,

> For a picture of the Romanzof Mountains, the original caption quoted
> Mr. Banerjee as saying, "The refuge has the most beautiful landscape I have

ever seen and is so remote and untamed that many peaks, valleys and lakes are still without names." The new version says, "Unnamed Peak, Romanzof Mountains." . . . Shortly after the [failed] vote, the Smithsonian . . . sent a letter to the publisher, saying that the Smithsonian no longer had any connection to Mr. Banerjee's work. (p. A20)

After attorneys for the museum insisted that he remove all mention of the Smithsonian from his book, Banerjee spoke to reporters. "I was told that my work was just too political" (Bailey, 2003, p. 16). In fact, museum staff had objected that his photos and their captions constituted advocacy: "'We do not engage in advocacy,' said Randall Kremer, a museum spokesman. 'And some of the captions bordered on advocacy'" (Egan, 2003, p. A20).

In one important sense, Kremer's criticism of Banerjee's photographs was correct. Photographs may be powerful, rhetorical statements and, as DeLuca and Demo (2000) argued, they can constitute a context for understanding and judgment. Especially when accompanied by captions that encourage a particular meaning, photos can embody a range of symbolic resources that sustain or challenge prevailing viewpoints. Some observers felt that Banerjee's photos of Alaska's wilderness had this potential. A book reviewer for the *Planet* in Jackson Hole, Wyoming, observed of these photos, "Sometimes pictures have a chance to change history by creating a larger understanding of a subject, thus enlightening the public and bringing greater awareness to an issue" (Review, 2003).

Both Carlton Watkins' 19th-century photographs of the "pristine" West and Subhankar Banerjee's scenes of Alaska's wildlife and indigenous peoples help to constitute a context of meaning and implicitly embody multiple streams of discourses. As a result, visual media's ability to affect contexts of understanding and appreciation exemplify well what I earlier described as the constitutive role of rhetorical agency.

Conclusion

Over the centuries, people have described their relations to the environment in dramatically different ways—"a hideous & desolate wilderness," "pristine," "the places where we live, work, play, and learn," and a "natural resource" for human use. These meanings have been the subject of political debate, art, imagination, advertising, scientific research, and fantasy. The rhetorical shaping of the environment and our relation to it reminds us that, whatever else they may be, *nature* and *environment* are powerful ideas whose meanings are always being defined and contested.

In the first section of this chapter, we described four historical periods in which individuals and groups challenged prevailing definitions of the environment. We called these periods of questioning and challenge *antagonisms*, which reveal limits of the prevailing views of society:

1. The late 19th- and early 20th-century questioning of nature as repugnant by advocates wishing to *preserve* the wilderness and others who articulated an ethic of *conservation* or efficient use of natural resources.

2. The growth of an ecology movement in the 1960s and 1970s, which criticized a system of poorly regulated industrial behavior that contributed to human health problems from chemical contamination and other forms of air and water pollution. This movement built upon efforts of 1920s environmental health pioneers such as Alice Hamilton.

3. A community-based movement for environmental justice in the 1980s that challenged mainstream views of nature as "a place apart" from the places where people work, live, learn, and play.

4. A growing, multinational movement to protect local communities and the global commons in the face of some forms of globalization.

In the second section, we developed a rhetorical perspective by looking at the idea of rhetorical agency: pragmatic and constitutive efforts by different forces to influence society's attitudes and behaviors through the distinctly human modes of communication available to us—persuasion, public debate, narrative, art, and other modes of symbolic action.

Related to this sense of rhetorical agency are two other concepts—discourse and symbolic legitimacy boundaries. *Discourses* are the recurring patterns of speech or systems of representation that circulate a coherent set of meanings; they may achieve a dominant status in society when they coalesce around particular viewpoints and naturalize a way of behaving toward the environment. We called these particular patterns of speech *dominant discourses*. During some periods, other voices arise that question and challenge these discourses; such *insurgent discourses* present an alternative vision or point of view.

Closely related to the work of dominant discourses are *symbolic legitimacy boundaries*. These are the symbolic associations—words, metaphors, images, and other sources of meaning—that encourage perceptions of a policy, idea, or institution as reasonable, appropriate, or acceptable. Much of the rhetorical work of an insurgent discourse is its challenge to these symbolic associations.

Finally, we explored some of the ways in which visual rhetorics such as art and photographs embody symbolic resources that can shape our perceptions of nature. As we saw in the photographs of a "pristine" West and scenes of Alaska's wildlife and peoples, visual rhetorics may impart an ideological disposition toward specific definitions of nature and thereby help to constitute the context in which political decisions take place.

KEY TERMS

Antagonism: Recognition of the limit of an idea, a widely shared viewpoint, or an ideology that allows an opposing idea or belief system to be voiced.

Apocalyptic narrative: A literary style used by some environmental writers to warn of impending and severe ecological crises; evokes a sense of the end of the world as a result of the overweening desire to control nature.

Common sense: What people assume to be the views of "everybody," or what is generally agreed to be true; a source of legitimacy.

Conservation: The term used by early–20th-century forester Gifford Pinchot to mean the wise and efficient use of natural resources.

Direct action: Physical acts of protest such as road blockades, sit-ins, and tree spiking.

Discourse: A pattern of speaking, writing, or other symbolic action that results from multiple sources. Discourse functions to circulate a coherent set of meanings about an important topic.

Dominant discourse: A discourse that has gained broad or taken-for-granted status in a culture, for example, the belief that growth is good for the economy; its meanings help to legitimize certain policies or practices.

Dominant Social Paradigm (DSP): A dominant discursive tradition of several centuries that has sustained attitudes of human dominance over nature. The DSP affirms society's belief in economic growth and its faith in technology, limited government, and private property.

Earth Summit: The 1992 United Nations Conference on Environment and Development in Rio de Janeiro, Brazil.

Insurgent discourse: Modes of representation that challenge society's taken-for-granted assumptions and offer alternatives to prevailing discourses.

Legitimacy: A right to exercise authority.

National Environmental Policy Act: Requires every federal agency to prepare an environmental impact statement and invite public comment on any project that would affect the environment. Signed into law by President Nixon on January 1, 1970, NEPA is the cornerstone of modern environmental law.

New Environmental Paradigm (NEP): An insurgent discourse emerging in popularity after Earth Day, 1970, which emphasizes beliefs and values such as "the inevitability of 'limits to growth,' . . . the importance of preserving the 'balance of nature,' and the need to reject the anthropocentric notion that nature exists solely for human use." (Dunlap & Van Liere, 1978, p. 10).

Preservationism: The movement to ban commercial use of wilderness areas and to preserve wild forests and other natural areas for appreciation, study, and outdoor recreation.

Principles of Environmental Justice: Sixteen principles adopted by delegates at the First National People of Color Environmental Leadership Summit in 1991 that enumerated a series of rights, including "the fundamental right to political, economic, cultural, and environmental self-determination of all peoples."

Public interest: The symbolic marker of legitimacy for actions that are taken in the name of the nation's people or the common good.

Rhetoric: The faculty (power) of discovering the available means of persuasion in the particular case.

Rhetorical perspective: A focus on purposeful and consequential efforts to influence society's attitudes and ways of behaving through communication, which includes public debate, protests, news stories, advertising, and other modes of symbolic action.

Rio Declaration: A document adopted by representatives at the Earth Summit that reaffirmed an earlier Declaration of the United Nations Conference on the Human Environment, adopted at Stockholm in 1972, and pledged to work "towards international agreements which respect the interests of all and protect the integrity of the global environmental and developmental system."

Sublime: An aesthetic category that associates God's influence with the feelings of awe and exultation that some experience in the presence of wilderness.

Sublime response: Term used to denote (1) the immediate awareness of a sublime object (such as Yosemite Valley), (2) a sense of overwhelming personal insignificance and awe in its presence, and (3) ultimately a feeling of spiritual exaltation.

Superfund: Legislation enacted in 1980 authorizing the Environmental Protection Agency to clean up toxic sites and hold the responsible parties accountable for the costs.

Symbolic legitimacy boundaries: The symbolic associations that politicians, business, and the public attach to a proposal, policy, or person; such boundaries define a particular policy, idea, or institution as reasonable, appropriate, or acceptable.

Terministic screens: The means whereby our language orients us to see certain things, some aspects of the world and not others. Defined by literary theorist Kenneth Burke (1966) to mean, "if any given terminology is a *reflection* of reality; by its very nature as a terminology it must be a *selection* of reality; and to this extent it must function also as a *deflection* of reality."

Transcendentalism: Belief that a correspondence exists between a higher realm of spiritual truth and a lower one of material objects, including nature.

Tree spiking: The practice of driving metal or plastic spikes or nails into trees in an area that is scheduled to be logged, to discourage the cutting of the trees.

Utilitarianism: Theory that the aim of action should be the greatest good for the greatest number.

Visual rhetoric: The capacity of visual images and representations to influence public attitudes toward objects such as the environment.

DISCUSSION QUESTIONS

1. Is wilderness merely a symbolic construction? Does this matter?

2. Do you agree with historian William Cronon that wilderness represents the "false hope of an escape from responsibility, the illusion that we can . . . return to the tabula rasa that supposedly existed before we began to leave our marks on the world"? Does the idea of wilderness as a place apart from civilization divert your attention from everyday problems, or does this idea provide a source of renewal or a challenge to civilization's shortcomings?

3. Does rhetoric constitute reality? How? Is it possible to "know" something without the aid of language?

4. Do environmental problems exist before someone names them as problems? For example, is the burning of hospital biochemical wastes an acceptable risk for those living in nearby neighborhoods? How do you explain the fact that not everybody agrees on which things are problems?

5. How would you characterize the dominant discourse or prevailing viewpoint about the environment today? Do you know of any who are challenging this viewpoint?

6. Other than the "dolphin safe" label on tuna cans, what other products carry, or should carry, labels attesting to their environmental impacts? Coffee? Sneakers? Clothes from sweatshops?

7. Do visual media function rhetorically to construct an ideological orientation toward nature or the environment? Brainstorm to identify the different visual representations you see today in media today—for example, on MTV, on news shows, in Hollywood films, in ads for SUVs or cars.

SUGGESTED READINGS

For detailed accounts of U.S. environmental history and U.S. and global environmental groups, see

- Samuel P. Hays, *Beauty, Health, and Permanence: Environmental Politics in the United States, 1955–1985* (1987)
- Carolyn Merchant, *The Columbia Guide to American Environmental History* (2002)
- Philip Shabecoff, *A Fierce Green Fire: The American Environmental Movement* (2003)
- Robert Gottlieb, *Forcing the Spring: The Transformation of the American Environmental Movement* (1993)
- Luke W. Cole and Sheila R. Foster, *From the Ground Up: Environmental Racism and the Rise of the Environmental Justice Movement* (2001)
- Robert J. Brulle, *Agency, Democracy, and Nature: The U.S. Environmental Movement from a Critical Theory Perspective* (2000)
- Bron Raymond Taylor, *Ecological Resistance Movements: The Global Emergence of Radical and Popular Environmentalism* (1995)
- Paul Wapner, *Environmental Activism and World Civic Politics* (1996).

Information on the life of Dr. Alice Hamilton and her advocacy for industrial health in the 1920s can be found in her autobiography, *Exploring the Dangerous Trades: The Autobiography of Alice Hamilton, M.D.* (1943).

REFERENCES

Alston, D. (1990). *We speak for ourselves: Social justice, race, and environment.* Washington, DC: Panos Institute.

Andrews, R. N. L. (1999). *Managing the environment, managing ourselves.* New Haven, CT: Yale University Press.

Axelrod, R. S., Downie, D. L., & Vig, N. J. (2004). *The global environment: Institutions law & policy* (2nd ed.). Washington, DC: CQ Press.

Bailey, H. (2003, May 5). Pictures of controversy: The Smithsonian. *Newsweek*, p. 16.

Banerjee, S. (2003). *Arctic National Wildlife Refuge: Seasons of life and land.* Seattle: Mountaineer Books.

Biesecker, B. A. (2002). Remembering World War II: The rhetoric and politics of national commemoration at the turn of the 21st century. *Quarterly Journal of Speech, 88*, 393–409.

Bookchin, Murray (1990). *Remaking society: Pathways to a green future.* Boston: South End.

Bradford, W. (1952). *Of Plymouth plantation, 1620–1647.* (S. E. Morison, Ed.). New York: Alfred A. Knopf. [Originally published 1898.]

Brulle, R. J. (2000). *Agency, democracy, and nature: The U.S. environmental movement from a critical theory perspective.* Cambridge: MIT Press.

Buck, S. J. (1996). *Understanding environmental administration and law.* Washington, DC: Island Press.

Bullard, R., & Wright, B. H. (1987). Environmentalism and the politics of equity: Emergent trends in the black community. *Midwestern Review of Sociology, 12*, 21–37.

Burke, K. (1966). *Language as symbolic action: Essays on life, literature, and method*. Berkeley: University of California Press.

Campbell, K. K., & Huxman, S. S. (2003). *The rhetorical act* (3rd ed.). Belmont, CA: Thomson Wadsworth.

Carson, R. (1962). *Silent spring*. Greenwich, CT: Fawcett Crest.

Clark, G., Halloran, M., & Woodford, A. (1996). Thomas Cole's vision of "nature" and the conquest theme in American culture. In C. G. Herndl & S. C. Brown (Eds.), *Green culture: Environmental rhetoric in contemporary America* (pp. 261–280). Madison: University of Wisconsin Press.

Clinton, W. J. (1994, February 16). Federal actions to address environmental justice in minority populations and low-income communities. Executive Order 12898 of February 14, 1996. *Federal register, 59*, 7629.

Cole, L. W., & Foster, S. R. (2001). *From the ground up: Environmental racism and the rise of the environmental justice movement*. New York: New York University Press.

Cooper, L. (1960). *The rhetoric of Aristotle*. New York: Appleton-Century-Crofts.

Cox, J. R. (1980). Loci communes and Thoreau's arguments for wilderness in "Walking" (1851). *Southern Speech Communication Journal, 26*, 1–16.

Cox, J. R. (in press). Golden tropes and democratic betrayals: Prospects for environmental justice in neoliberal "free trade" agreements. In P. C. Pezzullo & R. Sandler (Eds.). *Environmental justice and environmentalism: Contrary or complimentary?* Cambridge: MIT Press.

Cronon, W. (1996). The trouble with wilderness, or, getting back to the wrong nature. In W. Cronon (Ed.), *Uncommon ground: Rethinking the human place in nature* (pp. 69–90). New York: W. W. Norton.

DeLuca, K. M. (1999). *Image politics: The new rhetoric of environmental activism*. New York: Guilford Press.

DeLuca, K., & Demo, A. T. (2000). Imaging nature: Watkins, Yosemite, and the birth of environmentalism. *Critical Studies in Mass Communication, 17*, 241–260.

Di Chiro, G. (1996). Nature as community: The convergence of environment and social justice. In W. Cronon (Ed.), *Uncommon ground: Rethinking the human place in nature* (pp. 298–320). New York: W. W. Norton.

Dunlap, R. E., & Mertig, A. G. (Eds.). (1992). *American environmentalism: The U.S. environmental movement, 1970–1990*. Philadelphia: Taylor & Francis.

Dunlap, R. E., & Van Liere, K. D. (1978). The "new environmental paradigm": A proposed instrument and preliminary analysis. *Journal of Environmental Education, 9*, 10–19.

Dunlap, R. E., Van Liere, K. D., Mertig, A. G., & Jones, R. E. (2000). Measuring enforcement of the new ecological paradigm: A revised NEP scale. *Journal of Social Sciences, 56*, 425–442.

Eder, K. (1996). The institutionalization of environmentalism: Ecological discourse and the second transformation of the public sphere. In S. Lash, B. Szerszynski, & B. Wynne (Eds.), *Risk, environment, and modernity: Towards a new ecology* (pp. 203–223). London: Sage.

Egan, T. (2003, May 3). Smithsonian is no safe haven for exhibit on Arctic Wildlife Refuge. *New York Times*, p. A20.

Ehrlich, P. R. (1968). *The population bomb*. San Francisco: Sierra Club Books.

Ehrlich, P. R. (2002). Human natures, nature conservation, and environmental ethics. *BioScience, 52*(1): 31–43.

Esty, D. (1994). *Greening the GATT: Trade, environment, and the future.* Washington, DC: Institute for International Economics.

Fiske, J. (1987). *Television culture.* London: Methuen.

Flippen, J. B. (2003). Richard Nixon and the triumph of environmentalism. In L. S. Warren (Ed.), *American environmental history* (pp. 272–289). Oxford, UK: Basil Blackwell.

Francesconi, R. A. (1982). James Hunt, the Wilmington 10, and institutional legitimacy. *Quarterly Journal of Speech, 68,* 47–59.

Gottlieb, R. (1993a). *Forcing the spring: The transformation of the American environmental movement.* Washington, DC: Island Press.

Gottlieb, R. (1993b). Reconstructing environmentalism: Complex movements, diverse roots. *Environmental History Review, 17*(4): 1–19.

Gottlieb, R. (2002). *Environmentalism unbound: Exploring new pathways for change.* Cambridge: MIT Press.

Hamilton, A. (1925). *Industrial poisons in the United States.* New York: Macmillan.

Hamilton, A. (1943). *Exploring the dangerous trades: The autobiography of Alice Hamilton, M.D.* Boston: Little, Brown.

Hariman, R., & Lucaites, J. L. (2002). Performing civic identity: The iconic photograph of the flag raising on Iwo Jima. *Quarterly Journal of Speech, 88,* 363–392.

Hariman, R., & Lucaites, J. L. (2003). Public identity and collective memory in U.S. iconic photography: The image of "accidental napalm." *Critical Studies in Media Communication, 20,* 35–66.

Hays, S. P. (1987). *Beauty, health, and permanence: Environmental politics in the United States, 1955–1985.* Cambridge, UK: Cambridge University Press.

Helvarg, D. (1994). *The war against the greens: The "wise use" movement, the new right, and anti-environmental violence.* San Francisco: Sierra Club Books.

Herndl, C. G., & Brown, S. C. (1996). Introduction. In C. G. Herndl & S. C. Brown (Eds.), *Green culture: Environmental rhetoric in contemporary America* (pp. 3–20). Madison: University of Wisconsin Press.

Hill, J. (n.d.). Julia Butterfly Hill. Downloaded August 16, 2005, from www.venus project.com/books_authors/julia_butterfly_hill.html

Jasinski, J. (2001). *Sourcebook on rhetoric: Key concepts in contemporary rhetorical studies.* Thousand Oaks, CA: Sage.

Jehl, D. (2001, March 21). E.P.A. to abandon new arsenic limits for water supply. *New York Times,* p. A1.

Kazis, R., & Grossman, R. L. (1991). *Fear at work: Job blackmail, labor and the environment* (New ed.). Philadelphia: New Society.

Kidd, D. (2003). Become the media: The global IMC network. In A. Opel & D. Pompper (Eds.), *Representing resistance: Media, civil disobedience, and the global justice movement* (pp. 224–240). Westport, CT: Praeger.

Killingsworth, M. J., & Palmer, J. S. (1996). Millennial ecology: The apocalyptic narrative from Silent Spring to Global Warming. In C. G. Herndl & S. C. Brown

(Eds.), *Green culture: Environmental rhetoric in contemporary America* (pp. 21–45). Madison: University of Wisconsin Press.

Laclau, E., & Mouffe, C. (1985). *Hegemony and socialist strategy: Toward a radical democracy.* London: Verso.

Lee, C. (1993). Beyond toxic wastes and race. In R. D. Bullard (Ed.), *Confronting environmental racism: Voices from the grassroots* (pp. 41–52). Boston: South End Press.

Lee, C. (1996). Environment: Where we live, work, play, and learn. *Race, Poverty, and the Environment, 6, 6.*

Limbaugh, R. (1992). *The way things ought to be.* New York: Pocket Books.

M., R. (May/June 2003). Tuna meltdown. *Sierra, 88*(3), 15.

Manes, C. (1990). *Green rage: Radical environmentalism and the unmaking of civilization.* Boston: Little, Brown.

McGee, M. C. (1975). In search of "the people": A rhetorical alternative. *Quarterly Journal of Speech, 61,* 235–249.

Merchant, C. (2002). *The Columbia guide to American environmental history.* New York: Columbia University Press.

Miller, C. (2004). *Gifford Pinchot and the making of modern environmentalism.* Washington, DC: Island Press/Shearwater Books.

Nash, R. F. (2001). *Wilderness and the American mind* (4th ed.). New Haven: Yale University Press.

National Environmental Justice Advisory Council Subcommittee on Waste and Facility Siting. (1996). *Environmental justice, urban revitalization, and brownfields: The search for authentic signs of hope.* EPA 500-R-96–002. Washington, DC: U.S. Environmental Protection Agency.

Now Only You Can Save Grand Canyon From Being Flooded . . . For Profit. (1966, June 9). *New York Times,* p. 35.

Oravec, C. (1981). John Muir, Yosemite, and the sublime response: A study in the rhetoric of preservationism. *Quarterly Journal of Speech, 67,* 245–258.

Oravec, C. (1984). Conservationism vs. preservationism: The "public interest" in the Hetch Hetchy controversy. *Quarterly Journal of Speech, 70,* 444–458.

Parsons, T. (1958). Authority, legitimation, and political action. In C. Friedrich (Ed.), *Authority* (pp. 197–221). Cambridge: Harvard University.

Pezzullo, P. C. (2001). Performing critical interruptions: Rhetorical invention and narratives of the environmental justice movement. *Western Journal of Communication, 64,*1–25.

Pirages, D. C., & Ehrlich, P. R. (1974). *Ark II: Social response to environmental imperatives.* San Francisco: W. H. Freeman.

Proceedings: The first national people of color environmental leadership summit. (1991, October 24–27). Washington, DC: United Church of Christ Commission for Racial Justice.

Review. (2003, June 5). Subhankar Banerjee, Arctic National Wildlife Refuge: Seasons of Life and Land. *Planet* (Jackson Hole, WY). Downloaded July 17, 2004, from www.mountaineersbooks.org/productdetails.cfm?PC=524

Sale, K. (1993). *The green revolution: The American environmental movement 1962–1992*. New York: Hill & Wang.

Schueler, D. (1992). Southern exposure. *Sierra, 77,* 45–47.

Schulzke, E. C. (2000, March 26). Policy networks and regulatory change in the 104th Congress: Framing the center through symbolic legitimacy conflict. Paper presented at the meeting of the Western Political Science Association, San Jose, CA.

Schwab, J. (1994). *Deeper shades of green: The rise of blue-collar and minority environmentalism in America*. San Francisco: Sierra Club Books.

Shabecoff, P. (1996). *A new name for peace: International environmentalism, sustainable development, and democracy*. Hanover, NH: University Press of New England.

Shabecoff, P. (2000). *Earth rising: American environmentalism in the twenty-first century*. Washington, DC: Island Press.

Shabecoff, P. (2003). *A fierce green fire: The American environmental movement* (Rev. ed.). New York: Hill & Wang.

Shaiko, R. G. (1999). *Voices and echoes for the environment: Public interest representation in the 1990s and beyond*. New York: Columbia University Press.

Smith, A. (1910). *An inquiry into the nature and causes of the wealth of nations* (Vol. 1). London: J. M. Dent & Sons. (Original work published 1776.)

Solnit, R. (1992). Up the river of mercy. *Sierra, 77,* 50, 53–58, 78, 81, 83–84.

Stone, D. (2002). *Policy paradox: The art of political decision making* (Rev. ed.). New York: W. W. Norton.

Taylor, B. C. (2003). "Our bruised arms hung up as monuments": Nuclear iconography in post-cold war culture. *Critical Studies in Media Communication, 20,* 1–34.

Taylor, B. R. (1995). *Ecological resistance movements: The global emergence of radical and popular environmentalism*. Albany: State University of New York Press.

Thoreau, H. D. (1893). Walking. In *Excursions: The writings of Henry David Thoreau* (Riverside ed., Vol. 9, pp. 251–304). Boston: Houghton-Mifflin. (Original work published 1862).

Tindall, D. B. (1995). What is environmental sociology? An inquiry into the paradigmatic status of environmental sociology. In M. D. Mehta & É. Ouellet (Eds.), *Environmental Sociology: Theory and Practice* (pp. 33–59). North York, Ontario: Captus Press.

Turner, T. (1991). *Sierra Club: 100 years of protecting nature*. New York: Harry N. Abrams.

Waddell, C. (Ed.) (2000). *And no birds sing: Rhetorical analyses of Silent Spring*. Carbondale: Southern Illinois University Press.

Wapner, P. (1996). *Environmental activism and world civic politics*. Albany: State University of New York Press.

Warren, L. S. (Ed.). (2003). *American environmental history*. Oxford, UK: Basil Blackwell.

White House. (1994, February 11). Executive Order 12898: Federal actions to address environmental justice in minority populations and low-income populations. Office of the Press Secretary.

White House. (2002, August 22). President announces Healthy Forest Initiative. Office of the Press Secretary. Retrieved June 24, 2003, from www.white house.gov/news/releases/2002/08/20020822–3.html

White, L., Jr. (1967). The historical roots of our ecological crisis. *Science, 155,* 1203–1207.

Wigglesworth, M. (1662). God's controversy with New England. In *Proceedings of the Massachusetts Historical Society, 12* (1871), p. 83, in Nash (2001), p. 36.

Zakin, S. (1993). *Coyotes and town dogs: Earth First! and the environmental movement.* New York: Penguin.

Appendix A

Major Public Lands and Wildlife Laws

1897   Forest Management (Organic) Act
Permitted timber cutting, mining, and water use on "forest reservations."

1916   National Parks Service Act
Created National Park Service to manage national parks and monuments.

1960   Multiple-Use Sustained-Yield Act
Declared that the purposes of National Forests are outdoor recreation, range, timber, watershed, and fish and wildlife; directs the Secretary of Agriculture to administer forest resources for their multiple use and sustained yield.

1964   Wilderness Act
Designated certain lands as wilderness and allowed for future areas to be added to the system.

1968   Wild and Scenic Rivers Act
Protected "free flowing, undammed rivers that had outstanding scenic, geologic, historic, recreational, or wildlife features."

1973   Endangered Species Act
Gave the Department of the Interior the authority to designate threatened and endangered species and to protect their habitat.

1976   Federal Land Policy and Management Act
Gave the Bureau of Land Management (BLM) the authority to "set grazing, preservation, and mining policy" on public lands, mainly in West.

1980   Alaska National Interest Lands Conservation Act (ANILCA)
Protects Alaskan lands with "scenic, historic, or wilderness values" and permits Native Alaskans "to continue a subsistence way of life."

1994   California Desert Protection Act
Protects millions of acres of the state's desert habitat as wilderness.

1996   Grand Staircase-Escalante National Monument
Sets aside 1.7 million acres in southern Utah as wilderness.

SOURCE: Merchant (2002), pp. 256, 258, 261–264.

Appendix B

Major Environmental and Public Health Laws

1970   National Environmental Policy Act (NEPA)
Signed into law on January 1, 1970, NEPA required "every federal agency to prepare an Environmental Impact Statement (EIS) for any legislation or project that would affect the quality of the human environment."

1970   Environmental Protection Agency (EPA)
A federal agency formed to regulate air and water quality, pesticides, chemical hazards, and solid-waste disposal under the federal environmental laws for these areas.

1970   Clean Air Act (CAA)
Regulated air emissions and authorized the EPA "to establish National Air Quality Standards . . . to protect public health and the environment."

1972   Clean Water Act (amended in 1977)
Regulated discharges of pollutants into U.S. waters and set the goal of "fishable and swimmable" waters.

1976   Toxic Substances and Control Act
Regulated the exposure of the public to toxic materials, including pesticides and chemicals.

1980   Comprehensive Environmental Response, Compensation, and Liability Act (CERCLA, or "Superfund")
Authorized the EPA to designate and manage the cleanup of toxic waste sites and to hold liable the responsible parties; also created a federal fund to help finance cleanup from a tax on industrial chemicals (now expired).

1986   Emergency Planning and Community Right-to-Know Act
Required industries to report their discharge of toxic chemicals and established the Toxic Release Inventory (TRI) to report publicly this data.

1990   Clean Air Act Amendments
Covered additional air pollutants, including smog, acid rain, airborne toxins, and ozone-depleting chlorofluorocarbons (CFCs); also established emissions trading permits for air emissions.

SOURCES: Merchant (2002), pp. 262–265; and Buck (1996), pp. 105–106.

Appendix C

Major International Environmental Treaties and Actions

1973 Convention on International Trade in Endangered Species (CITES)
      This treaty prohibited international commercial trade in endangered species
      or products from these species.

1982 International Whaling Commission moratorium on commercial whaling.

1987 Montreal Accord on Ozone
      An agreement signed by the United States and 23 other nations to phase out
      the production of chlorofluorocarbons (CFCs) that contribute to the deplet-
      ing of the earth's ozone layer.

1989 Basel Convention on Hazardous Wastes
      This agreement controlled the movement of hazardous wastes across interna-
      tional boundaries.

1992 Earth Summit
      The United Nations conference in Rio de Janeiro, Brazil, that discussed plans
      for addressing global environmental, economic, and social problems; also
      adopted the first draft of the "Earth Charter," a vision for an environmentally
      sustainable planet.

1994 World Trade Organization
      Replaced the earlier General Agreement on Trade and Tariffs; provided new
      protections for economic investments; also limited some nations' authority to
      impose health and environmental rules on business activities.

1997, Kyoto Accord on Global Warming
2005   An agreement by nations at the Climate Change Conference in Kyoto, Japan,
       that would set legally binding limits on pollutants affecting climate change.
       The Kyoto Accord went into effect in 2005 when the required number of
       nations had ratified it. (The United States officially withdrew from the Accord
       in 2001.)

SOURCES: Merchant (2002), pp. 265–266; and Axelrod, Downie, and Vig (2004). *The Global
Environment: Institutions Law & Policy.*

NOTES

1. This attitude of dominance was evident in the actions of officials in the U.S. government in their treatment of nature and Native Americans in the West. Helvarg (1994) recounts the strategy of elimination of Western tribes and animals they relied on: "Between 1600 and 1890 . . . more than two hundred major battles would be fought between indigenous groups and the settlers, some four hundred treaties signed and broken, and three-quarters of the Native American population destroyed. . . . [T]he Europeans' utilitarian approach to nature . . . included . . . resource denial ('Kill a buffalo, starve an Indian' was a motto favored by General George Crook's cavalry forces in the West). The near elimination of the buffalo as part of a strategic belief that it was "God's will that man [sic] exploit nature for his proper ends" (p. 1205). Such repugnance for nature provided fertile soil as it nurtured, along with the growth of commerce in a young nation, a dominant language that saw wild nature as a commodity to be conquered and exploited. (Note: We'll observe a number of different interpretations of biblical texts in the struggle over the environment; for example, in Chapter 1 we saw a very different attitude toward creation when U.S. Interior Secretary Bruce Babbitt drew on the biblical story of Noah to urge respect for nature.)

2. In 1872, President Ulysses S. Grant signed a law designating 2 million acres for Yellowstone National Park, the nation's first national park. And 13 years later, the state of New York set aside 715,000 acres for a forest preserve in its Adirondack Mountains. Still, these first acts were less motivated by an aesthetic or spiritual appreciation of wilderness than by a desire to protect against land speculation and, in the case of New York, a need to protect the forest watersheds for New York City's drinking water (Nash, 2001, p. 108).

3. Tree spiking is the practice of driving spikes or long nails into some trees in an area that is scheduled to be logged. (The metal—or, sometimes, plastic—spikes do not actually hurt the trees.) Tree spiking can discourage loggers from cutting the trees because of possible damage to their chain saws or, later, to the machinery in timber mills when saw blades strike the (hidden) spikes.

4. The 1971 Urban Environment Conference (UEC) was one of the first successful efforts to link environmental and social justice concerns. A coalition formed by Senator Philip Hart of Michigan, the UEC sought "to help broaden the way the public defined environmental issues and to focus on the particular environmental problems of urban minorities" (Kazis & Grossman, 1991, 247; Gottlieb, 1993a, pp. 262–263). I will address this history in more detail in Chapter 8.

5. Although the State of North Carolina completed the landfill in Warren County, NC, in 1982, local activists persisted in calling for its detoxification. Two decades later, in 2004, their efforts finally paid off when the state cleaned up the landfill.

PART II

Citizen Voices
and Public Forums

3

Public Participation in Environmental Decisions

Make diligent efforts to involve the public . . .

—National Environmental
Policy Act (Section 1506.6 [a])

Cindy King, a mother of two, walked to the microphone at a crowded public hearing in Salt Lake City. Utah's governor and members of the state's delegation to the United States Congress were seated on the stage in the large auditorium listening to citizens comment on a proposed federal law that would designate areas of Utah's wild forests and canyon lands as protected wilderness. The law, however, would also leave many wilderness areas unprotected. For this reason, a majority of the citizens speaking at the public hearing criticized the proposed law as too weak. Yet, the officials seemed not to be listening. When she reached the microphone, King said she would stand silently for her allotted time out of respect for the wildlife and living forests that were unable to speak. She added, "Since you are not listening, I will stand in silence to demonstrate the unfairness to those you have not heard." After three minutes of electrifying silence, the packed auditorium erupted in cheers and foot-stomping in support for the young mother's silent "statement" (C. King, personal communication, March 29, 2005). Later, lawmakers rejected the flawed wilderness bill when it came to a floor vote in the Senate.

One of the most striking features of the U.S. political landscape during the last 35 years has been the growth in participation by citizens, environmental organizations, business groups, scientists, and community activists in decisions about the environment. Environmental historian Samuel Hays (2000) noted that people have been "enticed, cajoled, educated, and encouraged to become active in learning, voting, and supporting [environmental] legislation and administrative action, as well as to write, call, fax, or e-mail decision makers at every stage of the decision-making process." Hays explained that all this has been "a major contribution to a fundamental aspect of the American political system—public participation" (p. 194). In fact, such involvement by members of the public and environmental groups often has been the critical element in efforts to protect threatened wildlife habitats, achieve cleaner air and water, and ensure a safer workplace.

Building on the idea of the public sphere, this chapter describes some of the legal guarantees and forums for communication that enable citizens to participate publicly in decisions about the environment. Here, I define **public participation** as the ability of individual citizens and groups to influence environmental decisions through (1) access to relevant information, (2) public comments to the agency that is responsible for a decision, and (3) the right, through the courts, to hold public agencies and businesses accountable for their environmental decisions and behaviors.

Beyond the First Amendment rights of freedom of speech, press, and peaceable assembly, U.S. laws and court rulings now accord citizens an unprecedented degree of access to information and opportunities to comment upon (and object to) official actions by state and federal environmental agencies. These procedural rights are an attempt to institutionalize the three aspects of public participation by recognizing their underlying principles of (1) *transparency,* or openness of governmental actions to public scrutiny, (2) *direct participation* in official decisions, and (3) *accountability*, the requirement that political authority meet agreed-upon norms and standards. (These tenets are summarized in Table 3.1.)

The first three sections of this chapter identify legal rights that have proved particularly important for citizen communication in environmental decisions: (1) the right to know, (2) the right to comment publicly about proposed projects or rules, and (3) the right of standing to object to a government agency's actions. **Standing** is the legal status accorded a citizen who has a sufficient interest in a matter, whereby the citizen may appear in court to protect that interest.

The fourth section describes in greater detail one of the most commonly used modes of public participation, citizen testimony in public hearings, as well as proposals to expand the rights of participation. In the final section, I conclude by describing some of the changes implemented since September 11, 2001, that restrict important aspects of public participation.

Table 3.1   Modes of Public Participation in Environmental Decisions

Legal Right	Mode of Participation	Authority	Democratic Principle
Right to Know	Written requests for information; access to documents online, etc.	Freedom of Information Act, Toxic Release Inventory, Clean Water Act, "Sunshine" laws	Transparency
Right to Comment	Testimony at public hearings, participation in advisory committees; written comment (letters, e-mail, etc.)	National Environmental Policy Act	Direct participation
Right of Standing	Plaintiff in lawsuit, *amicus* brief (third party) in legal case	Clean Water Act and other statutes; Supreme Court rulings (*Sierra Club v. Morton*, etc.)	Accountability

A final note on the focus of this chapter: I describe federal law primarily because most states reflect federal standards for public access to information and public participation generally. For example, the EPA delegates to the states the administration of laws regulating clean air and water, and these state programs fall under many of the same requirements for public participation as their federal counterparts. Finally, access to information from local industry about pollution sources is often available to any citizen through federal right-to-know laws.

The Right to Know: Access to Information

There is probably no more firmly held norm of democratic society than the principle of **transparency**. Simply put, this is openness in government and citizens' right to know information that is important to their lives. In regard to the environment, the United Nations has declared that the principle of transparency "requires the recognition of the rights of participation and access to information and the right to be informed. . . . Everyone has the right of access to information on the environment with no obligation to prove a particular interest" ("Declaration of Bizkaia on the Right to the Environment," 1999, n.p.). Violations of this principle have led to demands to strengthen public right-to-know guarantees. A recent case involving the American meat industry and the Environmental Protection Agency illustrates the type of situation that affects the environment yet sometimes take place out of public view.

On June 11, 2002, representatives of the livestock and poultry industry sent a confidential proposal to EPA officials that would shield large animal factories from U.S. pollution laws. The industry's proposed Safe Harbor Agreement would exempt many so-called factory farms or concentrated animal feeding operations (CAFOs) from violations of the Clean Air Act and the Superfund law. For a year, closed-door discussions occurred among EPA officials, meat industry representatives, and clean air administrators of many states. However, in May 2003, state officials walked out of the secret negotiations in Washington, D.C., convinced that the industry's proposal was fatally flawed. At the same time, a copy of the industry's confidential plan was publicly released by an anonymous source "concerned with the consequences of exempting animal factories from basic environmental protections" (Sierra Club, 2003, para. 1). (You can find more information on this issue at www.sierraclub.org/pressroom/cafo_papers/.)

Using the newly disclosed plan, environmentalist and citizens' groups mounted public pressure to bring an end to the EPA's private negotiations with the meat industry. The groups included Environmental Defense; the Center on Race, Poverty, and the Environment; and the Association of Irritated Residents (AIR). They announced that they were objecting to a "sweetheart deal" between EPA and the meat industry, drafted without input from the public, that would allow the industry to evade environmental laws (N. Garrett, personal communication, May 5, 2003). State and local air pollution officials also sent a letter to the EPA administrator, Christine Whitman, expressing "serious concern" over the industry request for a "safe harbor" exempting it from sanctions in the Clean Air Act (Sierra Club, 2003, p. 1). Despite this, the EPA proceeded to issue new regulations that closely mirrored the draft Safe Harbor Agreement negotiated privately with industry (Janofsky, 2005, p. A8).

The disclosure of secret negotiations by a U.S. government agency with an industry it is charged with regulating also illustrates the growing importance of information—and who controls it—in shaping environmental policies. Hays (2000) has noted that political power lies increasingly in an ability to understand the complexities of environmental issues, and "the key to that power is information and the expertise and technologies required to command it." As a result, Hays said, the most interesting political drama of recent years has been "the continued struggle between the environmental community and the environmental opposition over the control of information" (p. 232).

Especially in disputes over air pollution or toxic chemical spills, the lack of information and technical expertise can be disempowering for ordinary citizens and other nonspecialists. For example, urban planner Robert Gottlieb (1993) reported that participants in the environmental coalition that pushed for passage of the Clean Air Act in 1970 discovered they were at a disadvantage compared to industry lobbyists. The lobbyists made use of their access to technical knowledge to "amend and otherwise limit the legislation" (p. 133). In contrast, environmental advocates were accustomed to dealing with national parks and the aesthetics of wilderness; but, as Gaylord Nelson, the founder of Earth Day, explained, dealing with complex subjects such as air pollution required a "level of sophistication and expertise that the [environmental] groups had just not acquired" (Gottlieb, 1993, p. 133).

By the late 20th century, however, a move toward transparency in government affairs and greater public access to expertise had begun to reshape the discussion of U.S. environmental policy. New **sunshine laws**, intended to shine the light of public scrutiny on the workings of government, required open meetings of most government bodies, and several important acts of the U.S. Congress threw open the doors to government records more generally. In environmental affairs, the Clean Water Act of 1972 for the first time required federal agencies to provide information on water pollution to the public. And, as we'll see below, new requirements under the National Environmental Policy Act to provide environmental impact statements about proposed actions, such as highway construction or the filling of wetlands, proved critically important to groups who monitored government agencies.

Two laws in particular have provided important guarantees of the public's **right to know**—that is, their right of access to information about environmental conditions or actions of government that potentially affect the environment. These are the Freedom of Information Act of 1966 and the Emergency Planning and Community Right to Know Act of 1986, which established the Toxic Release Inventory.

The Freedom of Information Act

The move toward greater transparency in government had its roots in an earlier law, the **Administrative Procedure Act (APA)** of 1946. In the 1940s, in response to charges of agency favoritism and corruption, the APA laid out new operating standards for U.S. government agencies. It required that proposed actions—such as agency regulations to implement a law—be published in the *Federal Register* and that the public be given an opportunity to respond before the action took effect. Nevertheless, there was no accompanying requirement that these agencies make available to the public any records or documents related to their decisions.

As a result of growing public pressure for access to federal documents, Congress passed the **Freedom of Information Act (FOIA)** in 1966. FOIA provides that any person has the right to see the documents and records of any federal agency (except the judiciary or Congress). Agencies whose records are typically requested by environmental groups include the U.S. Forest Service, the Fish and Wildlife Service, the Bureau of Land Management, the EPA, and the Departments of Energy and Defense. Upon written request, an agency is required to disclose records relating to the requested topic, unless the agency can claim an exemption from disclosure as allowed by the Act. The FOIA also grants requesting parties who are denied their request the right to appear in federal court to seek the enforcement of the act's provisions.

In 1996, the Congress amended FOIA by passing the **Electronic Freedom of Information Amendments**. The amendments require agencies to provide public access to information in electronic form. This is done typically by posting a guide for making a FOIA request on the agency's website. (See FYI: How to Make a Request Under FOIA.) Individual states have adopted similar procedures governing public access to the records of state agencies.

FYI: How to Make a Request Under FOIA

For information on the Freedom of Information Act, see the Environmental Protection Agency's manual on FOIA, www.epa.gov//foia/docs/foiamanual.pdf, and its how-to web page on requesting documents under the FOIA, www.epa.gov/foia.

To request information from other agencies, see the website for that agency. For example, if you want to know what the U.S. Forest Service office in your area has done to enforce the Endangered Species Act in a recent timber sale, go to the Forest Service's website for FOIA requests (www.fs.fed.us/im/foia/). There you will find instructions for submitting your request for information. For example, it must be in writing. The site requires that you send your request to the Forest Service regional office or research station that is likely to have the information, or you may send it to the national USFS office if you are unsure. The website gives the addresses of these offices and research stations.

The Forest Service website also includes a sample FOIA request letter and details on FOIA procedures in the Forest Service.

Under the Freedom of Information Act, individuals, public interest groups, scientists, and others routinely gather information from public agencies in the course of monitoring their decisions and enforcement of permits. Individuals and environmental groups also may be interested in investigating management plans for forests, actions taken in designating species as endangered, or plans to decommission military bases. For example, citizens from a community contaminated with toxic chemicals may consider bringing a tort action against the polluter. An **environmental tort** is a legal claim for injury or a lawsuit, such as those depicted in the films *Erin Brockovich* and *A Civil Action*. In researching such a tort, a group may access information held by the EPA. Under federal law, the EPA is required to maintain records on any company that handles hazardous waste, including records of inspections of its facilities, notices of permit violations, and records of other legal actions taken against the company (Cox, 2000, para. 2). As the group prepares its legal case, it can request all of these documents from the EPA under the agency's procedures for complying with the Freedom of Information Act.

Public interest and environmental groups also may be interested in information about the actions of the U.S. government itself. A typical case occurred in 2002 when the Alaska Wilderness League, the Sierra Club, the Wilderness Society, and the Defenders of Wildlife submitted two FOIA requests for information about the Department of the Interior's plans to develop the Arctic National Wildlife Refuge. The FOIA requests called for release of records of any communications between Interior Department officials and oil industry associations or lobbying groups about proposals to open the refuge's coastal plain to oil drilling. Drilling for oil in the Arctic had been the centerpiece of the energy policy in President George W. Bush's administration, and the environmental groups reasoned that, "the public deserves to know how and why that decision was made" (Willett, Huffines, Devries, & Keogh, 2003).

Although an important tool for information, a FOIA request may not always be successful. An unsuccessful but high-profile Freedom of Information Act case involved the conservative group Judicial Watch and the Sierra Club, who jointly filed a lawsuit against Vice President Richard Cheney. The two groups had requested the disclosure of documents from closed-door meetings between Vice President Cheney and officials from Enron and other energy companies in 2001 as part of the vice president's energy task force. The vice president's office refused to provide the requested documents. The lawsuit therefore asked the courts to direct the vice president's office to honor the FOIA request. The Sierra Club and Judicial Watch contended that the administration was required to disclose information about the energy task force's members and its decision-making process because the task force helped to draft energy legislation that went to

Congress. The case went all the way to the U.S. Supreme Court, which ruled in 2005 limiting the grounds for the use of the Freedom of Information Act in the case of the vice president. The Supreme Court then sent the case back to the lower court, which later dismissed the lawsuit (Stout, 2005).

The Emergency Planning and Community Right to Know Act

In 1984, thousands of people were killed when two separate plants released toxic chemicals—one a Union Carbide plant in Bhopal, India, the other a chemical plant in West Virginia. These two incidents fueled public pressure for accurate information about the production, storage, and release of toxic materials in local communities by such companies. Responding to this pressure, Congress passed the **Emergency Planning and Community Right to Know Act** in 1986, known simply as the Right to Know Act. The law requires industries to report to local and state emergency planners the use and location of specified chemicals at their facilities.

The Right to Know Act also requires the Environmental Protection Agency to collect data annually on any releases of toxic materials into the air and water by designated industries and to make this information easily available to the public through an information-reporting tool, the **Toxic Release Inventory (TRI)**. In the 20 years since the TRI debuted, the EPA has expanded its reporting and now collects data on approximately 650 different chemicals (Environmental Protection Agency, 2003b). The EPA regularly makes this data available through online tools such as its TRI Explorer (www.epa.gov/triexplorer). Other public interest groups also use the TRI database to offer user-friendly links on their own websites for individuals wanting information about the release of toxic materials into the air or water in their local communities.

Act Locally!

Use the Toxic Release Inventory to check for the presence of toxic chemicals in the air, soil, or water in the community where you live or attend school.

To access the TRI database, use either the EPA's TRI Explorer at www.epa.gov/triexplorer or the user-friendly Scorecard at www.score card.org. Sponsored by Environmental Defense, Scorecard makes it possible for you to send faxes (free) to the polluters in your area or e-mail to state and federal decision makers. Scorecard also links you to volunteer opportunities and directories of environmental organizations in your area.

Also see the EPA's Enforcement & Compliance History Online (ECHO) at www.epa.gov/echo. This site allows you to know, for a specific facility, whether the EPA or state or local governments have conducted inspections at the facility, whether violations were detected or enforcement actions were taken, and whether penalties were assessed in response to environmental law violations.

Many community activists as well as scholars believe that the Toxic Release Inventory may be the single most valuable information tool available to citizens who are concerned with pollution from industrial plants in their communities. Stephan (2002) reports that the motivation for many of those who pushed for information disclosure laws was the principle that "citizens have a right to know whether the actions of private industry have a negative impact on their lives" (p. 192; Hadden, 1989). For that reason, one of the assumptions of the Toxic Release Inventory is that public access to information can be a means of ensuring community and industry safety. The goal of the Toxic Release Inventory, the EPA states, "is to empower citizens, through information, to hold companies and local governments accountable in terms of how toxic chemicals are managed" (2003b, p. 1).

Sometimes, information disclosure alone may affect polluters' behavior. For example, Stephan (2002) found that public disclosure of information about a factory's chemical releases or violation of its air or water permit may trigger a "shock and shame" response. If community members found out that a local factory was emitting high levels of pollution, their "shock" could push the community into action. Furthermore, Stephan explained that a factory itself (that is, those who work there) may feel shame from disclosure of its poor performance. However, he conceded another explanation might be that industry fears a backlash from citizens, interest groups, or the market (p. 194).

Overall, the public's access to important government information about the environment through the Freedom of Information Act and the Toxic Release Inventory has been a major advance both for the principle of transparency and for environmental protection.

Figure 3.1   The Toxic Release Inventory gives citizens access to information about the presence of many toxic chemicals in their communities

(Photo courtesy of Getty Royalty Free Images)

The Right of Public Comment

Town hall meetings and public comments before city councils are a long-standing tradition in the United States. When it comes to the environment, that tradition received a significant boost in 1970, the year millions of citizens first celebrated Earth Day. The National Environmental Policy Act guaranteed that the public would have an opportunity to comment directly to federal agencies before those agencies could proceed with any actions affecting the environment. At its core, the new law promised citizens that a kind of "pre-decisional communication" would occur between them and an agency that is responsible for decisions that impact the environment (Daniels & Walker, 2001, p. 8).

Public comment typically takes the form of testimony at public hearings, exchanges of views at open houses and workshops, written communications (letters, faxes, e-mails, research reports, and memos), and participation on citizen advisory panels. In this section, I'll focus on the *procedural right to comment,* provided under the National Environmental Policy Act and under President Clinton's 1994 Environmental Justice Executive Order. We'll examine the characteristics—and the limitations—of public hearings more fully in the next section. I'll describe the role of citizens' advisory panels in Chapter 4.

The National Environmental Policy Act

The core authority for the public's right to comment or participate directly in federal environmental decision making comes from the **National Environmental Policy Act,** commonly referred to as NEPA. Passed by Congress in 1969 and signed into law by President Nixon on January 1, 1970, NEPA was the first effort to involve the public in environmental decision making in a comprehensive manner. Political scientists Matthew Lindstrom and Zachary Smith (2001) explained that NEPA's sponsors wanted the public not only to be aware of and informed about projects that might be environmentally damaging but also to have an active role in commenting on alternative actions that an agency had proposed. Thus, NEPA and its regulations "act like other 'sunshine' laws . . . in that they require full disclosure to the public as well as extensive public hearings and opportunities for comment on the proposed action" (p. 94).

Two NEPA requirements are intended to give members of the public an opportunity to communicate about a proposed federal environmental action: (1) a detailed statement of any environmental impacts must be made public, and (2) concrete procedures for public comment must be implemented.

Environmental Impact Statements

As implemented by the Council on Environmental Quality, the National Environmental Policy Act requires federal agencies to prepare a detailed **environmental impact statement (EIS)** for any proposed legislation or major actions "significantly affecting the quality of the human environment" (Council on Environmental Quality, 1997, Sec. 102. [1][c]). Such actions range from constructing a highway to adopting a forest management plan.

Regardless of the specific action that is proposed, all EISs must describe three things: (1) the environmental impact of the proposed action, (2) any adverse environmental effects that could not be avoided should the proposal be implemented, and (3) alternatives to the proposed action (Sec. 102 [1][c]). (In some cases, a less detailed environmental assessment may be substituted.)

Public Comment on Draft Proposals

NEPA also requires that, before an agency completes a detailed statement of environmental impact, it must "make diligent efforts to involve the public" (CEQ, 1997, Section 1506.6 [a]). That is, the agency must take steps to ensure that interested groups and members of the public are informed and have opportunities for involvement prior to a decision. As a result, each federal agency must implement specific procedures for public participation in any decisions made by that agency that impact the environment. For example, citizens and groups concerned with natural resource policy ordinarily follow the rules for public comment developed in accordance with NEPA by the U.S. Forest Service, the National Park Service, the Bureau of Land Management, or the Fish and Wildlife Service. Community activists who work with human health and pollution issues are normally guided by Environmental Protection Agency and state rules. The states are relevant because the EPA delegates to them the authority to issue air and water pollution permits for plants, and construction permits and rules for managing waste programs (landfills and the like).

FYI: Requirements for Public Involvement in NEPA

Public Involvement (Section 1506.6 [a] [b]): Agencies shall:

(a) Make diligent efforts to involve the public in preparing and implementing their NEPA procedures.

(b) Provide public notice of NEPA-related hearings, public meetings, and the availability of environmental documents so as to inform those persons and agencies who may be interested or affected. . . .

(c) Hold or sponsor public hearings or public meetings whenever appropriate or in accordance with statutory requirements.

Inviting Comments (Section 1503.1 [a] [4]):

(a) After preparing a draft environmental impact statement and before preparing a final environment impact statement, the agency shall . . . (4) Request comments from the public, affirmatively soliciting comments from those persons or organizations who may be interested or affected.

SOURCE: Council on Environmental Quality (http://ceq.eh.doe.gov/nepa/regs/ceq/toc_ceq .htm) and Walker (2004, p. 116).

The requirements for public comment or communication under NEPA typically occur in three stages: (1) issue surfacing, (2) notification, and (3) comment on draft decisions (Daniels & Walker, 2001). These steps are guided by the rules adopted by the Council on Environmental Quality to ensure that all agencies comply with basic requirements for public participation that are implied in the NEPA statute itself. (See "FYI: Requirements for Public Involvement in NEPA.")

The process normally starts with **issue surfacing**. This is a preliminary stage in an agency's development of a proposed rule or action. Also called **scoping**, it involves canvassing interested members of the public about some interest— for example, a plan to reallocate permits for water trips down the Colorado River in the Grand Canyon—to determine what the concerns of the affected parties might be. Such scoping might involve public workshops, field trips, letters, and agency personnel speaking one on one with members of the public.

When an agency has a proposal ready for consideration, it must provide **notification** to the public. The intent to receive public comments on the proposal or action is announced in the media and in special mailings to interested parties; a formal notice also is published in the *Federal Register*. Typically, a notice describes the proposed regulation, management plan, or action and specifies the location and time of a public meeting or the period during which written comments will be received by the agency.

Finally, NEPA rules require agencies to actively solicit **public comment** on the draft proposal. Public comments on the draft proposal or action usually occur during public hearings and in written comments to the agency in the form of reports, letters, e-mails, postcards, or faxes. The public also may use this opportunity to comment on the adequacy of any environmental impact statement accompanying the proposal, or it may use the information in the

EIS to assess the proposal itself. In response, the agency is required to assess and consider comments received from the public. It must then respond in one of several ways: (1) by modifying the proposed alternatives, (2) by developing and evaluating new alternatives, (3) by making factual corrections, or (4) by "explain[ing] why the [public] comments do not warrant further agency response" (Sec. 1503.4).

The success of NEPA's public participation process obviously depends on how well agencies comply with the law's original intent. For example, in its study of NEPA's effectiveness, the Council on Environmental Quality observed that, "the success of a NEPA process heavily depends on whether an agency has systematically reached out to those who will be most affected by a proposal, gathered information and ideas from them, and responded to the input by modifying or adding alternatives throughout the entire course of a planning process" (CEQ, 1997, p. 17).

A successful illustration of NEPA's effectiveness occurred in 2001 when the Clinton administration announced its sweeping "roadless rule." The rule, adopted by the U.S. Forest Service, prohibited road building and restricted commercial logging on nearly 60 million acres of U.S. national forest lands in 39 states, including Alaska's Tongass National Forest. The final rule was adopted on January 5, 2001, after a year and a half of public review and comment. (Here, I must admit a personal interest, having participated as president of the national Sierra Club in helping to mobilize individuals to participate in the public comment process. A more critical review of the process used in the roadless rule can be found in Walker, 2004).

By the end of the process, the U.S. Forest Service had held more than 600 public meetings and had received an unprecedented two million comments from members of the public, environmentalists, businesspeople, sports groups and motorized recreation associations, local residents, and state and local officials. As a result of the public's review and comment on successive drafts, the rule grew stronger, expanding the amount of protected forest land. After the final rule was adopted, Forest Service chief Mike Dombeck reflected, "In my entire career, this is the most extensive outreach of any policy I've observed" (Marston, 2001, p. 12, in Walker, 2004, p. 114). (For the final roadless rule, see http://roadless.fs.fed.us/documents/rule/index.shtml.)

Following its adoption, the Clinton roadless rule has been both praised and criticized for its public participation process, and its implementation initially was delayed by court challenges from logging interests and Western state officials. Environmentalists praised the rule not only for its substantive protections but also for the quality of its process for public comment. "This is a day to celebrate participatory democracy at its finest," said the Oregon Natural Resources Council's Ken Rait (Ash, Merritt, & Rait, 2000, para. 1). Others claimed that the process used for the roadless rule missed a chance for a more collaborative process involving the public. For example, environmental communication scholar Gregg Walker (2004) argued that the process "exemplified a business as usual approach rather than innovation and civic deliberation" (p. 135). (In May, 2005, the U.S. Forest Service dropped the roadless rule altogether after a hasty NEPA process. Environmental groups challenged this ruling, and the case is before the courts as this book goes to press.)

At the heart of the controversy has been a fierce debate over the meaning of public participation and the goals it is intended to serve. Walker asks, "Does the number of public meetings and amount of comment letters received provide sufficient evidence of meaningful public participation?" (p. 115). Similarly, in 2002 the Forest Service proposed a rule change that would disallow counting postcards and form letters as public comments for the purpose of complying with NEPA. (For the status of the rule, see www.fs.fed.us/emc/nfma/index3.html.) I'll take up this question more generally in the next chapter by describing some of the criticisms of public comment in environmental decision making.

The Executive Order on Environmental Justice

A more recent source expanding the right of public comment is President Clinton's 1994 **Executive Order on Environmental Justice.** Shortly after entering office, the president directed all federal agencies to "study the impact of proposed actions [permits for plants, etc.] related to the environment and public health on minority communities and to implement an agency 'strategy' for public participation" (Clinton, 1994, p. 7629). The executive order specifically directed each agency to develop an agency-wide environmental justice strategy that included opportunities for public participation and access to information. (See "FYI: The Executive Order on Environmental Justice.")

One successful use of the Executive Order occurred in 2002 when the public watchdog group Public Employees for Environmental Responsibility (PEER) invoked it in requesting that the EPA's inspector general issue a report on the environmental justice impacts of President George W. Bush's proposed Clear Skies Proposal. (The Clear Skies Proposal would revise federal regulations under the Clean Air Act that control emissions from older electric utility plants and refineries.) Clinton's executive order also has encouraged the development of guidelines by federal agencies for involving minority communities in decisions about the environment. For example, the EPA's National Environmental Justice Advisory Council (2000) has published a "Model Plan for Public Participation" to guide federal agencies working with such communities (see www.epa.gov/compliance/resources/publications/ej/model_public_part_plan.pdf. I'll provide more information about the calls for environmental justice in Chapter 8.)

FYI: The Executive Order on Environmental Justice

The American Bar Association maintains a website for news related to environmental justice, including official government statements and pending cases of enforcement of President Clinton's Executive Order on Environmental Justice. See www.abanet.org/environ/committees/envtab/ejupdates.html.

See also EPA's Environmental Justice Public Participation Checklist, www.epa.gov/epaoswer/hazwaste/permit/pubpart/appendd.pdf.

This checklist lays out ways to identify, inform, and involve stakeholders from communities of color.

The effectiveness of an executive order may be somewhat limited. On the other hand, there is no doubt that the National Environmental Policy Act has proved to be one of the most empowering laws passed by the U.S. Congress. In terms of its scope and involvement of members of the public, NEPA has been the cornerstone of the principle of direct participation in governance through the right of citizens to comment directly to agencies responsible for decisions affecting the environment. There remains one other right of public participation, to which I now turn.

The Right of Standing: Citizen Suits

Beyond the right to know and public comment is a third route for citizen participation in environmental decisions: the right of standing. A right of standing is based on the presumption that an individual having a sufficient interest in a matter may "stand" before legal authority to speak and seek protection of that interest in court. In both common law and provisions under U.S. environmental law, citizens—under specific conditions—may have standing to object to an agency's failure to enforce environmental standards or to hold a violator directly accountable.

Standing and Citizen Suits

The right of citizens to standing developed originally from common law, wherein individuals who have suffered an **"injury in fact"** to a legally protected right could seek redress in court (Buck, 1996, p. 66). The definition of injury required under common law normally meant a concrete, particular injury that an individual had suffered due to the actions of another party. One of the earliest cases of standing in an environmental case involved William Aldred, who in 1611 brought suit against his neighbor Thomas Benton. Benton had built a hog pen on an orchard near Aldred's house. Aldred complained that "the stench and unhealthy odors emanating from the pigs drifted onto [his] land and premises" and were so offensive that he and his family "could not come and go without being subjected to continuous annoyance" (9 Co. Rep. 57, 77 Eng. Rep. 816 [1611], in Steward & Krier, 1978, p. 117–118). Although Benton argued that, "one ought not have so delicate a nose, that he cannot bear the smell of hogs," the court sided with Aldred and ordered Benton to pay for the damage caused to Aldred's property.

Aldred was able to pursue his claim before the court as a result of his and his family's injury in fact from the offensive odors. But in the 20th century, the principle of injury in fact would be expanded in ways that allowed wider access to the courts by environmental interests. Two developments modified the strict common-law requirement of concrete, particular injury, allowing a greater opening for citizens to sue in behalf of environmental values. First, the 1946 Administrative Procedure Act broadened the right of judicial review for persons "suffering a legal wrong because of agency action, or adversely affected or aggrieved by agency action" (5 U.S.C. § 702, in Buck, 1996, p. 67). This was so because, under the APA, the courts generally have held that an agency must "weigh all information with fairness and not be 'arbitrary and capricious'" in adopting agency rules (Hays, 2000, p. 133). Thus, when an agency's actions depart from this standard, they are subject to citizen complaints under the APA; that is, citizens have standing under the "arbitrary and capricious" standard for what constitutes an injury. In succeeding years, this provision of the Administrative Procedures Act would be an important tool enabling environmental groups to hold agencies accountable for their actions toward the environment.

The second expansion of standing came in the provision for **citizen suits** in major environmental laws. The provision for such lawsuits enables any citizen to go into a federal court to ask that an environmental law be enforced. For example, the Clean Water Act confers standing on any citizen or "persons having an interest which is or may be adversely affected" to challenge violations of clean water permits in federal court if the state or federal agency fails to enforce the statutory requirements (Stearns, 2000, para. 378). Using this provision, citizens in West Virginia invoked their right of standing by filing citizen suits against the practice of mountaintop removal, in which coal companies literally push earth from the tops of mountains into nearby valleys, filling streams, in their search for coal (Trial Lawyers for Public Justice, 2002). Other environmental laws that allow citizen suits include the Endangered Species Act, the Clean Air Act, the Toxic Substances Control Act, and the Comprehensive Environmental Response Compensation and Liability Act (the Superfund law).

The purpose of a citizen suit is to challenge an agency's lack of enforcement of environmental standards; local citizens and public interest groups are empowered to sue the agency directly to enforce the law. Jonathan Adler (2000), a senior fellow at the Competitive Enterprise Institute, explained the rationale behind this. When federal regulators "overlook local environmental deterioration or are compromised by interest group pressure, local groups in affected areas are empowered to trigger enforcement themselves" (para. 48). This is especially important in cases of **agency capture,** in which a regulated industry pressures or influences officials to ignore violations of a corporation's permit for environmental performance (e.g., its air or water discharges).

Landmark Cases on Environmental Standing

Citizens' claims to the right of standing are subject not only to the provisions of specific statutes (e.g., the Clean Water Act), but also to judicial interpretations of the **cases and controversies clause** in Article III of the U.S. Constitution. Despite its arcane title, this requirement serves an important purpose. The cases and controversies clause "ensures that lawsuits are heard only if the parties are true adversaries, because only true adversaries will aggressively present to the courts all issues" (Van Tuyn, 2000, p. 42).

To determine if a party is a "true adversary," the U.S. Supreme Court uses three tests: (1) persons bringing a case must be able to prove an injury in fact, including a legal wrong as allowed by the APA; (2) this injury must be "fairly traceable" to an action of the defendant; and (3) the Court must be able to redress the injury through a favorable ruling (p. 42). Although environmental statutes grant a right of standing, citizens still must meet these three constitutional tests before proceeding.

The main question in granting standing in environmental cases has been the meaning of the Court's test of "injury in fact." What qualifies as injury where individual citizens seek to enforce the provisions of an environmental law? The Supreme Court has worked out an uneven and, at times, confusing answer to this question in several landmark cases.

Sierra Club v. Morton (1972)

The Supreme Court's ruling in **Sierra Club v. Morton** provided the first guidance for determining standing under the Constitution's cases and controversies clause in an environmental case. In this case, the Sierra Club sought to block plans by Walt Disney Enterprises to build a resort in Mineral King Valley in California. Plans for the resort included the building of a road through Sequoia National Park. In its suit, the Sierra Club argued that a road would "destroy or otherwise adversely affect the scenery, natural and historic objects, and wildlife of the park for future generations" (Lindstrom & Smith, 2001, p. 105). Although the Supreme Court found that such damage could constitute an injury in fact, it noted that the Sierra Club did not allege that any of its members themselves had suffered any actual injury, and therefore they were not true adversaries. Instead, the Sierra Club had asserted a right to be heard simply on the basis of its interest in protecting the environment. The Court rejected the group's claim of standing in the case, ruling that a long-standing interest in a problem was not enough to constitute an injury in fact (Lindstrom & Smith, 2001, p. 105).

Despite its ruling in *Sierra Club v. Morton,* the Supreme Court spelled out a liberal standard for what might constitute a successful claim of standing. It observed that in the future, the Sierra Club need only allege an injury to its members' *interests*—for example, that its members would no longer be able to enjoy an unspoiled wilderness or their normal recreational pursuits. The Sierra Club immediately and successfully amended its suit against Disney Enterprises, arguing that such injury would occur to its members if the road through Sequoia National Park were to be built. (Subsequently, Mineral King Valley itself was added to Sequoia National Park, and Disney Enterprises withdrew its plans to build the resort.)

An interesting footnote to legal history occurred in a famous dissent in the original Morton case. Arguing for a more expansive standard, Justice William O. Douglas argued that even trees should have standing. He noted that U.S. law already gave standing to some inanimate objects such as ships and corporations and that environmental goals would be enhanced if citizens could sue on behalf of environmental objects (Buck, 1996; for more information about this argument, see Stone, 1996).

The Court's liberal interpretation of the test for injury in fact in *Sierra Club v. Morton* and other cases, along with the right of standing in many environmental laws, produced a 20-year burst of environmental litigation by citizens and environmental groups. This trend continued until the Supreme Court issued a series of conservative rulings that narrowed the basis for citizens' standing.

Lujan v. Defenders of Wildlife (1992)

In the 1990s, the U.S. Supreme Court handed down several rulings that severely limited citizen suits in environmental cases. In perhaps the most important case, **Lujan v. Defenders of Wildlife,** the Court rejected a claim of standing by the conservation group Defenders of Wildlife under the citizen suit provision of the Endangered Species Act. The ESA declares that "any person may commence a civil suit on his own behalf (A) to enjoin any person, including the United States and any other governmental instrumentality or agency . . . who is alleged to be in violation of any provision" of the Act (ESA, 1973, §1540 [g] [1].) In its lawsuit, Defenders of Wildlife argued that the secretary of the interior (Lujan) had failed in his duties to ensure that U.S. funding of projects overseas—in this case, in Egypt—did not jeopardize the habitats of endangered species, as the law required (Stearns, 2000, p. 363).

Writing for the majority, Justice Antonin Scalia stated that Defenders had failed to satisfy constitutional requirements for injury in fact that would grant standing under the ESA. He wrote that the Court rejected the view that the citizen suit provision of the statute conferred upon "*all* persons an abstract, self-contained, noninstrumental 'right' to have the Executive observe the procedures required by law" (Lujan, 1992, p. 573). Rather, he explained, the plaintiff must have suffered a tangible and particular harm not unlike the requirement in common law (Adler, 2000, p. 52). This ruling overturned the standard in *Sierra Club v. Morton*, in which Sierra Club members needed only to prove injury to their interests—that is, that they couldn't enjoy their recreational pursuits or enjoyment of wilderness.

Consequently, courts began to limit sharply citizen claims of standing under citizen suit provisions of environmental statutes. Writing in the *New York Times*, Glaberson (1999) reported that the Court's rulings in the 1990s were one of the most "profound setbacks for the environmental movement in decades" (p. A1).

Friends of the Earth, Inc. v. Laidlaw Environmental Services, Inc. (2000)

In a more recent case, the Supreme Court appeared to reverse its strict Lujan doctrine, holding that the knowledge of a possible threat to a legally recognized interest (clean water) was enough to establish a "sufficient stake" by a plaintiff in enforcing the law (Adler, 2000, p. 52).

In 1992, Friends of the Earth and CLEAN, a local environmental group, sued Laidlaw Environmental Services in Roebuck, South Carolina, under the Clean Water Act citizen suit provision. Their lawsuit alleged that Laidlaw had repeatedly violated its permit limiting the discharge of pollutants (including mercury, a highly toxic substance) into the nearby North Tyger River. Residents of the area who had lived by or used the river for boating and fishing testified that they were "concerned that the water contained harmful pollutants" (Stearns, 2000, p. 382).

The Supreme Court's majority in *Friends of the Earth, Inc. v. Laidlaw Environmental Services, Inc.* ruled that Friends of the Earth and CLEAN did not need to prove an actual (particular) harm to residents. Writing for the majority, Justice Ruth Bader Ginsburg stated that injury to the plaintiff came from lessening the "aesthetic and recreational values of the area" for residents and users of the river due to their knowledge of Laidlaw's repeated violations of its clean water permit (Adler, 2000, p. 56). In this case, the plaintiffs were not required to prove that Laidlaw's violations of its water permit had contributed to actual deterioration in water quality. It was sufficient that they showed that residents' knowledge of these violations had discouraged their normal use of the river.

With this ruling, the Supreme Court reaffirmed the rationale of citizen suits that local groups and citizens have an interest in the enforcement of environmental quality under the provisions of specific laws such as the Clean Water Act. However, disagreement over the criteria for citizen standing in environmental cases is likely to continue. At stake are differing interpretations of injury in fact and the rights of citizens of standing to compel the government to enforce environmental laws.

Citizens' Communication and Public Participation

Access to information, public comment, and the right of standing are basic procedural rights of public participation in U.S. environmental decision making, but they shed little light on the communication that occurs as individuals pursue these rights. Here and in the following chapter, I'll describe some of the characteristics of this communication. The most frequently used modes of individual citizen communication on environmental matters are (1) testimony at public hearings, (2) participation on advisory panels, and (3) collaboration with other parties with an interest in an environmental decision. This section focuses on citizen testimony in public hearings and recent proposals to expand the rights of participation. Chapter 4 will explore the increasing use of citizen advisory panels and informal collaboration by citizens, businesses, agencies, and environmental groups to mediate disputes in environmental conflicts.

Public Hearings and Citizen Testimony

Public hearings, workshops, and meetings undoubtedly are the more common modes of participation by ordinary citizens in environmental decision making at both the federal and state levels. Typically, these are forums for public comments to an agency before the agency takes action that might significantly

Figure 3.2   Citizens' comments at a public hearing are the most common form of public participation

impact the environment. As we saw earlier, the National Environmental Policy Act requires federal and some state agencies to actively solicit public comment before taking any action. In such cases, the agency normally conducts scoping sessions (workshops or open houses) and public hearings to establish a record of public comment. At the state and local levels, public hearings typically are held before an agency issues a permit for a company to discharge pollutants into the air or water, or to gather input before a town acts on a strictly local matter—for example, deciding the location of a municipal solid waste site, issuing a permit to widen a street, or approving funds to purchase land for a park.

The public hearings and meetings to address environmental questions mainly involve an exchange of information. Typically, an agency will inform citizens about its proposed action, and citizens then provide input or express their opinions about the proposal. Any interested citizen may attend these meetings. There are usually sign-in sheets for those wishing to speak. Before inviting comment from members of the public, the presiding official often will call agency staff or outside experts to testify and provide technical information on matters before the agency. Speakers are limited to a short time in which to comment orally or to read a statement. Some individuals will read from a prepared statement; others speak extemporaneously. Supporters and opponents of a proposal may attend, and both sides speak at the meeting.

The communication at public meetings and hearings may be polite or robust, restrained or angry, as well as informed, opinionated, and emotional. The range of comments reflects the diversity of opinion and interests of the community itself. Officials may urge members of the public to speak to the specific issue that is on the agenda, but the actual communication often departs from this, ranging from individual citizens' comments, emotionally charged remarks, personal research, and stories of their family's experiences, to criticism of opponents or public officials.

Some people may denounce the actions of the agency or respond angrily, even theatrically, to plans that affect their lives or community. At one particularly intense public hearing, I witnessed residents of a rural community place bags of garbage on the stage of the auditorium where elected officials were presiding, to protest plans to allow an out-of-state company to build a hazardous waste incinerator near their homes. The atmosphere in this public hearing was electric, with angry parents and other community members noisily confronting defensive and harried officials on the stage.

The communication in public hearings also can be affected by factors other than personal emotions or concerns about an issue. Ordinary citizens find themselves apprehensive about having to speak in front of large groups, perhaps with a microphone, to unfamiliar officials. They may face opponents or others who are hostile to their views. Sometimes, they must wait hours for their turns to speak. Those with jobs or small children face additional constraints because they must take time from work or find (and often pay) someone to watch their children. I'll return to these and other constraints in Chapter 8 when I describe some of the barriers to citizen participation in public hearings in low-income communities.

Due to the conditions that are typically imposed by crowded hearing rooms, limited time, volatile emotions, and long waiting times for speaking, many believe that public hearings are not an effective form of public participation. Matthews (1994) reports an all-too-frequent occurrence: "Officials usually make presentations, or get lectured to by some outraged individual. Little two-way communication occurs. And with no feedback, people don't think they have been heard. The prevailing sense is that a decision was reached long before the hearing was scheduled" (p. 23). Daniels and Walker (2001) go further. They contend that the methods used by some public lands management agencies such as the Forest Service exhibit a "Three-'I' Model . . . inform, invite, and ignore." For example, agency officials will inform the public about a proposed action, such as a timber sale, then "invite the public to a meeting to provide comments on that action, and ignore what members of the public say" (p. 9). Other critics have described this as a "decide, announce, and defend" attitude. That is, officials decide a policy beforehand, announce this decision, and then defend their decision at the public hearing. Walker and Daniels argue that such public hearings lack the basic characteristics of a "learning environment," instead fostering communication that "is intended to convince rather than explore" and therefore discourage citizens from participating (p. 85).

Local public meetings and hearings about environmental matters, although adversarial and impolite at times, reflect the diverse and messy norms of democratic life. At their best, meetings that invite wide participation by members of the public may generate comments and information that help agencies to shape or modify important decisions affecting the environment. Although they occasionally may be confrontational, such hearings provide many citizens their only opportunity to speak directly to government authority about matters of concern to them, their families, or their community.

On the other hand, a growing number of agency leaders and scholars are beginning to explore alternatives to the adversarial and one-way communication modes that characterize environmental public meetings. In Chapter 4, I will describe some of these alternative formats to formal public hearings. For now, I want to alert you to other proposals to strengthen the public's rights to information and participation in the "green" public sphere.

Act Locally!

Investigate the procedures and types of communication that occur in a local public hearing on the environment in your town, city, or county.

1. **Identify one local agency or committee and the environmental issue it is considering.** What committee or body in your local government deals with environmental problems? Are there upcoming meetings to consider proposals for bike paths? A permit to operate a medical waste incinerator near your campus? A vote to approve funds to purchase green space? A commission to study public transportation? Are its meetings publicly announced? Is the public invited to attend its meetings?

2. **Attend one of the public meetings, and observe the procedures for public comment.** Is the public welcome to comment publicly during the proceedings? Who gets to speak? For how long? What do individuals testifying include in their remarks? Do they present facts? Are they sometimes emotional? Do agency officials treat members of the public respectfully?

3. **Interview two or three members of the public who spoke at the public meeting, as well as an official who presided.** Did members of the public feel that their comments made a difference? Did the officials listen to them? How did the presiding official feel about the quality of communication at the meeting? What effects, if any, did you observe as a result of the public meeting?

Proposals to Expand the Green Public Sphere

Although some feel that the traditional models for public participation nurture adversarial communication, many community activists would like to change the current system in other ways. Many residents who live near hazardous facilities, in particular, have been pushing in recent years to expand the opportunities for public participation in four areas: (1) a right to know more, (2) a right to independent expertise, (3) a right to a more authoritative involvement, and finally (4) a right to act.

A Right to Know More

Since passage of the original Emergency Planning and Community Right to Know Act in 1986, community activists have asked for the **right to know more**. That is, they have tried to extend the provisions of the law to cover more industries and more types of chemicals. They have also urged that *other sources of potential danger* be covered under this law. Such dangers can result not only from the toxic chemicals inside the plants but from transport of raw chemicals into and out of plants and the disposal of products containing toxic chemicals. For example, Massachusetts, New Jersey, and the city of Eugene, Oregon, all have enacted laws requiring industries to report information about additional sources of potential exposure to toxic chemicals. As a result, the public interest group INFORM (2003) reports, "Communities located near these facilities have the ability to monitor plant operations and ensure that maximum efforts are being made to protect the environment and public health" (para. 1). (For more recent information about the right-to-know-more initiative and its status, see www.informinc.org/rtkm_00.php.)

A Right to Independent Expertise

Because the proof of harmful effects from exposure to toxic chemicals involves complex issues, advocates from communities with toxic waste sites long have sought access to sources of expertise to aid them in understanding the effects of these chemicals. Often, there is a disparity in the expertise that is available to government agencies or industry, on the one hand, and that which is available to local citizens, on the other. In response to this gap, Congress enacted the **Technical Assistance Grant (TAG) Program** in 1986. The TAG program is intended to help communities at Superfund sites. (Superfund sites are abandoned chemical waste sites that have qualified for federal funds for their cleanup.) Decisions about the cleanup of these sites are usually based on technical information that includes the type of chemical wastes and the technology available (EPA, 2003a). The purpose of TAG grants is to provide funds for citizen groups to hire consultants who can help them to understand and comment on the information provided by the EPA and the industries responsible for cleaning these sites.

As I learned in working with Superfund communities while I was president of the Sierra Club, the TAG program does not ensure that local citizens actually have a **right to independent expertise**. Such a right would allow the community to seek expertise from independent sources and to use this knowledge to assess the EPA or other government agencies' recommendations. For example, in working with the residents of a small town in Mississippi whose homes bordered an abandoned chemical plant, I learned that that their requests to use their TAG grant to hire experts to analyze their well water had been denied. They had been dissatisfied with the EPA's plans for cleanup of the toxic waste site and distrusted the data supplied to them by the agency. When they asked for support to consult their own experts, they were told the TAG program did not allow funds for communities to generate *new* (independent) data. Hence, the local activists could not use TAG funds to drill for soil samples to determine whether chemicals had traveled underground from the plant to their wells; nor could they use the TAG funds to conduct their own health studies of the residents in the community who were complaining of rare illnesses (C. Keys, 1995, personal communication).

Dissatisfaction with the limits on the EPA funds for hiring experts has led community activists from toxic sites around the country to push for greater flexibility in the use of TAG grants to secure independent experts to aid their efforts. (For more information about the EPA's Technical Assistance Grants program, see the "Frequently Asked Questions" about community involvement in decisions about local toxic waste sites at the EPA's website, www.epa.gov/superfund/tools/tag/faqs.htm.)

A Right to a More Authoritative Involvement

As we learned earlier, most public comment under NEPA and in public hearings is only advisory. Although agencies must consider such comments in reaching a decision, they are not legally bound to change a proposal or rule just because the public opposes it. For example, some advocates for environmental justice were especially critical of the failure of President Clinton's Executive Order on Environmental Justice to give their communities an "authoritative" role in defining a problem and the range of solutions that might be considered. Christopher Foreman (1998), a senior fellow at the Brookings Institution, expressed this sentiment when he wrote that officials who dealt with underrepresented groups, especially racial minorities, had found "a relatively safe haven in varieties of *consultative*—but, again, not *authoritative*—citizen participation: advisory boards, public forums, community outreach efforts, and access to information" (p. 45). Foreman explained, "By stressing nonbinding mechanisms of inclusion . . . officials pay homage to democratic values, signal benign intent, and hope to deflect criticism" (pp. 45–46; emphasis added).

A more **authoritative involvement** in environmental policymaking, on the other hand, would include citizens' input in an agency's initial framing or definition of a problem, as well as the development of a range of solutions and criteria by which officials and the public jointly reach a decision (Lynn, 1986; and Katz & Miller, 1996). For example, should communities be able to require, as a condition of a company's air permit, that it contribute to an independent monitoring service for future air pollution and a health fund to support local health clinics and hospitals? Should community groups be part of any team designing a public education campaign about health risks in their community? We'll explore alternative models for this authoritative public involvement in Chapter 6.

A Right to Act

Starting in the 1980s, labor, public health, and environmental activists focused on a new approach to workplace and community safety, one that labor leader Tony Mazzocchi of the Oil, Chemical, and Atomic Workers Union called the "right to act." Earlier, Mazzocchi had coined the phrase *right to know* (Engler, 2001, para. 1). In arguing for a new *right to act*, he pointed out that the government's reliance on permits, inspectors, and fines to enforce workplace environmental safety could not ensure that every chemical plant or hazardous facility in a community met safety and health regulations. Going beyond this traditional approach, the **right to act** asserted that workers and nearby residents should be allowed to inspect workplaces and then to negotiate measures to prevent chemical leaks and other hazards (Engler, 2001). While some unions had won a right to inspect plant operations and correct hazardous work conditions, communities historically have had no means to act directly to monitor facilities near their homes.

One incident in 1998, however, gave a boost to the right to act movement. After three chemical accidents near schools in Passaic, New Jersey, caused the hospitalization of elementary school students, the county enacted the nation's first right-to-act local ordinance. It allowed the creation of Neighborhood Hazard Prevention Committees made up of residents, workers, and management from local industries. At first, the new ordinance allowed the neighborhood committees to conduct unannounced inspections of plants or industries and to have the committee's own technical experts take part in the inspection. However, after criticism from industries, the county altered the ordinance by eliminating inspections that lacked prior permission by the plant or industry (Engler, 2001).

Overall, the prospects of wider opportunities for the public's participation in environmental decisions are uncertain. Although there have been some advances, new barriers to the right to know and public comment have been erected in recent years. In the final section, I will describe some of the restrictions on public participation that have occurred since the terrorist attacks on New York City and Washington on September 11, 2001. These restrictions have come from two sources: (1) actions taken to protect national security and their corresponding restrictions of civil liberties, and (2) a shift in the policies of environmental agencies that limit citizens' access to information and right of public comment.

Restricting Public Participation in the Post-9/11 Era

In the immediate aftermath of terrorist attacks on the United States in 2001, the U.S. Congress and the executive branch moved quickly to give new authority to federal law enforcement agencies and intelligence services. However, civil libertarians, public interest groups, and environmentalists soon learned that these actions had troublesome implications for civil society and the Bill of Rights. Historians Gerald Markowitz and David Rosner (2002) reported that, "in the wake of the September 11 attacks, the Bush administration acted to restrict public access to information about polluting industries and restricted journalists' and historians' access to government documents previously available through the Freedom of Information Act" (p. 303). One law in particular was responsible for many of these restrictions on the public's right to know: the Homeland Security Act.

Homeland Security and Restrictions on Public Participation

Scholars and individuals seeking information about the environment from sources that were available to the public before September 11, 2001, first noticed a shift in response by federal agencies. For example, *USA Today* reported,

When United Nations analyst Ian Thomas contacted the National Archives in March [2002] to get some 30-year-old maps of Africa to plan a relief mission, he was told the government no longer makes them public. When John Coequyt, an environmentalist, tried to connect to an online database where the Environmental Protection Agency lists chemical plants that violate pollution laws, he was denied access. (Parker, Johnson, & Locy, 2002, n.p.)

In fact, in the eight months following the 9/11 attacks, the federal government removed hundreds of thousands of public documents from its websites; in other cases, access to material was made more difficult. For example, documents reporting accidents at chemical plants, previously available online from the EPA, now may be viewed only in government reading rooms (Parker, Johnson, & Locy, 2002).

The shift to greater secrecy of information appeared to follow the release of a memorandum from the U.S. attorney general urging caution in disclosing material under the Freedom of Information Act. Within days of the 9/11 attacks, Attorney General John Ashcroft (2001) assured federal agencies that they should not fear that their deliberations would be made public, and added, "No leader can operate effectively without confidential advice and counsel" (n.p.). He then directed the agencies to carefully consider the protection of such values and interests when making disclosure determinations under the Freedom of Information Act.

The move to restrict public access to information gained a significant boost shortly after the first anniversary of the 9/11 attacks, when the U.S. Congress passed the **Homeland Security Act** of 2002. This law contains broad authority for the federal government to take steps to protect national security, including the right to restrict public access to any information that could be used to attack U.S. interests. Although differing political parties and interests agreed that national security measures were needed, the new law posed serious challenges to Americans' civil liberties. Certainly, the chief complaints against the law came from journalists, environmentalists, civil libertarians, and academics. Environmental groups focused particularly on provisions in the Homeland Security Act that permitted exemptions to the Freedom of Information Act (FOIA).

The FOIA exemptions are in a key provision of the Homeland Security Act, called **Critical Infrastructure Information (CII)**. Wishing to shield information about vulnerabilities in the nation's energy and transportation infrastructure, such as electrical transmission lines, airlines, and oil and gas pipelines, the law authorizes a level of "extraordinary secrecy" (Fagin, 2003, n.p.) from public scrutiny. Specifically, the CII section allows any federal agency to deny FOIA requests from journalists, environmental groups, and individuals for federal records of permit violations, fines, or other information about oil refineries, drinking water plants, oil and natural gas pipelines, and so forth. Furthermore, it protects from public scrutiny and prosecution any information that is voluntarily submitted to federal agencies by corporations. Some critics of the Homeland Security Act fear that this secrecy extends to violations of environmental, civil rights, consumer protection, worker health and safety, and other laws. That is, they fear that if information about such violations is voluntarily submitted to the EPA, the information might then be unavailable in any criminal or civil prosecution. (For other concerns about the implications of the Homeland Security Act of 2002, see the Society of Environmental Journalists' website, www.sej.org/foia/.)

The rationale for the secrecy allowed by the Homeland Security Act seemed to make sense to many in the aftermath of the 9/11 terrorist attacks. *USA Today* reporters seemed to capture the nation's mood: "Protecting maps and descriptions of nuclear power plants, hydroelectric dams, pipeline routes and chemical supplies seemed justified, for national security" (Parker, Johnson, & Locy, 2002, n.p.). Nevertheless, many reporters and environmentalists believed that an excessive secrecy also could undermine other vital interests, such as the need for transparency in alerting public agencies to potential safety problems. (See "Another Viewpoint: The Public Need for Critical Infrastructure Information.")

Another Viewpoint: The Public Need for Critical Infrastructure Information

On November 14, 2002, the Reporters Committee for Freedom of the Press and the Society of Environmental Journalists jointly released a letter to members of Congress, raising concerns about the restrictions on public information planned for the new Homeland Security Act of 2002. In particular, they were concerned about prohibition in the "Critical Infrastructure Information" (CII) section of the law. They wrote:

> The threat of terrorism is real . . . However, there exists a definite need for the public to be able to recognize vulnerabilities in order to avert them. Public demand for reliable [energy] infrastructures is possibly the greatest assurance that measures will be taken to strengthen them. . . . Media organizations have used freedom of information laws extensively to expose defects in pipelines and pipeline management. For example, records obtained by the *Austin American Statesman* after a 1994 pipeline explosion near Corpus Christi, Texas, showed that Koch, a large utility company entrusted with keeping its pipelines in proper working order, increased pressure in its pipeline "after being warned about corrosion and weaknesses in the steel."

They also showed that the company underestimated the amount of oil spilled, "a miscalculation of some 70,000 gallons" for nine days, an error that probably hindered cleanup efforts.

It is precisely this kind of information that would be closed to the general public under the proposed CII rules. Whether that information would be useful to terrorists is uncertain, but its usefulness in explaining to the public what did go or can go wrong is inestimable.

SOURCE: Society of Environmental Journalists (2002).

More recently, the Department of Homeland Security (DHS) has proposed a significant restriction of public participation under regulations that implement the National Environmental Policy Act. (The new department also was established in the Homeland Security Act of 2002.) In 2004, the DHS proposed rules allowing it to classify as secret certain information generated by the department, including potentially the environmental impact statements required for some of its proposed actions. Although the directive applies only to the DHS itself, it nevertheless affects broad areas related to the environment. For example, DHS jurisdiction includes such concerns as oil spills, transport and handling of hazardous materials, chemical plant security, and plans for responses to nuclear accidents. Such concerns would normally trigger an environmental impact statement or environmental assessment for any action proposed by the agency under the National Environmental Policy Act.

In summary, the government's response to the attacks of September 11, 2001, although ensuring critical safeguards, also raises serious concerns about the public's access to information. Although intended to limit information useful to terrorists, some of the restrictions on information also limit the ability of journalists and environmental groups to address perceived problems or to publicize inadequate performance by government agencies or private businesses. The public interest group OMB Watch (2004) stated this dilemma in its criticism of the Department of Homeland Security's proposed NEPA restrictions: "While it is understandable that classified and proprietary information, or information sincerely vital to national security should sometimes remain secret, a blanket exemption like this is prone to abuse and would hide vast amounts of environmental information" (n.p.). To follow developments in the DHS related to public access to information, see www.dhs.gov and www.ombwatch.org.)

Restricting Public Involvement in Environmental Agencies

Concern for national security has not been the only source of restrictions on the public's rights of public participation in the years since the 9/11 attacks. A second catalyst has been the shift in management by some federal environmental agencies. This shift was apparent very early in the second Bush administration when the President's Healthy Forests Initiative became public. The Healthy Forests Restoration Act, which became law in 2003, exempted some 10 million acres of forest land from the requirements under the National Environmental Policy Act for an environmental impact statement and public comment period. In other cases, the White House requested expedited environmental reviews of transportation and energy projects such as highway construction and oil and gas exploration on public lands. And, as noted earlier in this chapter, the Forest Service has revised its rules to ban the use of postcards or form letters in public comment under NEPA.

Perhaps the most far-reaching shift in environmental management that affects public participation occurred in the U.S. Forest Service. In late 2004, the Forest Service announced sweeping new rules to implement the **National Forest Management Act** (NFMA). The U.S. Congress enacted the NFMA in 1976 to reform management of the nation's 155 national forests. Specifically, it required that each forest "insure that land management plans be prepared in accordance with the National Environmental Policy Act of 1969" (16 USC 1604[g][1]). As I noted earlier in this chapter, NEPA requires an environmental impact statement and an opportunity for public comment prior to any action that may significantly impact the environment. Yet, the *New York Times* reported that the new Forest Service rules relax these "long-standing provisions on environmental reviews and the protection of wildlife on 191 million acres of forests and grasslands . . . [and] also cut back on requirements for public participation in forest planning decisions" (Barringer, 2004, p. 1A).

The stated intention of the new rules is to streamline the planning of forest managers, enabling them to revise forest plans faster and disallowing lengthy appeals by environmentalists. The desire to avoid appeals in the courts from environmentalists had been a goal of the second Bush administration from the outset. For example, in unveiling his Healthy Forests Initiative in 2002 to expedite timber sales, President Bush explained: "There's [sic] so many regulations, and so much red tape, that it takes a little bit of effort to ball up the efforts to make the forests healthy. And plus, there's [sic] just too many lawsuits, just endless litigation" (Izakson, 2003, n.p.).

On the other hand, many forest advocates believe the forest rule changes mean that the Forest Service can avoid public scrutiny for failures to respect relevant standards under such laws as the Endangered Species Act—for example, to allow logging in sensitive habitats of endangered species. Their concerns are based in the new rules' allowance of an exemption, or "categorical exclusion," from the NEPA process of certain types of forest planning. For example, when a local forest district wished to revise an existing management plan under the old rules, forest managers had to satisfy NEPA requirements for an environmental impact statement and public comment before proposed changes could be put into effect in that forest. Under the NFMA rule changes, they potentially can skip the entire NEPA process when revising an existing forest plan. In its review of the new rules, the nonprofit forest law firm Wildlaw (2005) explained that the final Forest Service regulations eliminate the requirement to prepare an environmental impact statement pursuant to NEPA "whenever a forest plan is revised or significantly amended. Instead, forest plans 'may be categorically excluded from NEPA documentation' [219.4(b)], which means that the Forest Service can entirely bypass the NEPA process whenever it revises or amends a forest plan" (para. 9). (For more information on the U.S. Forest Service changes and an extensive review of the new rules, see www.wildlaw.org/WildLaw_NFMA_Regs_White_Paper.doc.)

The changes to the National Forest Management Act illustrate the tension between an understandable desire, on the one hand, of forest managers to complete their planning in an efficient manner and the need, on the other hand, of journalists and environmental groups to scrutinize the work of a public agency to ensure its compliance with environmental standards and public safety.

Conclusion

In this chapter, I've identified some of the legal rights and forums that enable you and other citizens to participate directly and publicly in decisions about the environment. Guarantees of the right to know, the right to comment on proposed actions, and the right of standing in court reflect basic norms of a democratic society: transparency, direct participation, and accountability of political and corporate authority to law and agreed-on standards.

Basic to effective participation in environmental decisions is a right to know, to have access to information. One of the more powerful tools for citizens and groups of all kinds is the Freedom of Information Act, which in principle makes available any information or documents used by an agency of the executive branch of government. An even more powerful information tool for investigating sources of pollution where you live or work is the Toxic Release Inventory (TRI). By filing a FOIA request with a federal agency by using a website such as Environmental Defense's Scorecard, you can access information that may aid your understanding of a problem or help you prepare your remarks for a public hearing about an environmental issue in your town or city.

Second, the ability of citizens to question, comment, or testify publicly before governmental officials in public meetings has expanded dramatically since the passage of the National Environmental Policy Act in 1969. The requirements of NEPA to solicit the public's involvement before a proposed action may be the most important development in the last half-century for democratizing the process of environmental decision making. Along with citizen suits and the right of standing to enforce major environmental laws in court, these requirements give greater meaning and significance to the ideals of direct participation and accountability.

We also looked at the communication that typically occurs at public hearings, including the opportunity for any citizen to speak freely to governmental officials, as well as proposals to widen the public sphere by providing more opportunities for ordinary citizens to influence decisions about the environment. Many citizens in communities affected by environmental hazards are pushing for a greater level of public access and direct participation—a right to know more, a right to independent expertise, a right to more authoritative participation in public meetings, and a right to act to inspect hazardous facilities and to require correction of environmental problems.

Finally, we reviewed recent trends toward greater restriction of rights to public participation in environmental decisions. The impetus for new restrictions of the access to information and requirements under NEPA for an environmental impact statement and public comment come from two sources in the period after the terrorist attacks of September 11, 2001: actions taken to protect national security and their corresponding restrictions of certain civil liberties, and a shift in the management policy of environmental agencies in the second Bush administration that impede citizens' access to information and right of standing in the courts.

As you reflect on the dilemmas for an open society that are raised by these actions, I hope that you will try to identify ways in which the democratic ideals of transparency, participation, and accountability can still be realized or even strengthened as we strive for a society that is both secure and environmentally healthy.

KEY TERMS

Administrative Procedure Act: Enacted in 1946; laid out new standards for the operation of U.S. government agencies; required that proposed actions be published in the

Federal Register and that the public be given an opportunity to respond; also broadened the right of judicial review for persons "suffering a legal wrong" resulting from "arbitrary and capricious" actions on the part of agencies.

Agency capture: The pressuring or influencing of officials by a regulated industry to ignore violations of a corporation's permit for environmental performance (e.g., its air or water discharges).

Authoritative involvement: An approach to public participation that includes citizens' input to an agency's initial framing or definition of a problem and to the development of a range of solutions and criteria by which officials and the public jointly reach a decision.

Cases and controversies clause: The portion of Article III of the U.S. Constitution that ensures that lawsuits are heard by true adversaries in a dispute, on the assumption that only true adversaries will represent to the courts the issues in a case; an important test of true adversary status is whether persons bringing the action are able to prove an injury in fact.

Citizen suits: Action brought by citizens in federal court asking that provisions of an environmental law be enforced. The right to bring such suits is a provision of major environmental laws.

Critical Infrastructure Information (CII): A section of the Homeland Security Act of 2002 that allows any federal agency to deny FOIA requests for federal records of permit violations, fines, or other information about oil refineries, drinking water plants, oil and natural gas pipelines, etc.; also protects from public scrutiny and prosecution any information voluntarily submitted to federal agencies by corporations.

Emergency Planning and Community Right to Know Act (the Right to Know Act): Enacted in 1986; requires industries to report to local and state emergency planners the use and location of specified chemicals at their facilities.

Electronic Freedom of Information Amendments: Amendments to FOIA that require federal agencies to provide public access to information in electronic form. This is done typically by posting a guide for making a freedom of information request on the agency's website.

Environmental impact statement (EIS): Required by the National Environmental Policy Act for proposed federal legislation or actions significantly affecting the quality of the environment, an EIS must describe (1) the environmental impact of the proposed action, (2) any adverse environmental effects that could not be avoided should the proposal be implemented, and (3) alternatives to the proposed action.

Environmental tort: A legal claim for injury or a lawsuit related to an environmental harm.

Executive Order on Environmental Justice: President Clinton's 1994 order directing federal agencies to "study the impact of proposed actions (permits for plants, etc.) related to the environment and public health on minority communities and to implement an agency 'strategy' for public participation" (Clinton, 1994).

Freedom of Information Act (FOIA): Enacted in 1966; provides that any person has the right to see documents and records of any federal agency (except the judiciary or Congress).

Friends of the Earth, Inc., v. Laidlaw Environmental Services, Inc.: A 2000 case in which the Supreme Court reversed its strict Lujan doctrine, ruling that plaintiffs did not need to prove an actual (particular) harm; rather, the *knowledge* of a possible threat to a legally recognized interest (clean water) was enough to establish a sufficient stake in enforcing the law.

Homeland Security Act: Passed in 2002 shortly after the first anniversary of the 9/11 terrorist attacks, this law contains broad authority for the federal government to take steps to protect national security, including the right to restrict public access to any information that could be used to attack U.S. interests.

Injury in fact: One of three tests used by the courts to determine a plaintiff's standing or right to seek redress in court for a harm to a legally protected right; criteria for defining injury in fact have varied from the denial of enjoyment or use of the environment to a concrete, tangible harm to the plaintiff.

Issue surfacing: Canvassing members of the public interested in a proposal; a preliminary stage in a federal environmental agency's development of a proposed rule or action. Also called *scoping*.

Lujan v. Defenders of Wildlife: A 1992 case in which the Supreme Court rejected a claim of standing by the group Defenders of Wildlife under the citizen suit provision of the Endangered Species Act, ruling that the Defenders had failed to satisfy constitutional requirements for injury in fact because plaintiffs had not suffered a tangible and particular harm. Overturned the more liberal standard established in *Sierra Club vs. Morton.*

National Environmental Policy Act (NEPA): Enacted in 1970; involves the public in environmental decision making by federal agencies through (1) a detailed, public statement of any environmental impacts of a proposed action and (2) concrete procedures for public comment.

National Forest Management Act (NFMA): Enacted in 1976; required, among other things, that management plans for the nation's 155 national forests be prepared in accordance with the National Environmental Policy Act of 1969.

Notification: Announcement in the media, by special mailings to interested parties, and by formal notice in the *Federal Register* inviting public comment on a proposal or action; required of a federal agency under the National Environmental Policy Act when an agency has a proposal ready for consideration.

Public comment: Required of federal agencies under the National Environmental Policy Act; public input solicited by a federal agency on any proposal significantly affecting the environment; usually takes place at public hearings and in written reports, letters, e-mails, or faxes to the agency.

Public hearing: The common mode of participation by ordinary citizens in environmental decision making at both the federal and state levels; a forum for public comment to an agency before the agency takes any action that might significantly impact the environment.

Public participation: The ability of individual citizens and groups to influence environmental decisions through (1) access to relevant information, (2) public comments to the agency that is responsible for a decision, and (3) the right, through the courts, to hold public agencies and businesses accountable for their environmental decisions and behaviors.

Right to act: A right sought by labor unions, public health groups, and environmentalists that would allow workers and nearby residents of facilities to inspect workplaces and then to negotiate measures to prevent chemical leaks and other hazards.

Right to independent expertise: A right demanded by advocates from communities with toxic waste sites to access to sources of expertise that are independent of governmental agencies, to understand the effects of chemicals from these waste sites on the health of community residents.

Right to know: The public's right of access to information about environmental conditions or actions of government that potentially affect the environment.

Right to know more: A right that would be conferred under the proposed extension to the 1986 Emergency Planning and Community Right to Know Act to cover more industries and types of chemicals.

Scoping: See *issue surfacing*.

Sierra Club v. Morton: A 1972 case that established the first guidance for determining standing under the Constitution's cases and controversies clause in an environmental case; the Supreme Court held that the Sierra Club need only allege an injury to its members' interests—for example, that its members could not enjoy an unspoiled wilderness or their normal recreational pursuits.

Standing: The legal status accorded a citizen who has a sufficient interest in a matter, whereby the citizen may appear in court to protect that interest.

Sunshine laws: Laws intended to shine the light of public scrutiny on the workings of government, requiring open meetings of most governmental bodies.

Superfund sites: Abandoned chemical waste sites that have qualified for federal funds for their cleanup under the Comprehensive Environmental Response Compensation and Liability Act (commonly called the Superfund law).

Technical Assistance Grant Program: A program initiated in 1986 to help communities at Superfund sites by providing funds for citizen groups to hire consultants who can help them understand and comment on information provided by EPA and the industries responsible for cleaning these sites.

Toxic Release Inventory: An information-reporting tool established under the Emergency Planning and Community Right to Know Act (1986) that enables the

Environmental Protection Agency to collect data annually on any releases of toxic materials into the air and water by designated industries and to make this information easily available to the public.

Transparency: Openness in government; citizens' right to know information that is important to their lives. In regard to the environment, the United Nations has declared that the principle of transparency "requires the recognition of the rights of participation and access to information and the right to be informed. . . . Everyone has the right of access to information on the environment with no obligation to prove a particular interest" ("Declaration of Bizkaia on the Right to the Environment," 1999).

DISCUSSION QUESTIONS

1. Do you believe that information is power? Have you ever thought of requesting informtion from the federal government under the Freedom of Information Act? How difficult do you think that would be?

2. Have you ever attended a public hearing or spoken publicly about an environmental concern? Were you nervous? Did you think you made a difference?

3. Should trees have standing? That is, should citizens be able to seek legal remedies in court on behalf of trees and other environmental subjects (rivers, wildlife, etc.)?

4. Whether a citizen has standing in court depends upon differing interpretations of injury in fact. Should a person have to demonstrate a concrete, personal harm in order to gain standing? Or should the test of injury allow for a social purpose, that is, an interest in ensuring environmental quality through the enforcement of laws such as the Clean Water Act, the Clean Air Act, or the Endangered Species Act?

5. Do you believe that individuals in a community should have a right to act to gain entry into local plants to inspect them for violations of their air or water permits?

6. Does the executive branch of government have a right to restrict the public's access to information under the Freedom of Information Act on the grounds, for example, that release of information about vulnerabilities at chemical plants or oil refineries might aid terrorists?

REFERENCES

Adler, J. H. (2000, March 2–3). *Stand or deliver: Citizen suits, standing, and environmental protection.* Paper presented at the Duke University Law & Policy Forum Symposium on Citizen Suits and the Future of Standing in the 21st

Century. Retrieved August 20, 2003, from www.law.duke.edu/journals/delpf/articles/delpf12p39.htm

Ash, S., Merritt, R., & Rait, K. (2000). *Sweeping forest protection plan would protect 58.5 million acres in 39 states.* Oregon Natural Resources Council. Retrieved September 11, 2003, from www.onrc.org/press/017.roadsbanonrc.html

Ashcroft, John. (2001). *FOIA memorandum.* Washington, DC: United States Department of Justice Office of Information and Privacy. Available at www.usdoj.gov/oip/foiapost/2001foiapost19.htm

Barringer, F. (2004, December 23). Administration overhauls rules for U.S. forests. *New York Times,* pp. A1, A18.

Beierle, T. C., & Cayford, J. (2002). *Democracy in practice: Public participation in environmental decisions.* Washington, DC: Resources for the Future.

Buck, S. J. (1996). *Understanding environmental administration and law.* Washington, DC: Island Press.

Clinton, W. J. (1994, February 16). Federal actions to address environmental justice in minority populations and low-income communities. Executive Order 12898 of February 14, 1994. *Federal Register 59,* p. 7629.

Council on Environmental Quality (CEQ). (1997, January). *The national environmental policy act: A study of its effectiveness after twenty-five years.* Washington, DC: Council on Environmental Quality, Executive Office of the President. Available at http://ceq.eh.doe.gov/nepa/nepa25fn.pdf

Cox, W. S., III. (2000, June 23). *Litigating environmental tort claims* (Birmingham Bar Association Continuing Legal Education). Retrieved September 6, 2003, from www.birminghambar.org/data/Outlines/BuddyCoxArticle/Environmental June23.pdf

Daniels, S. E. & Walker, G. B. (2001). *Working through environmental conflict: The collaborative learning approach.* Westport, CT: Praeger.

Declaration of Bizkaia on the Right to the Environment. (1999, February 10–13). International Seminar on the Right to the Environment, held in Bilbao, Spain, under the auspices of UNESCO and the United Nations High Commissioner for Human Rights. Available at www.gurelurra.net/english/declar.html

Endangered Species Act of 1973, 16 U.S.C.A. §1531–1544.

Engler, R. (2001, October 28). *Beyond the right to know: Fighting for the right to act.* Report issued by the New Jersey Work Environment Council. Retrieved August 13, 2003, from www.ombwatch.org/rtkconference/right_to_act.htm

Environmental Protection Agency. (2003a). *Grants and financial assistance: Technical assistance grants.* Retrieved August 13, 2003, from www.epa.gov/region08/community_resources/grants/granttag/granttag.html

Environmental Protection Agency. (2003b). *What is the Toxics Release Inventory (TRI) program?* Retrieved September 8, 2003, from www.epa.gov/tri/whatis.htm

Foreman, C. H., Jr. (1998). *The promise and perils of environmental justice.* Washington, DC: Brookings Institution Press.

Gottlieb, R. (1993). *Forcing the spring: The transformation of the American environmental movement.* Washington, DC: Island Press.

Hadden, S. G. (1989). *A citizen's right to know: Risk communication and public policy*. Boulder, CO: Westview.

Hays, S. P. (2000). *A history of environmental politics since 1945*. Pittsburgh: University of Pittsburgh Press.

INFORM. (2003). *The community's right to know more*. Retrieved September 8, 2003, from www.informinc.org/rtkm_00.php

International Joint Commission (IJC). (1992). *Sixth biennial report on Great Lakes water quality*. Windsor, Canada: IJC.

Izakson, O. (2003, November). Smokescreen: Fire, forests and the Bush administration's "healthy forest" plan for increased logging. *Multinational Monitor, 24* (11), n.p. Retrieved April 4, 2005, from http://multinationalmonitor.org/mm2003/03november/nov03corp1.html

Janofsky, M. (2005, January 22). E.P.A. offers an amnesty if big farms are monitored. *New York Times*, p. A8.

Jefferson, T. (1907). Letter to William Charles Jarvis, 28 September, 1820. In E. Bergh (Ed.), *The writings of Thomas Jefferson*. Volume 19 (pp. 276–279). Washington, DC: Thomas Jefferson Memorial Association.

Katz, S. B., & Miller C. R. (1996). The low-level radioactive waste siting controversy in North Carolina: Toward a rhetorical model of risk communication. In C. G. Herndl & S. C. Brown (Eds.), *Green culture: Environmental rhetoric in contemporary America* (pp. 111–140). Madison: University of Wisconsin Press.

Lindstrom, M. J., & Smith, Z. A. (2001). *The national environmental policy act: Judicial misconstruction, legislative indifference, & executive neglect*. College Station: Texas A&M University Press.

Lujan v. Defenders of Wildlife, 504 U.S. 555 (1992).

Lynn, Frances M. (1986). Citizen involvement in hazardous waste sites: Two North Carolina success stories. *Environmental Impact Assessment Review, 7*, 347–361.

Markowitz, G., & Rosner, D. (2002). *Deceit and denial: The deadly politics of industrial pollution*. Berkeley: University of California Press.

Marston, B. (2001, May 7). A modest chief moved the Forest Service miles down the road. *High Country News, 33*(9). Retrieved August 25, 2003, from www.hcn.org.

Matthews, D. (1994). *Politics for people: Finding a responsible public voice*. Urbana: University of Illinois Press.

National Environmental Justice Advisory Council. (2000, February). *The model plan for public participation*. Washington, DC: Office of Environmental Justice, U.S. Environmental Protection Agency. Available at www.epa.gov/compliance/resources/publications/ej/model_public_part_plan.pdf

National Environmental Policy Act (NEPA). 42 U.S.C.A. § 4321 *et. seq.* (1969).

OMB Watch. (2004, June 29). DHS seeks exemptions from public disclosure requirements. *OMB Watcher, 5*(13). Retrieved April 4, 2005, from www.ombwatch.org/article/articleprint/2240/-1/218/

Parker, L., Johnson, K., & Locy, T. (2002, May 15). Post-9/11, government stingy with information. *USA Today*, p. 1A. Retrieved March 12, 2005, from www.usatoday.com/news/nation/2002/05/16/secrecy-usatcov.htm

Sierra Club. (2003, May 5). Animals factories using closed-door meetings. Retrieved August 15, 2003, from www.sierraclub.org/pressroom/2003/may/cafo_papers.asp

Society of Environmental Journalists. (2002, November 14). Comments of the Reporters Committee for Freedom of the Press and the Society of Environmental Journalists to proposed rules re: public access to critical energy infrastructure information. Retrieved March 23, 2005, from www.sej.org/foia/rcfp.htm

Stearns, M. L. (2000, March 2–3). From Lujan to Laidlaw: A preliminary model of environmental standing. Paper presented at the Duke University Law & Policy Forum Symposium on Citizen Suits and the Future of Standing in the 21st Century. Retrieved from www.law.duke.edu/journals/delpf/articles/delpf12p39.htm

Stephan, M. (2002). Environmental information disclosure programs: They work, but why? *Social Science Quarterly, 83*(1): 190–205.

Steward, R. B., & Krier, J. (Eds.). (1978). *Environmental law and public policy.* New York: Bobbs-Merrill.

Stone, C. (1996). *Should trees have standing? And other essays on law, morals & the environment* (Rep. ed.). Dobbs Ferry, NY: Oceana.

Stout, D. (2005, May 11). Appeals court backs Cheney in secrecy case. *New York Times,* pp. A1, A15.

Trial Lawyers for Public Justice. (2002, January 24). Press release. Retrieved December 22, 2003, from www.tlpj.org/pr/National_AD_Press_Release.htm

U.S. Environmental Protection Agency. (2003, August 18). *What is the toxics release inventory (TRI) program?* Retrieved August 18, 2003, from www.epa.gov/tri/whatis.htm

Van Tuyn, P. (2000). "Who do you think you are?" Tales from the trenches of the environmental standing battle. *Environmental Law, 30*(1): 41–49.

Waddell, C. (1996). Saving the great lakes: Public participation in environmental policy. In C. G. Herndl & S. C. Brown (Eds.), *Green culture: Environmental rhetoric in contemporary America* (pp. 141–165). Madison: University of Wisconsin Press.

Walker, G. B. (2004). The roadless areas initiative as national policy: Is public participation an oxymoron? In S. P. DePoe, J. W. Delicath, & M.-F. A. Elsenbeer (Eds.), *Communication and public participation in environmental decision making* (pp. 113–135). Albany: State University of New York Press.

Wildlaw. (2005, January 20). *Review of the new NFMA planning regulations.* Retrieved March 30, 2005, from www.wildlaw.org

Willett, D., Huffines, E., Devries, B., & Keogh, L. (2003, March 11). *Bush administration keeping secrets on arctic drilling plans: Groups must sue to enforce freedom of information act.* (Press release.) Washington, DC: Sierra Club, Wilderness Society, Defenders of Wildlife, Alaska Wilderness League.

4

Conflict Resolution Through Collaboration and Consensus

M any citizens, scientists, environmentalists, industry groups, and government officials have become frustrated with public hearings and other traditional forms of public participation. In recent years, many have begun to turn to alternative ways to manage environmental conflicts. For example, in southern Oregon, ranchers, environmentalists, and loggers work together in a voluntary association called the Applegate Partnership. Their goal is the ecological and economic health of the Applegate watershed, an area of farms, ranches, and national forests, and their guiding principle is "Practice Trust—Them Is Us" (Wondolleck & Yaffee, 2000, p. 139; for more information, see Shipley, 1995).

In hundreds of communities across the country, citizens, environmentalists, business leaders, and public officials are experimenting with new approaches to public participation in environmental disputes. They are talking with their opponents across the table, working through their differences, and in many cases resolving conflicts that have festered for years. These innovative forms of conflict management have been called by different names: partnerships, community-based collaboration, citizen advisory boards, consensus decision making, and alternative dispute resolution models. Usually, they involve a form of communication called **collaboration**. Collaboration has been defined generally as "constructive, open, civil communication, generally as dialogue; a focus on the future; an emphasis on learning; and some degree of power sharing and leveling of the playing field" (Walker, 2004, p. 123). In many cases of collaboration, participants will strive to reach agreement by **consensus**, which usually means that discussions will not end until everyone has had a chance to share their differences and find common ground.

The purpose of this chapter is to describe the adoption by many communities, environmentalists, and businesses of some form of collaboration to resolve environmental disputes. In the first section, I'll begin with some background—the growing dissatisfaction with traditional forms of public participation such as public hearings. I'll then identify a range of collaborative alternatives for resolving environmental disputes.

In the second section, I'll ask: When is collaboration appropriate? What communication skills are required for successful collaboration? I'll also look at several case studies of collaboration—some quite successful and one that has served as a cautionary tale for many environmental groups. And I'll introduce a key term that is important to the idea of collaboration: **stakeholder**. Stakeholders are those parties in a dispute who have a real or discernible interest (a stake) in the outcome. Finally, in the third section, I'll consider criticisms of collaboration and identify some of the circumstances in which collaboration may *not* be appropriate for resolving environmental conflicts.

When you've finished this chapter, you should be familiar with the benefits of collaborative approaches to resolving environmental disputes and with the communication skills needed for successful collaboration. You should also be aware of barriers to effective collaboration and circumstances under which collaborative approaches may not be appropriate. Indeed, in the end, disputes over deeply held values about the environment at times require collaboration with opponents; at other times, such disputes may call for advocacy and resistance to compromise.

From Advocacy to Collaboration

In the three decades since the passage of the National Environmental Policy Act (NEPA), the public's right to comment on government actions affecting the environment has been widely recognized; hence, forums for public involvement have proliferated. As we learned in the last chapter, public comment on an environmental proposal typically takes the form of public hearings, citizen testimony, and written comments. Yet, citizens and public officials alike feel that these processes sometimes produce more frustration and division than they do reasoned decision making. Officials and consultants often speak in technical jargon, using such phrases as "parts per billion" of chemical substances, and nonexpert members of a community sometimes feel that their concerns do not matter, that their efforts to speak are dismissed by public officials and experts. In this section, I'll examine some of the criticisms of traditional public hearings and identify some of the emerging alternatives for public involvement.

Criticism of Traditional Forms of Public Participation

Several years ago, public officials in a town near mine announced a public hearing after they had decided informally to build a hazardous waste facility near residential homes and a state hospital. Many of the area residents and patients' advocates understandably were upset at this. They staged a mass march through town, chanted slogans, and denounced local officials and the state's governor. At the public hearing, they voiced their anger at officials who sat stone-faced in the front of the auditorium. While some testified, other members of the audience shouted at the officials. One young man rushed to the front of the auditorium and dumped a bag of garbage in front of the officials to dramatize his objection to hazardous waste. Later, in an editorial, the state's leading newspaper characterized the citizens' testimony at the hearing as "heavy on emotion and often feather-light on solid technical grounds for objection" ("Waste Is Still with Us," 1991, p. 22A). (In Chapter 8, I'll explore further the question of emotion and the dismissal by some officials of residents' concerns as inappropriate.)

Are ordinary citizens really irrational? Or are public officials insensitive to the concerns of ordinary citizens, dismissing citizens' fears because they lack technical expertise? Certainly, some officials feel that the behavior of citizens is "overdramatized and hysterical" and that they must endure "the public gauntlet" of angry, shouting, sign-waving protesters (Senecah, 2004, pp. 17, 18). Yet, environmental communication scholar Susan L. Senecah (2004) poses the question differently: Are public hearings sometimes divisive or unproductive because of the way the public acts, *or is there something wrong with the process itself?* She suggests that, in many local conflicts, "a significant incongruity exists between the expectations for public participation raised by the laws . . . and the actual experiences of participants in these processes" (p. 18). Although NEPA procedures require officials to solicit the views of the public, formal mechanisms for public participation too often are simply ritualistic processes that give members of the public little opportunity to influence decisions. It's no surprise, then, that ordinary citizens so often experience "frustration, disillusionment, skepticism, and anger" (Senecah, 2004, p. 18).

What has gone wrong? Stephen Depoe, director of the University of Cincinnati's Center for Environmental Communication Studies, and John Delicath (2004) of the U.S. General Accounting Office have surveyed the extensive literature on the shortcomings of traditional modes of public participation, such as written comments and public hearings. They identify five primary shortcomings:

1. Public participation typically operates on technocratic models of rationality, in which policymakers, administrative officials, and experts see their roles as educating and persuading the public of the legitimacy of their decisions.

2. Public participation often occurs too late in the decision-making process, sometimes even after decisions have already been made.

3. Public participation often follows an adversarial trajectory, especially when public participation processes are conducted in a "decide–announce–defend" mode on the part of officials.

4. Public participation often lacks adequate mechanisms and forums for informed dialogue among stakeholders.

5. Public participation often lacks adequate provisions to ensure that input gained through public participation makes a real impact on decisions' outcomes. (pp. 2–3)

Although formal mechanisms for citizens' involvement in influencing environmental decisions have been effective on some occasions, on others they have fallen far short of citizens' expectations. Too often, disputes over local land use or the cleanup of communities contaminated by chemical pollution linger for years. In such cases, citizens, businesses, government agencies, and environmentalists have turned to alternatives to public hearings to resolve conflicts over environmental problems.

The Emergence of Alternative Forms of Public Participation

In the 1990s, new forms of public involvement in environmental decisions began to emerge, from local, neighborhood initiatives to EPA-sponsored collaborations with cities over new standards for safe drinking water.[1] As citizens, public officials, businesses, and some environmentalists have grown frustrated with traditional forms, they have begun to experiment with citizen advisory boards, facilitated meetings, partnerships, and negotiations over federal rules (Fiorino, 1989). Recently, President George W. Bush (2004) issued the executive order "Facilitation of Cooperative Conservation." This order requires federal agencies that deal with the environment, such as the EPA and the Departments of Interior, Defense, Agriculture, and Commerce, to collaborate with private landowners and local governments when formulating environmental rules that apply to these people's areas.

At the heart of these experiments is some version of community or place-based collaboration among the relevant parties. Earlier, we defined **collaboration** as "constructive, open, civil communication, generally as dialogue; a focus on the future; an emphasis on learning; and some degree of power sharing and leveling of the playing field" (Walker, 2004, p. 123). Supporters of collaboration believe that it reflects a commitment to the principles of participatory democracy, in which the objective is to enhance citizens' ability to participate and the quality of their participation in decisions that affect their communities and lives. Depoe and Delicath (2004) identify a set of values and assumptions, grounded in the ideal of participatory democracy, that some practitioners and scholars have proposed for evaluating these alternative models: "(1) people should have a say in decisions that will affect their lives; (2) early and ongoing, informed and empowered public participation is the hallmark of sound public policy; and (3) the public must be involved in determining how they will participate in choosing what forums and mechanisms will be used . . . to ensure informed participation" (p. 3).

Later, I'll identify characteristics of collaboration that help to explain its success or failure. But first, let's look at three specific forms that collaboration can take: (1) citizen advisory committees, (2) natural resource partnerships, and (3) community-based collaborations.

Citizens' Advisory Committees

One of the commonest types of citizen collaboration about environmental concerns is the **citizens' advisory committee**. Also called citizens' advisory panels or boards, these usually are groups that a government agency appoints to solicit input from diverse interests in a community—citizens, businesses, environmentalists—about a project or problem. For example, the Department of Defense uses restoration advisory boards (RABs) to advise military officials on the social, economic, and environmental impacts of military base closings and the restoration of military lands. The Defense Department uses RABs, which were initiated in 1994, to "achieve dialogue between the installation and affected stakeholders; provide a vehicle for two-way communication; and provide a mechanism for earlier public input" (Santos & Chess, 2003, p. 270). The Defense Department had established hundreds of these collaborations at sites across the United States and in other countries. One typical RAB is composed of interested parties in collaboration on the Department of Defense's plans to convert the Rocky Mountain Arsenal, a former chemical weapons facility, into a wildlife refuge (Johnson, 2004).

The impetus for involving communities in the work of federal agencies was one result of the Federal Advisory Committee Act of 1972 (Long & Beierle, 1996). This act's impact can be seen in other agencies that also use citizen advisory panels. For example, the Environmental Protection Agency uses citizen advisory panels to involve citizens in ongoing projects to clean up abandoned toxic waste sites. Similarly, the Department of Energy relies on site-specific advisory boards to involve nearby residents during the cleanup of toxic waste at former energy sites such as the nuclear weapons production facility in Fernald, Ohio. (For information about the DOE's use of site-specific advisory boards, see Williams, 2002; for case studies of the collaboration between citizens and the DOE at the Fernald site, see Hamilton, 2004, and Depoe, 2004.)

For most citizen advisory committees, the government agency selects participants to represent various interests or points of view or to be "representative, that is, a microcosm of the socioeconomic characteristics and the issue orientation of the public in [a] particular area" (Beierle & Cayford, 2002, pp. 45–46.). The committee's work normally takes place over time in meetings of the participants. The committee's decision-making process may or may not assume that consensus will be achieved, although that is often the stated objective. Typically, the outcome of collaboration is a set of recommendations to the agency (Beierle & Cayford, 2002; for an interesting account of a community's involvement with a citizens' advisory committee dealing with a hazardous waste landfill, see Pezzullo, 2001.)

Natural Resource Partnerships

Particularly in Western states, the idea of collaboration has taken off as diverse groups seek ways to manage differences over the use of public lands. Colorado-based *High Country News* (Jones, 1996) reported, "Coalitions of ranchers, environmentalists, county commissioners, government officials, loggers, skiers, and jeepers are popping up as often as wood ticks across the Western landscape" (p. 1). These **natural resource partnerships** are informal working groups organized around regions with natural resource concerns such as the uses of rangelands, forests, and water resources (including timber, agriculture, grazing, and off-road motorized recreation), as well as concerns for the protection of forests, wildlife, and watersheds. Such partnerships operate collaboratively to integrate their differing values and approaches to the management of natural resource issues.

Organized in 1992, the Applegate Partnership is one of the earliest models of natural resource collaboration. It was formed after years of conflict among ranchers, local government, loggers, environmentalists, and the Bureau of Land Management (BLM) in the watershed of southwestern Oregon and northern California. Feuding parties finally decided to take a different approach. Local BLM official John Lloyd explained, "We got to the point where we just had to sit down and start talking" (Wondolleck & Yaffee, 2000, p. 7).

As they talked, it became apparent that conservationists, loggers, and community leaders all shared a love of the land and a concern for the sustainability of local communities. An initial group of 60 people from all sides of the controversy agreed to discuss a plan to make the Applegate watershed "a demonstration site for ecologically and financially responsible resource management" (Wondolleck & Yaffee, 2000, p. 140). At its first meeting, the partnership agreed on a vision statement that foreshadowed a model later adopted by other communities in the West:

> The Applegate Partnership is a community-based project involving industry, conservation groups, natural resource agencies, and residents cooperating to encourage and facilitate the use of natural resource principles that promote ecosystem health and diversity.
>
> Through community involvement and education, the partnership supports the management of all lands within the watershed in a manner that sustains natural resources and that will, in turn, contribute to economic and community stability within the Applegate Valley. (Wondolleck & Yaffee, 2000, pp. 140–41)

The collaboration in a natural resource partnership such as the Applegate Partnership differs somewhat from the agency-appointed citizen advisory committee. Partnerships usually are voluntary and focus on a geographical region and a wider range of ecological concerns; unlike a citizen advisory committee, a partnership usually works on an ongoing basis to respond to new challenges and concerns about natural resources in its region.

Community-Based Collaboration

Occasions for local disputes over the environment are numerous: loss of green space, traffic planning, contamination of well water, pollution from manufacturing plants, lead paint in older buildings, tensions between automobile drivers and bicyclists, and so forth. Increasingly, local government, courts, and civic groups are encouraging the use of collaborative processes to avoid long, contentious conflicts that can drain resources, divide groups, and weaken community relationships. Such **community-based collaboration** usually involves individuals and representatives of affected groups, businesses, or other agencies in addressing a specific or short-term problem in the local community. Often operating by consensus, this kind of collaborative group identifies goals and issues of concern, forms subgroups to investigate alternatives, and seeks support for specific solutions. Besides being court-appointed or agency-sponsored associations, these community-based groups may be voluntary associations without legal sanction or regulatory power.

Although they have some features in common with natural resource partnerships, community-based collaborations tend to focus on specific, local problems that involve a shorter time frame; partnerships, on the other hand, usually require ongoing involvement with natural resource management. For example, in Sherman County, Oregon, a conflict arose over a proposal by Northwest Wind Power (NWWP) to locate a 24-megawatt wind farm in the community. A farming community with a population of 1,900, Sherman County lies directly in the path of relentless winds from the Pacific Ocean; for this reason, the area was proposed as a site for harvesting wind energy. In other communities, proposals for wind farms had generated considerable conflict—powerful, 200-foot-tall turbines can affect aviation, bird populations, cultural and historical sites, weed control, and other ecological matters (Policy Consensus Initiative, 2004b).

In the face of potential controversy, Oregon's governor invited local farmers, citizens' groups, landowners, the Audubon Society, and representatives from local, state, and federal agencies, NWWP, and other business concerns to engage in a collaborative process to decide the fate of the proposed wind farm. Working together, the group identified possible wind farm sites and related issues of concern, then formed subteams to address each issue. Their efforts eventually led to an agreement on a site that would have "minimal negative impacts on the community and environment" (Policy Consensus Initiative, 2004b, n.p.).

Each of these forms of participation—citizen advisory committees, natural resource partnerships, and community-based collaboration—share certain characteristics that contribute to their eventual success (or failure). Therefore, in the next section of this chapter, I'll identify some of the conditions that must be in place for successful collaboration, as well as the requirements for building trust among the participants and sustaining open, civil dialogue.

Collaboration and Consensus in Environmental Disputes

As we saw in the previous examples, collaboration clearly differs from the more traditional forms of public hearings and written comments. In their survey of successful cases of collaboration between governmental agencies and environmental groups, citizens, and business, Wondolleck and Yaffee (2000) observed that most of the successful collaborations "fostered two-way, interactive flows of information, and decision making occurred through an open, interactive process rather than behind closed agency doors. Such efforts actively involved people throughout a planning or problem-solving process so that they learned together, understood constraints, and developed creative ideas, trust, and relationships" (p. 105).

In this section, I'll build on Wondolleck and Yaffee's observations to describe some of the characteristics of successful collaboration and distinguish it from traditional forms of public participation. However, before going further, it may be helpful to distinguish collaboration from two other, closely related forms of conflict resolution: arbitration and mediation. **Arbitration** is usually court ordered and involves the presentation of opposing views to a neutral, third-party individual or panel that in turn renders a judgment about the conflict. **Mediation** is a facilitated effort entered voluntarily or at the suggestion of a court, counselors, or other institution. Most important, this form of conflict management involves an active mediator who helps the disputing parties find common ground and a solution on which they agree. Whereas collaboration may use a mediator on occasion, it requires active contributions from all participants.

Collaboration is also sharply distinguished from more adversarial forms of managing environmental conflict, such as litigation, advocacy campaigns, or contentious public hearings. One of the field's leading scholars in collaborative learning, Gregg Walker (2004, p. 124) identifies eight attributes that distinguish collaboration from traditional forms of public participation:

1. Collaboration is less competitive.

2. Collaboration features mutual learning and fact-finding.

3. Collaboration allows underlying value differences to be explored.

4. Collaboration resembles principled negotiation, focusing on interests rather than positions.

5. Collaboration allocates the responsibility for implementation across many parties.

6. Collaboration's conclusions are generated by participants through an interactive, iterative, and reflective process.

7. Collaboration is often an ongoing process.

8. Collaboration has the potential to build individual and community capacity in such areas as conflict management, leadership, decision making, and communications.

Walker's list helps us understand collaboration as a process that is distinctive from more adversarial forms of public participation in environmental decisions. With these distinctions in mind, let's look at the core conditions that are typically present when collaboration succeeds.

Requirements of Effective Collaboration

Most scholars and those who have participated in effective collaborations cite a number of conditions and participant characteristics that must be present for collaboration to succeed.

Relevant stakeholders are at the table. A collaborative process begins when the relevant stakeholders agree to participate in a collective effort to address some problem. As we noted earlier, stakeholders are those parties to a dispute who have a real or discernible interest (a stake) in the outcome. Sometimes, they're selected by a sponsoring agency to "sit at the table," usually to represent certain interests or constituents, such as local businesses, residents, environmental groups, the timber industry, and so forth. In other cases, stakeholders self-identify and volunteer to participate. In most collaborations, stakeholders are place based; that is, they live in the affected community or region. As we shall see below, this last condition constructs a potential barrier to participation by more distant but interested parties, such as national environmental groups. (For more information about the

Table 4.1   Core Requirements of Successful Collaboration

1. Relevant stakeholders are at the table.

2. Participants adopt a problem-solving approach.

3. All participants have access to necessary resources and opportunities to participate in discussions.

4. Decisions usually are reached by consensus.

5. Relevant agencies are guided by the recommendations of the collaboration.

concept of the stakeholder in environmental decision making, see Yosie & Herbst, 1998).

Participants adopt a problem-solving approach. Communication among participants strives to solve problems instead of being adversarial or manipulative. Problem solving uses discussion, conversation, and information, seeking to define the concrete problem, the relevant concerns, the criteria for appropriate solutions, and finally a solution that addresses the concerns of all parties. Although conflict is expected in the discussion, collaboration keeps the focus on the issues rather than on people. It discourages adversarial or overtly persuasive stances and instead favors listening, learning, and trying to agree on workable solutions.

All participants have access to necessary resources and opportunities to participate in discussions. In a collaborative effort, solutions cannot be imposed. If agreement is to be reached by all parties, all participants must have an opportunity to be heard, to challenge others' views, to question, and to provide input to the solution. If an individual stakeholder represents other individuals or groups, it is also important that the concerns of these constituencies be expressed to other stakeholders in the collaboration. Finally, the group must guard against the effects of different levels of power or privilege among the participants, to ensure that all voices are respected and have opportunities to contribute and influence the solution.

Decisions usually are reached by consensus. Most collaborative groups aim to reach decisions by **consensus**, which usually means that discussions will not end until everyone has had a chance to share their differences and find common ground. Consensus may sometimes mean that all participants agree; sometimes, it means that a decision is supported in different degrees by the participants. Daniels and Walker (2001) note that the Oregon Department of Land Conservation and Development uses a definition of consensus that leaves room for some differences of opinion. It defines *consensus* as "an agreement that is reached by identifying the interests of all concerned parties and then building a solution that maximizes satisfaction of as many of the interests as possible. . . . Consensus does not mean unanimity in that it may not satisfy each participant's interests equally . . . [but] addresses all interests to some extent" (p. 72, quoting Tarnow, Watt, & Silverberg, 1996, p. 113).

Consensus can be distinguished usefully from compromise, another form that groups use to reach decisions. As interpersonal communication scholar Julia Wood (2003) observes, "Members may differ in how enthusiastically they support a decision, but everyone agrees to accept a consensus decision"; whereas in a **compromise**, "members work out a solution that satisfies each person's minimum criteria but may not fully satisfy all members" (pp. 307, 308). In either case, a decision assumes some form of cooperation, requiring opposing interests to work together, a process that can take the form of "internal negotiations among participants" (Beierle & Cayford, 2002, p. 46).

Most successful collaborations go to considerable effort to avoid deciding by anything less than consensus, because support of all parties usually is necessary for solutions to work. When participants disagree, discussion typically continues until an agreement is reached or until all objections have been explored thoroughly. If the disagreement continues, groups may drop the matter, perhaps returning later, or may decide by majority vote. For these reasons, Wood (2003) advises that consensus is "inappropriate for trivial decisions, emergency issues, or decisions on which members cannot come to agreement" (p. 308).

Relevant agencies are guided by the recommendations of the collaboration. The results of a collaborative effort usually are advisory to the agency that appointed the group, for example, the report of a citizens' advisory committee to the governmental agency handling the cleanup of a toxic waste site. The recommendations are not legally binding in most cases. However, in some cases an agency may agree to implement the results of a consensus-based process. The prospect of their solution's implementation is a powerful incentive for participants to invest the time and work required for successful collaboration. When a group's recommendations are not implemented, those who participated in the collaboration often feel frustrated or angry at the energy wasted in a process the outcome of which was ignored. (For an excellent case study illustrating this problem and the requirements for successful collaboration, see Depoe, 2004.)

Successful collaboration among parties with diverse interests is not always possible, particularly in environmental disputes where the stakes are high or the parties are too deeply divided by a history of discord or entrenched opposition. Scholars and practitioners who work with collaboration have identified a number of conditions that must be present for collaboration to work. Long-time mediator Gerald Mueller of Missoula, Montana, shared his experience with *High Country News*. He observed that citizen collaboration is more likely when key parties have "a feeling that something must change [and] a shared vision or focus on a desired future" (Jones, 1996, p. 8).

On the other hand, collaboration may not always be possible. Guy Burgess and Heidi Burgess (1996), co-directors of the Conflict Research Consortium at the University of Colorado at Boulder, observed, "While consensus building can be very effective in low-stakes disputes . . . , it does not work as well when the issues involve deep-rooted value differences, very high stakes, or irreducible win-lose confrontations" (p. 1). They explain, "Learning to distinguish when conflicts are 'ripe' for consensus resolution and when they are not is one of the most critical skills advocates should have" (p. 1). (For further information and case studies, see "Suggested Readings" at the end of this chapter.)

Two Case Studies of Collaboration

It may be helpful to look at two case studies of collaboration, both of which involve a citizen advisory committee. The first is a successful case in Ohio that resolved a dispute over water quality standards. The second case illustrates a failed collaboration over plans to deepen the Port of Savannah in Georgia. In each case, we'll identify the presence or absence of the core requirements for effective collaboration and illustrate the importance of these to a successful outcome.

Reaching Consensus on Water Quality Standards in Ohio

The state of Ohio borders on Lake Erie and is therefore one of eight states subject to a stringent agreement called the Great Lakes Water Quality Initiative. For years, large portions of the Great Lakes have been dying biologically. Pollution runoff from factories, agricultural fields, and urban sources surrounding the Great Lakes has contaminated the water and led to high levels of toxins in fish. In 1995, the Environmental Protection Agency issued its far-reaching Great Lakes Water Quality Initiative, which required the states to adopt strict standards for waste disposal and discharge into the lakes. Although the EPA gave states such as Ohio two years to come up with rules to implement the new standards, the initiative caused considerable controversy among affected industries, environmentalists, and the states' governors (Policy Consensus Initiative, 2004a).

In an attempt to reach an agreement, Ohio's governor appointed a group of 25 diverse stakeholders as a citizen advisory committee. The members included representatives of business and industry, environmental groups, universities, local and state government, and the Ohio EPA. The charge to this External Advisory Group (EAG) was to seek consensus on the new water quality rules that would satisfy the requirements of the Great Lakes Water Quality Initiative.

The task before the advisory group was daunting. In addition to the diverse interests among the 25-member group, the EAG had to resolve a total of 99 issues, many technically complicated. For example, they had to establish the numerical levels, or "parts per billion," of chemicals that could be present in waters discharged into Lake Erie (Policy Consensus Initiative, 2004a, para. 1), as well as the mix of aquatic species that would indicate a healthy recovery of the Great Lakes. The Director of the Ohio EPA gave the EAG a strong incentive: "If the group achieved consensus on an issue, and if the recommendation was consistent with state and federal law, [the Ohio EPA] would implement it. If the group could not reach consensus, [the director] would make a decision," taking into account the recommendations of both the agency's technical staff and the majority of the advisory group (Policy Consensus Initiative, 2004a, para. 1).

As they started, EAG members agreed on the ground rules to guide their deliberations and encourage consensus. Two facilitators were assigned to assist the group. At first, the level of trust among participants was not high enough to make progress on the 99 issues facing them. As a result, they formed subcommittees, each with its own facilitator, to begin discussions. As the subcommittees made progress, they reported their recommendations to the full group, and when agreement was reached with the Ohio EPA staff on a specific issue, the issue was crossed off the list. As progress continued, the relationships among group members improved. One facilitator reported that, from then on, the group was able to spend time on the nonconsensus issues. In the end, the state of Ohio adopted new rules for waste disposal and discharge into the Great Lakes. One facilitator summed up the two-year process: "All perspectives had been thoroughly aired, and the interest groups were confident that they had been heard" (Policy Consensus Initiative, 2004a, n.p.).

The conditions for successful collaboration clearly were present in the Ohio experience. At the outset, all parties were aware of the need to reach agreement on rules to implement the EPA-mandated Great Lakes Water Quality Initiative. If they failed, the state EPA office would choose the rules. The right people were present, along with appropriate leadership and authority to recommend rules to the Ohio EPA. The two-year deadline also served to motivate the search for agreement.

In addition, the requirements for effective collaboration were satisfied:

1. Relevant stakeholders were invited to the table (and nonrelevant people were absent).

2. EAG members agreed to use a problem-solving approach rather than advocacy. They agreed early on ground rules for discussion and had the assistance of "impartial, skilled facilitators" (Policy Consensus Initiative, 2004a, para. 2).

3. As a result of these ground rules, the presence of facilitators, and use of sub-committees in the early period, the participants learned to work with one another and felt they had an equal opportunity to participate in discussions.

4. Most of the recommendations of the EAG were reached by consensus.

5. The relevant agency, the Ohio EPA in this case, honored its pledge to implement the committee's recommendations.

The Port of Savannah and Failed Collaboration

A less successful case of collaboration occurred in 1999 in Savannah, Georgia, over a controversial plan to deepen the Savannah River to allow large container ships to enter the city's harbor. The Georgia Ports Authority's (GPA) plan to increase the harbor's depth by eight feet brought opposition from many in the community. City officials were concerned that deepening the Savannah River could puncture the underlying aquifer and cause saltwater contamination of the area's source of fresh water. Local conservationists and the EPA feared that increased salinity (saltwater) and a decrease in the level of dissolved oxygen in the river would cause a "catastrophic collapse" of local fisheries and "the loss of over half of the tidal freshwater marsh which forms the centerpiece of the Savannah National Wildlife Refuge" (quoted in Toker, 2004, p. 183). As a result of this opposition, the GPA created a citizens' advisory committee called the Stakeholder Evaluation Group (SEG). It consisted of representatives of local government, business, and the citizenry, whose role would be to examine the proposal's environmental impacts and to develop a plan for alleviating them. However, as environmental communication scholar Caitlin Wills Toker (2004) concluded in her study of the controversy, the actual communication in the SEG meetings failed to meet this vision for resolving the dispute.

When it created the Stakeholder Evaluation Group, the Georgia Ports Authority announced that the group would be a mechanism to ensure two-way communication between the GPA and representatives of the local citizenry, businesses, and government in developing "an environmentally acceptable mitigation plan" (quoted in Toker, 2004, p. 184). In the second meeting of the SEG, the facilitator reaffirmed the ideal of collaboration, "characterizing all stakeholders as equal with 'everybody' having the 'chance to speak up and be heard'" (Toker, 2004, p. 186). Nevertheless, Toker discovered that, as the actual process unfolded, inconsistencies between the ideal and the practice surfaced in two areas: (1) unequal relationships, in which the GPA had greater authority and voice than the local stakeholders participating in the collaboration, and (2) disagreement over the meaning of "stakeholder," specifically the inability of SEG members to attend certain meetings.

The first problem arose when SEG representatives asked for a list of concerns about the deepening of the harbor that had been expressed during the earlier public comment period. They argued that these comments had revealed impacts other than those identified by the Georgia Ports Authority for the group's deliberation, and that "these comments were the very basis for the SEG's existence" (Toker, 2004, p. 187). However, the GPA representatives insisted that these concerns already had been adequately addressed and that they were "historical issues" (p. 187). Toker notes that by defining certain topics as historical issues, the GPA representative "worked to set the agenda for the SEG rather than allowing members to begin with a list of all issues" (p. 187).

A second inconsistency between the ideal of collaboration and actual practice occurred when some stakeholders were prohibited from attending the meetings of a technical group that the Georgia Ports Authority had created. The purpose of this group was to model the impacts of the deepened harbor on fisheries and the environment, a task directly related to the announced purpose of the stakeholders' group. When a business representative in the Stakeholder Evaluation Group asked to attend these meetings, he was told that everyone was already represented because the technical group was committed to "outreach" through e-mail, hard copies of materials, and Web page postings (Toker, 2004, pp. 193, 194).

Throughout the Savannah collaboration, it became clear that some SEG participants, such as the EPA and other agencies involved in the technical research, were considered "primary agencies" with "significant interests" (Toker, 2004, p. 194). In order to accommodate the "busy schedules" of these stakeholders, the GPA's consultant explained that the technical review meetings would be held in Atlanta, Georgia—four hours' drive—because two agencies were located there, and "they're really the two important agencies that really have to get involved" (quoted in Toker, 2004, p. 194).

In the end—and despite claims of an open, equal process—some in the Stakeholder Evaluation Group discovered that they lacked the ability to address certain topics and that they were prohibited from attending important technical meetings about impacts of the proposed deepening of the Savannah harbor. Toker (2004) concludes that although the Georgia Ports Authority continued to use a vocabulary that spoke favorably of a collaborative process for decision making, in practice it gave more authority to "primary agencies" and "scientific folks" and excluded "less knowledgeable stakeholders from the technical deliberations" (p. 197). (In many ways, this problem illustrates the clash between the technical sphere and the public sphere mentioned in Chapter 1.) In order to finish its work by the deadline, the Stakeholders Evaluation

Group "ultimately transformed itself from an egalitarian, consensus-based group into an exclusive and efficient decision-making group" (p. 198). But in the process, it moved away from the principles of collaboration.

Limits of Collaboration and Consensus

As we've just seen, not all attempts at collaboration and consensus-based solutions are successful. Following, we'll examine a case that initially appeared to be a very successful experiment in bringing together loggers, environmentalists, and local business and community leaders but which was criticized almost immediately for excluding relevant stakeholders. However, before we look at this case, it may be helpful to identify some benchmarks by which to evaluate collaborative efforts and assess the reasons for their failures, where these occur.

Act Locally!

Role Simulation of an Environmental Conflict

Check these websites and others that offer case studies or exercises that simulate environmental conflict. These simulations allow you to role-play the different parties to a conflict—for example, ranchers, neighborhood residents, local businesses, or environmentalists—as you collaborate to reach agreement in an environmental dispute.

- One of the best sites is maintained by the Program on Negotiation at Harvard University Law School: www.pon.org/catalog/index.php?cPath=27. Harvard's Program on Negotiation has dozens of role simulations of environmental conflicts and sells role-play exercises of these conflicts for a minimal fee.
- An excellent simulation also is available from the University of Arizona's Udall Center for Studies in Public Policy. *Trouble in Tortuga! A Rangeland Conflict Simulation* simulates a conflict among ranchers, developers, and conservationists over the fate of grasslands in the far West. This simulation is available from www.udallcenter.arizona.edu/publications/tortuga/summary.html. The site provides a summary of the conflict, instructions, and confidential information for all roles.

The case studies on these websites involve issues ranging from radioactive waste, western grasslands, and hazardous waste facilities to billboards and conflicts over Native American rights and development of sacred lands.

Evaluating Collaboration and Consensus-Based Decisions

In recent years, environmental scholars have begun to address some of the recurring problems of the traditional forums for public participation and the newer models of consensus-based decisions. For example, Daniels and Walker (2001) have proposed a modification of the collaborative process that recognizes that environmental conflicts are inevitable, often irresolvable, but manageable. Rather than taking conflict resolution as the goal, their model of **collaborative learning** is more modest in viewing collaboration as a process of conflict management.

As environmental decisions almost always involve controversy and conflict, Daniels and Walker propose that "our task is to learn how to *manage* their conflict dimensions so that rancor does not begin to dominate the discussion and diminish the possibility of substantive improvements" (p. 16). For an example of a successful use of Daniels's and Walker's collaborative learning model, see their case study of controversy over off-road vehicle use in the Oregon Dunes National Recreation Area (pp. 227–244).

Recently, Senecah (2004) has offered a three-part model for assessing the different forms of public participation in environmental decisions, called the **Trinity of Voices (TOV)**. The TOV builds on the importance of the stakeholder and on many of characteristics we identified above for effective collaboration. Therefore, I believe it can be used as a guide to plan and assess collaboration and consensus-based approaches. Overall, the model holds that the key to an effective participation process is "an ongoing relationship of trust building to enhance community cohesiveness and capacity [to reach] good environmental decisions" (p. 23). Specifically, the TOV model refers to three elements that most effective participatory processes seem to share and that empower a stakeholder: access, standing, and influence. Senecah (2004) explains that **access** refers to the minimum resources that citizens need to exercise fully their opportunity to participate, including convenient times and places, readily available information and technical assistance to help them understand the issues, and continuing opportunities for public involvement. By **standing**, Senecah does not mean the right to bring a legal complaint in court (see Chapter 3). Instead, she explains, standing is "the civic legitimacy, the respect, the esteem, and the consideration that all stakeholders' perspectives should be given" (p. 24). Finally, **influence** is the element felt by many to be most often missing in traditional models of public participation. Influence refers to participants' opportunity to be part of a "transparent process that considers all alternatives, opportunities to meaningfully scope alternatives, opportunities to inform the decision criteria, and thoughtful response to stakeholder concerns and ideas" (p. 25).

Let's use Senecah's TOV model to evaluate a high-profile effort that was launched by community members who attempted to develop a consensus approach for managing national forest lands. The case ended by moving in a different, more adversarial direction. The Quincy Library Group experience is a provocative case of community-based collaboration that is worth examining in some detail.

The Quincy Library Group: Collaboration in the Sierra Nevada Mountains

The rural town of Quincy (fewer than 50,000 residents) is located 100 miles northeast of Sacramento, California. More important, it lies in the geographical center of the "timber wars" in the Plumas, Lassen, and Tahoe National Forests of the Sierra Nevada Mountains. Although logging increased from the 1960s through the 1980s in the three national forests around Quincy, the timber cut fell sharply in the 1990s due to shifting market demands and to Forest Service restrictions that protected old-growth trees and habitat for spotted owls and other endangered species.

As logging declined and local sawmills shut down, the area began to experience sharp conflicts between timber interests and environmentalists. For example, loggers and their families blamed the Forest Service for restricting the level of timber cuts and organized the Yellow Ribbon Coalition to lobby for their interests. Charges and counter-charges also flew between the coalition and environmentalists over instances of tree spiking (see Chapter 2) and the use of nail clusters embedded on forest roads to stop logging trucks (Wondolleck & Yaffee, 2000, p. 71). Plumas County Supervisor Bill Coates expressed the fears of many in local communities: "Our small towns were already endangered. This [decline in logging] was going to wipe them out" (Wondolleck & Yaffee, 2000, p. 71).

Initial Success: Collaboration in Quincy

Despite the controversy, some in the community began to suggest that the different camps might share a larger set of interests and values. Michael Jackson, an environmental attorney and member of Friends of Plumas Wilderness, was one of the earliest. In 1989, he wrote a letter to the local newspaper, the *Feather River Bulletin*, "arguing that environmentalists, loggers, and business needed to work together for 'our mutual future'" (quoted in Wondolleck & Yaffee, 2000, p. 71). In his letter, Jackson invited loggers to work with environmentalists toward a set of common goals:

What do environmentalists believe we have in common with the Yellow Ribbon Coalition? We believe that we are all honest people who want to continue our way of life. We believe that we all love the area in which we live. We believe that we all enjoy beautiful views, hunting and fishing and living in a rural area. We believe that we are being misled by the Forest Service and by large timber, which controls the Forest Service, into believing that we are enemies when we are not. (quoted in Wondolleck & Yaffee, 2000, pp. 71–72)

By 1992, a few individuals in each of the warring camps—forest industry, community and business leaders, and environmentalists—began to talk about the impacts of declining timber production on the community. Initially, three men agreed to talk among themselves: Bill Coates (Plumas County Supervisor and a business owner who supported the timber industry), Tom Nelson (a forester for Sierra Pacific Industries), and Michael Jackson, the environmental attorney and a passionate environmentalist. The three "found more common ground than they had expected, and decided to try to build at least a truce, maybe even a full peace treaty, based upon that common ground" (Terhune & Terhune, 1998, para. 8).

Soon other people joined the discussions of Coates, Nelson, and Jackson. Later observers recalled that these "early meetings had some very tense moments, and some participants were very uncomfortable at times" (Terhune & Terhune, 1998, p. 8). Meeting in the public library, they began calling themselves the Quincy Library Group. "Some only half-jokingly [noted] that meeting in a library would prevent participants from yelling at each other" (Wondolleck & Yaffee, 2000, p. 72).

By 1993, members of the Quincy Library Group (www.qlg.org) had agreed among themselves on the Community Stability Plan, which the group hoped would guide management practices in the Plumas, Lassen, and Tahoe National Forests. Although this plan had no official status—the Forest Service was not involved in the discussions—it reflected the group's belief that "a healthy forest and a stable community are interdependent; we cannot have one without the other" (Terhune & Terhune, 1998, p. 11). The purpose of the Community Stability Plan was to integrate these values into a common vision: "to promote the objectives of forest health, ecological integrity, adequate timber supply, and local economic stability" (Wondolleck & Yaffee, 2000, p. 72). The group's plan set forth a series of recommendations to the Forest Service for implementing its vision:

The plan would . . . prevent clear-cutting on Forest Service land or in wide protection zones around rivers and streams and would require group and single tree selection [logging] intended to produce an "all-age, multi-storied, fire-resistant forest approximating pre-settlement conditions." Under the plan, local timber mills would process all harvested logs. The plan also included provisions to reduce the amount of dead or dying plant material, which the group believed was posing a significant threat of fire to the area. (Wondolleck & Yaffee, 2000, p. 72)

The Community Stability Proposal was the result of many meetings, difficult conversations, and the desire of all participants to reach consensus where possible. Their agreement was unusual among the (previously) contentious parties in Quincy and its surrounding communities. Nevertheless, the Quincy Library Group confronted resistance from others that would shift it to a more adversarial process. Most importantly, the Forest Service—which had not participated in the collaborative process—refused to entertain the group's Community Stability Proposal.

Frustrated by resistance from the Forest Service and criticisms from other environmentalists, QLG members turned to the legislative process in Washington, D.C. After successive lobbying trips, they persuaded Congress to enact a version of the Community Stability Proposal. In an unprecedented move, the new law also directed the Forest Service to include this version in its management planning for the three national forests in the Quincy area.

Although I'll return to some of the criticisms of this experience, it is important to note that initially the Quincy Library Group received considerable praise for its collaborative work. Prompted by the feeling that "something had to change," individuals in Quincy believed that conditions were ripe for some alternative mechanism for resolving the long-simmering dispute over logging in the area's national forests. Using Senecah's (2004) TOV model, we can assess favorably the group's effort to find consensus: Participants felt they had full *access* to all meetings, information, and ongoing opportunities to participate. Despite their initial suspicions, business and community leaders, timber industry personnel, and local environmentalists learned to respect and work with each other. In Senecah's (2004) term, they had acquired *standing* in one another's eyes. And, throughout the process, participants themselves exercised *influence* in determining the vision, the criteria to be used in their deliberations, and the final set of recommendations in the Community Stability Plan.

As they looked at their work, Quincy Library Group members Pat and George Terhune (1998) admit they weren't sure why their collaboration worked or whether it could be exported to other communities. Nevertheless, their assessment closely mirrored many of the characteristics we've identified for effective collaboration. They offered these five reasons for why they believed the Quincy group worked:

1. A project of great importance was taken on. . . .

2. Convergence of attention on the issues chosen [i.e., "tight focus" on a short list of issues out of the larger problem]. . . .

3. Decision by true consensus. . . .

4. Maintaining "unofficial" status. . . . QLG has found much greater power in having complete flexibility to choose when and where to put pressure on the system. . . .

5. And . . . the luck of having the right size community or having the right people show up. (pp. 32–33)

Terhune and Terhune (1998) stressed that it is hard to overstate the importance of consensus in keeping the group together and focused. "Votes are not taken until the group is pretty well convinced that the decision will be unanimous. If it isn't, then more discussion takes place, and if anybody is still opposed, the decision is either dropped or postponed for still more discussion" (p. 32).

Criticisms of the Quincy Library Group

Not everyone was pleased with the Quincy Library Group's process or with its vision for management of the national forests. Environmentalists were upset that the QLG's proposal would double the levels of logging in the Lassen, Plumas, and Tahoe National Forests (Brower & Hanson, 1999). Others objected that the process used by the Quincy group excluded key stakeholders—particularly environmental groups concerned with the national forests—therefore allowing local interests to set national standards for managing natural resources. (See "Another Viewpoint: A Skeptic Looks at Collaboration.") Based on these criticisms, community-based collaborations such as the Quincy Library Group would violate the principle of access in Senecah's (2004) TOV model—certain citizens (outside the local area) were not a part of the process for setting standards for these natural resources. Such exclusions can lead to mistrust of the collaboration's outcomes by those excluded, as well as prevent access to the resources that these other (outside) citizens can provide. For example, environmentalists David Brower and Chad Hanson (1999) charged that the QLG had allowed industry interests to capture the decision process: "The Quincy plan is based on the premise of letting industry groups in rural timber towns dictate the fate of federally owned lands, essentially transferring decision-making power from the American people and into the hands of extractive industries" (p. A25). Similar criticism came from other environmentalists, editorials, and scholars studying collaborative processes. For example, Wondolleck and Yaffee (2000) observed that, instead of being "a model collaborative effort, the QLG suddenly became the focus of an acrimonious debate" (p. 265).

Another Viewpoint: A Skeptic Looks at Collaboration

In a highly publicized article printed in the western *High Country News*, the Sierra Club's former executive director, Michael McCloskey (1996), argued that collaborative processes such as the Quincy Library Group give small local groups "an effective veto" over entire national forests. McCloskey cited two shortcomings of local or place-based collaboration:

1. Placed-based collaboration *excludes key stakeholders.* They ignore "the disparate geographical distribution of constituencies" (p. 7). That is, those who are sympathetic to environmental values often live in urban areas; therefore, they are not invited to participate in collaborative processes in the communities near the national forests where there is a dispute.

2. Placed-based collaboration *undermines national standards* for managing natural resources such as national forests. By transferring the power to decide the direction for public lands to small, local groups, local collaboration evades the need to hammer out "national rules to reflect majority rule in the nation" (p. 7).

As a result, McCloskey argued, such models are an abdication of the role of government to represent the national (public) interest.

The charge by Brower and Hanson (1999) that local groups can capture the decision-making process affecting U.S. public lands also illustrates a dilemma posed by place-based collaboration. To what extent do such models provide a mechanism for resolving contentious disputes, and to what extent do they exclude key stakeholders and ignore national standards? The Quincy experience is not encouraging in this regard. As a result of the congressionally mandated use of the QLG's proposal, some feared that "local efforts will preempt national interests, bypassing environmental safeguards and the opportunity for non-participants' review and comment along the way" (Coughlin, Hoben, Manskopf, & Quesada, 1999, p. 4).

Common Criticisms of
Collaboration and Consensus

Although community-based collaborations have many advantages, Daniels and Walker (2001) have observed that they have not been universally accepted as a model for handling conflicts over natural resources. In closing, it may be useful to review some of the common criticisms of the use of collaboration and consensus decision making in environmental conflicts. (For a discussion of the limits of consensus-based approaches in wildlife conservation conflicts, see Peterson, Peterson, & Peterson, 2005). Environmental scholars and facilitators who work with such disputes have found seven complaints or occasions on which collaboration may not be appropriate:

1. *Stakeholders may be unrepresentative of wider publics.* Some scholars have suggested that the "more intensive" modes of alternative participation, such as citizen advisory councils and consensus-seeking groups, may be able to reach agreement, but they often do so only by excluding wider publics. For example, Beierle and Cayford (2002) report that, "the exclusion of certain groups, the departure of dissenting parties, or the avoidance of issues ultimately made consensus possible—or at least easier—in 33%" of the cases they studied involving consensus-based efforts in which conflict was reported (p. 48). Environmental communication scholar William Kinsella (2004) also observes that highly involved individuals who serve on citizen advisory boards "do not necessarily represent the larger public"; furthermore, as they serve for long time periods, "they may lose contact with the communities and values that they are presumed to represent" (p. 90). In other situations, the questions of who is a stakeholder and who should set environmental policy lie at the heart of many local, national, and global environmental controversies.

2. *Place-based collaboration may encourage exceptionalism or a compromise of national standards.* As we witnessed in the Quincy Library Group case, the exclusion of the representatives of national environmental groups gave local interests greater control over the management of national resources. Daniels and Walker (2001) reported that such cases may "preclude meaningful opportunities for non-parties to review and comment on proposals" (p. 274), encouraging a kind of **exceptionalism,** or the view that because a region has unique or distinctive features, it is exempt from the general rule. The concern by some critics is that, if place-based decisions reached at the local level in one area become a precedent for exempting other geographical areas,

they may compromise more uniform, national standards for environmental policy.

3. *Power inequities may lead to co-optation.* One of the most common complaints about collaboration and consensus approaches is that power inequities among the participants may lead to the co-optation of environmental interests. Some argue that the greater resources in training, information, and negotiation skills often brought to collaboration processes by industry representatives and government officials make it harder for ordinary citizens and environmentalists to defend their interests (Moldavi, 1996; Coughlin, Hoben, Manskopf, and Quesada, 1999). Environmentalists such as McCloskey (1996) are especially critical of such inequities in power and resources: "Industry thinks its odds are better in these forums [place-based collaboration] . . . It believes it can dominate them over time and relieve itself of the burden of tough national rules" (p. 7).

4. *Pressure for consensus may lead to the "lowest common denominator."* As we saw in cases of successful collaboration, groups striving for consensus may drop contentious issues or defer them until later. However, some critics fear that this tendency can go too far, that vocal minorities are given an effective veto over the process. "Any recalcitrant stakeholder can paralyze the process . . . Only lowest common denominator ideas survive the process" (McCloskey, 1996, p. 7). Instead of a win–win solution, agreement on the least contentious parts is simply a deferral of the real sources of conflict to other forums or other times.

Conversely, a pressure for conformity among the group's members can lead to what psychologist Irving Janis (1977) called **groupthink**, that is, excessive cohesion that impedes critical or independent thinking. The result of groupthink often is an uninformed consensus. One tragic example is the admission by FBI director Robert Mueller after the September 11, 2001, terrorist attacks on the United States that the attacks were not inevitable. Mueller said FBI agents had not exercised critical thinking and "had fallen prey to the illusion that they and America were invulnerable" (Wood, 2004, p. 265).

5. *Consensus tends to de-legitimize conflict and advocacy.* Conflict can be unpleasant. For many people, civil dialogue in forums where collaboration is the rule may be a safe harbor from controversy. The desire to avoid disagreement is closely related to groupthink and may lead to a premature compromise in a collaborative setting, thus postponing the search for long term solutions. As a result some charge that the desire for consensus "may serve to de-legitimize conflict and co-opt environmental advocates" (Daniels & Walker, 2001, p. 274).

6. *Collaborative groups may lack authority to implement their decisions.* In the Ohio water quality standards case discussed earlier, the state pledged to implement any recommendation that the Great Lakes External Advisory Group reached by consensus. But this is not always the case. Many citizens' advisory committees deliberate for extended periods without the assurance that their decisions will be accepted or implemented by federal agencies. The Quincy Library Group ran into immediate resistance from the Forest Service when it presented its proposal. The simple fact is that most collaborative groups are composed of nonelected citizens and other individuals whose authority—when present—is contingent upon the very governmental agency they are seeking to influence.

7. *Irreconcilable values may hinder agreement.* I suggested earlier that collaborative approaches do not work well when the issues involve deep-rooted value differences, very high stakes, or irreducible, win–lose confrontations. Each of us has values that we believe we cannot or should not compromise—for example, the health of our children, liberty, biodiversity, private property rights, or the right of people to be safe from industrial poisons. In his book *The Politics of Environmental Mediation,* Douglas Amy (1987) observes that some aspects of the natural environment have been compromised enough, such as the continuing loss of wilderness. For Amy and others, further compromises presumably are non-negotiable.

In a larger sense, efforts to move toward consensus on environmental values confront what social theorist Chantal Mouffe (2000) has called the **democratic paradox.** This paradox results from the core tension within liberal democracy itself: the *liberal* tradition of respect for individual liberties (for example, freedom of speech and property rights) and the *democratic* tradition of equality and the respect for the will of the majority. This "intrinsic conflict" between individual liberty and democratic majorities thus prevents an ideal solution in some environmental conflicts (Peterson, Allison, Peterson, Peterson, & Lopez, 2004, p. 744). One example is the conflict that sometimes exists between private property owners and democratic majorities that support restrictions on property in order to protect habitat for endangered species. (See "FYI: The Democratic Paradox and Florida's 'Toy Deer.')

In summary, the attractiveness of collaboration and consensus models for managing environmental conflicts should not overshadow the difficulties these processes may involve. For example, even when all parties with a stake in the conflict are involved, it may not be possible to level the playing field between citizens and the skilled representatives of industry or to identify solutions to conflicts between different or deeply rooted values.

FYI: The Democratic
Paradox and Florida's "Toy Deer"

Figure 4.1   Sometimes called "toy deer," Key deer are the smallest deer in North America and are found only in the lower Florida Keys. (Adults are only 24 to 32 inches tall at the shoulder.)

(Photo courtesy of Ken Araujo, www.K101images.com)

Continued

Humans began clearing densely wooded land in Key deer habitat for farming and other purposes in the mid-to-late 1800s. . . . In conjunction with increasing human density, [this] encouraged settlers to perceive deer as pests and expanded the use of deer as food. The 1934 Ding Darling cartoon captioned "The Last of the 'Toy' Deer of the Florida Keys" elicited a strong public response resulting in the Florida legislature banning Key deer hunting in 1939. Local residents ignored and even resisted efforts to save the deer, including the ban on hunting, and by the 1950s the population was estimated at 25 deer. . . . Key deer were placed on the federal list of endangered species in 1967. By 1974, Key deer numbers had increased to 300–400 . . .

The state of Florida declared the Keys an Area of Critical State Concern in 1975, and Monroe County [only location of Key deer] adopted a land-use plan and a policy of preservation and reduced growth. . . . The community itself was divided between . . . groups supporting environmental preservation and those supporting private property rights . . . [A resident] said, "You have people here who bought land, and Americans tend to think that if they own land they have the right to do whatever they want with it . . . I think there is another side of people who think more environmentally conservation oriented" . . . [When the U.S. Fish and Wildlife Service invited community members to join in drafting a habitat plan to protect Key deer on private property, residents initially] began habitat conservation planning expecting consensus to emerge . . . [But they] left disillusioned with the process and more polarized than ever.

SOURCE: Peterson, Allison, Peterson, Peterson, & Lopez (2004, pp. 746, 748).

Conclusion

As a result of their frustration with public hearings and other traditional forms of public participation, many communities, environmentalists, business leaders, and government agencies have begun to turn to alternative forms for addressing environmental conflicts. In the 1990s, alternative forums for public involvement in environmental decisions began to emerge, such as citizens' advisory committees, natural resource partnerships, and community-based collaborations. At the heart of these experiments is some version of *collaboration* among the relevant parties, which we defined as a "constructive, open, civil communication, generally as dialogue; a focus on the future; an emphasis on learning; and some degree of power sharing and leveling of the playing field" (Walker, 2004, p. 123).

Although successful collaborations on environmental matters have varied widely, they generally have been seen as requiring five conditions: (1) that all relevant stakeholders are at the table; (2) that the participants adopt a problem-solving approach; (3) that all participants have equal access to resources and opportunities to participate in discussions; (4) that decisions usually are reached by consensus; and (5) that the relevant agencies are guided by the recommendations of the collaborating group.

Although the collaboration and consensus approaches have been helpful in resolving numerous disputes, those who have helped to facilitate such groups or who have participated in them also have reported a number of recurring complaints and problems. These range from failure to include key stakeholders to pressure toward the lowest common denominator in order to reach consensus. Indeed, we found that collaboration may not always be possible, especially when a conflict involves deep differences over values or irreducible win–lose confrontations.

In the end, the most successful instances of collaboration assume that not all conflict is bad and not all controversy should be avoided in group deliberations. Indeed, what communication scholar Thomas Goodnight (1991) has called **dissensus** may serve an important communication role. Dissensus is a questioning of, refusal of, or disagreement with a claim or a premise of a speaker's argument. Goodnight suggests that, rather than bringing a discussion to a halt, dissensus can be generative. If properly handled, it may invite more communication about the areas of disagreement between the differing parties.

Our ability to manage the conflicts that arise in human relationships with the environment may require us to listen to one another and perhaps learn new ways to narrow the scope of our differences. As we've seen in the successful cases of collaboration in this chapter and also in the failures, our communication behaviors have consequences—whether we choose to listen to certain voices and not others, speak up for a different perspective, or find common ground with others. Neither collaboration nor the more adversarial forms of communication provide a magic answer to the difficulties that arise from the complex human–environment relationship. Indeed, in the end, disputes over deeply held values about the environment may require both conflict and conversation—collaboration with opponents and, at other times, advocacy of values that cannot or should not be compromised. Collaboration—like advocacy—has a place in managing environmental conflicts, but no single mode is always the most appropriate or effective path to a solution.

KEY TERMS

Access: The minimum resources that citizens need to exercise fully their opportunity to participate, including convenient times and places, readily available information and technical assistance to help them understand the issues, and continuing opportunities for public involvement.

Arbitration: The presentation of opposing views to a neutral, third-party individual or panel that, in turn, renders a judgment about the conflict; usually court ordered.

Citizens' advisory committee: Also called a citizens' advisory panel or board, a group appointed by a government agency to solicit input from diverse interests in a community—for example, citizens, businesses, and environmentalists—about a project or problem.

Collaboration: "Constructive, open, civil communication, generally as dialogue; a focus on the future; an emphasis on learning; and some degree of power sharing and leveling of the playing field" (Walker, 2004, p. 123).

Collaborative learning: An approach to collaboration that recognizes that environmental conflicts are inevitable, often irresolvable, but manageable; rather than taking conflict resolution as the goal, this approach is more modest in enabling participants to learn how to manage their conflict so that rancor does not dominate the discussion and diminish the possibility of substantive improvements.

Community-based collaboration: An approach to problem solving that involves individuals and representatives of affected groups, businesses, and other agencies in addressing a specific or short-term problem defined by the local community. Like natural resource partnerships, collaborative groups are usually voluntary associations without legal sanction or regulatory powers.

Compromise: An approach to problem solving in which participants work out a solution that satisfies each person's minimum criteria but may not fully satisfy all.

Consensus: The assumption that discussions will not end until everyone has had a chance to share differences and find common ground; may sometimes mean that all participants agree.

Democratic paradox: Term used by social theorist Chantal Mouffe (2000) to refer to the tension between two different traditions in Western societies: the liberal tradition of respect for individual liberty, and the democratic tradition of equality and respect for the will of the majority.

Dissensus: Term coined by communication scholar Thomas Goodnight, meaning a questioning of, refusal of, or disagreement with a claim or a premise of a speaker's argument.

Exceptionalism: The view that, because a region has unique or distinctive features, it is exempt from the general rule. Some critics are concerned that place-based decisions reached at the local level in one area can become a precedent for exempting other geographical areas and thus compromise more uniform, national standards for environmental policy.

Groupthink: Term coined by psychologist Irving Janis (1977) referring to an excessive cohesion in groups that impedes critical or independent thinking, often resulting in uninformed consensus.

Influence: In Senecah's Trinity of Voices model, a term referring to participants' opportunity to be part of a "transparent process that considers all alternatives, opportunities to meaningfully scope alternatives, opportunities to inform the decision criteria, and thoughtful response to stakeholder concerns and ideas" (Senecah, 2004, p. 25).

Mediation: A facilitated effort, entered into voluntarily or at the suggestion of a court, counselors, or other institution, that involves an active mediator who helps the disputing parties find common ground and a solution upon which they can agree.

Natural resource partnerships: Informal working groups organized around regions with natural resource concerns such as the uses of rangelands, forests, and water resources for timber, agriculture, grazing, off-road motorized recreation, as well as concerns for protection of forests, wildlife, and watersheds. Partnerships operate collaboratively to integrate their differing values and approaches to the management of natural resource issues.

Stakeholders: Those parties to a dispute who have a real or discernible interest (a stake) in the outcome.

Standing: A term in Senecah's Trinity of Voices model that refers to the civic legitimacy—the respect, esteem, and consideration that all stakeholders' perspectives should be given; in this context, the term does not refer to legal standing in a court of law.

Trinity of Voices: Senecah's model for assessing the quality of public participation processes; holds that the key to an effective participation process is an ongoing relationship of trust building to enhance community cohesiveness and the capacity to reach good environmental decisions. The model poses three elements— access, standing, and influence—that empower stakeholders and are shared by most effective participatory processes.

DISCUSSION QUESTIONS

1. "Go tell town hall!" has been the rallying cry for years of those with concerns about their water bills, taxes, or other problems. But how effective for making environmental decisions are traditional forms of public participation such as public hearings or e-mail to officials? Can talking to elected officials about environmental concerns such as contamination of a stream, the need for more

bicycle lanes, or problems with air pollution get results, or does it simply lead to frustration?

2. Are members of the public uninformed or irrational if they use emotion or lack technical information about an environmental matter in speaking of their concerns at a public hearing?

3. Would you feel comfortable speaking up or disagreeing with the majority in a collaborative process? Would you still support a group consensus even if your preferred solution was not adopted, as long as you felt that the group had fairly considered your views before it reached its decision?

4. McCloskey (1996) is critical of the inequities in power and resources between representatives of industry and others in consensus groups. "Industry thinks its odds are better in these forums . . . It believes it can dominate them over time" (p. 7). Do you agree? In consensus groups, can ordinary citizens and industry representatives truly have equal access to resources and equal influence on decisions?

5. Is compromise or consensus possible in environmental conflicts over logging in national forests, over oil drilling in times of energy crisis in wilderness areas like the Arctic National Wildlife Refuge, or over protecting critical habitat for endangered species on private property?

SUGGESTED READINGS

The following books contain helpful case studies and resources for collaboration in environmental disputes:

Amy, D. J. (1987). *The politics of environmental mediation*. New York: Columbia University Press.

Daniels, S. E., & Walker, G. B. (2001). *Working through environmental conflict: The collaborative learning approach*. Westport, CT: Praeger.

Williams, B. A., & Matheny, A. R. (1995). *Democracy, dialogue, and environmental disputes*. New Haven: Yale University Press.

Wondolleck, J. M., & Yaffee, S. L. (2000). *Making collaboration work: Lessons from innovation in natural resource management*. Washington, DC: Island Press.

Yosie, T. F., & Herbst, T. D. (1998). *Using stakeholder processes in environmental decision making*. ICF Incorporated. Available online at www.gdrc.org/decision/nr98ab01.pdf

In addition, a number of nonprofit associations offer online resources and case studies of successful collaboration. A useful site is maintained by the National Policy Consensus Center, which provides a database of collaboration by citizens, government agencies, businesses, and conservation groups at www.policyconsensus.org/casestudies/index.html

REFERENCES

Amy, D. J. (1987). *The politics of environmental mediation.* New York: Columbia University Press.

Beierle, T. C., & Cayford, J. (2002). *Democracy in practice: Public participation in environmental decisions.* Washington, DC: Resources for the Future.

Brower, D., & Hanson, C. (1999, September 1). Logging plan deceptively marketed, sold. *San Francisco Chronicle,* p. A25.

Burgess, G., & Burgess, H. (1996). *Consensus building for environmental advocates.* Working Paper #96–1. Boulder: University of Colorado Conflict Research Consortium.

Bush, G. W. (2004, August 26). Executive Order 13352, Facilitation of cooperative conservation. Washington, DC: The White House, Office of the Press Secretary.

Coughlin, C., Hoben, M., Manskopf, D., & Quesada, S. (1999). *A systematic assessment of collaborative resource management partnerships: A Master's project report.* Ann Arbor: University of Michigan School of Natural Resources & Environment. Retrieved September 10, 2004, from www.snre.umich.edu/ecomgt/pubs/crmp.htm

Daniels, S. E., & Walker, G. B. (2001). *Working through environmental conflict: The collaborative learning approach.* Westport, CT: Praeger.

Depoe, S. P. (2004). Public involvement, civic discovery, and the formation of environmental policy: A comparative analysis of the Fernald citizens task force and the Fernald health effects subcommittee. In S. P. Depoe, J. W. Delicath, & M-F. A. Elsenbeer (Eds.), *Communication and public participation in environmental decision making* (pp.157–173). Albany: State University of New York Press.

Depoe, S. P., & Delicath, J. W. (2004). Introduction. In S. P. Depoe, J. W. Delicath, & M-F. A. Elsenbeer (Eds.), *Communication and public participation in environmental decision making* (pp. 1–10). Albany: State University of New York Press.

Depoe, S. P., Delicath, J. W., & Elsenbeer, M-F. A. (Eds.). (2004). *Communication and public participation in environmental decision making.* Albany: State University of New York Press.

Eilperin, J. (2004, April 14). Groups unite behind plan to protect Idaho wilderness. *Washington Post,* p. A2.

Fiorino, D. J. (1989). Technical and democratic values in risk analysis. *Risk Analysis, 9,* 293–299.

Goodnight, G. T. (1991). *Controversy.* In D. Parson (Ed.), *Argument in controversy* (pp. 1–12). Annandale, VA: Speech Communication Association.

Hamilton, J. D. (2004). Competing and converging values of public participation: A case study of participant views in Department of Energy nuclear weapons cleanup. In S. P. Depoe, J. W. Delicath, & M-F. A. Elsenbeer (Eds.), *Communication and public participation in environmental decision making* (pp. 59–81). Albany: State University of New York Press.

Janis, I. L. (1977). *Victims of groupthink.* Boston: Houghton Mifflin.

Johnson. K. (2004, April 19). Weapons moving out, wildlife moving in. *New York Times,* p. 15.

Jones, L. (1996, May 13). "Howdy, Neighbor! As a last resort, Westerners start talking to each other. [Colorado] *High Country News, 28,* pp. 1, 6, 8.

Kinsella, W. J. (2004). Public expertise: A foundation for citizen participation in energy and environmental decisions. In S. P. Depoe, J. W. Delicath, & M-F. A. Elsenbeer (Eds.), *Communication and public participation in environmental decision making* (pp. 83–95). Albany: State University of New York Press.

Long, R. J., & Beierle, T. C. (1996). *The federal advisory committee act and public participation in environmental policy*. Resources for the Future. Retrieved September 10, 2004, from www.rff.org/documents/RFF-DP-99–17.pdf

McCloskey, M. (1996, May 13). The skeptic: Collaboration has its limits. [Colorado] *High Country News, 28*, p. 7.

Moldavi, N. (1996). Mediation of environmental conflicts in Hawaii: Win-win or co-optation? *Sociological Perspectives, 39*, 301–316.

Mouffe, C. (2000). *The democratic paradox*. London: Verso.

Peterson, M. N., Allison, S. A., Peterson, M. J., Peterson, T. R., & Lopez, R. R. (2004). A tale of two species: Habitat conservation plans as bounded conflict. *Journal of wildlife management, 68*(4), 743–761.

Peterson, M. N., Peterson, M. J., & Peterson, T. R. (2005). Conservation and the myth of consensus. *Conservation Biology, 19*, 762–767.

Pezzullo, P. C. (2001). Performing critical interruptions: Rhetorical invention and narratives of the environmental justice movement. *Western Journal of Communication, 64*, 1–25.

Policy Consensus Initiative. (2004a). Reaching consensus in Ohio on water quality standards. Retrieved September 4, 2004, from www.policyconsensus.org/casestudies/pdfs/OH_water.pdf

Policy Consensus Initiative. (2004b). State collaboration leads to successful wind farm siting. Retrieved September 6, 2004, from www.policyconsensus.org/casestudies/pdfs/OR_wind.pdf

Santos, S. L., & Chess, C. (2003). Evaluating citizen advisory boards: The importance of theory and participant-based criteria and practical implications. *Risk Analysis, 23*, 269–279.

Senecah, S. L. (2004). The trinity of voice: The role of practical theory in planning and evaluating the effectiveness of environmental participatory processes. In S. P. Depoe, J. W. Delicath, & M-F. A. Elsenbeer (Eds.), *Communication and public participation in environmental decision making* (pp. 13–33). Albany: State University of New York Press.

Shipley, J. (1995). Applegate Partnership. Retrieved September 17, 2004, from www.watershed.org/news/sum_95/applegate.html

Tarnow, K., Watt, P., & Silverberg, D. (1996). *Collaborative approaches to decision making and conflict resolution*. Salem, Oregon: Department of Conservation and Development.

Terhune, P., & Terhune, G. (1998, October 8–10). *QLG case study*. Prepared for workshop "Engaging, Empowering, and Negotiating Community: Strategies for Conservation and Development." Sponsored by The Conservation and Development Forum, West Virginia University, and the Center for Economic Options. Retrieved August 12, 2004, from www.qlg.org/pub/miscdoc/terhunecasestudy.htm

Toker, C. W. (2004). Public participation or stakeholder frustration: An analysis of consensus-based participation in the Georgia Ports Authority's stakeholder evaluation group. In S. P. Depoe, J. W. Delicath, & M-F. A. Elsenbeer (Eds.),

Communication and public participation in environmental decision making (pp.175–200). Albany: State University of New York Press.

Walker, G. B. (2004). The roadless area initiative as national policy: Is public participation an oxymoron? In S. P. Depoe, J. W. Delicath, & M-F. A. Elsenbeer (Eds.), *Communication and public participation in environmental decision making* (pp. 113–135). Albany: State University of New York Press.

Waste is still with us. (1991, June 13). [Raleigh, NC] *News & Observer,* p. 22A.

Williams, B. A., & Matheny, A. R. (1995). *Democracy, dialogue, and environmental disputes.* New Haven: Yale University Press.

Williams, W. L., Jr. (2002). *Determining our environments: The role of Department of Energy citizen advisory boards.* Westport, CT: Praeger.

Wondolleck, J. M., & Yaffee, S. L. (2000). Making collaboration work: Lessons from innovation in natural resource management. Washington, DC: Island Press.

Wood, J. T. (2003). *Communication in our lives.* (3rd ed.) Belmont, CA: Wadsworth.

Wood, J. T. (2004). Communication mosaics: An introduction to the field of communication. (3rd ed.) Belmont, CA: Wadsworth.

Yosie, T. F., & Herbst, T. D. (1998). *Using stakeholder processes in environmental decision making.* ICF Incorporated. Available online at www.gdrc.org/decision/nr98ab01.pdf

NOTE

1. President Clinton's administration (1993–2001) sponsored several collaboration and consensus-based projects, including the Environmental Protection Agency's Project XL (a national pilot program that invited state and local governments, businesses, and federal agencies to develop innovative strategies for achieving environmental protection and public health). In 1995, in his Reinventing Government Initiative, President Clinton also identified consensus and the inclusion of stakeholders as the preferred method of public participation (Toker, 2004).

PART III

Media Coverage
of the Environment

5

Media and Environmental Journalism

The environment story is one of the most complicated and press-ing stories of our time. . . . It concerns the very future of life as we know it on the planet. Perhaps more than most stories, it needs careful, longer-than-bite-sized reporting and analysis, now.

—Stocking & Leonard (1990, p. 42)

Acid rain, hazardous waste . . . they're the kind of big bureau-cratic stories that make people's eyes glaze over. There's no clear solution, no clear impact. They're not sexy.

—Senior editor of a newspaper, quoted in Ryan (1991, p. 31)

B y now, we've seen that our perceptions and attitudes toward nature and environmental problems are mediated by many sources—popular cul-ture, news shows, scientific reports, film, political debate, college courses, and so forth. The most important sources of information about the envi-ronment are mainstream news and entertainment media. By **mainstream media,** I mean major television and cable news and entertainment program-ming, commercial films, wide-circulation newspapers, magazines, advertis-ing, and radio news and talk shows. **Alternative media,** such as Internet news services, Web TV, blogs, independent journalists, and environmental groups, have arisen to challenge the mainstream media's control of information about the environment.

Historically, news media in particular have played a critical role in educating the public about environmental problems, from asbestos and lead poisoning of children to logging of ancient forests and global warming. For example, the *Seattle Post-Intelligencer* ran a series of investigative news stories in 1999 that blew the whistle on severe human exposure to asbestos in Libby, Montana. (Asbestos is made of microscopic, fibrous particles and is used in fireproofing, building materials, and electrical insulation. When these tiny particles lodge in human lungs, they cause serious health problems.) The *Post-Intelligencer* exposé helped to pressure local and national officials to address the problem (Schwarze, 2003). As with newspaper reports about asbestos, television news and editorials have served as bright spotlights of attention, arousing members of the public to demand action from health and environmental authorities.

Yet, at the heart of U.S. environmental journalism is a dilemma. Communication and journalism professor Sharon Friedman recently observed that environmental journalists today must deal with a "shrinking news hole while facing a growing need to tell longer, complicated and more in-depth stories" (p. 176). In journalistic parlance, a **news hole** is the amount of space that is available for a news story relative to other demands for the same space. Friedman argues that competition for shrinking news space increases pressure on journalists to dramatize issues to ensure that a story gets out. As a result, few mainstream media have the space to document less dramatic problems, such as loss of biodiversity or the impacts of new synthetic chemicals. Thus, although the environment may be an important concern, news media are pressured to underreport environmental problems or to cover them in highly dramatized ways.

What, then, are we to think about the role of the news media and commercial programming about the environment? How extensive—and accurate—is coverage of the environment? What effects (if any) do media representations of environmental issues have on the public's perceptions, attitudes, and behavior? Finally, what are the alternatives to mainstream, commercial media for environmental news and information?

This chapter examines the role of the news media and, to a lesser extent, commercial programming in mediating our perceptions, attitudes, and behavior regarding the environment. The first section of this chapter looks at the ways nature is depicted in news media and in entertainment programs. The second section identifies some of the constraints on news production that dictate the manner in which stories are composed, as a result of the norms of objectivity and balance, media frames, and the requirements for newsworthiness. The third section then describes some of the research on media effects and the debate about the importance of the media in influencing specific attitudes and behavior related to environmental topics. I'll also examine surprising studies of the effects of frequent television viewing on viewers' interest in the environment. Finally, in the fourth section, I'll consider the alternative media for environmental news, made possible by environmental groups, independent media and journalists, and the proliferation of Web sites and news services.

When you have finished this chapter, you should be aware of some of the factors that influence the production of news and media programming about the environment, as well as the media's rhetorical construction of nature and environmental problems. You should also be able to raise questions about the possible influence of media in shaping our perceptions, attitudes, and behavior, as well as media's potential for public education about important environmental concerns.

Media Depictions of Nature

The mainstream media's portrayal of nature is hardly uniform. Images of oil spills on the nightly news clash with ads depicting the latest sports utility vehicle climbing a rugged mountain ridge. *National Geographic* filmmakers capture hungry lions stalking gazelles even as television ads for Caribbean travel showcase a more innocent nature. In this section, I'll explore some of the images and depictions of nature in mainstream news, commercials, and entertainment programs.

Media Representations of Nature

By the 1960s, media references to and photographic images of environmental concerns had become prominent: An oil spill off the coast of Santa Barbara, California, in 1969; scenes across the country on Earth Day, 1970; whales trapped in ice in 1988; and oil coating sea birds and shorelines from the wreck of the *Exxon Valdez* in 1989 were only some of the more dramatic images. However, the trend began to change, and by the 1990s it had become clear that mainstream media's interest in environmental themes had waned.

Frequency of References to the Environment

Shabecoff (2000) reports that not only had environmental stories not grown at that time, but the total number of news stories about the environment carried by newspapers and television networks had declined substantially. For example, Douglas (1997) reported the results of a study of local television news conducted by the *Detroit News*. Although it noted the prevalence of stories about shootings, fires, and mayhem, the study found that the 11 P.M. half-hour news shows in Detroit devoted only 2% of their content to government or politics (an average of 18 seconds), whereas environmental problems, poverty, education, and race relations received no coverage at all over a two-month period. More recently, a survey of environmental reporters in New England found that shrinking news holes were cited as one of the most frequent barriers to coverage of environmental news (Sachsman, Simon, & Valenti, 2002).

Similarly, in their study of fictional and non-news entertainment television shows, media scholars Katherine A. McComas, James Shanahan, and Jessica S. Butler (2001) found that environmental themes received little attention and that this attention had been decreasing since 1993. They looked at programs from 7 P.M. to 11 P.M. on local affiliates of ABC, CBS, NBC, and (in 1997) Fox TV in the study period of 1991 to 1997. They rated the number of environmental episodes (defined as any part of a show in which the characters' speech or physical actions explicitly focused on the environment) for each show. Out of 510 programs, McComas and her colleagues found a total of 72 environmental episodes. Furthermore, each episode itself was very brief: "Forty-seven of the 72 episodes lasted less than 15 seconds, most actions were over in less than 1 minute, and only 6 episodes lasted longer than 6 minutes" (p. 538). In short, the total time devoted to environmental themes—positive *or* negative—in prime-time television entertainment programs is glaringly low. McComas and colleagues concluded, "If all of the episodes were played back to back as one long episode, the 2 hours and 22 minutes of environmental references would not outlast one Monday Night Football game" (p. 539).

An intriguing variation of this trend is the different accounts of public support for environmental values over time. That is, has support for the environment steadily increased, declined, or been uneven over time? A somewhat skeptical account is Anthony Downs's (1972) model of the **issue-attention cycle** and what is termed the "natural decline" of the public's concern with environmental issues (Dunlap, 1992, p. 90). Writing shortly after Earth Day in 1970, Downs predicted that the public's attention to environmental issues would go through the same stages as most social problems, from the public's lack of awareness to active engagement to disinterest. Dunlap summarizes Downs's five-stage progression:

1. the pre-problem stage

2. alarmed discovery and euphoric enthusiasm

3. realization of the cost of significant progress (the stage in which public support wanes)

4. a gradual decline in intense public interest

5. the post-problem stage, in which the issue moves into "a twilight of lesser attention" (Downs, 1972, p. 40)

In fact, research indicates that public interest in environmental problems has neither disappeared nor remained constant over the years. Rather, the public's environmental concern seems to go through bursts of support as well as periods of lesser interest, "at times shifting around definitive peaks and troughs" (Guber, 2003, p. 57). This shifting pattern is reflected in the post–September 11, 2001, swing of news coverage to focus on terrorism and the war in Iraq. Friedman (2004) reports that almost all the environmental journalists with whom she consulted agreed that "the events of September 11 have shrunk the [environmental] news hole even further" (p. 179). However, political scientists Norman Vig and Michael Kraft (2003) conclude that, although such developments may divert the public's interest from environmental issues short term, over time "one can see the continuity of strong public support for environmental protection and expanding environmental authority" (p. 10). I mention these accounts of shifting public interest in environmental concerns because they raise the question of whether the frequency of media coverage might affect the salience or level of concern about environmental problems. I'll return to this question later in this chapter.

Differing Views of Nature in Media

Beyond simple frequency of environmental themes, what is actually said or shown about nature itself in news and entertainment programs? Do these depictions invite concern for environmental values or a quest to dominate or manage nature? In Chapter 2, we saw that rhetorically nature can be presented in different ways, from the fearsome sermons of early colonial preachers to the passion for wild areas of preservationists such as John Muir. In her book *What Is Nature?* British philosopher Kate Soper (1995) observed that mainstream media project both popular and contradictory images onto nature:

Nature is both machine and organism, passive matter and vitalist agency. It is represented as both savage and noble, polluted and wholesome, lewd and innocent, carnal and pure, chaotic and ordered. Conceived as a feminine principle, nature is equally lover, mother and virago: a source of sensual delight, a nurturing bosom, a site of treacherous and vindictive forces bent on retribution for her human violation. Sublime and pastoral, indifferent to human purposes and willing servant of them, nature awes as she consoles, strikes terror as she pacifies, presents herself as both the best of friends and the worst of foes. (p. 71)

If popular media images depict nature as both "the best of friends and the worst of foes," does this mean that there are no problems in the media's representations of nature? Or are there stable and recurring trends in media's depictions?

The research is somewhat mixed, as might be expected. For example, in their study of television entertainment programs noted earlier, McComas, Shanahan, and Butler (2001) rated 46% of the episodes from these shows "neutral," 40% "concerned," and 13% "unconcerned" about the environment (p. 538). More recently, Meisner (2004) surveyed images of nature in a comprehensive study of Canadian media that included newspapers, magazines, and prime-time television shows (news, drama, documentaries, comedy, science fiction, and current affairs). He reported that the most prominent representations of nature found in these media could be classified according four major themes: (1) nature as a victim, (2) nature as a sick patient, (3) nature as a problem (threat, annoyance, etc.), and (4) nature as a resource.

Meisner found that, not unlike Soper's account, these themes offered two competing views of nature: "Sometimes there seems to be a strong admiration and desire for Nature. At other times there is a hatred. Sometimes there is a strong injunction to connect with or care for Nature. At other times the injunction is to fight or exploit it" (p. 17). Overall, however, he found that the frequency of images valuing nature positively outweighed negative images by a ratio of 3 to 1.

Although the themes in this study appear contradictory at times, Meisner argues that there is an overarching theme: a "symbolic domestication of nature" (p. 19). By **symbolic domestication**, he means the rhetorical construction of nature as something tame and useful but also fragile and in need of human care and protection. He observes that these depictions invite a narrow range of possible human relationships with nature that are consistent with symbolic domestication. The relationships included Care for Nature, Protect Nature, Control Nature, Manage Nature, Use Nature, and Enjoy Nature (p. 431). Overall, Meisner concludes, these relationships suggest that a strong technological optimism guides human relations with nature, and this optimism cultivates in us the view of nature as something to protect, control, use, or enjoy. Indeed, he suggests that these images sustain an **anthropocentric-resourcist ideology,** by which Meisner means that they help to "justify the continued human control and domination" of nature solely as a benefit for humans (pp. 1, 17). (For other accounts of the different constructions of nature, see Cronon, 1996.)

A related example of such cultural representations of nature from prime-time entertainment media might be *The Simpsons* cartoon television show. *Entertainment Weekly* has called *The Simpsons* "guerrilla TV, a wicked satire masquerading as a prime-time cartoon" (Korte, 1997, p. 9). We could also say that from an environmental communication perspective, the show transfers themes in news and public debate over the environment to the satiric form embodied in its key episodes. This is the view of communication critic Anne Marie Todd (2002) in her critical study of *The Simpsons*. Todd argues that the show "presents a strong ideological message about nature as a symbol—as an object for human exploitation" (p. 77). In particular, she singles out the character of Lisa, the brainy daughter whose concern for the environment often emerges as a humorous counterpoint to the **anthropocentricism** of her father, Homer. (As used by many environmentalists, *anthropocentricism* is the belief that nature exists solely for the benefit of humans.) For example, "When Lisa bemoans the crashing of an oil tanker on Baby Seal Beach, Homer comforts her . . . 'It'll be okay, honey. There's lots more oil where that came from'" (Appel, 1996, in Todd, 2002, p. 78).

Todd notes that, overall, *The Simpsons'* characters display a disregard for the environment and often oppose nature. Homer's only concern about the oil tanker's wreck is whether there will be enough oil left for our usual lifestyle. Through its humorous exaggeration, *The Simpsons* also highlights the tensions inherent in each of us as television viewers—as consumers and citizens. That is, its subversive humor opens a space in which we are invited to re-examine the environmental consequences of our actions toward the environment, a reminder that, as citizens, our judgments and actions require a viewpoint larger than that of mere consumption (Torgerson, 1999).

But why certain views of nature and not others? One influence on media depictions of its subjects is the ease with which reporters can convey the subject's importance to viewers or readers who may know or care little about it. The challenge is that many environmental problems are *unobtrusive*; that is, it is not easy to link their relevance concretely to our lives. This makes it difficult to fit these concerns into the media's conventions for reporting and entertaining. Let's examine this further.

Unobtrusive Environmental Threats

In 1979, reports of a possible meltdown of the reactor core at the Three Mile Island nuclear plant became breaking news and captured headlines worldwide. The movie *The China Syndrome*, about a threatened nuclear plant meltdown, had just appeared in theaters, fueling the public's imagination about the horrors of an accident at a nuclear plant. But most environmental threats are usually far less dramatic. Chemical contamination, the loss of biodiversity, climate change, and other threats to human health and ecological systems are less visible and often go unnoticed for years or decades. These are **unobtrusive events** because they are remote from one's personal experience. For example, Hays (1987) reported that toxic chemicals are "surrounded by mystery" because their effects are not easily observed (p. 173). Because many toxic chemicals are invisible and their effects on us delayed, we rarely notice such toxins in our everyday lives. Such contamination also may be a nonissue for government officials and the media because of this invisibility and lack of immediate impact.

As a result of the unobtrusiveness of many environmental concerns, the mainstream media have difficulty covering these issues and often report or represent issues in sensational ways. For example, Wilkins and Patterson (1990) found that newspapers frequently cover "slow-onset hazards," such as ozone depletion or global warming, in the same ways as traditional news stories, as *specific events* rather than as longer-term developments. I recall learning of scientists' discovery of the gradual warming of the earth's atmosphere many years ago by seeing a news story, "The Dunes of Durham," on a local television station in North Carolina. The news segment showed a reporter standing atop a sand dune (several hundred miles from the television station). I remember the reporter excitedly announcing that a new study warned that the earth's temperature was rising and that melting polar ice caps would flood our coastal areas. If true, he predicted, Durham residents wouldn't have to travel quite as far to enjoy the state's beaches!

Another Viewpoint: Environmental Reporting

There is some evidence of a move away from simple or dramatic news coverage of the environment. Sharon Friedman (2004), who is director of the Science and Environmental Writing Program at Lehigh University in Bethlehem, Pennsylvania, obtained evidence from senior environmental journalists that the earlier, event-driven sort of story may be giving way to more complex coverage of the environment. She explains:

"In the last half of the [1990s], some journalists turned more frequently to longer-term investigative projects . . . talking to epidemiologists, toxicologists, and other scientists. . . . All 12 senior environmental journalists who provided information . . . maintained that the range of environmental topics today is not only more complex but also broader than in the early 1990s."

> Such stories now include "wide-ranging issues such as land man-
> agement, sustainability, climate change, endocrine disruptors, new
> technologies such as hybrid cars, overfishing, invasive species, energy
> efficiency, farm practices, and suburban sprawl" (p. 179–180).

"The Dunes of Durham" was probably more sensational than many news media accounts of unobtrusive concerns. Still, news stories about the loss of biodiversity often focus not on moss or insects but on threats to charismatic fauna (the polar bear, the panda, the bald eagle), whereas stories about the pollution of the oceans may focus not on the cumulative effects of multiple industrial sources but on a dramatic oil spill or discharges from a well-known cruise liner. To cover unobtrusive events, news media often must find an event to link to the story, and such event-centered stories usually attribute the problem to one-time actions by individuals or corporations rather than to longer-term social and economic developments (Wilkins & Patterson, 1990).

I don't mean to suggest that there is little or no value in mainstream news reporting on environmental problems. Clearly, that is not the case. Awareness of global warming has increased, and the dangers of chemical contamination have become part of our national consciousness. For example, recent coverage of mercury contamination from old, coal-fired power plants and its effects on human health has been exemplary. Yet, even in these cases, the effects observed by Wilkins and Patterson can be seen in stories that center on specific people and events rather than on the less visible, less immediate sources of mercury contamination. For example, a recent report in *USA Today* on the health dangers of mercury carried the headline, "Pregnant Women Eating Too Much Fish" (Weise, 2004, p. 3A). *USA Today's* opening paragraph reduced the slow-onset danger of mercury contamination to the conventional event–people story line: "Of the 4 million babies born in the USA in 2000, more than 300,000 of them—and as many as 600,000—may have been exposed to 'unacceptable' levels of methyl mercury because their mothers ate a diet rich in fish, a study finds" (p. 3A). The story line appears to blame mothers for the toxic poisoning of their babies, and the story offers no explanation of how mercury gets into fish in the first place, nor does it mention steps that public authorities are taking (or not taking) to reduce the source of mercury emissions from aging power plants.

The *USA Today* story about mercury poisoning of infants raises important questions about the forces that shape the production of news. Therefore, it is important for us to look at influences on the reporting of environmental subjects and also at the effects of these constraints on viewers' and readers' perceptions and behavior.

News Production and the Environment

Representations of nature and of environmental problems such as toxic levels of mercury in pregnant women are shaped by an array of forces that influence and often limit the way these topics are covered by media. In her study of environmental journalism, *Media, Culture, and the Environment,* British sociologist Allison Anderson (1997) observed that the production of environmental news is influenced by various constraints ranging from "advertising pressure, editorial policy and ownership, to stylistic conventions, news cultures and the limitations of time and space" (p. 56). In this section, we'll look at five factors that constrain news production generally and environmental news in particular: (1) media political economy, (2) gatekeeping and the environmental beat, (3) criteria for newsworthiness, (4) media frames, and (5) norms of objectivity and balance.

Political Economy

The term **media political economy** refers to the influence of ownership and the economic interests of the owners of news stations and television networks on the news content of these sources. In her critical study of corporate influence on the media, Australian environmental scholar Sharon Beder (1997) noted that most commercial media organizations are owned by multinational corporations with financial interests in other businesses that are often affected by environmental regulations, such as forestry, energy companies, pulp and paper mills, oil wells, real estate, electric utilities, and so forth. With increasing consolidation of media ownership, some media managers and editors may feel pressure from owners to choose (or avoid) stories and to report news in ways that ensure a favorable political climate for these business concerns. In turn, such editors and managers "become the proprietor's 'voice' within the newsroom, ensuring that journalistic 'independence' conforms to the preferred editorial line" (McNair, 1994, p. 42).

Consider the example of General Electric (GE), one of the world's largest corporations and owner of NBC television and its business channel CNBC. Beder (1997) found that General Electric is by no means a hands-off owner of its networks. Instead, she reported, GE officials regularly insert the business's interests into network editorial decisions. Although GE has had environmental problems, "NBC journalists have not been particularly keen to expose GE's environmental record" (p. 224). For example, when the Environmental

Protection Agency found GE responsible for discharging more than a million pounds of polychlorinated biphenols (PCBs) into New York's Hudson River and proposed that GE pay for a massive cleanup, "the company responded with an aggressive campaign aimed at killing the plan," spending, by its own estimates, 10 to 15 million dollars on advertising (Mann, 2001, para. 2). And, while the president of its NBC television network lobbied government officials in New York City urging them to oppose the EPA's plan, NBC news programs "offered little national coverage of the Hudson cleanup" (para. 4). Such relationships of corporate ownership and news content underscore the belief of some media scholars that "mainstream mass media are agents of social control for dominant institutions and value systems" (Demers & Viswanath, 1999, p. 419). In this sense, media political economy also determines the size of the news hole available for certain kinds of stories.

Media influence on environmental news is not always as direct as in the GE case. Marhefka, Salimbene, and Pollock (2002) observe that, although a good deal of the literature on media has emphasized the political economy of ownership, media increasingly have been receptive to the concerns of women, labor, environmentalists, minorities, and gays. This shift in political economy research is reflected in community structure research, which emphasizes the influence on media coverage of demographic traits and interests of residents and other stakeholders in the communities. The results of these **community structure studies** suggest that community characteristics, such as political affiliation, income, education, and unemployment rates, are directly linked to the content of reporting on political and social issues that appears in local newspapers (Marhefka et al., 2002).

To test the influence of community structure on newspaper coverage of environmental issues, Marhefka et al. (2002) examined newspaper coverage of oil drilling in the Arctic National Wildlife Refuge (ANWR) in 13 cities nationwide from 2000 to 2001. News stories were rated according to their "direction" as favorable, unfavorable or balanced/neutral on drilling in the ANWR. Results showed positive correlations between political affiliation and the direction of news coverage: Cities with larger populations of Democratic voters had less news coverage favoring oil drilling in ANWR, whereas cities with more Republican voters had more favorable news coverage. The authors also found that in cities with more unemployed people, news coverage was more pro-drilling, suggesting that "the unemployed see drilling as an opportunity for more jobs and as lower fuel prices" (p. 28).

Gatekeeping and the Environmental Beat

The decisions of editors and media managers to cover or not to cover certain environmental stories illustrates what has been called the **gatekeeping** role of news production. Simply put, the metaphor of gatekeeping is used to suggest that certain individuals in newsrooms decide what gets in and what stays out. White's classic study "The 'Gatekeeper': A Case Study in the Selection of News" (1950) launched the tradition in media research of tracking the structure and routines of the newsroom and the informal forces that set priorities for and help shape news stories. Gatekeeper studies thus focus on the routines, habits, and informal relationships among editors and reporters and among reporters' background, training, and sources.

Many editors and newsrooms find it particularly difficult to deal with the environmental beat (or assignment) for two reasons: First, as we saw earlier, the unobtrusive nature of many environmental problems makes it hard for reporters to fit these stories into conventional news formats. The former president of the Society of Environmental Journalists, Rae Tyson, observed that one problem was the nature of the environmental beat itself. He recalled a Midwestern editor once quipping, "There's no one building to go to, no meeting to attend, no homicide of the day" (R. Tyson, personal communication, July 28, 1997). There is seldom a breaking story or a definitive event or crisis on the environmental beat.

Second, environmental news can be difficult to report because few reporters have training in science or knowledge of complex environmental problems such as groundwater pollution, animal waste, urban sprawl, genetically modified crops, or cancer and disease clusters. Few news organizations have the financial means to hire such talent. Thus, they face a dilemma: "As the public becomes increasingly aware of and worried about the environment, editors and reporters cannot rely on a 'seat-of-the-pants' approach when reporting on environmental issues. Stories must be technically accurate . . . Yet few newspapers or broadcast stations can assign a full-time reporter to environmental stories" (West, Lewis, Greenberg, Sachsman, & Rogers, 2003, p. vii).

As a result of these constraints, reporters and editors have begun to turn to Internet sources and electronic databases for information and as guides to environmental reporting. Also, manuals such as Michael Frome's (1998) *Green Ink: an Introduction to Environmental Journalism,* Bernadette West et al.'s (2003) *The Reporter's Environmental Handbook,* and Lori Luechtefeld's (2005) *Covering Pollution: An Investigative Reporter's Guide* offer briefings on environmental topics and guides to environmental laws to aid journalists. For example, *Covering Pollution: An Investigative Reporter's Guide,* produced in cooperation with the Society of Environmental Journalists, focuses on how to use Web-based federal databases to get information for investigations of local sources of pollution. In other cases, reporters are turning to independent sources on the Web such as Greenwire (www.greenwire.com) and the Environmental News Network (www.enn.com), as well as other databases maintained by the Society of Environmental Journalists. (I'll discuss these newer sources at the end of this chapter.)

Newsworthiness

One of the most important of the gatekeeper practices that affect environmental news reporting is what editors describe as the news value, or *newsworthiness*, of a story. **Newsworthiness** is the ability of a news story to attract readers or viewers. In their popular guide to reporting, *Reaching Audiences: A Guide to Media Writing*, Yopp and McAdams (2003) identify the conventions, found in most U.S. media guidelines, that determine newsworthiness. Reporters and editors are likely to draw on one or more of these criteria for selecting, framing, and reporting environmental news: (1) prominence, (2) timeliness, (3) proximity, (4) impact, (5) magnitude, (6) conflict, (7), oddity, and (8) emotional impact.

As a result, editors feel they must strive to fit or package environmental problems according to these news values. For example, the persistent problem of ground-level ozone may be difficult to explain in normal reporting, but a new EPA rule offered a timely way to package this problem: The news headline "Ground-Level Ozone Too High For New Standard in 31 States" (ENS, 2004) taps into the news values of impact, proximity, and magnitude. On the other hand, stories of confrontations between forest activists and loggers typically evoke images of conflict. Importantly, the newsworthiness of a story may not be the same as its economic, scientific, personal, or ethical importance. For example, the headline "Pregnant Women Eating Too Much Fish" may draw readers not so much with the scientific finding of mercury contamination but with the emotional impact or personal relevance of this news.

Act Locally!

How many stories about environmental topics do the newspapers and local television stations in your area cover in a one-week period? Are the references to nature or the environment in these stories favorable, unfavorable, or neutral?

Try an experiment. Each evening for one week, tape a local news show on one channel. (Or collect the front page of a local newspaper each day.) Review these tapes or newspapers at the end of the week. Then, do the following:

Continued

1. Count the number of news stories that mention environmental concerns.

2. For the local television show, count the number of seconds of each story. What is the average length of these stories? For newspaper articles, count the column inches of each story. What is the average length of these stories?

3. Now, try to characterize each reference to nature or the environment in these stories. Is it favorable, unfavorable, or neutral?

4. Finally, note whether the stories ran at the beginning, middle, or end of a newscast. Similarly, for newspapers, note whether the story is "above the fold," or in the top half of the paper, and whether a photograph accompanies the story.

Overall, Anderson (1997) found that environmental news coverage tends to feature stories that are (1) event-centered (e.g., oil spills and publicity stunts), (2) characterized by strong visual elements (pictures or film), and (3) closely tied into a 24-hour daily cycle. An event-centered approach focusing on disasters such as the Bhopal chemical accident in India and the *Exxon Valdez* oil spill seemed to characterize environmental news coverage in the 1970s and 1980s in particular. However, Friedman (2004) suggested that this pattern may be changing in recent years as "the obvious stories [give] way to more complex issues like particulate air pollution, climate change, endocrine disruption, and non-point water pollution" (p. 179).

Anderson emphasizes that a bias toward visual elements and the 24-hour news cycle still characterizes environmental news coverage and can be a particular challenge for reporting environmental stories on television. She cites the example of a BBC News correspondent who complained, "We're about pictures . . . Above all environment stories need good pictures . . . global warming is very difficult because you can't actually see global warming" (pp. 121–122). Most environmental problems do not naturally fit these requirements for newsworthiness, because they involve slower, more diffuse and drawn-out processes or because they lack visual quality.

On the other hand, mainstream media's heavy reliance on visual images also provides an opening for environmentalists and journalists alike to fulfill the newsworthiness standard through the coverage of dramatic visual events. Environmental communication scholar Kevin DeLuca (1999) has called these **image events**. Image events fully take advantage of television's hunger for pictures, such as footage of large banners draped from a corporate head-quarters proclaiming, "End clear-cutting of rain forests!" DeLuca quotes a veteran Greenpeace campaigner who explained that such image events succeed by "reducing a complex set of issues to symbols that break people's comfortable equilibrium, get them asking whether there are better ways to do things" (p. 3).

Despite the occasional success of image events, the newsworthiness of environmental news itself has come under fire. Why must such news meet standards—such as conflict, oddity, and emotional impact—that seem more relevant to entertainment than to news? One reason is that many editors and station owners insist there is little or no interest among the public in environmental stories. Yet, some evidence suggests otherwise. For example, a survey by the Roper Center for Public Opinion Research (1997) found that 59 percent of respondents said that they were "extremely" or "very" interested in environmental news, "ranking the environment just below local news and crime but well above sports, national and international affairs, business and money issues, and politics" (Shabecoff , 2000, p. 72). If there is such public interest, why is there so little coverage of environmental news? Perhaps the answer lies partly in Vig and Kraft's (2003) finding that, although over time the public supports environmental protection, short-term developments may divert the public's interest from environmental issues. Editors are acutely aware of this, and such shifting interest is reflected in the size of the news hole. In the end, many journalists believe that the challenge of environmental journalism remains to make environmental news both accurate and newsworthy in the face of other pressures for news space.

Media Frames

In his classic study, *Public Opinion* (1922), Walter Lippmann was perhaps the first to grasp a basic dilemma of news reporting when he wrote,

> The real environment is altogether too big, too complex, and too fleeting for direct acquaintance. We are not equipped to deal with so much subtlety, so much variety, so many permutations and combinations. And although we have to act in that environment, we have to reconstruct it on a simpler model before we can manage it. *To traverse the world men [sic] must have maps of the world.* (p. 16, emphasis added)

As a result, journalists have sought ways to simplify, frame, or make "maps of the world" to communicate their stories.

The term *frame* was first popularized by Erving Goffman in his book *Frame Analysis: An Essay on the Organization of Experience* (1974). Goffman defined **frames** as the cognitive maps or patterns of interpretation that people use to organize their understanding of reality. Building on Goffman's insight, Pan and Kosicki (1993) defined **media frames** as the "central organizing themes . . . that connect different semantic elements of a news story (headlines, quotes, leads, visual representations, and narrative structure) into a coherent whole to suggest what is at issue" (Rodríguez, 2003, p. 80). By providing this coherence, media frames help people cope with new or problematic experiences, relating them to familiar ideas and assumptions about the way the world works.

For our study of environmental communication, it is important to note that different parties who have a stake in news stories—environmentalists, property owners, citizens, corporations, scientists, and so forth—compete to influence the framing of a story. Miller and Riechert (2000) explain that opposing stakeholders try to gain public support for their positions, often "not by offering new facts or by changing evaluations of the facts, but *by altering the frames or interpretive dimensions for evaluating the facts*" (p. 45, emphasis added).

An example of industry's success in framing news stories occurred in debates over the opening of the Arctic National Wildlife Refuge to oil drilling. As a vote neared in the U.S. Congress in 2001 and again in 2005, oil industry sources argued that the drilling would have little impact on the environment. Touting advances in technology, industry spokespeople insisted, "With sideways drilling and other advances, the oil beneath the 1.5 million-acre coastal plain can be tapped with a 'footprint' on the surface no larger than 2,000 acres" (Spiess & Ruskin, 2001, para. 1). The *Anchorage Daily News* reported that the oil industry's footprint metaphor "proved to be a potent piece of rhetoric," implying that drilling would affect less than 1 percent of the coastal plain (para. 18).

The footprint metaphor is an example of one stylistic device journalists use in framing news stories. Gamson and Modigliani (1989) suggest that media communication can be thought of as a set of "interpretive packages" that give meaning to a particular issue. Such a media package is organized by a symbol or stylistic device that provides an overarching frame for the story (for example, the footprint). Gamson and Modigliani identify five framing devices that aid thinking about an issue: metaphors, exemplars (historical examples from which lessons are drawn), catchphrases, depictions, and visual images (p. 3). As we saw in the photos of Alaska's Arctic National Wildlife Refuge in Chapter 2, visual images can add powerfully to a frame.

Other parties to a controversy may attempt to displace a media frame by proposing their own exemplar, visual image, or metaphor to organize a news story. For example, opponents of the plan to drill in the Arctic National

Figure 5.1   Dillon oil rig, Cook Inlet, Alaska. Oil rigs such as this one, along with supply roads and other support facilities, would be built on the fragile tundra of the coastline in the Arctic National Wildlife Refuge.

(© Greenpeace / Robert Visser)

Wildlife Refuge objected to the footprint metaphor and countered with their own metaphor and media frame: "Oil extraction, much like open heart surgery, is a very messy business" (Ferris, 2001, para. 3). The critics' argument was that the figure of 2,000 acres for the impact from oil drilling was misleading because it did not count the large area covered by roads, connecting pipelines, worker housing, garbage dumps, water use, and other intrusions. And, like open heart surgery, the result of such drilling could be "messy."

Finally, media frames often function rhetorically to sustain dominant discourses about the environment. In his book *Image Politics*, DeLuca (1999) argues that commercial news networks such as *ABC World News Tonight* tend to negatively frame—and thus marginalize—radical environmental groups such as Earth First! that criticize timber and mining interests and challenge the U.S. Forest Service. Nevertheless, DeLuca suggests that, even in such media framing, there remain possibilities for insurgent discourses as well. For example, at the height of the cold war, Greenpeace activists in small Zodiac boats confronted Russian whaling ships in attempts to disrupt the Russians' harpooning of whales. In the television news reports of these confrontations on

Figure 5.2   A Greenpeace zodiac maneuvers itself between two Russian whaling ships. Harpooned whales are being transferred from catcher vessels to the factory processing ship.

(© Greenpeace / Rex Wyler)

the high seas, it would have been easy to dismiss Greenpeace as extreme or strange, but DeLuca points to the larger frame of the cold war ideology of the United States versus the evils of communism. In that frame, "Greenpeacers are embraced as heroes, intrepid individuals (thirteen people against a Russian fleet) who went to war against the Soviet Union and returned victorious" (p. 96). Although framed in terms of cold war politics, "Greenpeace performs and gets favorably aired [on television] an image event that is a radical critique of industrialism [and] nature as a storehouse of resources" (p. 100).

In both instances—negative framing of Earth First! and favorable framing of Greenpeace—it is still media frames "that connect different semantic elements of a news story (headlines, quotes, leads, visual representations, and narrative structure) into a coherent whole to suggest what is at issue" (Rodríguez, 2003, p. 80).

Norms of Objectivity and Balance

The twin values of **objectivity and balance** have been the bedrock norms of journalism for almost a century. In principle, these are the commitments by news media to provide information that is accurate and without reporter bias and, where there is uncertainty or controversy, to balance news stories with statements from all sides of the issue. In practice, these norms run into difficulty. Particularly in environmental journalism, reporters struggle to maintain genuine objectivity. Although specific facts of a story on deforestation may be accurate, a kind of bias already has occurred in the selection of *this* story versus others, in its framing, and in the choice of sources that have been interviewed. As Lee and Solomon (1990) point out, "value judgments infuse everything in the news media," ranging from the choice of which stories out of an infinite number to cover and which facts to include in the story, to what prominence to give it (whether on the front page or buried inside) (p. 16).

Some critics have suggested that what passes for objectivity is merely the prevailing consensus about what is real in a given time and society. For example, Craig L. LaMay (1991), the former editor of the *Gannett Center Journal,* noted that news reports of the nation's consumption—how much we spend on certain products—are taken to be an objective measure of its social and economic health. In contrast, why not measure the nation's health in terms of other variables, such as the literacy rate, the number of people in poverty, or the amount of energy conserved? LaMay explains that measures such as consumption "are objective only in the sense that they represent society's dominant values, largely agreed upon by government, commerce and other institutions—including the media. Objectivity as consensus . . . is a kind of Orwellian notion in which consensus belongs to those with the power to make it" (p. 108).

As a result of the inability to achieve objectivity generally and to cover complex environmental issues in particular, news media try to balance stories by quoting multiple or differing sources. This refers to the practice of balancing a controversial report or statement with an opposing viewpoint. For example, a *New York Times* (2004) story on the destruction of Brazil's rain forest cited the Brazilian environmental minister, who claimed that the government had kept the rate of destruction from accelerating. Although deforestation remained, the *Times* reported that, in 1995, the level was still below that of the worst year for total acreage destroyed. Then, the *Times* sought to balance the government's optimism by quoting a spokesperson for the environmental group Friends of the Earth Brazil: "Never in history has the tropical rain forest disappeared at such a rapid rate" ("Destruction of Brazil's Rain Forest Seems to Slow, 2004, p. A4).

Still, some critics charge that the assumption that there are two sides of an issue sometimes can be misleading. For example, former *New York Times* environmental reporter Phil Shabecoff (1994) argued that, ironically, such balance may undermine any claim to accurate reporting. He offered this example of reporting on global warming:

The findings of the International Panel on Climate Change—a body of some 200 eminent scientists named by the World Meteorological Organization of the United Nations Environment Program—is generally considered to be the consensus position. But I have seen a number of stories where its conclusions are given equal or less weight than those of a single scientist who has done little or no significant peer-review research in the field, is rarely, if ever, cited on those issues in the scientific literature, and whose publication is funded by a fossil-fuel industry group with an obvious axe to grind. . . . For a reporter, at this stage of the debate, to give equal or even more weight to that lonely scientist with suspect credentials is, in my view, taking sides in the debate. (p. 204)

Such criticism has prompted increasing debate among some environmental journalists over the limits of objectivity and the purpose of environmental reporting. Of special note is what LaMay (1991) has called the **objectivity-advocacy debate**, which has become a feature of journalism conferences lately. At the heart of this debate is a clash between defenders of objectivity in news and the call by some journalists for a right to *evaluate* competing arguments in an environmental controversy. They insist that what the public needs is not necessarily more information but better or more usable information about an issue. Rather than merely reporting, "X said this, and Y said that" (a balancing of opposing viewpoints), a news story would assess the quality of the information and potential biases of sources. Those supporting this more explicit advocacy role for the media believe that media have a duty to educate and empower, to provide answers and to equip readers and viewers with "a better argument" about crucial topics (pp. 104–05).

The call for more explicit advocacy, as well as the other constraints on news production that we've reviewed here, presume that media affect or impact consumers of news in certain ways. Do news reports or media viewpoints actually influence their readers' and viewers' attitudes and behavior toward the environment? It is to the debates over such media effects that we now turn.

Media Effects

Earlier, in Chapter 1, I said that our understanding and behavior toward the environment depend not only on ecological science but also on media representations and public debate as well as ordinary conversation. Clearly, news and entertainment media have been forces in affecting our perceptions of the environment. And there is some evidence that the news media have played a key role in influencing public opinion about particular environmental issues

(Anderson, 1997). Nevertheless, there is also intense controversy about the possibility of **media effects.** By this phrase, I mean the influence of different media content, frequency, and forms of communication on audiences' attitudes, perceptions, and behaviors. In particular, there is doubt whether we can pinpoint particular media content as the *cause* of specific opinions or behavior (Anderson, 1997; Shanahan & McComas, 1999).

We will enter the debate over the impact of environmental media by reviewing three broad theories of the effects of news and media programming on the public's attitudes and behavior. These theories are (1) the direct transmission model, (2) agenda setting, and (3) narrative framing and cultivation theory. Overall, these approaches provide little evidence of direct, causal effects on audiences' beliefs and behaviors; rather, they suggest that media's impact is both cumulative and a part of a wider context of social influence that helps to construct our interest in and understanding of the environment.

Direct Transmission (The Hypodermic Model)

Early theories of media effects operated from a model that assumed that communication is a **direct transmission.** This model described media effects as the result of the direct transmission of information from a sender (source) to a receiver. This early theory viewed audiences as highly susceptible to manipulation and typically viewed people "as a homogenous mass of damp sponges, uniformly soaking up messages from the media" (Anderson, 1997, pp. 18–19). Direct transmission, also called the **hypodermic model,** likened the media to a syringe that "injected" messages into an audience, assuming that individuals would respond in predictable ways (p. 19).

Although there is little evidence of a direct transmission effect, the early communication model served practical needs. It allowed researchers to look for effects from specific campaigns to impart information or change attitudes or behavior. For example, do public information campaigns teach farmers important information about soil conservation? Do pleas to the public to recycle change people's behavior? Generally, such research failed to find evidence of direct, causal effects on audiences. For example, Allen and Weber (1983) reported that President Jimmy Carter's 1979 television campaign to persuade the public to turn down their thermostats and conserve energy was largely ineffective (p. 104). In other cases, information campaigns may succeed in encouraging positive attitudes about conservation—for example, strengthening the public's *intentions* to recycle—but such campaigns may not necessarily alter people's actual behavior.

Because the direct transmission model has not proved particularly useful in explaining the influence of environmental media, other accounts have emerged. These accounts move beyond the study of specific effects on individuals to broader influences of media in shaping perceptions of issues and in constructing social narratives about the environment. We turn now to the first of these, the agenda-setting theory.

Agenda Setting

Perhaps the single most influential theory of media effects that applies to environmental news is agenda setting. Cohen (1963) first suggested the idea of **agenda setting** to distinguish between individual opinion (*what* people believe) and the public's perception of the salience or *importance* of an issue. News reporting "may not be successful much of the time in telling people *what to think,* but it is stunningly successful in telling its readers *what to think about*" (p. 13, emphasis added; see also McCombs & Shaw, 1972). In their study of television, Iyengar and Kinder (1987) defined agenda setting in this way: "Those problems that receive prominent attention on the national news become the problems the viewing public regards as the nation's most important" (p. 16). In other words, the public's perception of what is important influences the media less than media influence the public's priorities (Ader, 1995, p. 300).

The agenda-setting hypothesis has been influential in much environmental communication research on the effects of media, though the results sometimes have been conflicting. On the one hand, Iyengar and Kinder (1987) found firm evidence of the agenda-setting effect in their study of evening news on television, in which viewers rated the importance of the environment higher *after* viewing increased coverage of news of environmental pollution (p. 19). Atwater, Salwen, and Anderson (1985) found support for agenda setting even at the "sub-issue" level, where increased coverage of the individual aspects of environmental issues led to higher levels of saliency for these issues (p. 397). Finally, Eyal, Winter, and DeGeorge (1981), and Ader (1995) discovered that the agenda-setting effect is especially strong for unobtrusive issues. This effect is most apparent in media's enhancement of the public's perceptions of risk or danger from environmental sources. (I'll examine news media coverage of risk in Chapter 6.)

On the other hand, Gooch's (1996) study of the coverage of environmental issues by Swedish newspapers did not find evidence of an agenda-setting effect. Although reports about water pollution and waste received the greatest amount of news coverage in the press, the public rated other environmental concerns, such as air quality, as more serious. Similarly, Suhonen

(1993) found a negligible relationship between the levels of environmental coverage in newspapers in Finland and levels of readers' concern about the environment. He suggests that one reason might be the influence of broader social forces in influencing the levels of concern at any one time. Finally, and somewhat surprisingly, Iyengar and Kinder (1987) found no support for the *vividness* of news reports in affecting television viewers' perception of the importance of environmental issues. In this case, a story that featured a link between a toxic waste site and a stormy interview with a mother and her sick child produced no more viewer concern than a pallid version in which a reporter merely discussed a possible connection between the chemical site and catastrophic illness.

However, some environmental communication scholars caution against a rejection of agenda-setting effects based on these studies. Ader (1995) observes that real-world conditions may affect perceptions of the seriousness of a problem independently of news coverage of these concerns. Anderson (1997) also points out that other influences, such as friends and family, may affect the public's perception of the importance of environmental issues and that agenda-setting research should take these factors into consideration.

In an attempt to refine agenda-setting theory, Ader (1995) investigated the relative influence of real-world conditions, public opinion, and the media's agenda in a study of news reports about the environment in the *New York Times* from 1970 to 1990. She asked two questions: (1) Is the public's concern about environmental problems driven by real-world conditions rather than media reports? (2) Do public attitudes influence the amount of media coverage of an issue rather than the other way around? Using data from Gallup polls during this period, Ader identified problems that the public periodically rated as the "most important problem facing the nation today." To control for the influence of public opinion and real-world conditions on media coverage, Ader examined the length and prominence of news reports of pollution in the *Times* for three months before and three months after each Gallup poll was conducted, as well as data from independent sources documenting real-world conditions for disposal of wastes, air quality, and water quality in these same periods.

Ader's findings affirmed the presence of a strong agenda-setting effect, even when real-world environmental conditions and prior public opinion both were taken into account. That is, even though objective measures showed that overall pollution had declined for the period studied, the *Times* increased its coverage of news stories about pollution, and the greater length and prominence of these stories correlated positively with a subsequent increase in readers' concerns about this issue. However, the opposite was not true; that is, the media did not appear to be mirroring public opinion. Ader concluded, "The findings suggest that *the amount of media attention devoted to pollution influenced the degree of public salience for the issue*" (p. 309, emphasis added).

While the agenda-setting hypothesis may explain the importance of an issue to the public, it doesn't claim to account for what people think about this issue. Therefore, it is important for us to look at other theories that focus on the role of the media in constructing meaning or ways of understanding environmental concerns.

Narrative Framing and Cultivation Analysis

Media communicate not only facts about the environment but also wider frameworks or guides for understanding and making sense of these facts. Theories of media effects that focus on such sense making emphasize the importance of discourse in coherently organizing our experience of the world and our relationship to the environment. Such theories do not argue that discourse "causes" public opinion; rather, they claim that "media discourse is part of the process by which individuals construct meaning" (Gamson & Modigliani, 1989, p. 2). In this section, we'll look at two related approaches to the role of media discourse in our sense making: narrative framing and cultivation analysis.

Narrative Framing

Unlike the direct transmission model, a narrative model takes seriously the perspective of media frames that provide central organizing themes to connect different elements of a news story into a coherent whole. **Narrative framing** refers to the ways in which media organize the bits and facts of phenomena through stories to aid audiences' understanding, and the potential for this organization to affect our relationships to the phenomena being represented. The principal proponents of this approach, James Shanahan and Katherine McComas (1999), observe that environmental media coverage is "hardly ever the simple communication of a 'fact,'" because "journalists use narrative structures to build interesting environmental coverage. Hence, studies of environmental communication show that media portrayals of environmental issues are presented from the start as stories; because journalists and media programmers must interest audiences, they must present their information in narrative packages" (pp. 34–35). Such "packages" structure our understanding of the environment along certain lines rather than others, and it is this selective portrayal and its potential impact that interest environmental media scholars.

A case in point is Harold P. Schlechtweg's (1992) study of a Public Broadcasting Service (PBS) program on Earth First! protesters. In May 1990,

Figure 5.3   Earth First! activists protest logging in Oregon's old-growth forests
(copyright Getty Images: Redwood Summer and Earth First! #772023)

the *Earth First! Journal* announced the start of Redwood Summer, a mobilization of activists who would flood into California's northern redwood
forests and "nonviolently blockade logging roads, [and] climb giant trees to
prevent their being logged" (Cherney, 1990, p. 1). Earth First! organizers
stressed that anyone who disagreed with nonviolence would be barred from
Redwood Summer. Earth First! also tried to open a dialogue with loggers,
suggesting they shared a common interest in sustainable logging from
new-growth forests rather than the older-growth areas (Schlechtweg, 1992).
Nevertheless, tensions grew among loggers, Earth First! activists, and rural
communities that summer. On July 20, 1990, the PBS program *The MacNeil-
Lehrer NewsHour* ran "Focus–Logjam," a report about the protests. It is this
report and its narrative framing of loggers, Earth First! protesters, community
people, and violence that Schlechtweg explored.

In his detailed textual analysis of "Focus–Logjam," Schlechtweg identified the key visual and verbal terms that disclosed the broadcast's thematic
frame. These included scenes of pristine forests, references to "small-town
economies" that depended on "lumber," close-up shots of an ax or hatchet
pounding a spike into a tree, and the PBS reporter's voice-over announcing
that "Earth First! has a record of civil disobedience, injuring private timberlands, sabotaging logging machinery, and . . . writing about putting metal
spikes in trees so they can't be logged" (pp. 266–267). By the end of the

9-minute, 40-second news report, "Focus–Logjam" had established clear identities for "protagonists" and "antagonists" in a tense confrontation that suggested the real prospect of violence.

Protagonists in the broadcast were portrayed through key identity and value terms: The report introduces "workers, "timber people, and "regular people" who depended on "timber harvests" and "small town economies" for "jobs," "livelihood," and their "way of life" (p. 273). Conversely, the report identified Earth First! protesters as "apocalyptic," "radical," "wrong people," "terrorists," and "violent" people who engaged in "confrontation," "tree spiking," "sabotage," and "civil disobedience" to save "tall, beautiful" trees (p. 273). Schlechtweg argued that as a result of these and other verbal and visual terms, "Focus–Logjam" implicitly constructed a narrative that pitted "regular people" against a "violent terrorist organization, willing to use sabotage . . . and tree spiking to save redwood forests" (pp. 273, 274).

In exploring the narrative identities and structure of "Focus–Logjam," Schlechtweg stated that his primary interest was to identity the *effect* of such portrayals of protesters and rural communities in fostering an atmosphere that worked to foreclose dialogue among activists, community people, and loggers and that "constructed violence as a reasonable and thus legitimate response to Earth First! demonstrations" (p. 265). He concluded that the broadcast "undercut Earth First!'s attempt to establish common ground with loggers" by not giving air time to the protesters' argument that industry practices threatened jobs. By casting Earth First! "as deviant, criminal, and violent, the report inspired fear and . . . provided justification . . . should there be violence against Earth First! members" (p. 274).

Act Locally!

Interestingly, Schlechtweg's (1992) claim that he is interested in the effects of PBS's broadcast "Focus–Logjam" raises an important question in the study of environmental media effects:

Can we determine the likely or actual impact of a broadcast like "Focus–Logjam" on people in the real world by inspecting the media text (its language, sounds, and images) only, or must there be an empirical study of the television viewers who watched this particular broadcast on July 20, 1990?

Identify a scheduled television program on an environmental theme. Invite a group of friends or fellow classmates to view this program with you, or record it and play it later for them. Afterward, ask those who viewed it,

- What effect did the program have on their thinking about the topic?
- How do they believe the program would affect others?
- What about the program do they think accounts for these responses?
- Can they identify particular narrative terms or structures that help to explain possible effects?
- How confident are they that they can generalize these accounts of effects to other audiences or viewers?

Cultivation Analysis

Akin to narrative theory is a cultivation model of media influence. Shanahan (1993) describes **cultivation analysis** as "a theory of story-telling, which assumes that repeated exposure to a set of messages is likely to produce agreement in an audience with opinions expressed in . . . those messages" (pp. 186–187). As its name implies, cultivation is not a claim about immediate or specific effects on an audience; instead, it is a process of gradual influence or cumulative effect. The model is associated with the work of media scholar George Gerbner (1990), who stated, "Cultivation is what a culture does. That is not simple causation, though culture is the basic medium in which humans live and learn. . . . Strictly speaking, cultivation means the specific independent (though not isolated) contribution that a particularly consistent and compelling symbolic stream makes to the complex process of socialization and enculturation" (p. 249). Gerbner's own research looked exclusively at the long-term effects of viewing violence on television—the cultivation of a worldview that he called the "mean world syndrome." This is a view of society as a dangerous place, peopled by others who want to harm us (Gerbner, Gross, Morgan, & Signorielli, 1986).

Similarly, environmental communication scholars who use cultivation analysis are interested in the longer-term effects of media on environmental attitudes and behavior. Perhaps surprisingly, this research suggests that heavy media exposure is sometimes correlated with *lower levels of environmental concern* (Novic & Sandman, 1974; Ostman & Parker, 1987; and Shanahan & McComas, 1999). In a study of college students' television viewing, Shanahan and McComas (1999) report that heavy exposure to television may actually retard the cultivation of pro-environmental attitudes:

Most correlations with amount of television viewing were negative and significant: heavier viewers consistently expressed lower levels of environmental concern. . . . This tends to go against the suggestion that media attention to the environment results in greater socioenvironmental [sic] concern. That television's heavy viewers tended to be less environmentally concerned suggests the opposite: Television's messages place a kind of "brake" on the development of environmental concern, especially for heavy viewers. (p. 125)

Interestingly, Shanahan and McComas (1999) found that the decrease in environmental concern among heavy television viewers is stronger among politically active students. This finding appears to contradict what we said earlier about the effects of agenda setting; that is, the more frequent the coverage of a subject, the more salience it gained. How is this explained? Cultivation researchers explain this pattern as **mainstreaming,** or a narrowing of differences toward a cultural norm. Shanahan and McComas suggested that, in the case of environmental media, television's consistent stream of messages may actually draw groups closer to the cultural mainstream, with the mainstream (as represented by television programs) being "closer to the lower end of the environmental concern scale" (1999, p. 130).

In a second study, Shanahan and McComas (1999) found more mixed results regarding a cultivation effect for environmentalism. However, when they looked closely at some subgroups, they found the same pattern as in the earlier study. For example, although women were more willing than men to sacrifice financially for environmental reasons, as they viewed television more often, they were less willing to do so. Similarly, urban dwellers were more willing than rural residents to sacrifice for the environment, but as more frequent viewers, they were less willing to do so (pp. 132–145).

A second explanation for the decrease in environmental concern among heavy viewers of television is what Shanahan (1993) terms **cultivation in reverse.** This is the media's cultivation of an anti-environmental attitude through a persistent lack of environmental images or by directing viewers' attention to other, nonenvironmental stories. By ignoring or passively depicting the natural environment, television tends to marginalize its importance. Cultivation theorists (Shanahan & McComas, 1999) also call this phenomenon **symbolic annihilation**—the media's erasure of the importance of a theme by the indirect or passive de-emphasizing of that theme.

It can be difficult to detect specific effects of media on viewers' beliefs or behaviors, at least in the short run. Nevertheless, theories such as agenda setting and the longer-term cultivation of viewers' outlooks do suggest broader effects. These indirect effects include the increased salience of issues (when spotlighted by media) or the adoption of mainstream views on the environment as a result of frequent exposure to television programs. But these broader influences may be significant. Meisner (2004) observes, "While it is unclear that the mass media have any significant short-term direct effects on individuals' environmental behaviors and choices, there is a growing consensus that there are long term systemic cultural impacts of mediated environmental discourse" (p. 5). Perhaps because of this influence, journalists and environmental groups alike have felt the need for alternative sources of news and information about the environment, and it is to this development that I now turn.

The Rise of Alternative Environmental Media

Although commercial newspapers, radio, and television coverage of the environment is uneven, these outlets are not the only sources of environmental news and information. In their study of environmental media, Shanahan and McComas (1999) observe that, despite an elite control of the commercial media, outlets in media for environmental opposition have been growing. They draw upon Downing's (1988) idea of an **alternative public sphere** for environmental communication, by which they mean that environmental and other groups have the ability to articulate for themselves a space within society in which "their own discourse can be privileged and their own knowledge pursued" (p. 45).

One of the reasons for the growth of alternative news sources is that environmental groups, science advocacy groups, and working journalists themselves have grown frustrated with the insufficient depth, range, and accuracy of commercial media coverage of environmental topics. Indeed, with the erosion of mass circulation and broadcast outlets such as commercial network news, more and more individuals are proactively seeking the kinds of information not found in traditional media or on specific subjects in which they're interested, such as the environment. In establishing alternative news sources, they often abandon the traditional media frames of objectivity and balance in favor of more insurgent discourses about the environment. (I described insurgent discourses briefly in Chapter 2.) Such alternative voices now appear regularly in independent newspapers and film, from online environmental news services, and in the videos, magazines, and books distributed by environmental groups themselves.

In this final section, I'll look at three sources of independent news and information about environmental topics: (1) environmental groups and independent newspapers and film; (2) professional societies for environmental journalists; and (3) online, independent environmental news services.

Environmental Groups and Independent Newspapers and Film

Magazines, books, films, and websites about the environment now seem to proliferate across the landscape. However, in the early 20th century, environmental groups were almost alone in providing news and information about important environmental issues (Hays, 2000, pp. 101–102). The early preservationist John Muir started publication of the *Sierra Club Bulletin* (now *Sierra*) in 1893. *Bird-Lore,* predecessor of the modern-day *Audubon* magazine, followed in 1899, and by the end of World War Two other nature and environmental groups had begun to issue their own newsletters and magazines. Still, it was not until 1960 that the Sierra Club, under David Brower, burst upon the book publishing scene with Ansel Adams's and Nancy Newhall's *This Is the American Earth.* Today, hundreds of environmental, scientific, and other publishers, such as Earthscan and Island Press, routinely publish thousands of environmental book titles each year.

At the local and regional level, independent newspapers, journals, and news magazines have appeared in recent years to fill what many citizens feel is a vacuum in environmental news and information in their areas. According to Hays (2000), the oldest and best known of these regional papers is *High Country News,* "a newspaper independent of environmental organizational affiliation and free from the burdens of advertising income, that provided unique coverage of environmental issues in the Rocky Mountain region" (p. 102). In the past decade, other regional daily and weekly papers have began to appear: the *Cascadian Times* (Seattle), the *Maine Times,* and *Appalachian Voices* (covering the southern Appalachian region of North Carolina, Virginia, Kentucky, Tennessee, and West Virginia). The *Bay Journal,* serving the Chesapeake Bay area of Maryland and Virginia, covers scientific and policy news about this important natural area, providing "one of the best examples of environmental knowledge organized around a specific regional set of circumstances" (Hays, 2000, p. 102).

Finally, local and national environmental groups alike now routinely have websites that feature news and information about their organizations, their campaigns, and resources for members or the general public (for example, the Sierra Club's extensive site is at www.sierraclub.org). Some groups have started their own blog sites. For example, the Natural Resources Defense Council (NRDC) unveiled its blog in early 2005 (http://blog.nrdcaction fund.org/).

Separately, a number of independent film companies have begun producing documentary films that address environmental issues. During the last two decades, for example, Bullfrog Films (www.bullfrogfilms.com) has emerged as a leading U.S. distributor of independently produced environmental videos that cover issues ranging from endangered species to global warming and environmental ethics. The smaller production company High Plains Films (www.highplainsfilms.org), on the other hand, focuses mainly on films that document threats to America's wild lands, forests, and endangered species. More recently, Sierra Club Productions (www.sierraclub.org/

scp) launched an ambitious film effort with its award-winning production of Ansel Adams and other documentary films on food safety, urban transportation, and other environmental topics.

Professional Societies for Environmental Journalists

Journalists in particular have felt the need for more accurate sources of information and timelier briefings about environmental topics. In the United States, the main source of support for working journalists and editors is the Society of Environmental Journalists (SEJ). Its primary goal is "to advance public understanding of critically important environmental issues" by providing the resources for a network of professional journalists and editors who cover environment-related issues. (See SEJ's homepage at www.sej.org). For example, SEJ maintains the Integrity in Science Database for journalists who want to investigate possible conflicts of interest on the part of scientists who publish on controversial environmental topics such as global warming. The database lists scientists' affiliations with principal funding sources, including chemical, gas, oil, food, drug, and other companies. It also lists nonprofit groups and universities that receive industry funding.

Internationally, similar networks for environmental journalists exist. The most prominent network is the Asia Pacific Forum of Environmental Journalists (www.environmentaljournalists.lk/apfej). This organization coordinates the national environmental journalist forums of 37 countries in the Asia–Pacific region. Its members include journalists working for newspapers, magazines, and broadcast media, as well as environmental groups and government departments and agencies. Another is the International Federation of Environmental Journalists, an umbrella group of member associations from forty nations (www.ifej.org/).

Online Environmental News Services

Newer online and electronic sources offer the widest access to independent environmental news and information. Friedman (2004) observes that many of the changes related to improved information and sources for environmental journalists can be traced to the Internet and the World Wide Web. One senior environmental reporter claimed that the Internet "drastically changed the way journalists do their job" (p. 183).

The first of this new genre was the Environmental News Service (ENS), the original daily, international wire service reporting environmental news. Established in 1990, ENS is an independently owned and Web-based service with more than 400 websites featuring its news stories. Its chief claim is that it offers "late-breaking environmental news in a fair and balanced manner." (See ENS's home page at www.ens-news.com.) ENS covers news stories from countries around the world on such topics as environmental politics, lawsuits, international agreements, and demonstrations, plus a range of environmental subjects—science and technology, air quality, public health, drinking water, oceans and marine life, land use, wildlife, natural disasters, toxics, nuclear issues, recycling, transportation, and environmental economics.

ENS was soon followed by other news services, listservs, and specialty coverage of subareas of environmental policy. The latter service is of particular interest to environmental and business groups, policymakers, and others who follow environmental legislation in the U.S. Congress. For example, Environment and Energy (E&E) Publishing provides detailed coverage of energy, public lands issues, and other issues before the courts or Congress. Its *Land Letter* (www.landletter.com) specializes in natural resources (wilderness, oil and gas drilling on public lands, etc.), and its *Environment and Energy Daily* report (www.eedaily.com) focuses on air, water, and energy issues. E&E Publishing also sponsors *Greenwire* (www.greenwire.com), which many journalists consider the leading daily news source for environmental stories. It offers both original reporting and a daily compilation of print, television, and online news stories and editorials about a wide range of environmental subjects.

More recently, E&E Publishing has added a Web TV forum (www.EandE.TV). This is a daily update of news about the environment via flash TV. Topics range from the effects of mercury on wildlife, opening of the Arctic National Wildlife Refuge to oil drilling, a new transportation bill in the Congress, and whether Congress has allocated enough funds to fight wildfires in the West. The lineup for the day's news is announced through daily e-mail alerts.

Although online sources provide many working journalists, institutions, and others with detailed information about current environmental issues, some of these are available only by subscription.

Other general-purpose environmental news and analysis websites are available free to anyone online. The choices are wide-ranging and seemingly endless. Here are just a few:

• *Rachel's Environment & Health News* (www.rachel.org), named for Rachel Carson; known for its incisive reports on toxic chemicals, environmental justice, worker healthy and safety, and other health-related issues.

• *Environmental News Network* (www.enn.com), a broader online service whose goal since its inception in 1993 has been "to educate the

world about environmental issues facing our Earth" (www.enn.com/
aboutenn); offers a variety of resources for online users from environmental news, live chats, and interactive quizzes to forums for debate and audio
and video reports.

- *EnviroLink Network* (www.envirolink.org) bills itself as "the online
environmental community," a nonprofit organization that provides access
to online environmental resources. For example, a headline about orcas (so-
called killer whales) boosting their calls to each other in order to be heard
above boat noise might direct the user to the British Broadcasting Channel for
the breaking story, or those interested in organic gardening might find links
to dozens of nonprofit groups for resources, new ideas, and information.

- *The Gallon Environment Letter* (www.cialgroup.com/gallonletter.html),
a twice-monthly Web environmental policy bulletin from Canada that is sent
to e-mail addresses around the world; it explores issues of sustainable development (balancing economic, environmental, and social aspects of society)
with a strong emphasis on the environment.

- *Grist Magazine* (www.grist.org) supports nonprofit, independent
columns that feature biting commentary, for example, about politicians
claiming to be "green," and a story in its "Powers that Be" column about
"hipster environmentalism"—a young couple turns an abandoned ware-
house in Brooklyn into an environmentally friendly dwelling with a rainwa-
ter collection system, a high-efficiency condensing boiler, and solar energy.

In addition, there are a number of independent news services that cover
the environment as well as other social issues. Perhaps the best-known online
site is the Independent Media Center, or Indy Media, as it is popularly
known. Indy Media is a collection of independent, progressively oriented
journalists and media organizations "offering grassroots, non-corporate
coverage" (www.indymedia.org).

In many ways, alternative media—Internet services such as the Environmental News Service, other Web sites, and blogs—are challenging conventional media theory about such topics as political economy and the gatekeeper
function. With the unlimited availability and interconnectivity of Internet sites,
scholars will need to rethink who—if anyone—controls access to news and
information and what determines newsworthiness. Indeed, environmental
issues may be "paving the way for the restructuring of the political economy
of the news and information media" (S. Depoe, personal communication,
March 9, 2005).

Conclusion

I've noted several times that environmental communication mediates our understanding and appreciation of nature and the environment. Because few of us encounter directly the problems of global warming, loss of biodiversity, or mercury poisoning, we rely upon the reports and representations of others, especially mainstream media: television, newspapers, radio, and popular websites, film, and magazines. Clearly, these media do influence in some ways our perceptions and the meaning of these and other issues.

Yet, these media are neither innocent nor neutral in their representations of the environment. In the first section of this chapter, we discovered that the mainstream media present different and even contradictory images of nature—as both nurturing and treacherous, sublime and dangerous, as victim, sick patient, a problem (threat), and a resource. These differing views may reflect the viewpoint of one or more gatekeepers. However, the content and shape of environmental news also reflect influences associated with the production of news itself.

In the second section, we saw that news coverage of the environment is subject to some of the same powerful constraints that affect news reports generally: (1) the economic interests of owners (political economy), (2) norms and routines of newsrooms (gatekeeping), (3) accepted criteria for news worthiness, (4) media frames, and (5) the news conventions of objectivity and balance. In some cases, environmental problems are unobtrusive because their invisibility and delayed effects make news coverage difficult. These constraints limit both the ability to present some stories at all, and, if reported, they influence powerfully the selection, angle, shaping, content, and hence the meaning of issues or concerns.

This chapter also asked whether news media coverage or programming about the environment has particular effects on audiences and, if so, what kinds of effects? In the third section, we looked at different approaches to the study of media effects—the impact of different media content on audiences' attitudes, perceptions, and behaviors. Whereas some older theories of media effects, such as the direct transmission (hypodermic) model, have gone out of favor, recent approaches have turned up interesting and unexpected results. For example, the agenda-setting hypothesis led researchers to explore media's ability to affect the public's perception of the importance of an issue. That is, media may not be successful in telling people *what* to think, but they often are successful in affecting what people think *about,* or the salience of issues.

Other approaches to the study of media effects, such as narrative theory and cultivation analysis, ask other questions: How do media narratives help to frame our understanding or sense making of an issue? Does repeated exposure to certain messages affect audiences' levels of concern about the environment? Some studies using cultivation analysis found that extended television viewing may lead to a lower level of concern or willingness to take action on behalf of the environment.

Finally, we observed that the rise of alternative media—Internet news services, Web flash TV, and blogs—are starting to challenge conventional media theory. With the broad access and interconnectivity of Internet sites, scholars will need to rethink who—if anyone— controls access and what determines newsworthiness.

For those of you who feel that the media can and should do a better job of educating the public about environmental issues, perhaps there is hope. Meisner (2004) calls our attention to a study of the long-running Canadian television show *The Nature of Things*. The study of its programs from 1960 to 1994 found that the early shows focused on nature as something to struggle against or to manage and exploit. But the shows changed over the years. In the 1980s and 1990s, *The Nature of Things* presented nature as something "to be understood in a spiritual as well as a scientific sense. It was presented as a fragile victim of our collective, wasteful and exploitive ways" (Wall, 1999, p. 70).

Likewise, the future of environmental coverage elsewhere will depend upon the public's demands for more accurate, thoughtful, and in-depth reporting and environmental programming. Both media professionals and their audiences (you) have a role to play in improving media representation of nature and the environment in the coming decade. In the next chapter, I'll look at one example of change as I describe some of the reforms in risk communication and efforts to communicate with vulnerable populations about hazards.

KEY TERMS

Agenda setting: An alleged effect of media on the public's perception of the salience or importance of issues, whereby news reporting, although it may not be successful in telling people *what* to think, is successful in telling them what to think *about*.

Alternative media: Sources that challenge the mainstream media's control of information about the environment, such as Internet news services, Web TV, blogs, independent journalists, and environmental groups.

Alternative public sphere: Term used by media scholars Shanahan and McComas (1999) to refer to a space within society, which environmental and other groups articulate for themselves, in which their own discourse can be privileged and their own knowledge pursued.

Anthropocentricism: The belief that nature exists solely for the benefit of humans; closely related to *anthropocentric-resourcist ideology.*

Anthropocentric-resourcist ideology: A view of nature that helps to justify the continued human control and domination of nature solely as a benefit for humans.

Community structure studies: Research suggesting that characteristics of communities, such as political affiliation, income, education, and unemployment rates, are directly linked to the content of reporting on political and social issues that appear in local newspapers.

Cultivation analysis: Associated with the work of media scholar George Gerbner (1990), the theory that repeated exposure to a set of messages tends to produce, in an audience, agreement with the views contained in those messages.

Cultivation in reverse: The media's cultivation of an anti-environmental attitude through the persistent lack of environmental images or by directing the attention of viewers and readers to other, nonenvironmental stories.

Direct transmission model: An early model that describes media effects as the result of a direct transmission of information from a sender (source) to a receiver; viewed audiences as highly susceptible to manipulation; also called the *hypodermic model,* it likened the media to a syringe that "injected" messages into audiences.

Frames: First defined by Erving Goffman (1974) to refer to the cognitive maps or patterns of interpretation that people use to organize their understanding of reality. See also *media frames.*

Gatekeeping: The role of editors and media managers in deciding to cover or not cover certain news stories; a metaphor used to suggest that individuals in newsrooms decide what gets in and what stays out.

Hypodermic model: See *direction transmission model.*

Image events: Actions by environmentalists that take advantage of television's hunger for pictures; such events often succeed by reducing a complex set of issues to (visual) symbols that break people's comfortable equilibrium, inviting them to ask if there is a better way to do things.

Issue-attention cycle: Anthony Downs's (1972) model of the "natural decline" of the public's concern with environmental issues; predicts that the public's attention to environmental issues goes through the same stages as most social problems, from the lack of awareness to active engagement to disinterest.

Mainstreaming: An alleged effect in consistent viewers of media whereby differences are narrowed toward cultural norms represented in media programs.

Mainstream media: Major television and cable news and entertainment programming, commercial film, large-circulation newspapers, magazines, advertising, and radio news and talk shows that carry news and information about the environment.

Media effects: The influence of different media content, frequency, and forms of communication on audiences' attitudes, perceptions, and behaviors.

Media frames: The central organizing themes that connect different semantic elements of a news story (headlines, quotes, leads, visual representations, and narrative structure) into a coherent whole to suggest what is at issue. See also *frames.*

Media political economy: The influence, on news content, of ownership and economic interests of the owners of news stations and television networks.

Narrative framing: Media's organization of phenomena through stories to aid audiences' understanding.

News hole: The amount of space that is available for a news story relative to other demands for this same space.

Newsworthiness: The ability of news stories to attract readers or viewers; often defined by such criteria for selecting and reporting environmental news as prominence, timeliness, proximity, impact, magnitude, conflict, oddity, and emotional impact.

Objectivity–advocacy debate: A debate between traditional defenders of objectivity in news and other journalists who call for the right to evaluate competing arguments in environmental controversies; the latter believe media have a duty to educate and empower, to provide answers and to equip readers and viewers with better arguments about crucial topics.

Objectivity and balance: Norms of journalism for almost a century; the commitment to which is made by news media to provide information that is accurate and without reporter bias and, where there is uncertainty or controversy, to balance news stories with statements from all sides of the issue.

Symbolic annihilation: Media's erasure of the importance of a theme by the indirect or passive de-emphasizing of that theme.

Symbolic domestication: The rhetorical construction of nature (by media) as something tame and useful but also fragile and in need of human care and protection.

Unobtrusive events: Events that are remote from one's personal experience, characterized by their invisibility and delayed effects, which individuals seldom notice in their everyday lives, such as contamination by toxins.

DISCUSSION QUESTIONS

1. Must environmentalists engage in dramatic image events to gain the attention of news media? Can you think of a television news story that provides in-depth coverage of an environmental concern?

2. Do media frames influence your understanding of environmental issues? Illustrate your answer by describing the different media frames used in news stories in campus or local newspapers and on a local radio or television station.

3. How did I frame this chapter? Does it present a particular viewpoint or representation of environmental media? Could this chapter have been framed differently?

4. How do you feel about the objectivity–advocacy debate—the call by some journalists for media's right to evaluate the competing arguments in an environmental controversy? What does *objective* mean to you? Do you believe that reporters have a duty to educate, to provide answers, and to equip readers and viewers with better arguments about crucial topics? Or should they be objective? Is this possible?

5. What effects (if any) does television have on your attitudes about and behavior toward the environment? Do popular programs such as *The Simpsons* affect your and others' attitudes about social and environmental issues such as nuclear power, vegetarianism, and corporations' environmental behavior?

6. To what extent are dominant ideologies reproduced by commercial news and entertainment media? Have you seen or heard mainstream media that question or challenge these ideologies?

7. Are there Internet sites that you rely upon for news and information about the environment other than those listed in this chapter?

REFERENCES

Ackerman, D. (1990, September 24). Albatrosses. *New Yorker, 24,* 61–88.

Ader, C. (1995). A longitudinal study of agenda setting for the issue of environmental pollution. *Journalism and Mass Communication Quarterly, 72,* 300–311.

Allan, S., Adam, B., & Carter, C. (2000). *Environmental risks and the media.* London: Routledge.

Allen, C., & Weber, J. (1983). How presidential media use affects individuals' beliefs about conservation. *Journalism Quarterly, 60,* 98–104.

Anderson, A. (1997). *Media, culture, and the environment.* New Brunswick, NJ: Rutgers University Press.

Atwater, T., Salwen, M., & Anderson, R. (1985). Media agenda setting with environmental issues. *Journalism Quarterly, 62,* 393–397.

Beder, S. (1997). *Global spin: The corporate assault on environmentalism.* White River Junction, VT: Chelsea Green Publishing Company.

Cherney, D. (1990, May 1). Freedom riders needed to save the forest: Mississippi summer in the California redwoods. *Earth First! Journal,* pp. 1, 6.

Cohen, B. C. (1963). *The press and foreign policy.* Princeton, NJ: Princeton University Press.

Cronon, W. (1996). (Ed.). *Uncommon ground: Rethinking the human place in nature.* New York: W. W. Norton & Company.

DeLuca, K. M. (1999). *Image politics: The new rhetoric of environmental activism.* New York: Guilford Press.

Demers, D., & Viswanath, K. (Eds.). (1999). *Mass media, social control, and social change: A macrosocial perspective.* Ames: Iowa State University Press.

Destruction of Brazil's rain forest seems to slow. (2004, April 8). *New York Times,* p. A4.

Douglas, S. (1997, April). Body-bag journalism. *The Progressive,* p. 19.

Downing, J. (1988). The alternative public realm: The organization of the 1980s anti-nuclear press in West Germany and Britain. *Media, Culture, and Society, 28,* 38–50.

Downs, A. (1972). Up and down with ecology–The "issue–attention" cycle. *Public Interest, 28,* 38–50.

Dunlap, R. E. (1992). Trends in public opinion toward environmental issues: 1965–1990. In R. E. Dunlap & A. G. Mertig (Eds.), *American environmentalism: The U.S. environmental movement, 1970–1990* (pp. 89–116). Philadelphia, Washington, DC, & London: Taylor & Francis.

ENS [Environmental News Service]. (2004, April 18). Ground-level ozone too high for new standard in 31 states. Retrieved April 18, 2004, from www.ens-news.com/0001.html

Eyal, C. H., Winter, J. P., & DeGeorge, W. F. (1981). The concept of time frame in agenda setting. In G. C. Wilhoit (Ed.), *Mass communication yearbook* (pp. 212–218). Beverly Hills, CA: Sage.

Ferris, B. (2001, February 22). Arctic oil: New technologies but still in the same messy business. TomPaine.com. Available at www.tompaine.com/feature2.cfm/ID/4070

Friedman, S. M. (2004). And the beat goes on: The third decade of environmental journalism. In S. Senecah (Ed.), *The environmental communication yearbook, 1,* 175–187. Mahwah, NJ: Erlbaum.

Frome, M. (1998). *Green ink: An introduction to environmental journalism.* Salt Lake City: University of Utah Press.

Gamson, W. A., & Modigliani, A. (1989). Media discourse and public opinion on nuclear power: A constructionist approach. *American Journal of Sociology, 95,* 1–37.

Gerbner, G. (1990). Advancing on the path to righteousness, maybe. In N. Signorielli & M. Morgan (Eds.), *Cultivation analysis: New directions in research* (pp. 249–262). Beverly Hills, CA: Sage.

Gerbner, G., Gross, L., Morgan, M., & Signorielli, N. (1986). Living with television: The dynamics of the cultivation process. In J. Bryant & D. Zillmann (Eds.), *Perspectives on media effects* (pp. 17–40). Mahwah, NJ: Erlbaum.

Gitlin, T. (1980). *The whole world is watching: Mass media and the making and unmaking of the new left.* Berkeley: University of California Press.

Goffman, E. (1974). *Frame analysis: An essay on the organization of experience.* Cambridge: Harvard University Press.

Gooch, G. D. (1996). Environmental concern and the Swedish press: A case study of the effects of newspaper reporting, personal experiences and social interaction on the public's perception of environmental risks. *European Journal of Communication, 11,* 107–127.

Guber, D. L. (2003). *The grassroots of a green revolution: Polling America on the environment.* Cambridge: MIT Press.

Hansen, A. (1993). *The mass media and environmental issues.* London: Leicester University Press.

Hays, S. P. (1987). *Beauty, health, and permanence: Environmental politics in the United States, 1955–1985.* Cambridge, UK: Cambridge University Press.

Hays, S. P. (2000). *A history of environmental politics since 1945.* Pittsburgh: University of Pittsburgh Press.

Herndl, C. G., & Brown, S. C. (1996). Introduction. In C. G. Herndl & S. C. Brown (Eds.), *Green culture: Environmental rhetoric in contemporary America* (pp. 3–20). Madison: University of Wisconsin Press.

Iyengar, S., & Kinder, D. R. (1987). *News that matters: Television and American opinion.* Chicago: University of Chicago Press.

Korte, D. (1997). The Simpsons as quality television. *The Simpsons archive.* Retrieved April 23, 2004, from www.snpp.com/other/papers/dk.paper.html

LaMay, C. L. (1991). Heat and light: The advocacy–objectivity debate. In C. L. LaMay & E. E. Dennis (Eds.), *Media and the environment* (pp. 103–113). Washington, DC, & Covello, CA: Island Press.

Lee, M. A., & Solomon, N. (1990). *Unreliable sources: A guide to detecting bias in news media.* New York: Carol Publishing Group.

Lippmann, W. (1922). *Public opinion.* New York: Harcourt, Brace.

Luechtefeld. L. (2005). *Covering pollution: An investigative reporter's guide.* Columbia, MO: Investigative Reporters and Editors Inc.

Mann, B. (Reporter). (2001, May 26). Bringing good things to life? *On the media.* New York: WNYC. Retrieved May 3, 2004, from www.onthemedia.org/transcripts/transcripts_052601_ge.html

Marhefka, M., Salimbene, D., & Pollock, J. C. (2002). Nationwide newspaper coverage of drilling in the Artic National Wildlife Reserve: A community structure approach. Paper presented at the annual conference of the National Communication Association, New Orleans, LA.

McComas, K., Shanahan, J., & Butler, J. (2001). Environmental content in prime-time network TV's non-news entertainment and fictional programs. *Society and Natural Resources, 14,* 533–542.

McCombs, M., & Shaw, D. (1972). The agenda setting function of the mass media. *Public Opinion Quarterly, 36,* 176–187.

McNair, B. (1994). *News and journalism in the UK.* London & New York: Routledge.

Meisner, M. (2004). Knowing nature through the media: An examination of mainstream print and television representations of the non-human world. In G. B. Walker & W. J. Kinsella (Eds.), *Finding our way(s) in environmental communication: Proceedings of the Seventh Biennial Conference on Communication and the Environment* (pp. 425–437). Corvallis: Oregon State University Department of Speech Communication.

Meister, M., & Japp, P. M. (Eds). (2002). *Enviropop: Studies in environmental rhetoric and popular culture.* Westport, CT: Praeger.

Miller, M. M., & Riechert, B. P. (2000). Interest group strategies and journalistic norms: News media framing of environmental issues. In S. Allan, B. Adam, & C. Carter (Eds.), *Environmental risks and the media* (pp. 45–54). London: Routledge.

Novic, K., & Sandman, P. M. (1974). How use of mass media affects views on solutions to environmental problems. *Journalism Quarterly, 51,* 448–452.

Opel, A., & Pompper, D. (Eds.). (2000). *Representing resistance: Media, civil disobedience, and the global justice movement.* Westport, CT: Praeger.

Ostman, R. E., & Parker, J. L. (1987). Impacts of education, age, newspaper, and television on environmental knowledge, concerns, and behaviors. *Journal of Environmental Education, 19,* 3–9.

Pan, Z., & Kosicki, G. M. (1993). Framing analysis: An approach to news discourse. *Political Communication, 10,* 55–76.

Price, J. (1999). *Flight maps: Adventures with nature in modern America.* New York: Basic Books.

Rodríguez, I. (2003). Mapping the emerging global order in news discourse: The meanings of globalization in news magazines in the early 1990s. In A. Opel & D. Pompper (Eds.), *Representing resistance: Media, civil disobedience, and the global justice movement* (pp. 77–94). Westport, CT: Praeger.

Roper Center for Public Opinion Research. (1997, February). *News junkies, news critics: How Americans use the news and what they think about it.* Arlington, VA: The Freedom Forum World Center.

Ryan, C. (1991). *Prime time activism: Media strategies for grassroots organizing.* Boston: South End Press.

Sachsman, D. B., Simon, J., & Valenti, J. (2002, June). The environment reporters of New England. *Science Communication, 23,* 410–441.

Schlechtweg, H. P. (1992). Framing Earth First! The MacNeil-Lehrer NewsHour and redwood summer. In C. L. Oravec & J. G. Cantrill (Eds.), *The conference on the discourse of environmental advocacy* (pp. 262–287). Salt Lake City: University of Utah Humanities Center.

Schwarze, S. (2003). Juxtaposition in environmental health rhetoric: Exposing asbestos contamination in Libby, Montana. *Rhetoric & Public Affairs, 6*(2), 313–335.

Shabecoff, P. (1994). Mudslinger on the earth-beat. *The Amicus Journal, 15*(4), 42–43.

Shabecoff, P. (2000). *Earth rising: American environmentalism in the 21st century.* Washington, DC: Island Press.

Shanahan, J. (1993). Television and the cultivation of environmental concern: 1988–92. In A. Hansen (Ed.), *The mass media and environmental issues* (pp. 181–197). Leicester, UK: Leicester University Press.

Shanahan, J., & McComas, K. (1999). *Nature stories: Depictions of the environment and their effects.* Cresskill, NJ: Hampton Press.

Soper, K. (1995). *What is nature?* Oxford, UK: Blackwell.

Spiess, B., & Ruskin, L. (2001, November 4). 2,000-acre query: ANWR bill provision caps development, but what does it mean? *Anchorage Daily News.*

Retrieved April 13, 2004, from www.adn.com/business/story/734443 p-781691c.html

Stocking, H., & Leonard, J. P. (1990). The greening of the press. *Columbia Journalism Review, 29,* pp. 37–44.

Suhonen, P. (1993). Environmental issues, the Finnish major press, and public opinion. *Gazette, 51,* 91–112.

Todd, A. M. (2002). Prime-time subversion: The environmental rhetoric of the Simpsons. In M. Meister & P. M. Japp (Eds.), *Enviropop: Studies in environmental rhetoric and popular culture* (pp. 63–80). Westport, CT: Praeger.

Torgerson, D. (1999). *The promise of green politics: Environmentalism and the public sphere.* Durham & London: Duke University Press.

Vig, N. J., & Kraft, M. E. (2003). Environmental policy from the 1970s to the twenty-first century. In N. J. Vig & M. E. Kraft (Eds.), *Environmental policy: New directions in the 21st century* (5th ed., pp. 1–32). Washington, DC: CQ Press.

Wall, G. (1999). Science, nature, and the nature of things: An instance of Canadian environmental discourse, 1960–1994. *Canadian Journal of Sociology, 24,* 53–85.

Weise, E. (2004, April 8). Study: Pregnant women eating too much fish. *USA Today,* p. 3A.

West, B. M., Lewis, M. J., Greenberg, M. R., Sachsman, D. B., & Rogers, R. M. (2003). *The reporter's environmental handbook.* New Brunswick, NJ: Rutgers University Press.

White, D. M. (1950). The "gatekeeper": A case study in the selection of news. *Journalism Quarterly, 27*(4): 383–390.

Wilkins, L., & Patterson, P. (1990). Risky business: Covering slow-onset hazards as rapidly developing news. *Political Communication and Persuasion, 7,* 11–23.

Yopp, J. J., & McAdams, K. C. (2003). *Reaching audiences: A guide to media writing* (3rd ed.). Boston: Allyn & Bacon.

6

Risk Communication

Nonexpert Publics and Acceptable Risk

Those who control the discourse on risk will most likely control the political battles as well.

—Plough & Krimsky (1987, p. 4)

Humans have always faced danger from natural events such as storms, earthquakes, disease, famine, and crop failure. However, with the rise of modern industrial society, we face ever-increasing danger from human sources as well—nuclear radiation, chemical contamination of water and food, asbestos and lead paint in older buildings, second-hand smoke from cigarettes, and more. As a result of growing public concern, since the 1970s federal agencies have begun to evaluate the risk of environmental hazards to the public's health and safety. Risk assessments typically ask such questions as, Will air pollution from this oil refinery affect the health of residents living within a half-mile radius? Can sewage treated to reduce the toxic chemicals in it be used safely as a fertilizer on farmers' fields? How can health agencies communicate information about such risks to residents, pregnant women, and other populations?

In sharing information about these and other potential hazards, health officials, media, scientists, and the general public engage in an important and sometimes controversial form of environmental communication called *risk communication.* The field of risk communication emerged in the 1980s in response to increasing environmental hazards and a growing discord between experts and the general public over what constitutes "acceptable risk." **Risk communication** is defined in its simplest form as "any public or private communication that informs individuals about the existence, nature, form, severity, or acceptability of risks" (Plough & Krimsky, 1987, p. 6). As we'll see, risk assessment actually involves more than that.

The chapter begins by describing what German sociologist Ulrich Beck (1992) has termed "risk society"—the growing threats to human health and safety from modern society itself. As we consider what it means to live in a risk society, we will explore the meaning of *risk* both as a technical construct and as a cultural construct. The differences in the meaning of *risk* have consequences for society's handling of its environmental dangers. As risk communication pioneers Alonzo Plough and Sheldon Krimsky (1987) pointed out almost two decades ago, "Those who control the discourse on risk will most likely control the political battles as well" (p. 4).

The second section of the chapter introduces the practice of risk communication. I'll take a critical look at some of the assumptions underlying the traditional model, which has been influenced by technical meanings of *risk*. I'll also discuss recent efforts to reform this model as we look at a risk communication campaign involving the experiences of groups who disproportionately face environmental hazards. Finally, the third section explores the ways that media reports may shape our perceptions of risks. In that section, I'll describe demands that news media open up spaces for the voices of residents, parents of sick children, and others who are most affected by environmental dangers.

When you have finished the chapter, you should be able to recognize some of the difficulties in defining "acceptable risk" and to appreciate the different perspectives on risk that are held by agencies such as the Environmental Protection Agency, by the news media, and by residents of communities themselves. In the end, society's ability to reduce environmental hazards may depend less on the language of technical risk—*parts per billion* and *dose exposures*—than upon the ability of experts and affected communities to speak honestly to one another about fairness and about who benefits (and who suffers) from dangerous environments.

Dangerous Environments: Assessing Risk

You may have seen the popular films *A Civil Action* and *Erin Brockovich*, which dramatize the experiences of two small towns in Massachusetts and

California where residents discovered that toxic contamination of their drinking water had caused leukemia, breast and uterine cancer, and other diseases. The films also portrayed the disillusionment and anger that many residents felt after they learned that official assurances that their water was safe to drink were untrue.[1] Both films portrayed the experiences of real communities, and both films call our attention to very real dramas about environmental risks. They also ask us to look more closely at the challenges to improving the communication among technical experts, the media, health officials, and the general public.

Risk Society

In his influential book *Risk Society: Towards a New Modernity,* sociologist Ulrich Beck (1992) argued that modern society has changed fundamentally in its ability to manage the consequences of its successful technical and economic development. He explained, "The gain in power from techno-economic 'progress' is being increasingly overshadowed by the production of risks" (p. 13). Unlike risks from nature or from 19th-century factories that affected specific individuals or groups, Beck characterizes today's **risk society** according to the large-scale nature of risks and the potential for irreversible threats to human life from modernization itself. These risks include such far-reaching and consequential hazards as nuclear power plant accidents, global climate change, chemical pollution, and the alteration of genetic strains from bioengineering.

In Beck's risk society, rapid scientific and technological changes entail unknown and unintended consequences. In addition, exposure to risks is unevenly distributed across the population. That is because the burden of coping with the hazards of new technologies and environmental pollutants often falls on the most vulnerable elements of the population: elderly people, children with respiratory problems, pregnant women, and residents of low-income neighborhoods with high concentrations of polluting facilities. As a result, a major environmental controversy of the 1980s occurred between the residents of at-risk communities and the technical experts and officials who too often assured them that polluting factories or buried toxic wastes posed no harm, when facts later proved such assurances false.

Too often, residents of affected communities felt that officials ignored the experiences and concerns of those suffering from environmental hazards. Lois Gibbs (1994), a former resident of Love Canal, New York, expressed the feelings of many: "Communities perceive many flaws in risk assessment. The first is who is being asked to take the risk and who is getting the benefit. From a community's perspective, risk assessments are 'the risks that someone else has chosen for you to take.' What is a life worth . . . but equally important is whose life" (pp. 328, 329).

Because many voices struggle to define risk, it is important to distinguish different meanings of risk and what constitutes acceptable risk for different parties. It is also important to appreciate the ways in which some evaluations of risk occur in the technical sphere (Chapter 1), whereas other approaches open risk assessment to a wider, public sphere. Indeed, there is heated controversy about whether risk is a technical matter that is determined objectively or a social construction that emerges from communication among experts, affected parties, and public agencies. Therefore, we will look at both technical and cultural meanings of *risk*, and in the next section we will examine the distinct approaches to risk communication invited by these differing meanings.

The Technical Model of Risk

By the 1980s, the public's fear of environmental hazards, along with the Environmental Protection Agency's mishandling of the health risks in high-profile cases such as Love Canal, had led to pressure on agencies to evaluate risk accurately and to do a better job in communicating with affected communities. In 1984, new EPA Administrator William Ruckelshaus proposed the terms *risk assessment* and *risk management* "as a common language for justifying regulatory proposals across the agency" (Andrews, 1999, p. 266). From a technical perspective, **risk assessment** is defined as the evaluation of the degree of harm or danger from some condition such as exposure to a toxic chemical, and **risk management** is defined as the implementation of steps to reduce the danger to the public and the environment.

In the years following Ruckelshaus's proposal, the EPA dramatically increased its technical analysis of the risks from nuclear power, pollution of drinking water, and pesticides and other chemicals in order to justify new health and safety standards for the commercial production, transport, and disposal of hazardous substances. Environmental policy professor Richard N. Andrews (1999) observed that, by the end of the 1980s, a "rhetoric of risk" had become the EPA's primary language for justifying its management of environmental hazards (p. 266).

Although the EPA is the major agency responsible for evaluating health and environmental risks, other federal agencies also have roles. Understanding the technical model of risk used by these agencies is important in its own right. In addition, understanding the restriction of this approach to the technical sphere of experts and agency personnel allows us to appreciate the type of risk communication that occurred in the 1980s and 1990s and why it generated so much controversy among the affected publics.

Risk Assessment

In everyday terms, *risk* is simply a rough estimate of the chances of something negative happening to us, such as an accident while driving on icy roads in the winter. Usually, our willingness to undertake something that may be dangerous suggests that we consider it to be an acceptable risk. For example, I'm still willing to drive in winter storms. However, for agencies such as the EPA or the Centers for Disease Control, risk is a quantitative concept. In this technical sense, **risk** is *the expected annual mortality* that results from some condition, such as exposure to a chemical substance. In other words, risk is a calculation of the probability that a certain number of people will die (usually from cancer) over a period of time (one year) from their exposure to a toxic chemical or other environmental hazard. But risk is not limited to mortality. It may include illness or injury as well. Risk communication scholar Katherine Rowan (1991) has noted that technical analysts view risk as "a multiplicative function of the severity of some hazard and its likelihood of occurrence (Risk = Severity × Likelihood)" (p. 303).

How do such agencies as the EPA, the federal Toxic Substances and Disease Registry, and the Centers for Disease Control know a risk's severity and its likelihood of occurrence? In such agencies, risk assessment occurs within a technical sphere of research labs and communication among experts such as toxicologists, epidemiologists, and other scientists. This process typically involves a **four-step procedure for risk assessment:**

1. *Hazard identification.* What is the potential source of danger? For example, does a waste incinerator emit highly toxic dioxins or other hazardous chemicals?

2. *Assessment of human exposure.* Are any human populations exposed to this hazard? If so, can the various routes or pathways of the hazardous substance to specific organs or tissues of human bodies be traced? Finally, how much (what dosage) of this substance enters these human bodies?

3. *Modeling of the dose responses.* What is the relationship between the dosage that is received and harmful responses or illnesses in the exposed population?

4. *Characterization of the overall risk.* What are the overall implications of the dose responses for the health of the exposed population? (Covello, 1993; Fischer, 2002)

The last step—the characterization of overall risk—usually seeks to combine the prior steps into an estimate of deaths or injuries expected annually from exposure to the hazard (Hornstein, 1992). Technical models of risk assessment use the resulting numerical value as the basis for judgments of **acceptable risk**. As we will see when we examine cultural models of risk, a judgment of acceptable or unacceptable risk inevitably involves values. Ultimately, acceptable risk is a judgment of the harms or dangers society is willing to accept (or not) and who is subject to this risk. Judgments of acceptable risk may involve a comparison with other risks, as well as estimates of the costs required to reduce these risks. As we'll see below, such judgments also involve questions of fairness and justice. For example, who bears the burden of exposure to a toxic waste incinerator, and who receives the benefit? Technical models of risk rarely consider such questions in arriving at an overall risk characterization.

One example of technical risk assessment occurred recently when the EPA announced that it would not regulate the presence of dioxins in sewage sludge used as fertilizer for farm crops. (Sewage sludge is a by-product of the process that some municipalities use to purify wastewater before releasing the water into local rivers. In the past, wastewater often contained the highly toxic chemical dioxin.) On October 17, 2003, the EPA summarized the results of its risk assessment for dioxins in sewage sludge.

First, the agency characterized the overall risk, announcing that "dioxins from this source [sludge] do not pose a significant risk to human health or the environment" (U.S. Environmental Protection Agency, 2003, para. 1). Second, it described the low probabilities of cancer in the different populations exposed to sewage sludge:

> The most highly exposed people, theoretically, are those people who apply sewage sludge as a fertilizer to their crops and animal feed and then consume their own crops and meat products over their entire lifetimes.
>
> EPA's analysis shows that even for this theoretical population, only 0.003 new cases of cancer could be expected each year or only 0.22 new cases of cancer over a span of 70 years. The risk to people in the general population of new cancer cases resulting from sewage sludge containing dioxin is even smaller due to lower exposures to dioxin in land-applied sewage sludge than the highly exposed farm family which EPA modeled. (U.S. Environmental Protection Agency, 2003, para. 1)

The EPA's decision not to regulate dioxin in sewage sludge set off a fierce controversy and raised questions not only about the limitations in technical risk analysis but also about the (lack of) involvement of the public in judgments about risk. While EPA officials commented that "the risk of new cancer cases from this source is small" (Heilprin, 2003, para. 3), a group of 73 environmental and farm worker groups petitioned the agency (unsuccessfully) for an immediate moratorium on the use of sewage sludge as a fertilizer for farm crops and animal feed (Werner, 2004). (For a skeptical background on the relationships between the EPA and industries pushing for the use of sludge for agricultural uses, see the book *Toxic Sludge Is Good for You! Lies, Damn Lies, and the Public Relations Industry,* by the editors of *PR Watch,* John Stauber and Sheldon Rampton [1995].)

Limitations of the Technical Model

The clash over sewage sludge helps to illustrate some of the difficulties with risk assessment that have surfaced in the last 20 years. In the case of sewage sludge, the National Research Council had criticized the EPA's reliance on outdated methods of detecting pathogens (harmful substances) and thus questioned the accuracy of the agency's risk assessment ("Government May Broaden the Regulating of Sewage Sludge," 2004). In other cases, the analysis of a particular risk, such as a recent acute or high-dose exposure to a toxic chemical, may not account for the health effects from a long-term, low-dose exposure to the same hazard. In other words, experiments in which high doses of the chemical were given to animals may not tell us much about the effects of long-term exposure of humans to smaller amounts of a harmful substance.

In the case of exposure to toxins such as dioxin or mercury, it also can be exceedingly difficult to trace the pathway (lungs, skin, etc.) by which individuals may be exposed or to measure with precision the cause–effect relationship between an exposure to toxins and specific damage to the body's respiratory, neurological, or reproductive systems. Gerald Markowitz and David Rosner, in *Deceit and Denial: The Deadly Politics of Industrial Pollution* (2002), observe that "it has often been difficult to show to the satisfaction of government regulators a direct correlation between particular chemicals from smokestacks and sewer pipes and the specific illnesses that clusters of people experience in particular communities" (p. 290).

The book *A Civil Action* and the Hollywood film based on it dramatized this problem in the town of Woburn, Massachusetts. There, the neighbors' exposure to toxic chemicals occurred years before any cases of childhood leukemia and other cancers became known. Yet, the technical sphere of experts and the legal system had difficulty determining which of the particular chemicals might have caused these illnesses and how seriously the victims had been exposed (Goldstein & Goldstein, 2002).

I encountered the same problem in the mid-1990s when I worked with the Jesus People Against Pollution (JPAP), a group of African American and white residents of a low-income community in Mississippi who lived next to an abandoned chemical plant. After the plant exploded and burned, the owners closed its doors and buried hundreds of chemical drums on the site and in the nearby countryside. Years later, residents began to complain of skin rashes, headaches, cancers, and reproductive problems. Many had inhaled toxic fumes when the plant caught fire and, later, had drunk water that they believed had been contaminated by chemicals seeping into the community's water source.

The efforts of JPAP to seek medical care for affected residents from state and federal health agencies were frustrated by the absence of any certainty that their illnesses had been caused by their exposure to the chemicals from the abandoned plant. At one meeting with staff from the Agency for Toxic Substances and Disease Registry, a clearly frustrated young African American woman pleaded for more accurate medical studies of the neighborhood, insisting, "The evidence is in our bodies!"

The Cultural-Experiential Model of Risk

The experience of these communities illustrates another difficulty with the technical model of environmental risk. The basic complaint of the individuals and communities that actually experience exposure to chemical hazards is that communication about risks is too often restricted to a technical sphere and thus excludes those who are most affected. That is, technical models equate *numerical risk* (expected annual mortality) with judgments about the experience of those forced to live with imposed or involuntary risks. Yet, as Beck (1998) explained, "There is a big difference between those who take risks and those who are victimized by risks others take" (p. 10). As a result, some public agencies have begun in recent years to solicit the experience and views of affected communities in their assessment of risks and judgments of what is an acceptable and unacceptable risk. It is this **cultural-experiential model of risk** that I will now describe, along with the role of a wider public sphere in assessing risk.

Environmental "Hazards" Versus "Outrage"

Political scientist Frank Fischer (2002) notes that experts often make assumptions about environmental risks that are quite removed from the experience of those affected by these risks. As a result, ordinary citizens' understanding of risk may be very different from a technical assessment. Fischer explains that the context in which a risk is embedded raises a number of questions that may affect one's judgment of whether a risk is acceptable or not: "Is the risk imposed by distant or unknown officials? Is it engaged in voluntarily? Is it reversible?" (p. 65).

Peter Sandman (1987), the former director of the Environmental Communication Research Program at Rutgers University, has made a similar point. Sandman proposed that risk be defined as a combination of technical risk and social factors that people often consider in judging risk. He suggested that what technical analysts call a "risk" instead be called a "hazard" and that other social and experiential concerns be called "outrage." **Hazard** is what experts mean by risk (expected annual mortality), and **outrage** refers collectively to those factors that the public considers in assessing whether their exposure to a hazard is acceptable. "Risk, then, is the sum of hazard and outrage" (p. 21).

Here are some of the main outrage factors that Sandman (1987) believed people consider in judging an environmental hazard:

1. *Voluntariness.* Do people assume a risk voluntarily, or is it coerced or imposed on them?

2. *Control.* Can individuals prevent or control the risk themselves?

3. *Fairness.* Are people asked to endure greater risks than their neighbors or others, especially without access to greater benefits?

4. *Process.* Is the agency defining the risk perceived as honest and concerned about the community, or as arrogant? Does the agency listen? Does the agency tell the community what's going on before making a decision?

5. *Diffusion in time and space.* Is the risk spread over a large population or concentrated in one's own community?

Sandman's model of Hazard + Outrage is particularly useful in calling our attention to the experiences of a community that might be left out of technical calculations. This model also suggests the difference that might result from enlarging the public sphere for the assessment of risk to include affected groups. Sandman's definition is not without its critics, however. Some have suggested that this definition subtly characterizes scientific or technical assessments of "hazards" as rational and the emotional "outrage" of communities as irrational. Therefore, they fear that such characterizations can be used to marginalize or trivialize community voices in debates about risk. (See "Another Viewpoint: Irrational Outrage?")

Another Viewpoint: Irrational Outrage?

Journalists Sheldon Rampton and John Stauber write and edit the quarterly newsletter *PR Watch: Public Interest Reporting on the PR/Public Affairs Industry*. In their recent book *Trust Us, We're Experts!* they take a critical look at the uses of Sandman's well-known formula ("Risk . . . is the sum of hazard and outrage") by the public relations industry.

Rampton and Stauber (2002) explain: By suggesting that the public's outrage is irrational, companies may be more interested in allaying outrage "rather than focusing on real hazards or harms to the public" (p. 105). They write:

> This deceptively simple formula [risk equals hazard plus outrage] has become a staple in PR industry discussions of risk communication. . . . By understanding that risk equals hazard plus outrage, [Thomas] Buckmaster [general manager of the public relations firm Hill & Knowlton] says, risk communicators can overcome the fear and hostility of "grassroots members, stakeholders, and the public at large." . . . Once people are outraged, they don't listen to hazard statistics . . . don't use numerical risk comparisons." In fact, he says, "managing the outrage is more important than managing the risk." (p. 106, quoting Buckmaster, 1997.)

Rampton and Stauber suggest that if businesses are more interested in managing the outrage than in focusing on real hazards or harms, they will invest in public relations campaigns rather than in changing the business practices that are causing public concern.

Cultural Rationality and Risk

When judgments about the social context and experience of exposed populations enter definitions of risk, a broader and more complex *cultural rationality* arises. Pioneering scholars in risk communication Alonzo Plough and Sheldon Krimsky (1987) define **cultural rationality** as a type of knowledge that includes personal, familiar, and social concerns in evaluating a real risk event. As distinct from technical analysis of risk, cultural rationality "is shaped by the circumstances under which the risk is identified and publicized, the standing or place of the individual in his or her community, and

Table 6.1   Factors Relevant to the Technical and Cultural Rationality of Risk

Technical Rationality	Cultural Rationality
Trust in scientific methods, explanations; evidence.	Trust in political culture and democratic process.
Appeal to authority and expertise.	Appeal to folk wisdom, peer groups, and traditions.
Boundaries of analysis are narrow and reductionistic.	Boundaries of analysis are broad; include the use of analogy and historical precedent.
Risks are depersonalized.	Risks are personalized.
Emphasis on statistical variation and probability.	Emphasis of the impact of risks on the family and community.
Appeal to consistency and universality.	Focus on particularity; less concerned about consistency . . .
Those impacts that cannot be uttered are irrelevant.	Unanticipated or unarticulated risks are relevant.

SOURCE: Plough & Kromsky (1987), p. 9.

the social values of the community as a whole (Fischer, 2002, pp. 132–133). Such rationality includes folk wisdom, the insights of peer groups, traditions, an understanding of how risk impacts one's family and community, and sensitivity to particular events as well as overall patterns. (See Table 6.1.)

Harvard University professors Phil Brown and Edwin J. Mikkelsen (1990) provide a disturbing example of the differences between risk assessments made in a restricted technical sphere and those made in a wider public sphere. In their classic study *No Safe Place: Toxic Waste, Leukemia, and Community Action*, they cite the experience of residents in Friendly Hills, a suburb of Denver, Colorado. In the early 1980s, mothers from the neighborhood wondered why so many of their children were sick or dying. After EPA and state health officials refused to study the problem, the women decided to canvass door to door to document the extent of the problem. They found that 15 children who lived in the neighborhood from 1976 to 1984 had died from cancer, severe birth defects, and other immunological diseases. The mothers suspected that the cause of these deaths was toxic waste discharge from a nearby industrial facility owned by Martin Marietta.

State health officials dismissed the mothers' findings and denied that there was any environmental or other unusual cause of the children's deaths. They insisted that all the illnesses were within "expected limits," and although there were more childhood cancer cases than expected, the officials said that "they might be due to chance" (Brown & Mikkelsen, 1990, p. 143). One week after the officials declared the waste discharges safe, "the Air Force, which runs a test facility on the Martin Marietta site, admitted that the groundwater was contaminated by toxic chemicals" (p. 143). Brown and Mikkelsen describe what happened next: "Residents found that Martin Marietta had a record of toxic spills. . . . Several months later, EPA scientists found serious contamination . . . in a plume, or underground wave, stretching from the Martin Marietta site toward the water plant" (pp. 143–144). The Harvard professors concluded, "The belated discovery of what residents knew long before is eerie and infuriating—and, sadly, it is common to many toxic waste sites" (p. 144).

The Friendly Hills case is not isolated. Environmental communication scholar Tarla Rai Peterson (1997) reported a similar experience among health workers along the Rio Grande River in Brownsville, Texas, and Matamoros, Mexico. This region is known for its high concentration of *maquiladoras,* or manufacturing plants, along the Mexican side of the border, encouraged by the North American Free Trade Agreement (NAFTA). Since 1990, environmentalists and health groups have been concerned about this region because of its polluted air, poor housing and sanitation, unsafe drinking water, and release of raw sewage and chemicals directly into local streams and the Rio Grande River.

Unfortunately, the area also has been known since 1991 for its high rate of anencephalic births. **Anencephaly** occurs during pregnancy, when the end of the fetus's neural tube fails to close, resulting in a partial or complete absence of the brain. "Babies who are born with this condition die within a few hours" (Peterson, 1997, p. 128). A controversial 1992 risk study by the Texas Department of Health (TDH) and the Centers for Disease Control (CDC) classified the outbreak of the area's anencephalic births as "a long-term incidence" (p. 129) rather than an epidemic. At the same time, the study admitted a major limitation in its findings due to incomplete records of birth defects in area hospitals and a lack of information about nonhospitalized births.

Health workers in Brownsville and Matamoros complained that TDH–CDC investigators' cultural insensitivity to people and their health practices had limited the potential of the study. In addition to use of an English-language survey instrument to interview Hispanic women, the study also overlooked other factors in characterizing the overall risk of anencephaly. Two of Peterson's (1997) informants from the region—Carmen de la Cruz Gomez and Rosa Ramirez—described some of these cultural factors:

> Ramirez maintained that the CDC "didn't know our culture" . . . and did not
> attempt to learn . . . Although "they're supposed to become sensitive to the
> particulars of the area, in terms of health care," she pointed out, the CDC, for

example, "didn't know about our parturas, our lay midwives" [who deliver a large percentage of the babies in the region]. . . . [Another] irritation, explained Gomez, was that "any environmental concern that we gave them was just completely ignored." . . .

She and Ramirez noted, for example, that all the mothers who had given birth to anencephalic infants during the past year had lived extremely near the Rio Grande during the early part of their pregnancies. When they mentioned this concern and provided THD–CDC with a map, they were told that it was irrelevant to the study. (p. 160)

Peterson (1997) concluded that the reports of CDC epidemiologists and the reassurances of the area's economic boosters conflicted with the stories of mothers and health workers regarding what was and was not relevant to the risk of anencephalic births. Technical risk models fragment "the body into independent pieces, such as 'age' and 'percent of neural tube development,'" whereas health workers such as Rosa Ramirez emphasized the social and cultural contexts in which these families lived (pp. 169–170).

In such cases as Friendly Hills and Brownsville, a cultural-experiential model for evaluating risk challenges the symbolic legitimacy boundaries (Chapter 2) of technical agencies and their methods. That is, the questioning by mothers or community health workers of the limited approaches of these agencies threatens the images of knowledge and authority that usually benefit the agencies. At the same time, I want to stress that *a reliance on cultural rationality does not reject technical assessments of risk.* Indeed, an understanding of the pathways of chemical hazards to the human body and the level of doses experienced is vitally important, even though it is challenging to identify these pathways and effects accurately. But a cultural-experiential approach expands the technical model of risk to include considerations of the contexts in which risks occur and the values of those who are asked to live with environmental dangers.

The differences between technical and cultural models of risk raise important questions about what we consider acceptable risk, how we assess risk, and ultimately how we convey information about risk to others. These differences matter in the larger society's treatment of risk. As environment and technology scholar Ortwin Renn (1992) explains, "If risk is seen as an objective property . . . the implications are obvious. Order risks according to 'objective' measures of probability and harm, and allocate resources to reduce the greatest risks first. If, on the other hand, risk is seen as a cultural or social construction, risk management . . . should reflect social values" (p. 54). These differences can be seen clearly in the ways public agencies choose to communicate with affected publics.

Risk Communication and Nonexpert Publics

As tensions grew between experts and at-risk communities over environmental pollution, scholars, activists, and agency officials began to pay closer attention to the communication practices of agencies like the EPA in describing these dangers. Although the study of risk communication barely existed before 1986, since then the field has grown steadily in response to increasing complaints about the quality, trustworthiness, and accuracy of experts' risk reports and interactions with affected communities. As we noted at the opening of this chapter, risk communication in its most general form is "any public or private communication that informs individuals about the existence, nature, form, severity, or acceptability of risk" (Plough & Krimsky, 1987, p. 6). However, as practiced by health and environmental agencies, risk communication has come to mean something more specific in its objectives and its assumptions about target audiences.

In this section, we'll look at two quite different models of risk communication that have emerged since the late 1980s, reflecting the technical and cultural meanings of risk we described in the first section of this chapter. These are (1) the traditional or technical model of risk communication, which seeks to translate numerical assessments of risk to public audiences, and (2) the cultural model of risk communication, which draws upon the experiences and local knowledge of affected communities as well as on laboratory models of risk assessment.

The Technical Model of Risk Communication

Early experiences with risk communication grew out of the need of federal managers of environmental projects (such as toxic waste site cleanups) to gain the public's acceptance of risk estimates. Other experiences grew from health agencies' need to communicate about risk to target populations (for example, pregnant women, smokers, or substance abusers). This early model of risk communication was influenced heavily by technical risk assessment. **Technical risk communication** is defined as the translation of technical data about environmental or health risks for public consumption, with the goal of educating a target audience. Communication is usually one-way: Information is channeled from experts to a general audience (Krimsky & Plough, 1988, p. 6). The EPA's press release announcing that "only 0.003 new cases of cancer could be expected each year" from dioxins in sewage sludge is an example of this technical approach to risk communication.

Inform, Change, and Assure

The main goal of technical risk communication is to educate public audiences about numerical risk. As used by the EPA and many health agencies, this goal traditionally has three objectives: to inform, to change, and (sometimes) to assure.

1. To *inform* local communities of an environmental or health hazard: The EPA's (2002) guide for its Superfund site mangers, *Superfund Community Involvement Toolkit: Risk Communication,* defines risk communication explicitly as "the process of informing people about the hazards of a Superfund site" (p. 1). The agency explains that the purpose of such communication is to help residents of affected communities understand risk assessment and the management of the cleanup of a contaminated site by forming "valid perceptions of the likely hazards" (p. 1, emphasis added). Similarly, hazard experts Michael Lindell and Ronald Perry (2004) have proposed a model of technical risk communication to inform target populations of the "hazards of extreme events" from natural events (e.g., hurricanes, floods, and earthquakes) as well as hazards transmitted through nature (e.g., industrial accidents that affect nearby residents) (p. 2). Their Protective Action Decision Model builds on traditional theories of communication similar to the direct transmission approach (Chapter 5); however, their model takes into account the social and behavioral factors influencing an audience's reception of a risk message. Importantly, technical risk communication occurs after the assessment of the effects of a hazard has been made. It is largely one-way communication (experts to laypeople). In addition to informing target populations, such communication is used in other phases of risk management. For example, managers of a toxic waste cleanup site may need the participation of community members if they are to gain permission to take water samples on private property or mobilize support for specific cleanup strategies at sites near residents' homes.

2. To *change* risky behavior: Public health agencies long have had as part of their mission the goal of educating the public about unsafe food products and risky personal behaviors (such as teen pregnancy, substance abuse, and driving without seat belts). This focus on health education has evolved in recent years and now targets at-risk populations with "slick national media campaigns developed by . . . advertising firms in conjunction with science-based strategies in the attempt to change 'unhealthy' behaviors" (Plough & Krimsky, 1987, p. 4). Nevertheless, the objective of health risk communication remains the same: "Don't eat fish from this lake," "Don't drink alcohol while pregnant," etc.

3. To *assure* those exposed to a perceived hazard that the risk is acceptable. Assuring local residents that a chemical plant or a waste landfill is safe is a controversial chapter in environmental history. The clashes between residents and public officials in Love Canal, Woburn, and Friendly Hills are woven into the memories of many environmental agencies today. As a result, the EPA now cautions its managers at Superfund sites to avoid terms such as safe and dangerous when speaking with residents in affected communities. Its risk communication manual advises, "Instead, explain risk numbers in ranges: 1–10 ppb [parts per billion] as 'low risk,' for example" (2002, p. 5).

A recent report of newly discovered contamination at the nation's Superfund waste sites led the EPA to issue a carefully nuanced statement to media, reassuring the public and, in particular, residents living near the waste sites. An Associated Press report handled the release this way:

> Almost one in 10 of the nation's 1,230 Superfund waste sites lack[s] [sic] adequate safety controls to ensure people and drinking water won't be contaminated, according to the Environmental Protection Agency. . . . [An EPA consultant said] the sites . . . "all have some contamination, but none . . . presents an imminent risk to human health" because of either emergency cleanup measures in place or the posting of fish advisories and other official warnings. (Associated Press, p. A3, 2004)

Despite the EPA's qualifications, the social context of risk communication suggests that there are often symbolic overtones of assurance embedded in the way that scientists and technical experts interact with at-risk communities. This was particularly the case in the tumultuous 1980s and early 1990s, when such communities fought with the EPA over risk assessments of hazardous waste sites. Plough and Krimsky (1987) observe that in some of these situations, "a scientist speaking to a community about the health risks of a chemical dump may be carrying out a ritual that displays confidence and control. The technical information . . . is secondary to the real goal of the communicator: 'Have faith; we are in charge'" (p. 7). (For an excellent case study of such failed assurances, see the discussion of the discourse surrounding the accident at the Three Mile Island nuclear plant in 1979 by Farrell & Goodnight, 1981.)

On the other hand, EPA has tried to assist communities in learning how to evaluate risks for themselves. Its recent manual, *How Safe Am I? Helping Communities Evaluate Chemical Risks* (1999) is one effort to provide local journalists and community leaders with guidance in assessing the risks associated with facilities such as oil refineries or manufacturing plants. (For a copy of this guide, see www.nsc.org/public/xroads/risk.pdf.)

Figure 6.1   Al Tuwaitha, Iraq—This girl is standing outside the Al-Majidat school for girls (900 pupils) next to the Tuwaitha nuclear facility

(© Greenpeace / Philip Reynaers)

The Assumption of the Irrational Individual

Technical approaches to risk communication sometimes make assumptions about the recipients of risk messages that appear to blame these persons. Under the technical model, "the success of risk communication is measured by the degree to which popular attitudes reflect the technical rationality of risk and the extent that popular behavior conforms to technocratic values" (Plough & Krimsky, 1987, p. 8). Conversely, such models seem to assume that any failure of technical risk communication is the result of public fear, irrationality, or other emotional factors.

Underlying this attitude on the part of some risk professionals is a specific assumption about laypeople who live near environmental hazards. Plough and Krimsky (1987) pointed out that both health and environmental risk agencies share the notion of the **irrational individual** (p. 6). That is, agency officials tend to assume that individuals underestimate the dangers of personal health behaviors such as smoking and not wearing seat belts, but in environmental affairs, the error is reversed: Agencies assume that individuals have exaggerated fears of chemical hazards, nuclear plant accidents, and so forth.

This view of the public's irrationality is fueled by a host of psychological studies of popular risk perceptions. Such studies typically have found that laypeople's perceptions of risk don't match (in the judgment of experts) so-called objective estimates of the likelihood of danger. "While scientists cite motor vehicle use, smoking, and alcohol consumption as three of the riski-est activities of modern life, laypeople instead believe nuclear power to top that list, often underestimating fatalities caused by less 'dramatic' accidents and diseases, while overemphasizing the magnitude of danger found in new technologies" (Guber, 2003, p. 7). For example, psychology professor David G. Myers (2001) reports, "National Safety Council data reveal that in the last half of the 1990s Americans were, mile for mile, 37 times more likely to die in a vehicle crash than on a commercial flight. . . . Flying understandably feels dangerous. But we have actually been less likely to crash and die on any flight than, when coin tossing, to flip 22 heads in a row" (paras. 5, 6).

This belief that the public is irrational in assessing risks has contributed to the dominance of the technical model of risk communication. Critics of risk management have argued that "without better risk communication from the top down, public attitudes toward environmental risks" will continue to pressure "scarce resources of time and money into all the wrong places" (Guber, 2003, p. 7; Breyer, 1993). The typical response of agency officials and experts to concerns about the public's acceptance of technical risk esti-mates has been to inject more expertise into the process, "either through increased grants of authority to experts or better citizen education, so that *the affected public might more rationally evaluate the risks they face with hazardous wastes or at least respect more the expertise of professional deci-sion makers*" (Williams & Matheny, 1995, p. 167, emphasis added).

But is this "elites-to-ignorant" model of risk communication (Rowan, 1991, p. 303) based on an accurate view of the public's judgments of risk? Many risk communication scholars, as well as community activists, argue that the technical model fails to acknowledge the concerns of those individuals who are most intimately affected by environmental dangers. (We will return later to this "elites-to-ignorant" approach in Chapter 8, "Environmental Justice: Voices from the Grassroots.")

The Cultural Model of Risk Communication

In his influential essay "Technical and Democratic Values in Risk Analysis," the EPA's senior policy advisor Daniel J. Fiorino (1989) argued that "the lay public are not fools" in judging environmental risks (p. 294). He identified three areas in which the public's intuitive and experiential judgments differed most from technical risk analysis:

1. "Concern about low-probability but high-consequence events": For example, a 1 percent chance that an accident will occur but a terrible death toll if it does.

2. A "desire for consent and control in social management of risks": The public's feeling that they have a say in decisions about risk is the opposite of a coerced or involuntary imposition of risk.

3. "The relationship of judgments about risk to judgments about social institutions": In other words, the acceptability of risk may depend on citizens' confidence in the institution that is conducting a study, managing a facility, or monitoring its safety. (p. 294)

Fiorino (1989) argued that public input to risk assessment often improves the quality of decisions about handling risks and also increases the likelihood that the decisions will be seen as legitimate. In each case, the concerns of the affected community are "expressions of democratic values, and . . . these values affect lay reactions to risk problems" (p. 294). As a result, risk communication that fails to take these judgments into account is less likely to win the confidence or support of the community.

FYI: Risk Communication at a Nuclear Waste Site

For a case study that examines the tensions between technical and democratic approaches to risk communication at a toxic waste site, see Jennifer Duffield Hamilton (2003), "Exploring Technical and Cultural Appeals in Risk Communication: The Fernald Radium Case," *Risk Analysis, 23,* pp. 291–302.

Hamilton argues that tensions in risk communication often result from the different "frames of acceptance" that scientists and residents use to understand environmental risks and their interests in the management of a toxic waste site. The case looks at the Department of Energy's nuclear weapons facility at Fernald, Ohio, and examines the different appeals that result from technical and cultural understandings of risk.

Citizen Participation in Risk Communication

In recent years, some agencies have recognized the need for a **cultural model of risk communication,** that is, an approach that involves the affected public in assessing risk and designing risk communication campaigns, and that recognizes the cultural knowledge and the experience of local communities. A major step toward defining such a model was taken in 1996, when the National Research Council released a report, *Understanding Risk: Informing Decisions in a Democratic Society*. The NRC report acknowledged that technical risk assessment was no longer sufficient to cope with the public's concerns about environmental dangers. It called for greater public participation and use of local knowledge in risk studies, and it pointedly noted that understanding environmental risk requires "a *broad understanding* of the relevant losses, harms, or consequences to the interested and affected parties, *including what the affected parties believe the risks to be in particular situations*" (National Research Council, 1996, p. 2, emphasis added).

Some health and environmental risk agencies have taken this tenet further to develop new practices in risk communication that recognize cultural knowledge and the experience of local communities. For example, communication scholars Jeffrey Grabill and Michelle Simmons (1998) propose a "critical rhetoric" for risk communication that entails three principles. Such an approach

1. sees risk as socially constructed and rhetorical . . . The meaning and value of risk in a given situation is [sic] a function of multiple and sometimes competing discourses. . . .

2. focuses on the processes of decision making . . . [especially] on the relations of power within decision-making processes, asking questions about who participates and in whose interests decisions are made[,]

   and . . .

3. seeks to contextualize and localize risk situations . . . [by encouraging] local participation. (pp. 428–429)

Similar concerns have begun to appear in risk communication, in particular from health agencies that work with vulnerable populations. In each case, the agencies usually identify community partners with whom to collaborate in designing communication campaigns that take a broad approach to the meanings of risk. One example of this model is the ongoing project with the Hmong community in Milwaukee.

Risk Communication and the Hmong Community

A culturally appropriate approach to risk communication has been unfolding in Milwaukee, Wisconsin. The University of Wisconsin's Marine and Freshwater Biomedical Sciences Center has been a regional leader in sharing knowledge of environmental and health risks with at-risk communities. In association with the National Institute for Environmental Health

Sciences, one of the center's objectives has been "to increase the knowledge and involvement of minority communities in environmental health issues, including awareness of the risks and benefits of fish consumption by the Hmong community in Milwaukee and understanding of the health risks of childhood obesity to Latino children" (NIEHS, 2003a, para. 1).

The Hmong are recent immigrants from Southeast Asia. In Vietnam, the Hmong culture depended heavily upon fish for their diets, and in their new home in the American Midwest they've turned to fishing in local waters and in the Great Lakes. Coming from a rural, relatively unpolluted country, they have little understanding of pollution and contamination of waters and fish in Wisconsin. As a consequence, the Center reports that Hmong fishers tend to "ignore the conventional warnings posted by the Department of Natural Resources about eating fish containing methyl mercury, PCBs and other chemicals" (NIEHS, 2003b, para. 2). The center also noted that the federal government recently had recommended lowering the safe level of exposure to methyl mercury in fish. This meant that families who depended upon fish from local waterways should reduce their weekly consumption of certain types of fish.

With the new warnings of the health risks from eating contaminated fish, the center felt that it was important to find effective means to communicate risks and benefits of fish consumption to the Hmong population. However, its approach departed from the traditional (technical) model of risk communication. Although its goal still was to inform the community about the hazards of eating fish contaminated with methyl mercury and PCBs, the university's Marine and Freshwater Biomedical Sciences Center proposed to work in collaboration with the community to design its communication campaign. The objective was to communicate in *a culturally sensitive way that results in active consideration of this issue within the context of the fishing practices of the Hmong people* (NIEHS, 2003a, para. 5, emphasis added). Collaboration between the center's scientists and the community included the Hmong American Friendship Association and the Sixteenth Street Community Health Center, the major health care provider for these residents.

The communication plan that grew from this interaction of scientists and members of the community relied on the Hmong native language and an awareness of Hmong cultural traditions. The main communication vehicle was a video titled "Beneath the Waters," which featured local Hmong residents "speaking to their community within a rich, cultural context that values fishing" (NIEHS, 2003b, para. 2). And because pregnant women and children were at higher risk, the center and its partners decided to develop approaches relating specifically to these populations. In addition, they relied upon Hmong focus groups to discuss the framing of the content of the communication campaign.

Table 6.2   Models of Risk Communication

	Technical Model	*Cultural Model*
Type of communication:	Usually one-way (experts-to-laypeople)	Collaborative (citizens-experts-agencies)
Source of knowledge of risk:	Science/technology	Science *plus* local, cultural knowledge and experience
Objectives:	1. To translate/inform	1. To inform by recognizing social contexts of meaning
	2. To change risky behavior	2. To change risky behavior when in the interests of affected groups
	3. To assure concerned groups	3. To involve affected groups in judgments of acceptable and unacceptable risks

Based on this collaboration, the center's risk communication campaign decided to include information about "the nutritional value of eating fish (benefits), the problems associated with eating contaminated fish (risks), how to recognize different species of fish, safer fishing areas and how to find them, and how to prepare fish to minimize exposure to contaminants" (NIEHS, 2003b, para. 2). The center and its community partners felt that a balanced presentation about pollution and fish consumption was important to gain a respectful hearing and not to alienate the Hmong people.

The center also relied upon volunteers in the Hmong community to distribute the video to households and local stores and to show it at Hmong festivals. Finally, the center and its partners worked with the local middle school to develop a module for its life science class that would educate inner-city students about eating contaminated fish. The risk communication project is ongoing among the Hmong community, largely as a result of the support and participation of local leaders, residents, and professionals in the community itself. As such, the project illustrates well the principal differences between the traditional (technical) form and the cultural model of risk communication. (For a summary of these differences, see Table 6.2.)

The University of Wisconsin–Milwaukee's Hmong risk communication approach reflects many of the democratic values in risk analysis first proposed by Fiorino (1989). Fiorino was concerned with the dilemma of "reconciling democratic ideals and citizen-centered values with the rationality of elite institutions and formal decision processes" (p. 293, quoting Plough &

Krimsky, 1987, p. 6). Whereas technical models of risk reflect numerical probabilities, the affected citizens living near a toxic waste site or fishing from polluted waters may desire to be part of the decision-making process and to have confidence in the social institutions responsible for managing risk. These are reflections of democratic values and must be part of any communication among scientists, agency officials, and members of an at-risk community.

Still, risk warnings that originate from the EPA, universities, or other governmental agencies do not occur in a vacuum. News reports of oil spills or the effects of eating contaminated fish also influence our perceptions of risk, prompting official actions and influencing the behavior of at-risk communities. I've explored some of the factors that influence media coverage of the environment in general in Chapter 5. Here, I'll describe specific, major concerns about media reports of environmental risk.

Media Reporting of Risk

With the growing awareness of environmental hazards, multiple interests and voices now compete to characterize risk: scientists, public health experts, parents of sick children, industry spokespersons, EPA officials, and others. In a real sense, media have become an important public sphere within which many voices and claims to rationality compete to evaluate and define risks (Cottle, 2000). News reports, talk shows, and Internet discussion boards and listservs often provide discursive space for communication about environmental dangers. Yet, such discourse is sometimes plagued by incomplete or misleading information about risks; sometimes it is intended to reassure a frightened public rather than to provide relevant information for public action.

A classic illustration of media confusion about serious risk occurred after the accident to the cooling system and subsequent damage to the reactor core at Pennsylvania's Three Mile Island nuclear plant on March 28, 1979. Rhetorical scholars Thomas Farrell and Thomas Goodnight (1981) described communication about the accident by media, government, and industry officials as "conspicuous confusion and failure" (p. 283). In their study of the discourse in response to this accident, they found that "reporters were unable to judge the validity of technical statements. Technicians often could not sense the relevance of reporters' questions. Government sources, frequently at odds with one another, could not decide what information to release . . . Some representatives of the nuclear power industry made misleading statements" (Farrell & Goodnight, 1981, p. 273).

As we saw in the last chapter, media themselves face significant constraints in covering the environment. Thus, while attempting to provide information about complex and serious hazards, reporters and editors also must negotiate a thicket of journalistic norms: Is the story newsworthy? How should it be framed? Will the story command the attention and interest of readers or viewers? Do sensational reports override substantive information? Furthermore, such factors influence not only *what* is reported about environmental risks, but they also affect *who* speaks about risk. For example, are cultural rationality claims of parents and other affected groups included in media reports? Not surprisingly, the answer to such questions is not a simple yes or no. In this section, I describe some of the ways in which risk is reported and factors that contribute to media coverage of environmental dangers.

Media Reports of Risk: Accurate Information or Sensational Stories?

A common criticism from scientists and risk managers is that news stories about risk often give readers inaccurate information or sensational images rather than substantive coverage of an environmental hazard. For example, accounts of exploding tanker trucks, oil spills off coastlines, or accidents at nuclear power plants call our attention to *low-probability but high-consequence* (acute) occurrences. That is, such risks occur only occasionally, but their effects on the environment and on human safety are significant when they do. Often, in these cases, news reports emphasize the impact on victims—sick children, oil-coated sea birds—but fail to explore contributing causes or the steps needed to prevent such dangers. Such tendencies to sensationalize news coverage of risk are accentuated by the importance of visual images, particularly for television. One study of television coverage of acute risks versus ongoing, low-impact, or chronic risks concluded, "Network evening news coverage surely tends to reinforce the public's overestimation of the health impact of acute risk events and underestimation of most chronic risk issues. The public's conception of risk is almost certainly distorted by television's focus on catastrophes and its dependence on films." (Greenberg, Sachsman, Sandman, & Salomone, 1989).

Some communication scholars have been critical of sensationalized risk news. Mass communication professor Donnalyn Pompper (2004) suggests that this type of story may play to understandable human interest, but it "absolves journalists of addressing the more complex environmental picture" of risk (p. 106). In other cases, scientists criticize news stories about risk for inaccuracy and misrepresentation of important data and conclusions. For example, Singer (1990) compared news about risk to the original research and found that a large percent of the stories had problems with accuracy: Forty percent of the stories contained an "outright error," while only 7% were completely accurate in characterizing findings about the hazards (quoted in Dunwoody and Peters, 1992, p. 207).

In fairness, journalists face difficult constraints in reporting risk issues. Dunwoody and Peters (1992) observed a decade ago that journalists tackle risk stories in ways that differ from the way scientists and agency officials think about risk: "A reporter's decisions about what topics to cover and how to construct the ensuing stories . . . reflect a rather complicated dance" (p. 209), including the needs of the media organization, the motivations of sources to get information to reporters, and resonance with readers.

The quality of the resulting news accounts can be decidedly mixed. On the one hand, many studies show weaknesses in news reports about the complexities of risk and, in particular, a failure to place risk in a wider perspective. (For example, is the risk of arsenic from the runoff from an abandoned mine that gets into drinking water greater or similar to the normal, or background level, of arsenic from naturally occurring sources? If the risk is greater, what can the area's residents do to avoid contamination?) Media scholar Sharon M. Friedman (2004) points out that the neglect of technical details and the failure to compare risks with more familiar circumstances means that readers and viewers are unable to "understand and judge their own risk levels" (p. 181). On the other hand, many reporters believe they're doing a good job. Friedman notes that a recent study found that 67% of journalists in New England "rejected a suggestion that environmental writers generally have overblown environmental risks, unduly alarming the public" (Friedman, 2004, p. 181; Sachsman et al., 2002). Finally, scientific research on risk itself may be ambiguous and hence difficult for reporters to interpret fairly or accurately for laypeople. Readers of local newspapers in the town of Teesside in northeastern England experienced the difficulties of media in the competing news headlines about a report linking air pollution possibly to cancer: "Air 'link' to cancer: report warns women" and "Illness: it's not the Teesside air. Poor health cannot be blamed on pollution, says new study." Other reports appeared in the environmental health trade press: "Teesside health study links lung cancer with air pollution"; yet another reported, "Teesside health study takes the blame off industry" (Phillimore & Moffatt, 2000, p. 105).

Two members of the original air quality research team, Peter Phillimore and Suzanne Moffatt (2000), observed that the differing interests of local government, industry, and public interest groups led the media to cover the report's conclusions from multiple and competing perspectives. For example, industry and local government attempted to play down suggestions that air pollution might cause cancer. Phillimore and Moffatt (2000) admitted that these attempts "were undoubtedly assisted by *our collective failure as researchers to summarize key findings effectively for the media and therefore ultimately for public consumption.* . . . Local government in particular seized on the evidence of poor health, in order to emphasize the significance of poverty . . . and personal lifestyle at the expense of any emphasis on the effects of pollution" (p. 115, emphasis added). The ambiguity and confusion in media reports about the risk from air pollution in Teesside ultimately led the researchers themselves to enter the public fray with a letter to the editor of one newspaper, leading that newspaper to report, "Teesside study 'misinterpreted,' say researchers" (p. 105).

Media Sources: Whose Voices Speak of Risk?

Our understanding of environmental dangers depends not simply on information but also on who speaks or interprets information about risk. A growing area of research in environmental communication is the nature of the sources used by media in reports about risks—government officials, scientists, at-risk publics, environmental groups, and so forth. Not surprisingly, the media sometimes echo some of the features of technical models of risk communication, using primarily government officials and experts to provide news about environment risks. As a result, stories too often rely on such sources to provide "objective" accounts of risks but use local residents or environmental groups for the nontechnical aspects of a story such as "color, emotion, and human elements" (Pompper, 2004, p. 106).

In a study of this tendency, Pompper (2004) surveyed 15 years of environmental risk stories in three national newspapers that target different social groups: the *New York Times, USA Today,* and the *National Enquirer.* Her major conclusion: Whereas mainstream media such as the *New York Times* and *USA Today* relied heavily upon government and industry sources, the *National Enquirer* relied most on members of the public (individuals, community members, etc.). This is significant because experts and community members framed the stories quite differently. Government and industry were more likely to frame their accounts of risk in terms of official assessments and assurances of safety. On the other hand, members of the public spoke about environmental and health hazards, such as cancer and industrial accidents.

The study also found that the two mainstream newspapers used frames that supported the status quo: Risk could be controlled, responsible agencies were providing oversight, and so forth. For example, industry sources stressed their ability to manufacture electrical power within a legal framework "designed to preserve natural resources, protect worker safety, and ensure that adequate research had been performed" (Pompper, 2004, p. 114). Pompper's conclusion is stark: "Voices of common people who live with environmental risks every day and voices of groups organized to save the environment from industrialism are drowned out by elites cited most often in environmental risk stories. For non-elites . . . this study's major finding has grim implications, indeed. The news media essentially ignore them" (p. 128).

Voices of the "Side Effects"

The dominance of government and industry spokespersons in environmental risk stories certainly affects the social definition of risk and raises an important question about the opportunities for cultural rationality in media outlets. Indeed, an important debate over media reporting of risk concerns what Beck (1992) has called the **voices of the "side effects"** (p. 61). Beck is referring to those individuals (and their children) who suffer the side effects of risk society, such as asthma and other illnesses from air pollutants, chemical contamination, and the like. Reflecting the tension between technical and cultural rationality that we discussed earlier, these voices of the "side effects" seek media recognition of a very different understanding of environmental dangers and the burdens of risk:

> What scientists call "latent side effects" and "unproven connections" are for them their "coughing children" who turn blue in foggy weather and grasp for air, with a rattle in their throat. On their side of the fence, "side effects" have *voices, fears, eyes,* and *tears*. And yet they must soon learn that their own statements and experiences are worth nothing so long as they collide with the established scientific [views]. . . . Therefore people themselves become small, private alternative experts in risks . . . The parents begin to collect data and arguments. The "blank spots" of modernization risks, which remain "unseen" and "unproven" for the experts, very quickly take form under their . . . approach. (p. 61)

Yet, it is not at all clear that these voices of the "side effects" are given the journalistic space to offer alternative cultural rationality in news accounts of environmental risks. Media communication scholar Simon Cottle (2000) looked at this possibility in a study of environmental news on British television. Unlike Pompper's study of newspapers, Cottle found that for television, "ordinary voices" were more frequently (37%) cited than either government sources or scientific sources. However, he concluded that such ordinary feelings and expressions of "lived experience" are used mainly to provide human interest or a "human face" for stories rather than substantive analysis.

Cottle cites a BBC2 *Newsnight* news story about a proposal for the British government to subsidize the purchase of new cars to reduce harmful emissions from the 7 million cars more than 10 years old that travel Britain's highways. The BBC station aired three reactions from "ordinary" viewers. One voice comes from a music student who expresses his/her personal experience and feelings about continuing to drive an older car: "I wouldn't be free without it; and I think that is the main thing. I wouldn't be able to do my degree, I wouldn't be able to go into work. It's just totally important to me and I do love it as well. It's not just the practical side of it. I love having a car" (p. 36).

The inclusion of personal interviews is important for human interest and thus news value in environmental stories. Nevertheless, these experiences are "sought out and positioned to play a symbolic role, not to elaborate a form of 'social rationality'" (Cottle, 2000, pp. 37–38). That is, they are used to provide color, variety, and human interest rather than to shed insight into a problem. For example, the voice of the British musician speaking about owning a car provides "a private-experiential statement" (p. 36) but does not reflect on the effects of pollution (risk).

Alternative Media and Risk

Partly due to the constraints on news production in the mainstream media (Chapter 5), more and more community and environmental groups are providing alternative forums for reports of risk and for residents to share their experiences in living with environmental hazards. For example, Rachel's Environment & Health News (www.rachel.org) provides regular reports of environmental threats to health and safety in communities and workplaces and shares news of efforts to address these concerns and barriers to doing so.

Typical is Peter Montague's (2005) report on the fears of health professionals to speak out about the risks of lead poisoning. He describes the case of Albert (a pseudonym), a public health worker assigned to reduce the sources of exposure to lead by children under 6 years of age who lived in a low-income community. Albert had discovered an alarming pattern of contaminated soils in the city from years of lead paint flaking off the old 1940s-era buildings and wind blowing lead into the air. Montague reported that, when the data Albert discovered are displayed, "every street in the city lights up like a Christmas tree. Essentially, all the children in the city have been poisoned to some extent by toxic lead" (p. 6). However, when others urged Albert to alert city officials or the media, he hesitated: "If you do that, I'll be fired for sure," he said (quoted in Montague, 2005, p. 6). Using a fictitious name for the city as well, Montague turned to *Rachel's Environment & Health News* to report the larger problem of intimidation and fear that limits health professionals in some areas from going public.

In other cases, community and regional environmental groups that report news about environmental dangers now exist in many parts of the country. In the southern Appalachian region, the Ohio Valley Environmental Coalition is a critical source of news and information about the environment. For example, in late 2003, OVEC (2003) published an alert online and in its newsletter about dangers from a massive West Virginia coal waste, or sludge, impoundment. Often, these large holding ponds of coal sludge are located in valleys directly above small communities. Sometimes, the impoundment walls burst after heavy storms, releasing the sludge, which destroys homes and businesses as it rushes down the valley. Using alternative means to inform members of the public and the mainstream news media, OVEC has launched a public campaign to require stricter safety regulations and inspections for such massive impoundments.

In summary, news media reports constitute a public sphere crisscrossed by competing claims about risk from scientists, government risk agencies, industry, and (less often) the voices of the "side effects" who are directly affected by environmental dangers. Reporters working in the mainstream media strive to balance not only these differing interests but also journalistic norms for newsworthiness. At times, such constraints push reporters to dramatize specific events and underreport chronic and longer-term conditions and causes of environmental and health risks. Partly as a result of these pressures, alternative media have arisen to offer communities and environmental groups a means to report risk and share information with those affected by these dangers.

Act Locally!

Communicating Risk on Campus

How would your college or university handle the discovery of a hazardous bacteria or mold in dormitory rooms on campus? How would campus officials determine whether it was harmful or an acceptable risk? Would students be able to live in the dorms, or would other accommodations be needed?

What communication should officials use to involve students and others in deciding whether to take action (such as moving students to local hotels while the dorms are cleaned)?

Identify the appropriate campus officials and state health officials to interview to answer these questions:

1. Who is responsible for environmental health in dorms?

2. What procedures do these officials use to assess the risk of such conditions (mold)?

3. Who is involved and what is considered in determining whether this is an acceptable risk?

4. What communication is used to decide how unacceptable risks are to be managed (e.g., relocating students to other housing)? Would any students be involved in this communication?

Conclusion

With the arrival of risk society (Beck, 1992), affected communities and government agencies such as the EPA have struggled to assess the dangers of modern hazards. The EPA and other federal agencies dramatically increased their use of technical methods to assess risk in the 1980s. Technical risk assessment determines the expected annual mortality (usually from cancer) from exposure to hazardous substances, such as chemicals that pollute a community's drinking water. Yet, inaccurate diagnoses and failure to warn the residents of health risks have provoked a firestorm of criticism of technical models of risk assessment.

As a result, health workers, residents, scholars, and other critics have helped develop a cultural model of risk analysis that takes into account broad factors that affect perceptions of the severity of risks. Plough and Krimsky (1987) have referred to this form of knowledge as *cultural rationality*. It involves such sources of insight as cultural experience, knowledge of local conditions, and the impacts on families and communities.

Differences in technical and cultural assessments of risk have influenced the practice of risk communication. The technical model of risk communication relies primarily upon one-way communication (experts to lay audiences) and seeks to translate numerical risk estimates for target populations. The cultural model of risk communication expands upon this technical awareness by involving members of at-risk groups in helping scientists and health agencies understand risk in terms of the community's values and cultural experiences. Representatives of affected groups also work with agencies to design communication campaigns that are appropriate for those affected by environmental hazards.

Finally, news media have become a public arena for many voices in evaluating and defining environmental risks—scientists, EPA officials, scholars, and the voices of the "side effects" (Beck, 1992), those who suffer directly the effects of modern environmental hazards. While mainstream media attempt to convey scientific findings and official health warnings, reporters are also influenced by the journalistic norms of newsworthiness and human interest, as well as other constraints. As a result, newer forms of media, such as the websites of local community and environmental groups, are arising to alert residents, to share information, and to provide opportunities for marginalized voices to draw attention to their concerns.

I hope this description of the technical and cultural approaches to risk communication has helped you appreciate some of the reasons for conflict among technical experts, public officials, scholars, the media, and communities exposed to environmental dangers. Equally, I hope you now have some appreciation of the improvements in risk communication that some agencies and universities are attempting today. The study of risk communication is essentially a study of the difficulties in defining *acceptable risk* in a way that acknowledges the different perspectives on risk evinced by agencies such as the EPA, by the news media, and by residents of communities.

At the beginning of this chapter, you read that "those who control the discourse on risk will most likely control the political battles as well" (Plough & Krimsky, 1987, p. 4). Some scientists and agency officials believe that the public's irrational fears of environmental risks will divert scarce funding from more serious problems, and thus they emphasize a technical model of risk communication that accurately conveys some aspects of risk. On the other hand, the residents of communities such as Brownsville, Texas, and Matamoros, Mexico, believe that risk researchers' ignorance of the cultural practices of *parturas* (lay midwives) and of reports of local health care advocates limited their ability to find links between environmental hazards and serious illness. Advocates of these voices of the "side effects" thus call for a cultural model of risk communication that considers a range of factors in characterizing risk. In the end, the ability of society to reduce environmental hazards may depend not only on the language of technical risk—*pathways* and *dose exposures*—but also on the willingness of scientists, risk experts, and affected communities to speak honestly to one another about the experiences of communities and who benefits (and who suffers) from dangerous environments.

KEY TERMS

Acceptable risk: From a technical perspective, a judgment based on the numerical estimate of deaths or injuries expected annually from exposure to a hazard. From a cultural perspective, a judgment of what harms society is willing or unwilling to accept and who is subject to this risk; such a judgment inevitably involves values.

Anencephaly: A condition occurring during pregnancy in which the end of the fetus's neural tube fails to close, resulting in a partial or complete absence of the brain and, usually death within a few hours of birth.

Cultural-experiential model of risk: See *risk (cultural-experiential)*.

Cultural model of risk communication: An approach that involves the affected public in assessing risk and in designing risk communication campaigns, and that recognizes cultural knowledge and the experience of local communities.

Cultural rationality: In Plough and Krimsky's (1987) view, a basis for risk evaluation that includes personal, familiar, and social concerns; a source of judgment that arises when the social context and experience of those exposed to environmental dangers enter definitions of risk.

Four-step procedure for risk assessment: Procedure used by agencies to evaluate risk in a technical sense; the four steps are (1) hazard identification, (2) assessment of human exposure, (3) modeling of the dose responses, and (4) a characterization of the overall risk. See *risk (technical)*.

Hazard: In Sandman's (1987) model of risk, what experts mean by *risk* (i.e., expected annual mortality). See *risk (technical)*.

Irrational individual assumption: The assumption among some risk professionals that laypeople tend to underestimate dangers to personal health (such as smoking) but exaggerate environmental dangers (such as chemical hazards).

Outrage: In Sandman's (1987) model, collective term for factors the public considers in assessing the acceptability of their exposure to a hazard. See *hazard*.

Risk (cultural-experiential): The effort by some public agencies to solicit the experience and views of affected communities in risk assessment.

Risk (technical): The expected annual mortality from some condition, such as exposure to a chemical substance; a calculation of the probability that a certain number of people will die (usually from cancer) over a period of time (one year) from their exposure to an environmental hazard; risk may include illness and injuries as well as death.

Risk assessment: The evaluation of the degree of harm or danger from some condition such as exposure to a toxic chemical.

Risk communication (general): Any public or private communication that informs individuals about the existence, nature, form, severity, or acceptability of risks.

Risk communication (technical): The translation of technical data about environmental or health risks for public consumption, with the goal of educating a target audience.

Risk management: The implementation of steps to reduce the danger to the public and the environment from a risk.

Risk society: Term coined by German sociologist Ulrich Beck to characterize today's society according to the large-scale nature of risks and the threat of irreversible effects on human life from modernization.

Voices of the "side effects": Term used by Beck (1992) to refer to those individuals (or their children) who suffer the "side effects" of the risk society, such as asthma and other illnesses from air pollutants, chemical contamination, etc.

DISCUSSION QUESTIONS

1. Should government be in the business of assessing the risks of technology or environmental hazards?

2. Do you trust government (or industry) warnings about the health risks of smoking, tanning salons, consuming alcohol while pregnant? Are these

communications effective? Do they give you useful information? Do they affect your own behavior?

3. Do people worry about the wrong risks? (For example, should we worry about exhaust from diesel trucks on the highways, or terrorists flying a plane into a nuclear reactor?) How do you judge what is an acceptable risk?

4. Is the public's outrage over environmental hazards rational? Although a toxic waste landfill may inconvenience those living near it, doesn't it have to go somewhere? Or does it? Does society manage fairly the risks associated with our chemical culture?

5. Do you feel there is a difference between the risks you choose to take as an individual (e.g., smoking or driving over the speed limit) and those risks about which you have not been given a choice (e.g., air or water pollution)?

6. Do you believe there is a cultural rationality about environmental risk? Should personal knowledge, experience, or cultural differences affect objective estimates of risk?

7. What precisely do the voices of the "side effects" have to contribute to risk communication? Are these voices merely emotional, or do they have relevant insight into risks in their environment?

REFERENCES

Allen, S., Adam, B., & Carter, C. (Eds.). (2000). *Environmental risks and the media*. London & New York: Routledge.

Andrews, R. N. L. (1999). *Managing the environment, managing ourselves: A history of American environmental policy*. New Haven: Yale University Press.

Associated Press. (2004, July 28). New Superfund concerns: Toxic exposure cited; in check at 80 percent of sites, officials say. *Richmond Times-Dispatch*, p. A3.

Beck, U. (1992). *Risk society: Towards a new modernity*. Newbury Park, CA: Sage.

Beck, U. (1998). Politics of risk society. In J. Franklin (Ed.), *The politics of risk society* (pp. 9–22). London: Polity.

Breyer, S. (1993). *Breaking the vicious circle: toward effective risk regulation*. Cambridge: Harvard University Press.

Brockovich, E. (2002). *Take it from me: Life's a struggle, but you can win*. New York: McGraw-Hill.

Brown, P., & Mikkelsen, E. J. (1990). *No safe place: Toxic waste, leukemia, and community action*. Berkeley: University of California Press.

Buckmaster, T. (1997, February 9–13). *Defusing sensitive issues through risk communication*. Paper presented at the Public Affairs Council's National Grassroots Conference for Corporate and Association Professions, Key West, FL.

Cottle, S. (2000). TV news, lay voices and the visualization of environmental risks. In S. Allan, B. Adam, & C. Carter (Eds.), *Environmental risks and the media* (pp. 29–44). London: Routledge.

Covello, V. T. (1993). *Risk assessment methods*. New York: Plenum Press.

Dunwoody, S., & Peters, H. P. (1992). Mass media coverage of technological and environmental risks: A survey of research in the United States and Germany. *Public Understanding of Science, 1,* 199–230.

Environmental Protection Agency. (1999). *How Safe Am I? Helping Communities Evaluate Chemical Risks* (EPA 550-B-99-D13). Author. Available at www.nsc .org/public/xroads/risk.pdf

Environmental Protection Agency. (2002). *Superfund Community Involvement Toolkit: Risk Communication*. Author. Retrieved June 4, 2003, from www.epa .gov/superfund/tools/pdfs/37riskcom.pdf

Environmental Protection Agency. (2003, October 17). *EPA makes final decision on dioxin in sewage sludge used in land applications.* (Press release). Retrieved July 20, 2004, from www.epa.gov/ost/biosolids/#rule

Farrell, T. B., & Goodnight, G. T. (1981). Accidental rhetoric: The root metaphors of Three Mile Island. *Communication Monographs, 48,* 271–300.

Fiorino, D. J. (1989). Technical and democratic values in risk analysis. *Risk Analysis, 9,* 293–299.

Fischer, F. (2002). *Citizens, experts, and the environment: The politics of local knowledge.* Durham: Duke University Press.

Friedman, S. M. (2004). And the beat goes on: The third decade of environmental journalism. In S. Senecah (Ed.), *The environmental communication yearbook, 1,* 175–187. Mahwah, NJ: Erlbaum.

Gibbs, L. (1994). Risk assessments from a community perspective. *Environmental Impact Assessment Review, 14,* 327–335.

Goldstein, I. F., & Goldstein, M. (2002). *How much risk? A guide to understanding environmental health hazards.* New York: Oxford University Press.

Government may broaden the regulating of sewage sludge. (2004, January 2). *New York Times,* p. A 13.

Grabill, J. T., & Simmons, W. M. (1998). Toward a critical rhetoric of risk: producing citizens and the role of technical communicators. *Technical Communication Quarterly, 7,* 415–441.

Greenberg, M. R., Sachsman, D. B., Sandman, P. M., & Salomone, K. L. (1989). Network evening news coverage of environmental risk. *Risk Analysis 9,* 119–125.

Guber, D. L. (2003). *The grassroots of a green revolution: Polling America on the environment.* Cambridge: MIT Press.

Hamilton, J. D. (2003). Exploring technical and cultural appeals in risk communication: The Fernald radium case. *Risk Analysis, 23,* pp. 291–302.

Harr, J. (1996). *A civil action.* New York: Vintage.

Hayes, S. P. (1987). *Beauty, health, and permanence: Environmental politics in the United States, 1955–1985.* Cambridge, UK: Cambridge University Press.

Heilprin, J. (2003, October 17). EPA won't restrict sludge fertilizer, despite possible cancer-causing dioxins. *SGGate.com.* Retrieved July 20, 2004, from www .sfgate.com/cgi-bin/article.cgi?file=/news/archive/2003/10/17/nationa11522ED

Hornstein, D. T. (1992). Reclaiming environmental law: A normative critique of comparative risk analysis. *Columbia Law Review, 92*, 562–633.

Krimsky, S., & Golding, D. (Eds.). (1992). *Social theories of risk*. Westport, CT: Praeger.

Krimsky, S., & Plough, A. (1988). *Environmental hazards: Communicating risks as a Social Process*. Dover, MA: Auburn House.

Lindell, M. K., & Perry, R. W. (2004). *Communicating environmental risk in multiethnic communities*. Thousand Oaks, CA: Sage.

Markowitz, G., & Rosner, D. (2002). *Deceit and denial: The deadly politics of industrial pollution*. Berkeley: University of California Press.

Montague, P. (2005, March 31). Public health professionals afraid to speak out. *Rachel's Environment & Health News, 814*. Retrieved May 28, 2005, from www.rachel.org/bulletin/index.cfm?issue_ID=2496

Myers, D. G. (2001, December). Do we fear the right things? *Observer* [American Psychological Society]. Retrieved July 31, 2004, from www.davidmyers.org/fears

National Institute of Environmental Health Sciences (NIEHS). (2003a). *University of Wisconsin Milwaukee Community outreach and education program*. Retrieved July 27, 2004, from www-apps.niehs.gov/centers/public/coep/ctr-182.htm

National Institute of Environmental Health Sciences (NIEHS). (2003b). *Fish consumption risk communication in ethnic Milwaukee*. Retrieved July 27, 2004, from www.niehs.gov/translat/envjust/projects/petering.htm

National Research Council. (1996). *Understanding risk: Informing decisions in a democratic society*. Washington, DC: National Academy Press.

Ohio Valley Environmental Coalition. (2003, October 19). *West Virginia's most massive coal waste impoundment*. Retrieved July 14, 2004, from www.ohvec.org/galleries/mountaintop_removal/008/

Peterson, T. R. (1997). *Sharing the Earth: The rhetoric of sustainable development*. Columbia: University of South Carolina.

Phillimore, P., & Moffatt, S. (2000). "Industry causes lung cancer": Would you be happy with that? Environmental health and local politics. In S. Allen, B. Adam, & C. Carter (Eds.), *Environmental risks and the media* (pp. 105–116). London & New York: Routledge.

Plough, A., & Krimsky, S. (1987). The emergence of risk communication studies: Social and political context. *Science, Technology, & Human Values, 12*, 4–10.

Pompper, D. (2004). At the 20th century's close: Framing the public policy issue of environmental risk. In S. L. Senecah (Ed.), *The Environmental Communication Yearbook, 1*, 99–134. Mahwah, NJ: Erlbaum.

Rampton, S., & Stauber, J. (2002). *Trust us, we're experts!* New York: Jeremy P. Tarcher/Putnam.

Renn, O. (1992). Concepts of risk: A classification. In S. Krimsky & D. Golding (Eds.), *Social theories of risk* (pp. 53–79). West Point, CT, & London: Praeger.

Rowan, K. E. (1991). Goals, obstacles, and strategies in risk communication: A problem-solving approach to improving communication about risks. *Journal of Applied Communication Research, 19*, 300–329.

Sachsman, D. B., Simon, J., & Valenti, J. (2002, June). The environmental reporters of New England. *Science Communication 23*(4), 410–441.

Sandman, P. (1987). Risk communication: Facing public outrage. *EPA Journal, 13*(9), 21–22.

Singer, E. (1990). A question of accuracy: How journalists and scientists report research on hazards. *Journal of Communication, 40,* 102–116.

Stauber, J., & Rampton, S. (1995). *Toxic sludge is good for you! Lies, damn lies, and the public relations industry.* Monroe, ME: Common Courage Press.

Werner, E. (2004, February 5). Whistleblower says EPA used unreliable data for sludge decision. *The Mercury News.* Retrieved August 1, 2004, from www.mercurynews.com/mld/mercurynews/news/local/7879338.htm?lc

Williams, B. A., & Matheny, A. R. (1995). *Democracy, dialogue, and environmental disputes: The contested languages of social regulation.* New Haven: Yale University Press.

NOTE

1. For an account of the real Erin Brockovich's story, see her autobiography, *Take It From Me: Life's a Struggle, But You Can Win* (2002). The story of Woburn, Massachusetts, is told in Phil Brown's and Edwin Mikkelsen's (1990) *No Safe Place: Toxic Waste, Leukemia, and Community Action*; and in Jonathan Harr's (1996) *A Civil Action*, on which the Hollywood movie version is based.

PART IV

Voices for Change

7

Environmental Advocacy Campaigns

SCENE 1: Zuni Pueblo, New Mexico, August 5, 2003

"It has been a long 20 year struggle . . . but we have had our voices heard," exclaimed Carlton Albert, the Zuni tribe's head councilman (quoted in Seciwa, 2003, p. 2). Albert had learned that a powerful utility company had dropped its plans for a coal mine near the sacred Zuni Salt Lake in western New Mexico. The lake was named for Ma'l Oyattsik'i (the Salt Woman), who, according to legend, for centuries had provided salt from the lake for religious ceremonies and for the well-being of area tribes. Surrounding land, called the Sanctuary, also contained burial sites and shrines sacred to the Zunis, the Navajos, the Lagunas, the Acomas, the Apaches, the Hopis, and other tribes. A coalition of these tribes and local conservationists had waged a campaign to halt the coal mine, including a people's hearing, radio ads, postcards to public officials, testimony at public hearings, and tribal runners carrying salt from Zuni Pueblo to the company's headquarters in Phoenix. Reflecting on their success, Albert said, "If there is a lesson to be learned, it is never to give up and [to] stay focused on what you want to accomplish" (quoted in Seciwa, 2003, p. 2).

SCENE 2: University of North Carolina at Chapel Hill, 2003 and 2005

Students at the University of North Carolina at Chapel Hill cheered in March 2003 as student government leaders announced the results of a campus-wide vote in favor of a green energy initiative. Approval of the initiative had been the objective of their campaign the previous year. The election results placed the university on a path to the use of alternative, clean energy sources and conservation measures that would lower energy use on the University of North Carolina campus. The continued campaign work paid off when students reaffirmed the green energy plan in 2005.

SCENE 3: The "Deep Ecology Platform"

Deep ecology is a philosophy of nature and a critique of mainstream environmentalism for its allegedly shallow approach to the environmental crisis. If you visit the website of the Foundation for Deep Ecology (www.deepecol ogy.org), you will see this brief excerpt from the "Deep Ecology Platform" by philosophers Arne Naess and George Sessions (n.d.):

> The well-being and flourishing of human and nonhuman life on Earth have value in themselves. These values are independent of the usefulness of the non-human world for human purposes. . . . Present human interference with the nonhuman world is excessive, and the situation is rapidly worsening. . . . Policies must therefore be changed. The changes in policies affect basic economic, technological structures. The resulting state of affairs will be deeply different from the present. (paras. 1, 4, 6)

These three scenes illustrate a form of environmental communication known as **advocacy,** the act of persuading or arguing in support of a specific cause, policy, idea, or set of values. The Zuni tribe and the University of North Carolina students engaged in advocacy by carrying out strategic campaigns to influence the plans of a utility company and a university. On the other hand, the Foundation for Deep Ecology's platform criticizes widely held values of the dominant society and articulates an alternative vision for that society. Communication scholar James Cantrill (1993) has described **environmental advocacy** generally as a kind of "symbolic discourse (i.e., legal, educational, expository, artistic, public and/or interpersonal communication) aimed at supporting conservation and the preservation of finite resources" (p. 68). I would broaden this somewhat by including in the definition of *environmental advocacy* support for both natural and human environments and the well-being of the life these environments sustain.

Although there are many forms of environmental advocacy, I'll focus in this chapter on one main form—the *environmental advocacy campaign*. An **advocacy campaign** can be defined broadly as a strategic course of action involving communication undertaken for a specific purpose. In the first section of this chapter, I'll describe advocacy in general, as well as the different modes of environmental advocacy from media events to corporate boycotts and community organizing. I'll also introduce and distinguish the advocacy campaign from other types of issue advocacy, such as public health campaigns. And I'll also contrast advocacy campaigns with critical rhetorics that, although they challenge dominant discourses, may decline to engage in strategic action or in campaigns on behalf of environmental objectives.

In the second section, I'll explore more closely the basic questions advocates must address in designing effective campaigns for the environment. The campaign is the form of advocacy most frequently used by local and national environmental groups to accomplish an objective, be it ending logging in a national forest or halting the use of growth hormones in the poultry sold to McDonald's. After we describe the design of a typical campaign, you'll have an opportunity to "Act Locally!" with exercises that allow you to apply the principles of the campaign to concerns in your community or on campus.

In the third section, I'll describe some of the dilemmas of persuasion faced by environmental advocates, particularly those who use critical and confrontational rhetorics, in mobilizing public support. For example, must a radical vision be articulated in socially acceptable language to gain a hearing? Does the use of such militant tactics as tree spiking make mainstream groups appear more reasonable and thus more acceptable, or do such tactics harm environmentalism by casting a negative light on the motives of all environmental groups?

My hope is that, when you have finished this chapter, you'll be more aware of the range of communication modes available to environmental advocates and that you'll also appreciate the challenges they face in questioning strongly held values and ideologies and in building public demand for environmental protection.

Environmental Advocacy

The practice of advocacy has a long tradition in the United States. In the 18th century, Samuel Adams's fiery pamphlets stirred colonists' anger against British rule and recruited patriots for the American Revolution. As the nation took form, trade guilds, political parties, charitable groups, and other associations emerged alongside more established institutions as advocates for workers, the poor, urban sanitation, and other social causes. A stream of advocacy campaigns and the critical questioning of social and economic practices characterized much of 19th- and 20th-century history, including campaigns for women's suffrage, for the right of workers to unionize and to bargain collectively, for civil rights, and to lower the voting age to 18.

Today, groups whose goals range from community support for the homeless to stopping sweatshop labor provide forums for newly emerging voices and concerns. Groups such as the Children's Defense Fund, the Humane Society, ACT-UP, and Behind the Label (a campaign against sweatshop labor) bring a variety of viewpoints to public attention and provide "a collective voice to those who lack the means or expertise to participate on their own" (Richardson & Joe, 1995, p. A19). Such groups hold public institutions accountable to democratic and humane principles and have often achieved important changes that protect vulnerable populations and interests, such as new medicines for people living with HIV or AIDS, or the agreement by some universities not to buy clothing from companies using sweatshop labor in third-world countries.

In providing a voice for those who may have no means of expression, advocacy groups act as intermediaries between individuals and the large, often impersonal institutions of public life. This has been particularly true of environmental groups. Former *New York Times* writer Philip Shabecoff (2000) argues that a chief role of environmental groups is to act as "intermediaries between science and the public, the media, and lawmakers" (p. 152). For example, students in the green energy group at the University of North Carolina drew on the expertise of economics and physics professors, as well as that of private firms working with solar thermal panels, to represent students in pressing the university to change its energy practices. As intermediaries, the green energy group enabled the concerns of a much broader group to gain expression.

Modes of Environmental Advocacy

Environmentalists engage in a wide variety of advocacy modes or forms of communication. These modes may differ dramatically in their goals, the media they use, their strategies of persuasion, and the audiences they target. They may include public education, campaigns to influence environmental legislation in Congress, community organizing, boycotts, and direct action protests such as sit-ins and hanging banners from corporate buildings. (See Table 7.1.)

Here and in the following chapter, I'll describe some of these modes of advocacy in more detail. For example, in Chapter 8 I'll describe the use of toxic tours, hosted by environmental justice groups who invite people to visit communities that are contaminated by toxic chemicals to see, smell, and feel what daily life is like for those who live there (Pezzullo, 2003, 2004). For now, I'll describe two broad forms of advocacy that cut across many of the modes in Table 1: advocacy campaigns and critical rhetorics. I'll also

Table 7.1   Modes of Environmental Advocacy

Mode of Advocacy	Objective
Political and Legal Channels:	
1. Political advocacy	To influence legislation or regulations
2. Litigation	To seek compliance with environmental standards by agencies and businesses
3. Electoral politics	To mobilize voters for candidates and referenda
Direct Appeal to Public Audiences:	
4. Public education	To influence societal attitudes and behavior
5. Direct action	To influence specific behaviors through acts of protest, including civil disobedience
6. Media events	To create publicity or news coverage to broaden advocacy effects
7. Community organizing	To mobilize citizens or residents to act
Consumers and the Market:	
8. Green consumerism	To use consumers' purchasing power to influence corporate behavior
9. Corporate accountability	Consumer boycotts, shareholder actions

distinguish environmental advocacy campaigns from other types of advocacy campaigns (such as public health campaigns) that target individual choices or behaviors.

Campaigns Versus Critical Rhetoric

Before an environmental advocacy campaign starts, there is often a period in which existing practices are questioned and a desire to find a better way is expressed. For example, Rachael Carson's classic book *Silent Spring* (1962) sharply criticized the practices of the pesticide industry and the government agencies that exposed the public to harmful chemicals. As a result of this questioning, public health advocates and groups such as Environmental Action began to campaign for federal legislation to curb DDT use and for stronger laws to protect air and water. Although they are different in some ways, campaigns and critical rhetorics can function in complementary ways, and it is therefore important to understand each of these modes of advocacy in more detail.

Critical Rhetoric

Critical rhetoric can be defined as the questioning or denunciation of a behavior, policy, societal value, or ideology; such rhetoric may also include the articulation of an alternate policy, vision, or ideology. Throughout the modern environmental movement, many voices—not part of any particular campaign—have questioned or denounced taken-for-granted views of and behavior toward nature. For example, biologist Paul Ehrlich (1968) challenged comfortable views of the future in his book *The Population Bomb*, predicting unsustainable population growth. Greenpeace activists have released *mind bombs* in the media since the 1970s to raise the world's consciousness of the cruelty of modern whaling. Greenpeace cofounder Robert Hunter defines **mind bombs** as simple images, such as Zodiac boats interposing themselves between whales and their harpooners, that "explode in people's minds" to create a new awareness (quoted in Weyler, 2004, p. 73).

A critical rhetoric may also include the articulation of an alternate policy, vision, or ideology. The Foundation for Deep Ecology urges such a vision, arguing that the basic economic and technological structures of society must change to the point that "the resulting state of affairs will be deeply different from the present" (Naess & Sessions, n.d.). And Rachel Carson's criticism of abuses of pesticides in *Silent Spring* (1962) led to stricter regulation of harmful chemicals such as DDT. Critical rhetorics frequently serve to expand the range of social choices and visions that are eclipsed in the day-to-day political struggles of a campaign.

Although the Foundation for Deep Ecology stated its criticisms of society's environmental abuse in polite language, critical rhetorics also have gained attention as a result of sharp denunciation of, or not-so-decorous challenges to, existing norms. Sometimes this has taken the form of what communication scholars Robert Scott and Donald Smith (1969) termed **confrontational rhetoric**, the use of strident language and actions such as sit-ins and the occupation of buildings to critique racism, war, or exploitation of the environment. Despite the controversy often surrounding such actions, Scott and Smith urge us to take seriously the criticisms they raise. They explain that sometimes the calls for ". . . civility and decorum serve as masks for the preservation of injustice . . . they condemn the dispossessed to nonbeing, and . . . they become the instrumentalities of power for those who 'have'" (p. 7).

Studies of confrontational rhetoric have examined marches, demonstrations, sit-ins, obscene language, and other forms of civil disobedience, as well as the destruction of logging equipment, SUVs, and animal research laboratories. Environmental communication scholar Kevin DeLuca (1999) has called these latter acts of destruction "ecotage" (p. 6). (See "FYI: Confrontation Rhetorics.")

FYI: Confrontation Rhetorics

For information on the use of confrontational rhetoric and other forms of critical rhetorics that challenge social norms and practices generally, see

- Haiman, F. S. (1967). The rhetoric of the streets: Some legal and ethical considerations. *Quarterly Journal of Speech, 53,* 99–114.
- Scott, R. L., & Smith, D. K. (1969). The rhetoric of confrontation. *Quarterly Journal of Speech, 55,* 1–8.
- Cathcart, R. S. (1978). Movements: Confrontations as rhetorical form. *Southern Speech Communication Journal, 43,* 233–247.
- Olson, K. M., & Goodnight, G. T. (2001). Entanglements of consumption, cruelty, privacy, and fashion: The social controversy over fur. *Quarterly Journal of Speech, 80,* 249–276.
- DeLuca, K. M. (1999). *Image politics: The new rhetoric of environmental activism.* New York: Guilford Press.

Advocacy Campaigns

Although campaigns, too, may take sweeping social changes as their ultimate goal, they differ from critical rhetorics in their approach and are organized instead around concrete, strategic actions that move us closer to those goals. As I stated earlier, an advocacy campaign can be defined broadly as a strategic course of action involving communication undertaken for a specific purpose. That is, a campaign is waged to win a victory or bring about a concrete outcome and thus goes beyond simply questioning a policy. For example, a campaign that aims to block the construction of a toxic waste landfill in a neighborhood might pursue this objective by organizing local residents to attend city council meetings and voice their opposition to the landfill's building permit. The difference between a campaign and critical rhetoric, then, is not simply the concreteness of the objective but the *strategic course of action* by which a campaign pursues such objectives.

In contemporary society, the campaign is a mode of communication used by many groups, agencies, and institutions, and the research literature about campaigns is extensive. (For example, see Rice & Atkin, 2001, and Klingemann & Römmele, 2002). Sometimes called *information* or *communication campaigns,* the basic campaign mode is used, among other purposes, to gain votes for political candidates, to stop littering, to prevent crime, to promote family planning, to reduce health risks from smoking, to encourage the use of designated drivers, to increase the installation of smoke detectors, and to encourage people to conserve energy by turning down their thermostats. Campaigns are employed by such widely diverse groups as the National Institute of Environmental Health Sciences (2003), which warned ethnic communities in Milwaukee about health risks from eating mercury-contaminated fish; researchers at Stanford University, who worked to reduce the incidence of heart disease by encouraging at-risk individuals to have medical checkups, alter their diets, and exercise more (Flora, 2001); and the U.S. Forest Service and Ad Council, whose slogan, "Remember, Only You Can Prevent Forest Fires" has warned outdoor users for decades about the danger of forest fires (Rice, 2001, p. 276).

Environmental advocacy campaigns share many of the characteristics of these other information campaigns, and it is important to recognize these similarities before looking at their differences. Communication scholars Everett Rogers and Douglas Story (1987) have identified four features shared by communication campaigns:

1. *A campaign is purposeful.* That is, "specific outcomes are intended to result from the communication efforts of a campaign" (p. 818).

2. *A campaign is aimed at a large audience.* A campaign's purpose usually requires an organized effort that goes beyond the interpersonal efforts of one or a few people to persuade another person or a small number of others.

3. *A campaign has a more or less specifically defined time limit.* A target audience's response to a campaign—a vote, a change in one's diet, or the purchase of a smoke detector, for example—will be made by some date, and the window for any further response will close. For example, Congress refused to raise fuel efficiency standards for cars and SUVs in 2005. (On the question of fuel standards, Congress has voted many times over the years, but in each case environmental and business groups waged new campaigns to affect the vote.)

4. *A campaign involves an organized set of communication activities.* The communication activities in a campaign are particularly evident in message production and distribution (Rogers & Storey, 1987). Messages are a form of persuasion particularly likely to resonate with a target audience. (We'll return later to the concept of message and its importance in advocacy campaigns.)

In summary, Rogers and Storey (1987) have identified four features common to a wide range of campaigns. They report that, at a minimum,

"(1) a campaign intends to generate specific outcomes or effects (2) in a relatively large number of individuals, (3) usually within a specific period of time and (4) through an organized set of communication activities" (p. 821).

Although they share these features with public health and other issue campaigns, environmental advocacy campaigns sometimes differ from them in basic ways. Two differences in particular stand out:

- First, most issue campaigns that aim to reduce risk or influence individual attitudes or behavior are institutionally sponsored; that is, they are initiated by a governmental agency such as the EPA, a health association, or a university such as the University of Milwaukee's Marine and Freshwater Biomedical Sciences Center (Chapter 6). Environmental advocacy campaigns, on the other hand, are usually waged by *noninstitutional* sources—concerned individuals, environmental organizations, or small community action groups.

- Second, most public relations and public health campaigns seek to change *individuals' attitudes and/or behaviors* (e.g., personal life style, consumer choices, diet, drug or alcohol use, or sexual practices). For example, Salmon and Kroger (1992) observe that health communication campaigns specifically focus on individual behavior rather than on system-level changes. Most environmental advocacy campaigns, on the other hand, seek to change either certain *external conditions*—for example, the cleanup of an abandoned toxic waste site—or *the policy or practice of a governmental or corporate body*. And although some environmental campaigns may seek to influence individual behaviors (encouraging the use of public transportation, for example), such attempts are often seen as steps toward systemic change in society's treatment of the environment (for example, more people using buses or commuter rail systems may build political support for more funding for public modes of transportation).

The campaign mode occurs as part of several of the advocacy forms listed in Table 7.1. For example, the campaign takes a familiar form in both legislative and electoral politics, and it also appears in public education efforts, community organizing, and corporate accountability campaigns. Business groups often launch public relations campaigns to influence the public debate over environmental problems such as global warming. On the other hand, a campaign itself may employ different forms of advocacy, such as education, direct action, and consumer boycott in its efforts to halt a corporation's use of sweatshop labor. The important idea is that a campaign may rely on multiple forms of advocacy as part of a strategic and time-limited course of action for a specific purpose.

Based on my own experience working with advocacy campaigns in the environmental movement, I believe this mode of communication is increasingly important in shaping public debate and decisions about environmental policy. Therefore, in the following section I'll describe in more detail the design of advocacy campaigns and the role of communication in undertaking a "strategic course of action involving communication undertaken for a specific purpose." Then, I'll explore the Zuni Salt Lake Coalition's campaign as an extended illustration of an environmental advocacy campaign.

Environmental Advocacy Campaigns

By the time of the first Earth Day in 1970, the environmental movement had begun to change the way that citizens communicated with public officials and with each other. Not content to rely simply on magazine articles, personal testimony, and nature programs on television to educate the public, many green groups began to design advocacy campaigns to achieve specific changes. One architect of this strategy was Michael McCloskey, the former executive director of the Sierra Club. In a 1982 interview, McCloskey reflected on his role in the environmental movement's turn to campaigns:

> What I have emphasized has been a serious approach toward achieving our ends. I thought that we were not here just to bear witness or to pledge allegiance to the faith, but in fact we were here to bring that faith into reality. . . . That means we could not rest content with having said the right things, or with having made our convictions known, but we also had to plan to achieve them. We had to know how the political system worked, how to identify the decision makers and how their minds worked. We had to have people concerned with all the practical details of getting our programs accomplished. (Gendlin, 1982, p. 41)

The shift described by McCloskey also reflected many environmental groups' interest in a more participatory approach that enabled citizens to take part in the decisions affecting their local and even national environments. Political scientist Ronald Shaiko (1999) noted that such groups' focus on campaigns includes "systematic mobilizations of their members to create public pressure for their legislative agendas. Letter-writing campaigns, telephone alerts, and other grassroots techniques are now standard items" in their campaigns (p. 140). Political scientists Kay Schlozman and John Tierney (1986) have called such mobilization of citizens to influence public or corporate officials "an ancient weapon" of democratic cultures (p. 197).

Underlying the different media and methods used by environmental and community groups is a more basic question about the design of an advocacy campaign. The question of **advocacy campaign design** is, What does a group need to do to implement a strategic course of action involving communication undertaken for a specific purpose? What concerns must it take into account in designing this strategic course of action? As I've noted, environmental campaigns—as opposed to other communication campaigns—usually target public officials or corporations in an attempt to influence practices or policies that affect the environment. Hence, the design of advocacy campaigns that I describe here[1] reflects the experience of environmental groups somewhat more than it does campaigns of health groups or governmental agencies.

In designing an advocacy campaign, environmental leaders usually ask, and then attempt to answer, three fundamental questions:

1. What *exactly* do you want to accomplish?

2. Which *decision makers* have the ability to respond, and what *constituencies* can hold these decision makers accountable?

3. What will *persuade* these decision makers to act on your objectives?

These three questions ask respectively about a campaign's (1) objectives, (2) audiences, and (3) strategies. I'll discuss each of these questions in turn.

Advocacy campaigns pursue three corresponding **communication tasks** in answering these three design questions. First, effective campaigns seek to create broader support or demand for their objectives, whether the objective is to block construction of a hazardous waste incinerator or to get funds approved to build a bicycle path. Second, campaigns strive to mobilize this support from relevant constituencies (audiences) to demand accountability. (It's important here to be aware that campaigns take place in the context of other, competing voices and counter-campaigns. Successful campaigns adapt their communication in this information environment.) Third, campaigns develop strategies to influence decision makers to deliver on their objectives.

In the remainder of this section, I'll describe these three questions and their corresponding communication tasks. (See Figure 7.1 for a model of the advocacy campaign.)

Create Demand for a Campaign's Objective

Effective advocacy campaigns usually require a focus on concrete objectives. For example, John Muir's famous preservation campaign to protect Yosemite Valley focused on the passage of a single bill in the U.S. Congress in 1890 that designated the mountains around Yosemite Valley as a national park. Campaigns flounder when their objectives are unclear or when they confuse a broad goal or vision with near-term, achievable, and specific

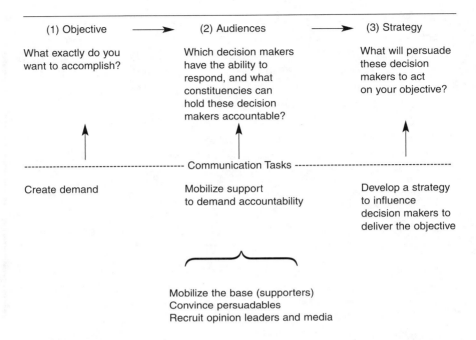

(1) Objective	→	(2) Audiences	→	(3) Strategy
What exactly do you want to accomplish?		Which decision makers have the ability to respond, and what constituencies can hold these decision makers accountable?		What will persuade these decision makers to act on your objective?

-- Communication Tasks --

Create demand	Mobilize support to demand accountability	Develop a strategy to influence decision makers to deliver the objective

Mobilize the base (supporters)
Convince persuadables
Recruit opinion leaders and media

Campaigns are time-limited actions that unfold in the context of other, competing voices and counter-campaigns

Figure 7.1   Design of the environmental advocacy campaign

actions or decisions. It is one thing to declare, "The United States should protect all old-growth forests," and quite another to mobilize citizens to persuade the U.S. Forest Service to issue a ruling halting the building of roads into these native forests, as occurred in the campaign for the roadless rule in the Clinton Administration. (See Chapter 4.) While stopping road building in national forests contributed to the broader goal of protecting America's wild lands, it is important to distinguish this objective from the broader effort that is presumably needed to protect permanently the remaining old-growth areas.

An advocacy campaign therefore begins by asking, "What *exactly* do you want to accomplish?" In answering this question, it is important to distinguish between a campaign's long-term goals and its specific objectives. As it is used here, the term **goal** refers to a long-term vision or value, such as the desire to protect old-growth forests, reduce arsenic in drinking water, or make economic globalization more democratic. While critical rhetorics are important in articulating these broader visions, they are not campaigns.

On the other hand, the term **objective** refers to a specific action or decision that moves a group closer to a broader goal. An objective is a concrete and time-limited decision or action. For example, the Environmental Protection Agency can issue a regulation imposing stricter limits on the number of parts per billion of arsenic allowed in drinking water. Thus, a question about a group's objective asks, "What *exactly* do you want to accomplish?" A campaign answers the first core question by identifying not only a longer-term vision or goal but, more importantly, an objective that is a concrete, specific, and time-limited action or decision. Such an objective might be to pass a referendum in support of clean water bonds, to persuade a city council to enact a zoning ordinance banning hazardous waste facilities within 10 miles of a school, or to appeal a Forest Service decision to allow a timber sale in an old-growth forest.

A campaign also has an important communication task to perform once it identifies its objective. It must create a broader public demand for its objective. A **public demand** is an active demonstration of support for the campaign's objective by key constituency groups, such as families with small children, voters in a key swing district, persons with respiratory problems, commuters, or members of a sports club. Although the American public generally supports clean air, clean water, and protection of natural resources, particular events and controversies often require the public's attention. Indeed, other voices and constituencies may be competing for the same support.

The Sierra Club's campaign manual (1999) explains that the challenge at this point "is to translate this passive support [for environmental values] into active participation" (p. 7). Indeed, for environmental campaigns the role of the public is often critical. The voting public particularly can be instrumental in influencing elected officials to respond to environmental concerns. Creating such a demand requires persuading the public that there is a specific and imminent threat to an environmental value, ecosystem, or human community that will motivate people to demand that it be protected and to demonstrate their concern to key decision makers.

The ability to create public demand for an environmental objective forces a campaign to address a second core question, Who has the ability to respond? And that, in turn, suggests the relevant constituencies and supporters whom a campaign must educate and mobilize as part of its strategy.

Mobilize Support to Demand Accountability

Once a campaign decides what exactly it wants to achieve, it must ask, Which *decision makers* have the ability to respond, and what *constituencies* can hold these decision makers accountable? In answering this question, campaign organizers must identify the decision makers who have the authority to act, as well as relevant constituencies (audiences) who are able to hold these leaders accountable. Here, it is important to distinguish between two different types of audiences: the **primary audience,** which is the decision makers who have the authority to act or implement the objectives of a campaign, and **secondary audiences** (also called public audiences), which are the various segments of the public, opinion leaders, and the media whose support is useful in holding decision makers accountable for the campaign's objectives.

A campaign cannot achieve an objective until someone with the ability or authority to decide on the objective responds favorably. These decision makers are a campaign's primary audience. If the objective is to fund bicycle paths along streets in Portland, Oregon, then the primary audience is most likely to be the members of Portland's city council. On the other hand, if a campaign wants tighter regulation of emissions of mercury from power plants, then the primary audience is the Environmental Protection Agency, which administers the Clean Air Act.

Once a campaign has answered the second question (Which decision makers have the ability to respond?), it faces an important communication task: *to mobilize the support of relevant constituencies to hold the primary audience accountable for its decisions.* The ability to fulfill this second task assumes that decision makers, in fact, are ultimately accountable to voters, to the media, or to other groups. This assumption goes to the heart of the discussion of the nature of legitimacy in Chapter 2. There, I defined *legitimacy* as a right to exercise authority. I observed there that an officeholder's legitimacy may be claimed by that person, but it is granted by others— voters, a group's members, or other constituencies. On the other hand, some decision makers may not be public officeholders and hence may be less susceptible to being held accountable by others. (For example, movements generally find it hard to influence corporate behavior. However, later I will describe one case in which environmental advocates did influence the behavior of a powerful corporation.)

In mobilizing the support of relevant constituencies to hold decision makers accountable, it is useful to distinguish between the media and opinion leaders, on the one hand, and members of the public, on the other. **Opinion leaders** are those whose statements often are influential with the media and members of the primary audience. For example, the Natural Resources Defense Council relies upon the well-known environmentalist Robert F. Kennedy, Jr., in many of its campaigns, and a grassroots community group may turn to a respected community leader to speak for it publicly.

More often, campaigns turn to members of the public. These may be neighbors, in a local campaign to block construction of a shopping mall in a wetlands area, or students, in a campaign to persuade administrators to adopt a green energy policy on campus. In each case, campaigns often distinguish between three types of public audiences: (1) the campaign's **base** (its core supporters), (2) the opponents of a campaign, and (3) **persuadables,** members of the public who are undecided but potentially sympathetic to a campaign's objectives. Persuadables often become important targets in mobilizing support.

It's important to note that, although persuadables potentially may be supporters of a campaign's objectives, they are initially undecided. They may lack awareness and information about the campaign, or they may be conflicted by different arguments. For example, persuadables may be exposed to information from the campaign's opponents and are thus unsure where they stand. Nevertheless, they are viewed as potentially open to information about a campaign's objective and hence are persuadable. Normally, a campaign does not attempt to persuade its opponents, as they are committed already to their own objectives. But persuadables constitute the heart of a campaign's communication because they often make the difference in the outcome of the campaign.

A campaign usually proceeds by mobilizing its base and preparing communication materials to educate key persuadables. In doing so, it is careful to adapt its strategy and message to the concerns of its different target audiences. For example, shortly we'll discuss a campaign by the Zunis and other indigenous tribes in New Mexico to protect their sacred lands. In carrying out their campaign, the Zunis adapted their basic message about the value of their lands to the concerns of their different audiences—environmentalists, churches and people of faith, consumers, and public officials. In other cases, audiences may have heard from a competing campaign—for example, the campaign by businesses to block U.S. action on global warming. In such cases, campaigns must adapt their communication to their persuadables by providing responses to opposing arguments from business groups, the media, and the frames in television news reports.

Such efforts to reach a group's base and persuadables often attract the attention of news media and therefore provide opportunities to influence the primary audience of decision makers. For example, environmental groups joined forces in 1996 to campaign against the efforts of some politicians in Congress to add **riders,** or amendments, to an EPA budget bill that cut funds for many environmental laws, including the Clean Water Act and the Superfund toxic cleanup program. In this session of Congress, Republicans constituted a majority in the House of Representatives, and undecided

Republican members thus were in a position to affect the final outcome. As a result, the environmental campaign identified these Republicans as its primary audience and began to mobilize supporters to hold accountable these undecided politicians.

Political scientist Eric Schulzke (2000) described the resulting "drumbeat" of opposition from voters and the news media mobilized by environmental groups to keep pressure on these key members of Congress to drop their support of the EPA riders:

> Terror grew as the rank and file became convinced that the party line was not resonating at home, while their opponents' message was. The [campaign] envisioned a "drumbeat" that would make Congress reverberate, through the media, from experts . . . from colleagues, and most importantly from home.
>
> The drumbeat proved to be an apt metaphor. More than one congressional staffer used that precise term in interviews. "It just didn't stop," said an aide to a Midwestern Republican who backed down on the EPA riders after being overwhelmed at home. . . . Staffers reported that the environmental message "hit a cord" at home, reflected not only in phone calls and mail, but also at town hall meetings and in feedback from Republican stalwarts. (p. 9.)

I mention this campaign because it was the first major advocacy campaign in which I participated, by helping to design its communication plan and serving as one of the spokespeople for the campaign. It is also an example of the synergy that is created when a campaign succeeds in mobilizing its base and thereby awakens the interest of the news media.

Therefore, a campaign answers the second question by mobilizing a network of supporters—particularly its base and persuadable audiences, opinion leaders, and the media—until sufficient influence is brought to bear on the primary audience of decision makers. At this point, it remains only to ask, What strategy is most likely to persuade this primary audience to act on the group's objective?

Develop a Strategy to Influence Key Decision Makers

The final question a campaign answers is, What will *persuade* these decision makers to act on your objective? This is a quintessential question of strategy. In the context of the environmental advocacy campaign, we can define **strategy** as a specific plan to bring about a desired outcome; it is the identification of the specific steps or means to an end. In implementing a strategy, a campaign often relies on educational and persuasive messages, spokespeople, and events to mobilize a group's base of support and persuadables, as well as opinion leaders and media, to influence the primary audience to act on the group's objective. (Later in this chapter, I'll discuss the dilemmas of persuasion that some groups face in carrying out the campaign's communication tasks in implementing its strategy.)

Environmental educator David Orr (1992) has observed that questions about strategy land us squarely in the realm of *praxis,* the study of efficient action or the best means to achieve an objective. At their core, environmental advocacy campaigns are about concrete outcomes—for example, the preservation of an old-growth forest or the disinvestment of a college's stocks from corporations with poor environmental performance. Whereas critical rhetorics may discredit the present and even help us to imagine a desired future, the basic question for a campaign's strategy is, How do we actually get to this future, step by step? How do community and environmental groups go about effecting specific changes in the world?

Orr proposed four broad ways to think about strategies that might lead to large-scale environmental change in society:

1. Strategies that regard change as inevitable and strategy as a kind of midwifery

2. Strategies that rely on markets and economic self-interest

3. Strategies that rely on public policy, government power, and regulation

4. Strategies that aim to change values through education.

In this book, I'll explore Orr's last three types of strategy, rather than assume that change is inevitable and that we need merely to help its birth. In particular, Orr's third kind of strategy focuses on the role of democratic politics in environmental policy. This involves attempts by advocacy groups to mobilize constituencies to influence public policy to protect the environment or to influence the performance of corporations. As we saw in Chapter 3, public participation in using the right to know, in providing public comments, and in holding both government and businesses accountable in court has been a major strategy for environmental change.

Some campaigns also rely on educating key audiences as part of their strategy. For example, some have used public information campaigns to encourage recycling, composting, and proper inflation of tires to increase gas mileage. Finally, we'll look at the strategic uses of market forces and economic self-interest to influence business performance affecting the environment. (For information on the use of market forces in effecting environmental change, see "Another Viewpoint: Green Conservatism.")

Another Viewpoint: Green Conservatism

In proposing what he calls a "conservative" approach to protecting the environment, communication scholar John Bliese (2001) calls for a strategy that relies upon the prudent use of the free market instead of government regulation:

> In sum, the proper role for conservatives is to use the market where it would work . . . as opposed to the liberals' penchant for command-and-control regulation . . . By making use of market-based mechanisms, tempered by the basic virtues of piety and prudence, conservatives could have the best policies for a much cleaner environment, a more efficient system with equitable assignment of costs ("the polluter pays"), sustainable use of natural resources, and a much better quality of life for ourselves and for countless generations to come. (p. 261)

An interesting illustration of a strategy that relied on both public education and the use of market forces is the case of McDonald's. In 2003, the fast-food chain acknowledged that the use of growth-stimulating antibiotics by large factory farms that raise and sell poultry and beef threatens human health. Many scientists believe that the overuse of these growth hormones in animals encourages the development of resistant strains of bacteria that may affect human immunity to disease. In its 2003 announcement, McDonald's agreed to phase out its purchase of poultry raised in this manner. The company's agreement was less specific for hogs and cattle (Greider, 2003, p. 8).

What brought about this change in the nation's largest purchaser of meat products? In the McDonald's case, a coalition of 13 environmental, religious, and public health organizations, including Environmental Defense, the Humane Society, and National Catholic Rural Life Conference, did not rely upon a campaign to target public officials; rather, they made innovative use of market forces. Their campaign pursued a strategy that drew on the power of consumers to change industry behavior, "not by one purchase at a time, but on a grand scale by targeting large brands in the middleman position" (Greider, 2003, p. 8). That is, they chose to influence the behavior of the meat industry by targeting one of the largest purchasers of its products, McDonald's.

Journalist William Greider (2003) closely studied the shift in strategy that occurred in this campaign. He observed that traditional "buy green" campaigns that rely on individual consumer purchases have had an exceedingly modest effect on corporate practices. "What has changed is an essential strategic insight" (p. 10). He explained:

> In . . . American capitalism, consumers are in a weak position and have very little actual leverage over the content of what they buy or how it is produced . . . Instead of browbeating individual consumers, new reform campaigns focus on the structure of industry itself and attempt to leverage entire sectors. The activists identify and target the larger corporate "consumers" who buy an industrial sector's output and sell it at retail under popular brand names. They can't stand the heat so easily, since they regularly proclaim that the customer is king. When one of these big names folds to consumer pressure, it sends a tremor through the supplier base, much as McDonald's has. (p. 10)

In the case of McDonald's, the campaign sought to use the purchasing power of the fast-food giant itself rather than individual consumers. By targeting the famous brand and familiar logo of this global icon, the campaign was able to leverage the buying power of McDonald's to influence the behavior of its suppliers. If the factory farms that sold meat products to McDonald's wanted to continue to do business, they would have to reduce their use of growth hormones in poultry and perhaps in other animals as well.

The campaign to persuade McDonald's to make a change is instructive for its creative strategy in using the leverage of a powerful corporation's brand and vulnerability to consumer pressure. Strategy is often the weak link of an advocacy campaign. In many cases, campaigns suffer when their strategy is unclear. In his discussion of this problem, Orr (1992) recalled the cartoon shown as Figure 7.2, which appeared in the journal *American Scientist*. Orr commented, "Most strategies of social change have similar dependence on the miraculous . . ." (p. 61).

Political theorist Douglas Torgerson (1999) suggests that dependence on the miraculous is particularly true of environmental strategies. He explains that a simple, though cynical, notion sometimes underlies green strategic thought: "Environmental problems are sure to get worse . . . and when they do, more and more people will be moved to join the green cause, thus enhancing its power and its chance of making a real difference" (p. 22). Torgerson believes that more is needed. I agree. Most successful advocacy campaigns specify the concrete steps required to move from the status quo to the specific decision or action that implements the campaign's objective. That specification of steps, rather than a reliance on the miraculous, is the meaning of strategy.

In designing its strategy, an advocacy campaign also has an important communication task. This task is *the identification of the appropriate*

"I think you should be more explicit here in step two."

Figure 7.2   A Miracle Needed?

(Reprinted with permission from Sidney Harris, copyright © www.Science
CartoonsPlus.com)

---

*educational and persuasive messages, spokespersons, materials, and media
for communicating with the campaign's primary audience of decision makers and its constituencies.* These materials help to mobilize a campaign's base
and persuade its persuadable audiences, opinion leaders, and media to influence the primary audience to act on the campaign's objective. For example,
in the McDonald's campaign, supporters circulated scientific research on
the overuse of antibiotics in farm animals, made persuasive appeals to consumers to protest outside McDonald's restaurants, issued reports to the news
media, and briefed officials at McDonald's corporate headquarters.

An important element of a campaign's strategic communication is its
message. As developed by many environmental groups, a **message** is usually
a phrase or sentence that concisely expresses a campaign's objective and the

values at stake in the decision of the primary audience. Although campaigns develop considerable information and arguments, the message itself is usually short, compelling, and memorable and accompanies all of a campaign's communication materials. Messages from the world of advertising are familiar to us for this reason: "Fly the Friendly Skies" (United Airlines), "Just Do It" (Nike), and "The Breakfast of Champions" (Wheaties). A message is not the complete communication, but it opens the door of attention on the part of a target audience to a campaign's other materials.

Environmental campaigns also have searched for ways to communicate a compelling message. In developing such messages, campaigns attempt to identify values and language that resonate with their bases and persuadables—those sympathetic to their objectives but undecided. For example, the message, "Extinction Means Forever" succinctly captured the values at stake in the Center for Environmental Education's campaign for a moratorium on commercial hunting of whales (Center for Environmental Education). Also, civil society groups in Asia, Europe, South America, and the United States have joined together in a "Water Is Life" campaign. The campaign opposes the move to turn over the world's water resources to the private sector through commercialization, privatization, and large-scale development. And for many years, the Sierra Club used one message to convey the values in each of its campaigns: "Protect America's Environment–For Our Families, For Our Future" (Sierra Club, 1999. p. 43).

The success of a campaign's communication depends largely upon its targeted audiences' responses to the campaign's message and other information. In studying the factors that affect the **reception of environmental advocacy** by audiences, environmental communication researcher James Cantrill (1993) identified three factors that influence audiences' perceptions of environmental messages: (1) sociocultural influences, such as values; (2) informational bases; and (3) "strategic-actional concerns" (p. 70). This last factor refers to "individuals' ways of thinking about themselves as participants in environmental settings," what they want and are willing to do to achieve in their environments (p. 82). Overall, Cantrill noted that cultural factors such as "deeply embedded environmental value systems" may be the most powerful influence on audience response to environmental messages (p. 71). (We'll look at the way one campaign drew upon relevant cultural values in the Zuni campaign later in this chapter.)

Messages are only one part of a campaign's communication, but they serve an important purpose. Messages summarize a campaign's objective, state its central values, and provide a frame for audiences' understanding and reception of the details of its other informational materials.

Act Locally!

Design a Campaign for Your Campus

What is one important step that your campus can take to support environmental values? Reduce the use of paper? Install energy-efficient light bulbs in classrooms? Disinvest or sell stock shares in companies that have poor environmental performance?

Imagine that the student government or administration on your campus has invited you to submit a campaign plan to pursue this interest. How would you answer the following questions?

1. What exactly do you want to accomplish?

2. Who has the ability to respond?

3. What will influence this person or authority to respond?

What groups are likely to be your base of support? Who are your persuadables? What types of appeals and message would be required to perform the related communication tasks of creating demand, mobilizing support to hold decision makers accountable, and designing a course of action to influence these authorities?

As an exercise in drafting a plan, work with several friends or classmates to draft an actual proposal to submit to a group that is interested in pursuing this campaign.

In summary, advocacy campaigns try to achieve concrete victories by building public demand for an important environmental objective, by mobilizing support, and by holding public officials, corporations, or other decision makers accountable for this objective. When they are designed well, strategic advocacy campaigns have several advantages over unplanned or spontaneous comments, protests, or criticism in general:

- By planning a strategic course of action, campaigns increase the chances of achieving their objectives.
- Campaigns draw on the collective strength of people and resources for both planning and implementing a course of action.
- Campaigns serve as intermediaries between individuals in their private lives and the large, often impersonal, institutions of public life.

Each of these strengths was demonstrated in the recent campaign of a coalition of Native Americans, religious groups, and environmental groups to oppose plans for a coal mine near sacred tribal lands in New Mexico.

The Campaign to Protect Zuni Salt Lake

On August 4, 2003, the Salt River Project, the third-largest electric power company in the United States, announced that it was dropping plans for an 18,000-acre coal mine located 10 miles from the Zuni Salt Lake in western New Mexico. The company's announcement was a victory for a coalition of Native American tribes, environmental and religious groups, and the Zuni people themselves, who had waged a multi-year campaign to protect the sacred Zuni Salt Lake and the surrounding lands from mining and other environmental threats.

I use this example because it clearly illustrates the three elements of design that advocacy campaigns must consider: (1) a clear objective, (2) a clearly identified decision maker and related constituencies, and (3) a strategy that is able to persuade the principal decision maker to act on its objective. The Zuni Salt Lake campaign also illustrates the ability of smaller groups, as well as larger environmental organizations, to use the principles of campaign design to carry out successful advocacy—an important objective of this textbook.

Zuni Salt Lake and a Coal Mine

The Salt River Project (SRP) company first proposed the massive Fence Lake Coal Mine in western New Mexico in 1981. Its plans called for strip-mining more than 80 million tons of coal from 18,000 acres of federal, state, and private lands. (**Strip mining** is the removal of large surface areas of land to expose the underlying coal seams.) To settle the coal dust that strip mining would produce, SRP planned to pump 85 gallons of water per minute from underground aquifers during the 40 years of the mine's planned operation (Valtin, 2003). The New Mexico Department of Energy, Minerals, and Natural Resources granted permits for the company to begin construction of the mine in 1996, although work did not immediately begin. By June 22, 2001, opposition to the mine had grown. The nearby Zuni tribe and its allies spoke against the mine when public hearings were held on the renewal of the mining permit.

To the Zuni people and area tribes, the Salt Lake is sacred. It has a special meaning derived from its history and culture. It is home to the Zunis' important deity *Ma'l Oyattsik'i,* the Salt Mother, who for centuries has provided salt for tribal religious ceremonies. The region surrounding the Zuni Salt Lake in western New Mexico is known to area tribes as the Sanctuary or *A:shiwi A:wan Ma'k'yay'a dap an'ullapna Dek'ohannan Dehyakya Dehwanne.* It is an area of burial grounds and other sacred sites, and it is laced with trails used by the Zunis, the Navajos, the Acomas, the Hopis, the Lagunas, the Apaches, and other Southwestern tribes to reach the Zuni Salt Lake. By tradition, the Sanctuary is a neutral zone where warring tribes put their weapons down and share in the gathering of "the salt which embodies the flesh of the Salt Mother herself" (Sacred Land Film Project, 2003, p. 1).

The strip mine would have been located in the heart of the Sanctuary, 10 miles from Zuni Salt Lake. Although the mine itself would not be on Zuni land, tribal leaders feared that the company's plans to pump large volumes of groundwater from the same desert aquifer that feeds the Salt Lake would dry up the lake. Malcolm Bowekaty, former Zuni Pueblo governor, told reporters, "If they vent a lot of pressure that's forcing the water up, we will no longer have the salt," (Valtin, 2003, p. 3).

Zunis also feared that the coal mine would disturb human burial remains and archaeological sites in the Sanctuary itself. Apart from the 18,000-acre site, the power company had to transport the mined coal to a generating station to produce electricity. To do this, SRP planned to construct a 44-mile railroad from the mine in Fence Lake, New Mexico, to a plant in St. John's, Arizona. Zuni leaders charged that construction of the railroad already had begun to destroy sections of pilgrimage trails and disturb some burial sites in the Sanctuary (Zuni Salt Lake Coalition, 2003, para. 1).

A Coalition's Campaign

By fall 2001, Zuni leaders had assembled a coalition of allies who would work together over the next two years to protect Zuni Salt Lake and the Sanctuary. From October 6th to 7th, the group met informally in the kitchen of one of the Zuni leaders to formulate an intensive, two-year advocacy campaign plan.[2] On November 30, 2001, leaders from the Zuni tribe, the Water Information Network, the Center for Biological Diversity, the Citizens Coal Council, Tonatierra (an indigenous community group), Friends of the Earth, the Sierra Club, and the Seventh Generation Fund for Indian Development publicly announced the formation of the Zuni Salt Lake Coalition. The Coalition would later grow to include councils of the Acoma, Navajo, Hopi, Laguna, and Apache tribes, as well as other conservation, church, and historic preservation groups. In what follows, I'll describe how this campaign embodied the core elements of design of advocacy campaigns.

Campaign Objectives: Creating Demand

From the beginning, members of the Zuni Salt Lake Coalition saw their long-term goal as "[to] get SRP to drop its plans for the Fence Lake Coal Mine [and to] protect Zuni Salt Lake for the long-term" (Zuni, 2001). More immediately, the coalition was faced with the prospect of SRP's imminent preparation of the mine site, including plans to drill into the underlying aquifer, which fed Zuni Salt Lake.

Therefore, the coalition identified two immediate *objectives:* (1) to "[m]ake sure that SRP does not tap Dakota Aquifer" [a key aquifer] and (2) to persuade the State of New Mexico and the Department of the Interior to deny the permits needed to open the coal mine and, if these were granted, to appeal the decisions in order to delay actual construction of the mine (Zuni, 2001). Coalition members felt that if they were successful in achieving either of these objectives, they could persuade SRP, in turn, to cancel its plans for the project.

Audiences: Mobilizing Support to Demand Accountability

The Zuni Salt Lake Coalition identified two sets of *primary decision makers.* Ultimately, they sought to persuade the SRP president and company officials to withdraw plans for the coal mine. Related to this longer-term goal and to the campaign's two objectives, the coalition also targeted Department of the Interior secretary Gale Norton and the New Mexico officials who oversaw the state's permitting process for the Fence Lake mine.

Key to influencing these decision makers would be the ability of the Zuni Salt Lake Coalition to *mobilize support from the appropriate constituencies* to hold these primary audiences accountable for their decisions. The effort to hold a powerful electric utility company accountable may seem unrealistic. SRP officials were not elected public figures and therefore were unaffected by voters or elections. Nevertheless, the coalition correctly saw that the company's continued *legitimacy* (Chapter 2) depended on key constituencies and regulators and that these could be mobilized or targeted. For example, investors or shareholders in SRP might worry about the costs to the company from protracted delays in construction of the coal mine; its customers might complain to state utility regulators; state and federal officials could delay or block SRP's permits, and, not least, key opinion leaders might begin to question the company's and its officials' credibility and moral standing in the community, an intangible but potentially important consideration.

Most immediately, the coalition had to reach out to its *base*–the Zuni people themselves and their allies among other area tribes. Also related to this base were several *persuadable* groups, including environmental groups, area churches, and people of faith in general (Zuni, 2001). In turn, support from these groups for the coalition's objectives would draw support from opinion leaders, the media, and, ultimately, key elected officials.

In creating a demand for its objectives and mobilizing key audiences, the coalition developed communication materials that drew on several sources of persuasion that acknowledged the cultural context and meaning of threats to the Zuni Salt Lake. Especially relevant to mobilizing its base and other supporters of the Zuni people, the coalition drew upon two important sources of persuasion: (1) spiritual and cultural values associated with the Zuni tribe's history and area indigenous cultures, and (2) an appeal to the irreparable nature of the threats to the Zuni Salt Lake. Rhetorically, the appeal to the irreparable consequences of a choice is an important way for a speaker or writer to enhance the importance of one choice over another. Elsewhere, I have defined the **irreparable** as a forewarning or opportunity to act before it is too late to preserve what is unique or rare before it is lost forever (Cox, 1982, 2001). Four characteristics appear to define an appeal to the irreparable nature of a decision or its consequences. A speaker identifies a decision as (1) threatening something that is unique or rare and thus of great value; (2) the existence of what is threatened is precarious, uncertain; (3) its loss or destruction cannot be reversed; therefore, (4) action to protect it is timely or urgent.

The campaign materials developed by the coalition reflect these sources of persuasive appeals. For the indigenous nations, the Zuni Salt Lake and nearby Sanctuary are very powerful places. Zunis describe them as a "church without walls," which evokes emotional commonalities across the divide of tribal and cultural differences (A. Bessler, personal communication, September 24, 2003). Zuni council member Arden Kucate captured this appeal to the area's indigenous cultures as well as the irreparable when he urged his coalition allies, "We have to start thinking in the tradition way. It is not the earth, it is Mother Earth. Zuni people will not sacrifice our Salt Woman for cheap coal to serve Arizona or California, because she is irreplaceable" (LaDuke, 2002).

Over the course of the first year of the campaign, Zuni leaders worked to secure its base and reach out to persuadable groups. First, they sent traditional runners to meetings of the councils of the Hopi, Acoma, Apache, Laguna, and Navajo tribes. Then, the coalition reached out to national federations of American Indians and to area churches to share their sense of the spiritual values at stake and the nature of the threats to Zuni Salt Lake.

As the campaign unfolded, resolutions of support arrived from area tribes, the Congress of American Indians, the Inter-tribal Council of Arizona, and the All-Indian Pueblo Council (Zuni, 2001). The executive director of the New Mexico Conference of Churches wrote an open letter to the Zuni tribe and the people of New Mexico sharing the conference's endorsement of the campaign to protect Zuni Salt Lake. The Reverend Barbara E. Dua wrote, "During this Lenten season, we ask New Mexicans to pray for peace and for the unity of the Zuni people to protect their Sacred Salt Lake and the adjoining Sanctuary District that contains the pristine aquifers, shrines, and burial sites at the proposed Salt River Project (SRP)/Fence Lake Coal Mine" (letter, March 13, 2002).

Finally, the Zuni Salt Lake Coalition reached out to other important secondary audiences. Most importantly, the campaign used the growing support of tribal and public constituencies to gain the attention of the news media and to enlist the support of public officials in New Mexico. I'll describe the importance of these groups as I identify the coalition's strategy.

Strategy: Influencing the Primary Decision Makers

Given its long-term goal to persuade SRP to withdraw its plans for the Fence Lake mine, the Zuni Salt Lake Coalition decided that the best strategy would be to *raise the costs* to the power company in its pursuit of permits for operating the mine. At its very first meeting, members of the coalition pledged to hold SRP accountable by "[making] *it so hard for them that they want to drop it. Make them feel that the Fence Lake project is a fruitless effort*" (Zuni, 2001). This strategy, in turn, focused the coalition's efforts on the campaign's two objectives: (1) to block SRP's ability to tap the aquifer that feeds Zuni Salt Lake and (2) to deny the permits for the mine to open and, failing this, to threaten to appeal. By organizing around these objectives, the coalition intended to place continual roadblocks in SRP's path and thereby increase the pressure on the company to cancel its plans for the coal mine.

Specifically, the coalition sought to influence SRP and the federal officials responsible for issuing the mine's permits (1) by introducing scientific evidence of the ecological effects on the Zuni Salt Lake of pumping water from the aquifer and (2) by launching an aggressive outreach to opinion leaders, news media, and New Mexico public officials.

The first element of the coalition's strategy was to use new evidence of environmental damage to Zuni Salt Lake as a basis for challenging the state and federal permits that had been issued. (By May 31, 2002, the Department of Interior had approved SRP's plan for the mine, allowing it to clear the final permitting hurdle. The State of New Mexico had previously given its permission. Mining at the Fence Lake site was expected to begin by spring

2003.) Coming forth with new research was a critical part of the effort to influence the Department of Interior's compliance with the requirement of the National Environmental Policy Act for an environmental impact statement before a permit could be granted. The research would lay a basis for an appeal of the decision in the event the agency continued to ignore the evidence of the impact of pumping large volumes of water from the aquifer. The threat to file a challenge to the agencies' failure to consider possible environmental impacts of pumping water from the underground aquifers promised to add more costs and delay to SRP's plans to start construction of the Fence Lake Coal Mine. (The importance of NEPA is described in Chapter 3.)

Therefore, the coalition challenged the adequacy of the studies used by the Department of Interior and commissioned independent research on the effects of using water from the aquifer. Ultimately, the coalition reported, "Every hydrological study, except SRP's own, shows that this pumping will detrimentally affect the lake" (Zuni, 2003). Based on its hydrological information (pumping tests), the coalition requested that Interior conduct a supplemental environmental impact study (Chapter 3). Similarly, it appealed the state's water permit pending completion of further pumping tests on the aquifer.

In its appeal to Interior officials, the coalition argued that the **precautionary principle**—an appeal to caution or prudence before taking a step that might prove harmful later—should apply in interpreting the results from models of differing effects of pumping from the aquifer. (I'll discuss the precautionary principle as a standard for guiding environmental actions in Chapter 9.) Throughout, SRP continued to forward its own scientific information and pressed for speedy resolution of the permitting process.

Because the Zuni Coalition members had to respond to its opponents' own communication, they turned to a second element of their campaign strategy—an aggressive outreach to the news media and New Mexico public officials. In part, this was to respond directly to SRP's counter-publicity. It was also to supplement the coalition's work inside government regarding the permits by keeping the issue of Zuni Salt Lake before the wider public. From the outset of the campaign, the coalition members sought creative ways to keep the issue alive.

At the heart of this effort were efforts to generate publicity, "lots of publicity" (Zuni, 2001). From 2001 to 2003, the Zuni Salt Lake campaign generated thousands of letters to newspapers, public officials, and allied groups; placed multilanguage radio ads and rented a mobile billboard; sent runners from Zuni Pueblo to SRP's corporate headquarters in Phoenix; and publicized resolutions of support from the tribal councils and the New Mexico

Conference of Churches. It also mounted two "fax attacks"—deluges of fax messages—on the Department of the Interior to press for delays in its approval of the mining plan and won the National Trust for Historic Preservation's listing of the area as one of America's most endangered places ("Victory," 2003, p. 6).

Typical of the campaign's public communication effort was the distribution of thousands of postcards for supporters to send to Interior Department secretary Gale Norton and SRP president William P. Schrader. The front of the postcard bore a photo of the Zuni Salt Lake and the message, "Save Zuni Salt Lake. Stop SRP's coal strip mine." The text of the postcard to Secretary Norton reminded her of the unique ecosystem of Zuni Salt Lake and its spiritual value to the Zuni, Hopi, Acoma, Laguna, Navajo, and Apache peoples, and it urged Norton to "fulfill your trust responsibilities to Native Americans and deny the life of mine permit for the Fence Lake strip mine."

Communication Message

In all their public communication materials, the campaign pressed its basic *message:* "SRP Is Targeting Our Sacred Lands. Save Zuni Salt Lake." Importantly, the campaign was able to adapt this core message to different audiences, such as church members and people of faith. Particularly in the American Southwest, many people are sensitive to the historical mistreatment of Native Americans. One example of such a cultural appeal was the text of the postcard to the SRP president. In it, the campaign drew on the respect of all religions for sacred sites and emphasized the irreparable nature of the sacrifice of Zuni Salt Lake. The postcard read, "People of faith don't want any sacred areas to be desecrated by a strip mine and railroad for cheap electricity from dirty coal: Not the Vatican, not Mecca, not Temple Square in Salt Lake City, . . . and **not Zuni Salt Lake**."

One of the campaign's best communication tools was a billboard truck that became a common sight as it drove through towns in Arizona and New Mexico. Valtin (2003) reports that after companies in Phoenix refused to accept the coalition's billboard ad, its organizers contacted a mobile company that placed the billboard on the back of a truck. The billboard bore a large photo of Zuni Salt Lake with the crosshairs of a rifle superimposed on the photo, and the campaign's message, "SRP is targeting our Sacred Lands. Save Zuni Salt Lake" (see Figure 7.3). Coalition organizer Andy Bessler explained, "We drove the truck around SRP headquarters and all over Arizona and New Mexico to tribal pueblos, and we got a lot of people to sign petitions" (quoted in Valtin, 2003, p. 3).

Figure 7.3   Members of the Zuni Salt Lake Coalition pose beside the mobile billboard truck used in their campaign

(Photo courtesy of the Zuni Salt Lake Coalition)

In an effort to keep the threat to Zuni Salt Lake before the public, the campaign continually sought creative ways to involve its supporters to generate coverage by the news media. Coalition organizer Bessler explained,

> Tribal members have a different approach, which made us think "outside the box." Where the Sierra Club might air a radio spot to convey our message, the Zuni suggested sending runners. And where we did run radio ads, we had scripts in English, Spanish, Zuni, Navajo, Hopi, and Apache so the spots could run on tribal radio stations as well as on mainstream stations in Phoenix and Albuquerque. (Quoted in Valtin, 2003, p. 3.)

Examples of such thinking "outside the box" included the use of traditional runners from Zuni Pueblo to SRP's corporate headquarters in Phoenix to generate public pressure for the power company to withdraw its plans for the coal mine. (See "Race for the Environment," following.) Another example, on July 19, 2003, was the campaign's scheduling of a People's Hearing on Zuni Salt Lake in Zuni Pueblo. The event included the showing of a video, updates on the campaign, and a People's Hearing. More than 500 people attended the informal hearing to offer their testimony. "At the conclusion of the hearing, the sky opened up and let loose a torrential down-pour, which the Zuni took as a blessing from heaven" (Valtin, 2003, p. 1).

"Race for the Environment: Native Americans Protest SRP's plans for Coal Mine"

(Daniel González, *The Arizona Republic,* July 13, 2002) Native Americans and environmentalists opposed to Salt River Project's plans to open a new coal mine near the Arizona-New Mexico border haven't given up their fight even though the utility has gained all the approvals it needs. In a symbolic gesture of their opposition, runners from Phoenix joined runners from the Hopi Nation and Zuni Pueblo on Friday in a 300-mile, three-day run that began at the Pueblo Grande Museum in east Phoenix and will end Monday at the Zuni Pueblo in New Mexico. "We are showing our support for Zuni and their fight against the mine," said one of the runners, Tupac Enrique, co-director of Tonatierra, a grass-roots group that advocates for the rights of immigrants and indigenous people.

The campaign's success in framing the news coverage (Chapter 4) of the controversy as a struggle over spiritual and ecological values by indigenous tribes began to pay dividends. Most importantly, the campaign's strategy of outreach to media and state officials succeeded in July 2003, when the entire New Mexico Congressional delegation sent a letter to Secretary of the Interior Norton asking her to stop the federal mining permit until new studies of the aquifer could be completed. Their letter also announced that they were planning to bring a lawsuit under NEPA if the department refused to prepare a supplemental environmental impact statement. The prospect of a federal lawsuit threatened to delay SRP's plans even further, carrying out the campaign's strategy of making it *"so hard for them that they want to drop"* the Fence Lake mine.

Success for Zuni Salt Lake

On August 4, 2003, just weeks after the New Mexico delegation's letter to Secretary Norton, SRP announced that the power company had canceled its plans for the Fence Lake mine and that it also would relinquish its permits and the coal leases it had acquired for the mine. This was a rare victory for both indigenous peoples and environmental groups, as such development projects usually proceed; and it is one of the reasons that study of this campaign is noteworthy.

After the announcement by SRP, Zuni tribal councilman Arden Kucate led a delegation to the edge of Zuni Salt Lake to pray and to make an offering of turquoise and bread to *Ma'l Oyattsik'i*, the Salt Mother. Back at Zuni Pueblo, the tribe's head councilman, Carlton Albert, expressed his feelings of relief and appreciation to allies who had worked with the Zuni Salt Lake campaign: "It has been a long 20 year struggle . . . but we have had our voices heard. I feel relieved and it sends shivers down my back to realize how long this struggle has been. . . . If there is a lesson to be learned it is to never give up and [to] stay focused on what you want to accomplish" (Seciwa, 2003, p. 2).

Dilemmas of Environmental Advocacy

Much of the advocacy in the Zuni Salt Lake campaign was carefully adapted to the audiences whose support was critical to the campaign. Yet, this is not always possible. In some cases, advocates may be sharply critical of the larger values held by audiences whose support is needed to effect change. The group Earth First! (2005) seemed to acknowledge this dilemma when it proclaimed, "Earth First!, in short, does not operate from a basis of political pragmatism, or what is perceived to be 'possible.' Wilderness is not something that can be compromised in the political arena. We are unapologetic advocates for the natural world, for Earth" (para. 6). Those who engage in more confrontational rhetorics or actions, such as tree spiking or the burning of ski resorts, face a dilemma of a different type: Does advocacy that may not be rhetorically effective still have consequences that aid the broader movement? Or do such actions harm the goals of environmentalism?

In this final section, I'll describe some of the dilemmas emerging from advocacy campaigns that challenge the beliefs and values of their audiences, as well as dilemmas posed by more confrontational rhetorics that engage in controversial, or even illegal, acts. I suggest that, as environmental advocacy pushes the edges of what is possible, it confronts two basic questions: (1) Must a campaign use language that is socially acceptable to gain a hearing when it pursues a vision that pushes beyond the status quo, or can it appeal to noninstrumental or idealistic values and still persuade others to embrace a radically different vision? (2) Do controversial or illegal actions such as Earth First!'s tree spiking and the Earth Liberation Front's SUV burning make mainstream groups appear more reasonable and thus more acceptable, or do such acts cast a negative light on the motives of all environmental groups?

Must Advocates Use Socially Acceptable Language to Gain a Hearing?

Must a campaign use language that is socially acceptable to gain a hearing when it pursues a vision that pushes beyond the status quo, or can it appeal to noninstrumental or idealistic values and still persuade others to embrace a radically different vision? This question raises a basic dilemma of persuasion: *If environmental advocates must use socially accepted premises or language in order to be credible, can they ever be critical of the status quo?* That is, if advocates must identify with their audiences by evoking beliefs and values that are part of the very system they're challenging, can they ever criticize these same values and beliefs? If they do, can they still receive a hearing from this audience?

Media critic Todd Gitlin (2003) posed this dilemma for social movements generally in his book *The Whole World Is Watching: Mass Media in the Making and Unmaking of the Left.* He observed,

> An opposition movement is caught in a fundamental and inescapable dilemma. If it stands outside the dominant realm of discourse, it is liable to be consigned to marginality and political irrelevance; its issues are domesticated, its deeper challenge to the social order sealed off, trivialized and contained. If, on the other hand, it plays by conventional political rules in order to acquire an image of credibility—if, that is, its leaders are well-mannered . . . and its slogans specific and "reasonable"—it is liable to be assimilated into the hegemonic political world view; . . . and its oppositional edge is blunted. (pp. 290–1)

For example, the Deep Ecology Foundation (2005) calls for dramatic cuts in society's consumer-driven lifestyle and insists, "The well-being and flourishing of human and nonhuman life on Earth have value in themselves . . . *Humans have no right to reduce this richness and diversity except to satisfy vital needs*" (para. 2; emphasis added). But in arguing for humans' noninterference with the natural world except to satisfy "vital needs," Deep Ecology faces a dilemma: Can it appeal to nonhuman values such as the rights of nature and still gain a hearing from those it must persuade? Or, if it uses appeals that are "well-mannered" and slogans that are "specific" and "reasonable," will their oppositional edge be blunted?

Certainly, the use of radical language and predictions of ecological collapse alienate some people. One public opinion researcher has cautioned,

"By using exaggerated doomsday warnings to motivate public awareness and concern, the environmental movement has sacrificed its own credibility by giving in to the politics of Chicken Little" (Guber, 2003, p. 4). Yet, many radical critics view the demand for reasonableness as a step toward co-optation by larger forces. For example, Earth First! cofounder Dave Foreman (1987) warned that "the American system is very effective at co-opting and moderating dissidents by giving them attention and encouraging them to be 'reasonable' so their ideas will be taken seriously. . . . [Yet,] we must resist the siren's offer of credibility, legitimacy, and a share in the decision making. We are thwarting the system, not reforming it" (p. 21).

Yet, the dilemma remains for groups such as Earth First! Is it possible to persuade those who do not share their vision by using uncompromising language, or can appeals to the rights of nature inspire these audiences? Perhaps no other dilemma so sharply divides advocates in the U.S. environmental movement.

Closely related to this first dilemma is a further question: Must advocates appeal to the self-interest of individuals to gain a hearing? Or can they appeal to more intrinsic values of nature? For example, Earth First! (2005) poses the question, "Why Wilderness?" In arguing for the value of wilderness, Earth First! rejects all self-interested rationales for wilderness, such as recreation or the discovery of medicines from rare plants or other motives that appeal to people's self-interest:

> Is it because wilderness makes pretty picture postcards? Because it protects watersheds for downstream use by agriculture, industry and homes? Because it cleans the cobwebs out of our heads after a long week in the auto factory or over the video display terminal? Because it preserves resource extraction opportunities for future generations of humans? Because some unknown plant living in the wilds may hold a cure for cancer? (p. 2)
>
> Earth First! proceeds to answer these questions with a firm "No," insisting that, "All natural things have intrinsic value, inherent worth. Their value is not determined by what they will ring up on the cash register . . . They are. They exist. For their own sake. Without consideration for any real or imagined value to human civilization" (pp. 3–4).

Responses to the dilemma of appeals to self-interest have varied. Canadian environmental studies scholar Neil Evernden (1985), for one, thinks that advocates must throw off appeals to narrow self-interest in winning long-term support for the environment. In his book *The Natural Alien,* Evernden warned that persuasion based on self-interest ("What is useful to me?") is short-sighted and dangerous: "By basing all arguments on enlightened self-interest . . . environmentalists have ensured their own failure whenever self-interest can be perceived as lying elsewhere" (p. 10). For example, the use of financial value as a rationale for preserving a natural area such as a mountain is risky: Is the mountain worth more as scenery or for the mining of minerals? Evernden cautioned, "As soon as its worth is greater as tin cans than as scenery, the case for the mountain vanishes" (p. 11).

Still, advocates face very real constraints in trying to persuade audiences whose support is needed to win concrete victories, such as preservation of old-growth forests or protection of sacred tribal lands. In his study of the sources of influence on audiences' reception of environmental messages, Cantrill (1993) warned that, if advocates are to be successful, they must "attend to the myriad of ways in which people make sense out of environmental discourse itself" (pp. 68, 71). In some cases, this means that advocates choose to appeal to their audiences' self-interest—the health or well-being of their families—for example, in seeking controls on harmful air pollutants. In other cases, advocates might choose to appeal to both idealistic *and* self-interested arguments. For example, advocates with the Zuni Salt Lake Coalition evoked the spirit of *Ma'l Oyattsik'i* and the cultural values of the lake and Sanctuary, but they also used appeals to SRP's self-interest in urging it to avoid further delays and high costs by dropping the Fence Lake mine.

One way to think about this first set of dilemmas is to appreciate the differences between campaigns and critical rhetorics. Campaigns inevitably seek support from key audiences to hold public officials and corporations accountable and must therefore be attuned to the pragmatic dimensions of communication. That is, campaigns cannot escape the basic rhetorical task to discover, *in the particular case,* what is most likely to persuade an audience whose support is important to its objectives. For those who are committed to such a *strategic* course of action, this means that a campaign will often pursue a series of short-term or incremental steps, persuading key audiences along the way, while using each victory to move toward a campaign's larger goal or vision. On the other hand, critical rhetorics have a different purpose. The contribution of groups such as the Deep Ecology Foundation is precisely their willingness to question existing values and to prod, cajole, or challenge society to go further and imagine a relationship with nature or a society different from what is possible now. Such visions, while questioning our current interests, at the same time hold open the prospect of a society that respects both the human community and the natural world.

Do Radical Actions Help Mainstream Groups Appear More Reasonable?

Environmental advocates sometimes face a second and very different question: Do radical tactics—even if unpersuasive—help mainstream groups to appear more reasonable and thus more acceptable? For example, do Earth First!'s use of tree spiking and destruction of logging equipment and Earth Liberation Front's burning of SUVs make the Audubon Society, Sierra Club, or the Wilderness Society appear more reasonable or acceptable, or do these actions hurt the environmental movement by casting a negative light on all environmental groups? Environmentalist David Brower came down decidedly on one side of this dilemma when he once remarked, "I founded Friends of the Earth to make the Sierra Club look reasonable. Then I founded Earth Island Institute to make Friends of the Earth look more reasonable. Earth First! now makes us [Earth Island Institute] look reasonable. We're still waiting for someone to come along and make Earth First! look reasonable" (quoted in Strand & Strand, 1993, pp. 59–60).

The claim that actions of radical groups make moderate groups look more reasonable and therefore acceptable is the thesis of what sociologists call a **radical flank effect** (see McAdam, 1996; Tarrow, 1998; and McAdam, Tarrow, & Tilly, 2001). The most common explanation of how the radical flank effect works is provided by social movement scholar Doug McAdam (1992):

> [A] movement stands to benefit when there is a wide ideological spectrum among its adherents. The basic reason for this seems to be that the existence of radicals makes moderate groups in the movement more attractive negotiating partners to the movement opponents. Radicalness provides strong incentives to the state to get to the bargaining table with the moderates in order to avoid dealing with the radicals. (n.p.; quoted in Gupta, 2002, p. 3)

As usually argued, a radical flank effect is presumed to have a *positive* effect on society's perceptions of the more mainstream groups. Indeed, this has been a basic claim of many writers and scholars sympathetic to radical environmentalism. For example, environmental author Rik Scare (1990) has argued that the effect of radical actions was a major reason behind the formation of Earth First! "Initially, the founders adopted the role of the extremists as a tactic to allow the mainstream groups to look less radical and achieve more protection for the environment" (pp. 6–7).

But this may not always be true. The radical flank effect can work in the other direction as well, that is, the actions of radical groups may produce *negative* views of more moderate groups. Political scientist Devashree Gupta (2002) points out that "there are cases where the presence of radicals in the same movement has deleterious effects on moderates' ability to gain access to decision makers and achieve some measure of success" (p. 6). For example, social movement scholar Herbert Haines (1984/1997) argued in his study of 1960s militant groups that groups such as the Black Panthers, while gaining popular media attention, negatively impacted the goals of more moderate civil rights groups.

Whether the radical flank effect occurs at all in the environmental movement—and whether its effect is positive or negative—has been sharply debated. Clearly, some environmental leaders believe that groups such as Earth First! and Greenpeace do help mainstream groups to appear reasonable and thus more acceptable. At the same time, some writers and politicians have tried to paint environmentalism broadly as a movement of "eco-terrorists," as a result of the actions of some. For example, conservative writer Lowell Ponte (2003) writes, "Once upon a time we tended to regard environmentalists as gentle idealists . . . But in the wake of 9/11, and as environmental extremism has mutated from this to the tree spikers of Earth First! to the firebugs of ELF [Earth Liberation Front], the laughter has ceased" (n.p.).

In other cases, a few states have considered legislation based on the model "Animal and Ecological Terrorism Act" drafted by the conservative American Legislative Exchange Council (www.alec.org). The proposed law is concerned with what its supporters refer to as "eco-terrorism," often referring to actions by the Earth Liberation Front. But the suggested language of the "Animal and Ecological Terrorism Act" appears to define environmental actions other than arson as criminal, and for this reason it has drawn criticism from editorial writers, environmentalists, and civil libertarians for painting environmentalism in general as eco-terrorism. For example, Karen Charman (2003), an investigative journalist writing for online journal *TomPaine.com*, argues that the proposed law "criminalizes virtually all forms of environmental or animal-rights advocacy" (para. 7). Charman explains that some versions of the law that were introduced into state legislatures defined an "animal rights or terrorist organization" as "two or more persons organized for the purpose of supporting any politically motivated activity intended to obstruct or deter any person from participating in an activity involving animals or . . . natural resources." She notes that in one bill, "'Political motivation' means an intent to influence a government entity or the public to take a specific political action."

Despite the attempts by the American Legislative Exchange Council to question environmentalism more broadly, questions of an actual radical flank effect remain unanswered in the environmental movement. To date, there has been no solid research on the impact—either positive or negative—of radical groups on the U.S. environmental movement. Gupta (2002) explains that, in the end, the actual impact of radical groups in a movement "depends on the ability and willingness of moderates to signal their distinctiveness from radical actors," as well as on the "the kind of policy change demanded by the moderates" (p. 4). In other words, moderate groups may well be judged on what media and members of the public think of these groups' own actions and objectives.

Conclusion

In this chapter, I have focused on the environmental advocacy campaign, defined as a strategic course of action involving communication undertaken for a specific purpose. Whereas critical rhetorics stress the questioning or denunciation of a behavior, policy, societal value, or ideology, campaigns strive to win concrete victories. To do this, environmental leaders usually ask, and then work to answer, three basic questions in designing a campaign:

1. What exactly do you want to accomplish?

2. Which decision makers have the ability to respond, and what constituencies can hold these decision makers accountable?

3. What will persuade these decision makers to act on your objectives?

Although similar in many respects to other types of advocacy campaigns, the environmental campaign differs in two respects: It is initiated not by business or government but by local communities and nonprofit groups, and it usually targets a change in governmental policy or corporate behavior rather than individual or consumer behavior. Correspondingly, campaigns face three communication challenges in answering these basic questions. First, campaigns must create *public* support for their objectives (what exactly they wish to accomplish). Second, they must mobilize relevant constituencies to demand accountability from public or corporate decision makers. Third, campaigns must develop strategies that will persuade these decision makers to act on the demands of these constituencies.

I don't want to leave the impression that addressing these communication tasks automatically produces a victory for the campaign. Advocates face many challenges in building public demand to secure protection for the environment. Deeply entrenched and powerful interests often resist change; and sometimes the broader public assumes that corporate or public officials will do the right thing, that there is no need for letter writing, lobbying, or the other communication tools of a campaign. In fact, environmental campaign victories are infrequent, and victories may be impermanent, like the defensive campaigns to protect the Arctic National Wildlife Refuge. Finally, environmental policy can be complex, and the maze of agencies and procedures for public involvement can discourage many citizens from participating in these forums.

Yet, every day many of these same citizens have been willing to speak up for their communities, for natural areas, and for remote wilderness areas that they may never see in their lifetimes. The Zuni people and their allies in Arizona and New Mexico told the nation's third-largest electric utility company to drop its plans to strip-mine coal on lands near the sacred Zuni Salt Lake. Like many community groups, leaders of the Zuni Coalition sat around a kitchen table to consider carefully what steps they needed to take to build public support for their objectives, how they might reach out to potential supporters, and what means of persuasion were available to them to influence a powerful corporation. The Zuni victory came from the vision and persistence of a people who were determined to fight to protect values sacred to them and to their ancestors, and to secure these values for their children, as the Zunis often said, "unto the seventh generation." Similarly, in urban neighborhoods, in rural communities, in the nation's capital, and throughout America, local citizens, environmental groups, and their supporters have protected local green spaces as well as old-growth forests, won victories strengthening the nation's laws for clean air and water, and protected the American bald eagle and thousands of lesser-known plants and mammals. At the same time, they have opened the file cabinets and computers of government agencies to ensure that citizens have the information they need to participate in decisions affecting their environment.

Several years ago, Greenpeace ran a series of emotionally charged, fast-paced video ads celebrating Earth Day on VH-1 cable stations. Shown in the various 60-second ads were ordinary people working in their communities to protect the environment. Typical of these ads were college students working to care for the fragile reefs of the Florida Keys, the residents of a low-income community poisoned by toxic chemicals who organized their neighbors to demand a cleanup and compensation for their homes, school kids in Washington, D.C., who organized ecology clubs at their middle school, and an elderly man in Florida who protected the nesting areas of endangered sea turtles. At the end of each ad, Greenpeace repeated the campaign's message, "Ordinary people are doing extraordinary things."

It is my hope that, when you have finished reading this chapter, you will appreciate some of the elements important in designing an advocacy campaign, as well as the challenge of critical rhetoric in questioning existing practices and ideologies. As a result, I hope you will feel inspired to work with others on your campus or in your community to do extraordinary things.

KEY TERMS

Advocacy: Persuasion or argument in support of a cause, policy, idea, or set of values.

Advocacy campaign: A strategic course of action involving communication undertaken for a specific purpose.

Advocacy campaign design: The directions for implementing a strategy that involves communication undertaken for a specific purpose. Campaign design asks three fundamental questions: (1) What *exactly* do you want to accomplish? (2) Which decision makers have *the ability to respond,* and what constituencies can hold these decision makers accountable? (3) What will *persuade* these decision makers to act on your objectives?

Audience (primary): Decision makers who have the authority to act or to implement the objectives of a campaign.

Audience (secondary): The various segments of the public, opinion leaders, and the media whose support is useful in holding decision makers accountable for the objectives of a campaign. Also called *public audiences.*

Base: A campaign's core supporters.

Communication tasks (of a campaign): (1) To create support or demand for the campaign's objectives, (2) to mobilize this support from relevant constituencies (audiences) to demand accountability, and (3) to develop a strategy to influence decision makers to deliver on their objectives.

Confrontational rhetoric: The use of nonconventional forms of language and action, such as marches, demonstrations, obscenity, sit-ins, and other forms of civil disobedience (for example, the occupation of a campus building), to critique social norms or practices such as racism, war, or exploitation of the environment.

Critical rhetoric: The questioning or denunciation of a behavior, policy, societal value, or ideology; may also include the articulation of an alternative policy, vision, or ideology.

Environmental advocacy: Symbolic discourse (legal, educational, expository, artistic, public and/or interpersonal communication) aimed at supporting conservation and the preservation of finite resources; aims also include support for both natural and human environments and the well-being of the life such environments sustain.

Goal (of a campaign): Describes a long-term vision or value, such as protection of old-growth forests, reduction of arsenic in drinking water, or making economic globalization more democratic.

Irreparable, appeal to the: A forewarning or opportunity to act before it is too late to preserve what is unique or rare before it is lost forever. Cox (1982, 2001) identified the four characteristics of an appeal to the irreparable nature of a decision or its consequences: A speaker establishes that (1) the decision threatens something unique or rare and thus of great value, (2) the existence of what is threatened is precarious and uncertain, (3) its loss or destruction cannot be reversed, and (4) action to protect it is therefore timely or urgent.

Message: A phrase or sentence that concisely expresses a campaign's objective and the values at stake in the decision of the primary audience. Although campaigns develop considerable information and arguments, the message itself is usually short, compelling, and memorable and accompanies all of a campaign's communication materials.

Mind bomb: Term coined by Greenpeace cofounder Robert Hunter referring to a simple image, such as Zodiac boats interposing themselves between whales and their harpooners, that "explodes in people's minds" to create a new awareness (quoted in Weyler, 2004, p. 73).

Objective (of a campaign): A specific action or decision that moves a group closer to a broader goal; a concrete and time-limited decision or action.

Opinion leaders: Those whose statements often are influential with the media and members of the primary audience.

Persuadables: Members of the public who are undecided but potentially sympathetic to a campaign's objectives; they often become primary targets in mobilizing support.

Precautionary principle: An appeal to caution or prudence before taking a step that might prove harmful later. (See Chapter 9 for a more detailed definition.)

Public demand: Active demonstration of support for a campaign's objective by key constituency groups, such as families with small children, voters in key swing districts, elderly persons suffering from respiratory problems, hunters, anglers, or urban commuters.

Radical flank effect: A result claimed for the actions of radical groups that such actions help moderate groups look more reasonable, rendering the latter more acceptable to the mainstream.

Reception of environmental advocacy: The factors that influence audiences' perception of environmental messages. Cantrill (1993) has identified three sources of influence on audience reception of messages: (1) sociocultural influences, (2) informational bases, and (3) strategic-actional concerns or "individuals' ways of thinking about themselves as participants in environmental settings" (p. 82).

Rider: An amendment to a bill in Congress.

Strategy: A specific plan to bring about a desired outcome; the specific steps or means to an end.

Strip mining: The removal of large surface areas of land to expose the underlying coal seams.

DISCUSSION QUESTIONS

1. What mode of advocacy do you believe is most effective in persuading the American public to support environmental proposals? Public education? Campaigns? Image politics? (See Table 7.1)

2. Do you agree with the claim that relying on the worsening of environmental problems to wake people up is an effective strategy for making real changes?

3. Do you as a consumer have power to affect environmental change? Journalist William Greider (2003) says that consumers are in a weak position and have very little actual leverage over the actions of large corporations. Do you agree?

4. Are corporations or government officials always the responsible parties? Do we share accountability for the smog created by our cars' emissions? For the clear-cutting of forests to supply paper for copiers, newspapers, and junk mail? For storm water runoff that carries oil, paint, and other solvents that we pour on the ground or into the street?

5. Do environmentalists use exaggerated rhetoric to gain attention? How can environmental advocates invite public awareness and concern without crying that the sky is falling?

6. Do radical flank attacks help or hurt the mainstream environmental move-ment? That is, do actions such as tree spiking and the Earth Liberation Front's SUV burning make mainstream groups appear reasonable by comparison and therefore more acceptable, or do these acts harm the credibility of all envi-ronmental groups? Do these actions turn people off or invite discussion by interrupting normal but complacent ways of thinking?

REFERENCES

Berger, P., & Neuhaus, R. (1977). *To empower people: The role of mediating struc-tures in public policy*. Washington, DC: American Enterprise Institute for Public Policy.

Bliese, J. R. E. (2001). *The greening of conservative america*. Boulder, CO: Westview.

Cantrill, J. G. (1993). Communication and our environment: Categorizing research in environmental advocacy. *Journal of Applied Communication Research, 21,* 66–95.

Carson, R. (1962). *Silent Spring*. Boston: Houghton Mifflin.

Cathcart, R. S. (1978). Movements: Confrontations as rhetorical form. *Southern Speech Communication Journal, 43,* 233–247.

Center for Environmental Education. (n.d.). *Will the whales survive?* [Brochure]. Author.

Charman, K. (2003, May 8). Environmentalists = terrorists: The new math. *Tompaine.com*. Retrieved May 6, 2005, from www.tompaine.com/feature2.cfm/ID/7748

Cox, J. R. (1982). The die is cast: Topical and ontological dimensions of the locus of the irreparable. *Quarterly Journal of Speech, 68*, 227–239.

Cox, J. R. (2001). The irreparable. In T. O. Sloane (Ed.), *Encyclopedia of rhetoric* (pp. 406–409). Oxford & New York: Oxford University Press.

Cox, J. R., & McCloskey. M. (1996). Advocacy and the Istook amendment: Efforts to restrict the civic speech of nonprofit organizations in the 104th Congress. *Journal of Applied Communication Research, 24*, 273–291.

Deep Ecology Foundation. (2005). *Deep ecology platform.* Retrieved March 3, 2005, from www.deepecology.org/deepplatform.html

DeLuca, K. M. (1999). *Image politics: The new rhetoric of environmental activism.* New York: Guilford Press.

Earth First! (2005). How deep is your ecology? *Earth First! Journal.* Retrieved May 4, 2005, from www.earthfirstjournal.org/efj/primer/Deep.html

Ehrlich, P. (1968). *The population bomb.* San Francisco: Sierra Club Books.

Evernden, N. (1985). *The natural alien: Humankind and the environment.* Toronto: University of Toronto Press.

Flora, J. A. (2001). The Stanford community studies: Campaigns to reduce cardio-vascular disease. In R. E. Rice & C. K. Atkin (Eds.), *Public communication campaigns* (3rd ed., pp. 193–213). Thousand Oaks, CA: Sage.

Foreman, D. (1987, November 1). *Earth First! Journal,* p. 21.

Foreman, D., & Haywood, B. (Eds.). (1987). *Ecodefense: A field guide to monkey-wrenching.* Tucson, AZ: Ned Ludd.

Gendlin, F. (1982). A talk with Mike McCloskey: Executive director of the Sierra Club. *Sierra, 67,* 36–41.

Gitlin, T. (2003). *The whole world is watching: Mass media in the making and unmaking of the new left.* Berkeley: University of California Press.

Glotfelty, C. (1996). Introduction: Literary studies in an age of environmental crisis. In C. Glotfelty & H. Fromm (Eds.), *The ecocriticism reader* (pp. xv–xxv). Athens: University of Georgia Press.

González, D. (2002, July 13). Race for the environment: Native Americans protest SRP's plans for coal mine. *The Arizona Republic,* n.p.

Greider, W. (2003, August 5). Victory at McDonald's. *The Nation,* pp. 8, 10, 36.

Guber, Deborah Lynn. (2003). *The grassroots making of a green revolution: Polling America on the environment.* Cambridge: MIT Press.

Gupta, D. (2002, March 14–16). Radical flank effects: The effect of radical-moderate splits in regional nationalist movements. Paper presented at the Conference of Europeanists, Chicago, IL. Retrieved April 2005 from http://falcon.arts.cornell.edu/sgt2/PSCP/documents/RFEgupta.pdf

Haiman, F. S. (1967). The rhetoric of the streets: Some legal and ethical considerations. *Quarterly Journal of Speech, 53,* 99–114.

Haines, H. (1997). Black radicalization and the funding of civil rights: 1957–1970. *Social Problems 32,* 31–43. In D. McAdam & D. A. Snow (Eds.), *Social movements: Readings on their emergence, mobilization, and dynamics* (pp. 440–449). Los Angeles: Roxbury. (Original work published 1984.)

Harris, S. (1977). *What's so funny about science?* Los Altos, CA: Wm. Kaufmann.

Hunter, R. (1971). *The storming of the mind.* Garden City, NJ: Doubleday.

Klingemann, H-D. & Römmele, A. (Eds.). (2002). *Public information campaigns and opinion research.* London: Sage.

LaDuke, W. (2002, November/December). The salt woman and the coal mine. *Sierra*, pp. 44–47, 73.

Luke, T. W. (1997). *Ecocritique: Contesting the politics of nature, economy, and culture.* Minneapolis: University of Minnesota Press.

Martin, M. (1990). Ecosabotage and civil disobedience. *Environmental Ethics, 12,* 291–310.

McAdam, D. (1992). Studying social movements: A conceptual tour of the field. *Program on Nonviolent Sanctions and Cultural Survival.* Weatherhead Center for International Affairs. Princeton, NJ: Harvard University Press. (As cited in Gupta, 2002.)

McAdam, D. (1996). The framing function of movement tactics: Strategic dramaturgy in the American civil rights movement. In D. McAdam, J. D. McCarthy, & M. N. Zald (Eds.), *Comparative perspectives on social movements: Political opportunities, mobilizing structures, and cultural framings* (pp. 339–334). Cambridge, UK: Cambridge University Press.

McAdam, D., Tarrow, D., & Tilly, C. (2001). *Dynamics of contention.* Cambridge, UK: Cambridge University Press.

Merchant, C. (2002). *The Columbia guide to American environmental history.* New York: Columbia University Press.

Naess, A., & Sessions, G. (n.d.). *Deep ecology platform.* Foundation for Deep Ecology. Retrieved October 8, 2003, from www.deepecology.org/deepplatform.html

National Institute of Environmental Health Sciences (NIEHS). (2003). Fish consumption risk communication in ethnic Milwaukee. Retrieved July 27, 2004, from www.niehs.gov/translat/envjust/projects/petering.htm

Olson, K. M., & Goodnight, G. T. (2001). Entanglements of consumption, cruelty, privacy, and fashion: The social controversy over fur. *Quarterly Journal of Speech, 80,* 249–276.

Orr, D. W. (1992). *Ecological literacy: Education and the transition to a postmodern world.* Albany: State University of New York.

Peterson, T. R., Witte, K., Enkerlin-Hoeflich, E., Espericueta, L., Flora, J. T., Loughran, T., & Stuart, R. (1994). Using informant directed interviews to discover risk orientation: How formative evaluations based in interpretive analysis can improve persuasive safety campaigns. *Journal of Applied Communication Research, 22,* 199–215.

Pezzullo, P. C. (2003). Touring "Cancer Alley," Louisiana: Performances of community and memory for environmental justice. *Text and Performance Quarterly, 23,* 226–252.

Pezzullo, P. C. (2004). Toxic tours: Communicating the "presence" of chemical contamination. In S. P. Depoe, J. W. Delicath, & M-F. A. Elsenbeer (Eds.),

Communication and public participation in environmental decision making. Albany: State University of New York Press.

Ponte, L. (2003, August 4). Eco-terrorism torch. *FrontPageMagazine.* Retrieved May 6, 2005, from www.frontpagemag.com/Articles/ReadArticle.asp?ID=9212

Rice, R. E. (2001). Smokey Bear. In R. E. Rice & C. K. Atkin (Eds.). *Public communication campaigns* (3rd ed., pp. 276–279). Thousand Oaks, CA: Sage.

Rice, R. E., & Atkin, C. K. (2001). *Public communication campaigns* (3rd ed.). Thousand Oaks, CA: Sage.

Richardson, E., & Joe, T. (1995, August 29). Reject that gag rule. *Washington Post,* p. A19.

Rogers, E. M., & Storey, J. D. (1987). Communication campaigns. In C. R. Berger & S. H. Chaffee (Eds.), *Handbook of communication science* (pp. 817–846). Newbury Park, CA: Sage.

Sacred Land Film Project. (2003). *Zuni salt lake.* Retrieved September 24, 2003, from www.sacredland.org/zuni_salt_lake.html

Salmon, C. T., & Kroger, F. (1992). A systems approach to AIDS communication: The example of the national AIDS information and education program. In T. Edgar, M. Fitzpatrick, & V. Freimuth (Eds.), *AIDS: A communication perspective* (pp.131–146). Hillsdale, NJ: Erlbaum.

Scare, R. (1990). *Eco-warriors: Understanding the radical environmental movement.* Chicago: Nobler Press.

Schlozman, K. L., & Tierney, J. T. (1986). *Organized interest and American democracy.* New York: Harper & Row.

Schulzke, E. C. (2000, March 26). Policy networks and regulatory change in the 104th Congress: Framing the center through symbolic legitimacy conflict. Paper presented at the meeting of the Western Political Science Association, San Jose, CA.

Scott, R. L., & Smith, D. K. (1969). The rhetoric of confrontation. *Quarterly Journal of Speech, 55,* 1–8.

Seciwa, C. (2003, August 5). *Zuni Salt Lake and sanctuary zone protected for future generations.* [News release]. Zuni Salt Lake Coalition.

Shabecoff, P. (2000). *Earth rising: American environmentalism in the 21st century.* Washington, DC, and Covelo, CA: Island Press.

Shaiko, R. G. (1999). *Voices and echoes for the environment: Public interest representation in the 1990s and beyond.* New York: Columbia University Press.

Sierra Club. (1999). *Grassroots organizing training manual.* San Francisco: Author.

Strand, P., & Strand, R. (1993). *The hijacking of the humane movement: Animal extremism.* Sun City, AZ: Doral.

Tarrow, S. (1998). *Power in movement: Social movements and contentious politics.* Cambridge, UK: Cambridge University Press.

Torgerson, D. (1999). *The promise of green politics: Environmentalism and the public sphere.* Durham, NC: Duke University Press.

Valtin, T. (2003, November). Zuni Salt Lake saved. *Planet: The Sierra Club Activist Resource* [Newsletter], 1.

Victory and new threats at Zuni Salt Lake, New Mexico. (2003, Winter). *The Citizen* [Newsletter of the Citizens Coal Council], 6.

Weyler, R. (2004). *Greenpeace: How a group of journalists, ecologists, and visionaries changed the world.* New York: Rodale.

Zuni Salt Lake Coalition. (2001, October 6–7). [Zuni Salt Lake Coalition's campaign plan: Edward's kitchen. Notes from first meeting of coalition members]. Unpublished raw data.

Zuni Salt Lake Coalition. (2003). [Website]. Retrieved September 23, 2003, from www.zunisaltlakecoalition.org/background.html

NOTES

1. I am indebted to the many leaders in the U.S. environmental movement with whom I've worked, as well as the Sierra Club Training Academy, in describing this approach to the design of an environmental advocacy campaign.

2. In describing the Zuni Salt Lake Coalition's campaign, I am indebted to the meeting notes of the coalition and its campaign materials, and to Andy Bessler, an organizer with the Sierra Club and coalition member who generously shared his recollections of the campaign in a personal interview, September 24, 2003.

8

Environmental Justice

Voices From the Grassroots

I heard words like "economic blackmail," "environmental racism." Somebody put words, names, on what our community was experiencing.

—Rose Marie Augustine (1993)

The ability to have one's symbols accepted by others is an important source of power. . . . The critical question becomes who controls the meaning of these key symbols, a battle with significant economic and social consequences. In this battle, language itself becomes a form of political action.

—Michael R. Reich, *Toxic Politics* (1991, p. 13)

In small towns and large cities, on Native American reservations, in the agricultural fields of California, at workplaces, in Appalachian communities, and in a heavily polluted industrial corridor in Louisiana called "Cancer Alley," voices at the community level have been speaking against "sacrifice zones" and "environmental racism" and demanding "environmental justice." On the front lines of such community struggles are

- Farmworkers in Kettleman City, California, who formed *El Pueblo para el Aire y Agua Limpio* (People for Clean Air and Water) to fight the spraying of toxic pesticides near farmworkers in the fields
- African American and white residents of Columbia, Mississippi, who organized as Jesus People Against Pollution to demand health studies and cleanup of an abandoned chemical plant that they believed had caused illnesses in their community
- The Mothers of East Los Angeles, a Chicana group formed in 1984, who led opposition to a proposed hazardous waste incinerator in their neighborhood
- Residents of West Virginia, who continue to oppose a form of coal strip mining called mountaintop removal, which threatens the safety of local communities
- Navajos in Northern Arizona and New Mexico who successfully halted mining on *Doko-oo-sliid,* a mountain they consider sacred, for the pumice used to make stonewashed jeans

Perhaps nowhere have efforts been more evident to redefine the meaning and significance of *environment* than in these and other community-based, multiracial struggles for environmental justice. As used by community activists and scholars studying the movement, the term **environmental justice** refers to (1) calls to recognize and halt the disproportionate burdens imposed on poor and minority communities by environmentally harmful conditions, (2) more inclusive opportunities for those who are most affected to be heard in the decisions made by public agencies and the wider environmental movement, and (3) a vision of environmentally healthy, economically sustainable communities.

The first section of this chapter[1] examines poor and minority communities' challenging of the mainstream environmental movement and larger society, which too often define *environment* as a place apart from the places where people live and work. I will introduce some of the voices that not only have criticized abandoned toxic waste sites, industrial pollution, unsafe work conditions, contaminated water, and destruction of sacred lands, but also have charged that the disproportionate presence of these environmental dangers in low-income neighborhoods and communities of color is environmental racism. I'll also examine the emergence of a discourse that articulates the values and vocabularies of both environmental protection and the struggle for social justice in a vision of environmental justice. In the second section, I'll explore some of the impacts of the new movement, including its efforts to build a network, or "a net that works," among grassroots groups facing similar struggles of environmental injustice. The third section of the chapter describes the recurring barriers faced by many residents in these communities when they voice their concerns about environmental problems. In expressing their opposition, members of low-income communities often are viewed as indecorous or inappropriate because they fail to adapt to official discourses of technical reason and economic benefits. Finally, in the fourth section, I'll illustrate the problem of the indecorous voice by looking at a case study of Louisiana's "Cancer Alley," where residents of a rural parish opposed the construction of a large chemical plant in their community.

When you have finished reading the chapter, you should appreciate a more robust meaning of *environment*, one that includes places where people live, work, play, learn, and, in many indigenous cultures, bury their dead. You should have a better understanding of the barriers that citizens from poor and minority communities often face when they call attention to environmental concerns; and you should understand why, in the end, the movement for environmental justice is also a movement for a more democratically open and inclusive society.

Whose Environment? Whose Voice?

The environmental movement in the United States historically has been concerned with wild places and the natural world. In the 1960s, we saw the beginning of a broadened focus of the movement that included human health and environmental quality. Nevertheless, the movement continued to offer "disjointed and at times contradictory" accounts of humans' place in nature, accounts that assumed a "long-standing separation of the social from the ecological" (Gottlieb, 2002, p. 5). Partly in response, by the 1980s activists in minority and low-income communities had opened a new antagonism by challenging society's view of nature as a place apart from the places where people live. In Chapter 2, we defined the term *antagonism* as the recognition of the limits of an idea or prevailing viewpoint; recognizing a limit creates an opening for alternative voices to redefine what is appropriate or just. This opening for new voices also fueled efforts to ensure that processes for environmental decision making are more inclusive, democratic, and just.

Challenging Environment as a Place Apart

By the 1960s, concerns had begun to emerge in the United States about the ecological effects related to new developments in large-scale chemical manufacturing and disposal of toxic wastes. Some scientists and citizens were skeptical of public institutions' ability to safeguard citizens' health in this new petrochemical society. Rachel Carson's (1962) best-selling book *Silent Spring* became the most visible text questioning the excessive use of powerful chemicals such as DDT by agricultural businesses and public

Figure 8.1   Woman with her child in front of her home in the Rocinha Favela.
Rio de Janeiro, Brazil

(Photo courtesy of Nigel Dickinson. © WWF–Canon / Nigel Dickinson)

health agencies, and it set off a national debate over the practices of the
pesticide industry. Two decades later, the small, upstate New York community of Love Canal became a metaphor for the nation's consciousness of the
hazards of its chemical culture.[2]

Increasingly, citizens had begun to feel themselves surrounded by what
environmental historian Samuel Hays (1987) termed "the toxic 'sea around
us'" (p. 171).[3] Many feared that the new synthetic chemicals were having devastating health effects—cancer, birth defects, respiratory illness, and neurological disorders—adding to the public's fears of "an environmental threat
that was out of control" (p. 200). Also, it quickly became evident that certain
communities—largely low-income and minority communities—were most
affected by toxic pollutants and the resulting health and social problems.

Challenging Traditional Language About Environment

Some attempts to call attention to the specific impacts of these environmental hazards occurred before a movement for environmental justice arose. In the
late 1960s and 1970s, a few civil rights groups, churches, and environmental
leaders tried to call attention to the particular problems of urban communities

and the workplace. Dr. Martin Luther King, Jr., went to Memphis, Tennessee, in 1968 to join with African American sanitation workers who were striking for wages and better work conditions—an event that sociologist and environmental justice scholar Robert Bullard (1993) called one of the earliest efforts to link civil rights and environmental health concerns. Also addressing the workplace environment was Congress's passage of the federal Occupational Safety and Health Act (OSHA) in 1970. This landmark law helped "stimulate the budding workplace environmental movements . . . as well as community-based organizations of activists and professionals such as the various Committees on Occupational Safety and Health . . . that sprang up in the early to middle 1970s" (Gottlieb, 1993, pp. 283, 285).

Other early efforts included the 1971 Urban Environment Conference (UEC), one of the early successful efforts to link environmental and social justice concerns. A coalition of labor, environmental, and civil rights groups, the UEC tried "to help broaden the way the public defined environmental issues and to focus on the particular environmental problems of urban minorities" (Kazis & Grossman 1991, p. 247). Other attempts to forge diverse coalitions included the 1972 Conference on Environmental Quality and Social Justice at Woodstock, Illinois; the 1976 United Auto Worker's Black Lake Conference, Working for Environmental and Economic Justice and Jobs; and the 1979 City Care conference on the urban environment in Detroit, jointly convened by the National Urban League, the Sierra Club, and the Urban Environment Conference.

Despite these early attempts to bring environmental, labor, civil rights, and religious leaders together to explore common interests, national environmental groups in the 1960s and 1970s largely failed to recognize and address the problems of urban residents or poor and minority communities. Part of the difficulty lay in the prevailing languages about the environment itself. Some community activists—particularly women of color—complained of obstacles when they tried to speak with traditional environmental groups. For example, in her account of efforts to stop the construction of a 1,600-ton-per-day solid waste incinerator in a south central Los Angeles neighborhood in the mid-1980s, Giovanna Di Chiro (1996) reported, "These issues were not deemed adequately 'environmental' by local environmental groups such as the Sierra Club or the Environmental Defense Fund" (p. 299). Di Chiro explained that, when residents of the predominantly African American and low-income community approached these groups, "they were informed that the poisoning of an urban community by an incineration facility was a 'community health issue,' not an environmental one"[4] (p. 299). Activists in other parts of the country similarly complained that "the mainstream environmental community [was] reluctant to address issues of equity and social justice, within the context of the environment" (Alston, 1990, p. 23). (For other accounts of such barriers, see Austin & Schill, 1994; Bullard, 1993; Pulido, 1996; and Schwab, 1994.)

Faced with indifference on the part of established environmental groups, in the 1980s residents and activists in some low-income neighborhoods and communities of color started to take matters into their own hands.[5] In the process, they began to redefine the meaning of *environment* to include the places "where we live, where we work, where we play, and where we learn" (Cole & Foster, 2001, p. 16).

"We Speak for Ourselves"

A key event in the beginnings of a movement for environmental justice was the 1982 protest by community members against a PCB (polychlori-nated biphenyl) toxic landfill in rural Warren County, North Carolina. In the late 1970s, the state discovered that PCB chemicals had been illegally dumped along miles of highways. To dispose of the toxics-laced soil, officials decided to bury it in a landfill in the predominantly poor and African American Warren County. Rather than accept this, local residents and sup-porters from national civil rights groups tried to halt the state's plan by plac-ing their bodies in the middle of the roads leading to the landfill, to block 6,000 trucks carrying the PCB-contaminated soil. More than 500 arrests occurred in what sociologists Robert Bullard and Beverly Hendrix Wright (1987) called "the first national attempt by Blacks to link environmental issues (hazardous waste and pollution) to the mainstream civil rights agenda" (p. 32; for background on Warren County as a symbolic birthplace of the environmental justice movement and its continued struggle against the toxic landfill, see Pezzullo, 2001).

Prompted by protests in Warren County and elsewhere, in the 1980s and 1990s federal agencies and academic scholars began to confirm patterns of disproportionate exposure to environmental hazards experienced by low-income populations and communities of color. For example, the U.S. General Accounting Office (1983) found that African Americans constituted the majority of populations living near hazardous landfills. In a follow-up study that looked at both commercially licensed and uncontrolled hazardous waste sites in the United States, the United Church of Christ's Commission for Racial Justice (Chavis & Lee, 1987) discovered a similar pattern. Among its key findings were these:

- "Race proved to be the most significant among variables tested in association with the location of commercial waste facilities. . . . Although socio-economic

Figure 8.2   Holy Rosary Cemetery, a stop on a toxic tour of "Cancer Alley," Louisiana. Since the towers of the industrial building in the background are so clearly mirrored in the religious icons of the graveyard that are positioned in the foreground, this tour stop rhetorically represents a symbolic elevation of environmental justice by juxtaposing the sacred and the profane, the progress promised by corporate development, and the incommensurable vulnerability of humans.

status appeared to play an important role in the location of [these] facilities, race still proved to be more significant." (p. xiii)

- "Three out of every five Black and Hispanic Americans lived in communities with uncontrolled toxic waste sites. . . ." (p. iv)
- "Approximately half of all Asian/Pacific Islanders and American Indians lived in communities with uncontrolled toxic waste sites." (p. xiv)

Other research on the racial and income characteristics of communities near environmental hazards soon followed. White (1998) reported that 87 percent of studies of the distribution of environmental hazards revealed racial disparities (p. 63). These studies concluded that minority and low-income populations not only are more likely to live near such hazards but also are "more severely exposed to potentially deadly and destructive levels of toxins from environmental hazards than others" (p. 63). There also appeared to be some disparity in the enforcement of environmental laws. In a study reported in the *National Law Journal*, Marianne Lavelle and Marcia Coyle (1992) found that "there is a racial divide in the way the U.S. government cleans up toxic waste sites and punishes polluters. White communities see faster action, better results and stiffer penalties than communities where Blacks, Hispanics and other minorities live" (pp. S1, S2).

With the heavy concentration of hazardous facilities, especially in low-income neighborhoods or communities of color, there began to appear new narratives of environmental harm. In many cases, such stories spoke of frustration in dealing with local officials and the search for words to express anger and suffering. Reports from community activists with whom I've spoken suggested that people in such circumstances tend to undergo five stages of political awareness:

1. Residents discover that they have been exposed to an environmental hazard and that local authorities withheld this information.

2. They suspect that local health problems may be linked to this exposure and seek answers from local officials.

3. Residents are met with silence, denial, or confrontation on the part of responsible health or public officials.

4. Many residents become angry; their consciousness is politicized.

5. They begin to search for language to explain their situation and for a vocabulary of redress for these grievances.

Many in such communities charged that they were suffering from a form of environmental discrimination. They spoke of being poisoned and complained that their communities were being targeted as human "sacrifice zones" that ignored people and invited sites for polluting industries. Bullard (1993) coined the term **sacrifice zones** to describe two characteristics shared by these communities: "(1) They already have more than their share of environmental problems and polluting industries, and (2) they are still attracting new polluters" (p. 12).

One particularly powerful term used by activists to describe the experience of their communities was **environmental racism**. At a 1991 summit of activists from the environmental justice movement, Benjamin Chavis of the United Church of Christ's Commission for Racial Justice searched for a way to describe "what was going on" in the persistent pattern of locating toxics in poor and minority neighborhoods: "It came to me—*environmental racism*. That's when I coined the term"[6] (quoted in Bullard, 1994, p. 278). Chavis described environmental racism as racial discrimination in environmental policy-making and the enforcement of regulations and laws, the deliberate targeting of people of color communities for toxic waste facilities, the official sanctioning of the life-threatening presence of poisons and pollutants in our communities, and the history of excluding people of color from leadership in the environmental movement. (quoted in Di Chiro, 1996, p. 304.)

While Chavis highlighted the "deliberate" targeting of people of color communities, others pointed out that discrimination also resulted from the *disparate impact* of environmental hazards on minority communities. The 1964 Civil Rights Act used the term **disparate impact** to recognize discrimination in the form of the disproportionate burdens that some groups experience, regardless of the conscious intention of others in their decisions or behaviors. In other words, racial (or environmental) discrimination results from *the accumulated impacts of unfair treatment,* which may include more than intentional discrimination or deliberate targeting.

Naming the problem as environmental racism was important. Residents in communities that suffered from environmental hazards often search for language to name their experiences. Rose Marie Augustine's experience in Tucson, Arizona, was typical. After trying unsuccessfully to get local officials to recognize the problems of polluted well water and illness in her neighborhood, Augustine attended a workshop for community activists in the Southwest. She said that for the first time, "I heard words like 'economic blackmail,' 'environmental racism.' Somebody put words, names, on what our community was experiencing" (Augustine, 1993, n.p.). In other cases, activists themselves began to call the conditions imposed on low-income communities a form of economic blackmail. For example, Bullard (1993) explained, "The plantation owner in the rural parishes was replaced by the petrochemical industry executive as the new 'master' and 'overseer'" (p. 12–13); "You can get a job, but only if you are willing to do work that will harm you, your families, and your neighbors" (p. 23). (For a debate about of this pattern, see "Another Viewpoint: Are Disparities Due to Environmental Racism?")

Another Viewpoint: Are Disparities Due to Environmental Racism?

An objection to the thesis of environmental racism is made by adherents of a market dynamics hypothesis. They pose the question, "Which came first, the environmental hazard or the racial/class makeup of the neighborhood?" (quoted in Cole & Foster, 2001, p. 60).

Continued

Adherents of the market dynamics theory argue that "'the dynamics of the housing and job markets' led people of color and the poor to 'come to the nuisance'—for example, to move to areas that surround waste facilities because those neighborhoods offered the cheapest available housing" (Cole & Foster, 2001, p. 60). These adherents argue that this "move in" hypothesis better explains the presence of low-income communities near polluting facilities. (For example, see Been, 1994; Anderton, et al., 1994; and Lambert & Boerner, 1997.)

Yet, the empirical evidence for this "move in" explanation of the racial and economic disparities among residents near hazardous facilities is decidedly mixed. For example, Vicky Been (1994), one of the early supporters of this view, has reported empirical research indicating that market forces do not lead people of color to "come to the nuisance." More importantly, Cole and Foster (2001) argue that the "move in" hypothesis assumes that individuals' choices about housing and residential locations are volitional instead of constrained by well-documented discrimination in housing and job markets.

As protests mounted against such patterns and the failure of the mainstream environmental movement to address the problems, activists began to insist that people in affected communities be able to "speak for ourselves" (Alston, 1990). In her book *We Speak for Ourselves,* social justice activist Dana Alston (1990) argued that environmental justice "calls for a total redefinition of terms and language to describe the conditions that people are facing" (quoted in Di Chiro, 1998, p. 105.). Indeed, what some found distinctive about the environmental justice movement was the ways in which it transformed "the possibilities for fundamental social and environmental change through processes of redefinition, reinvention, and construction of innovative political and cultural discourses" (Di Chiro, 1996, p. 303). Environmental justice attorney Deehon Ferris put it more bluntly when she said, "We're shifting the terms of the debate" (Ferris, 1993, n.p.).

One important attempt to shift the terms of debate occurred in 1990 when the SouthWest Organizing Project in New Mexico publicly criticized the nation's largest environmental groups, specifically those who belonged to the "Group of Ten."[7] Called "the single most stirring challenge to traditional environmentalism" (Schwab, 1994, p. 388), the letter ultimately was signed by 103 civil rights and community leaders. The letter accused the mainstream environmental organizations of racism in their hiring and environmental policies. A particularly stinging passage stated the signers' grievance with the mainstream groups:

> For centuries, people of color in our region have been subjected to racist and genocidal practices including the theft of lands and water, the murder of innocent people, and the degradation of our environment. . . . Although environmental organizations calling themselves the "Group of Ten" often claim to represent our interests . . . your organizations play an equal role in the disruption of our communities. There is a clear lack of accountability by the Group of Ten environmental organizations towards Third World communities in the Southwest, in the United States as a whole, and internationally. . . . (SouthWest Organizing Project, 1990, p. 1)

Coverage of the letter in the *New York Times* and other newspapers "initiated a media firestorm" and generated calls for "an emergency summit of environmental, civil rights, and community groups" (Cole & Foster, 2001, p. 31).

The First National People of Color Environmental Leadership Summit (1991)

A key moment in the new movement came when delegates from local communities and national leaders from social justice, religious, environmental, and civil rights groups met in Washington, D.C., for the **First National People of Color Environmental Leadership Summit** in October 1991. The summit is generally considered to be important for three reasons. First, it was a "watershed moment" in the history of the nascent environmental justice movement (Di Chiro, 1998, p. 113). For three days, activists from local communities shared stories of grievances and attempted to compose a collective critique of the narrow vision of the environment and the exclusion of people of color from decisions that affected their communities. Second, summit participants agreed upon the "Principles of Environmental Justice" that would powerfully shape the vision of the emerging movement. Finally, many viewed the meeting as a declaration of independence from the traditional environment movement. One participant declared, "I don't care to join the environmental movement, I belong to a movement already" (quoted in Cole & Foster, 2001, p. 31).

For the first time, different strands of the emerging environmental justice movement met together and, with leaders in the U.S. environmental movement,[8] challenged traditional definitions of environmentalism and composed a new discourse of environmental justice that would merge the values of social justice and environmental protection. For example, U.S. representative for the District of Columbia Eleanor Holmes Norton insisted, "We will not be defined out of any issues . . . The way not to be defined out is to define these issues ourselves for [our] own communities." Referring to the title of the meeting, the People of Color Environmental Leadership Summit, she explained, "we have all the names we need in there" (*Proceedings,* 1991, p. 13–14).

Most importantly, summit participants were able to insert their experiences of toxic poisoning into earlier narratives of the U.S. civil rights movement. Running on a monitor during the summit was a powerful example of such a critical rhetoric (Chapter 7). The video showed images of industrial pipes disgorging pollution into the air and water, along with scenes of African American residents of Reveilletown, Louisiana, a community established by freed slaves after the Civil War.[9] The historic community had become so badly polluted by wastes from a nearby chemical factory that it had to be abandoned in the 1980s. Janice Dickerson, an African American activist working with similar communities, provided a running narration as the video showed documentary film images of the Ku Klux Klan burning crosses in the 1960s:

> From the perspective of the African American, it's a civil rights matter; it's interwoven. Civil rights and the environment movement are both interwoven. Because, again, we are the most victimized . . . There's no difference in a petrochemical industry locating two, three hundred feet from my house and killing me off than there is when the Klan was on the rampage, just running into black neighborhoods, hanging black people at will. (Greenpeace, 1990)

By drawing on the "morally charged terrain" of the American civil rights movement, summit participants believed that they would be able to insert a powerful moral claim of justice into the public debate about the environment (Harvey, 1996, p. 387). In so doing, many activists believed that they could contest and/or redefine the meaning of environment itself.

Many of the speakers at the summit also urged participants to demand political representation and to speak forcefully to public officials, corporations, and the traditional environmental movement. At the summit, Chavis explained, *"This is our opportunity to define and redefine for ourselves* . . . What is at issue here is our ability, our capacity to speak clearly to ourselves, to our peoples, and forthrightly to all those forces out there that have caused us to be in this situation" (*Proceedings,* 1991, p. 59). On the last day, participants did so in a dramatic way by adopting 17 **"Principles of Environmental Justice,"** an expansive vision for their communities and the right to participate directly in decisions about their environment.

The principles began with the deeply ethical statement, "Environmental justice affirms the sacredness of Mother Earth, ecological unity and the interdependence of all species, and the right to be free from ecological destruction"

(*Proceedings*, 1991, p. viii). The principles developed an enlarged sense of the environment to include places where people lived, worked, and played and enumerated a series of rights, including "the fundamental right to political, economic, cultural, and environmental self-determination of all peoples" (p. viii). (For a copy of the principles, see http://saepej.igc.org/Principles.html.)

The inclusion of the right of self-determination in the summit's "Principles of Environmental Justice" was especially important to the emerging movement. Many of the summit's participants had criticized the officially sanctioned decision making in their communities for failing to provide meaningful participation "for those most burdened by environmental decisions" (Cole & Foster, 2001, p. 16). In adopting the principles, they insisted that environmental justice not only referred to the right of all people to be free of environmental poisons but that at its core is the inclusion of all in the decisions that affect their health and the well-being of their communities. One delegate remarked that the "Principles of Environmental Justice" represented "how people of color define environmental issues for ourselves, as social and economic justice" (*Proceedings*, 1991, p. 54).

In the decade following the First People of Color National Environmental Leadership Summit, the new movement for environmental justice would extend the new antagonism of questioning the view of environment as a place apart from the concerns of those places where people lived and worked. In doing so, the movement also began to see some successes. Urban planning scholar Jim Schwab (1994) observed that, "the new movement had won a place at the table. The Deep South, the nation, would never discuss environmental issues in the same way again" (p. 393). But the movement for environmental justice also would confront new obstacles and a need to identify new ways to communicate to pursue the vision put forward in the "Principles of Environmental Justice." The remaining sections of this chapter describe some of these successes and the challenges for an environmentalism that builds healthy, democratic communities.

Act Locally!

Do Groups Experience Different Environmental Burdens in Your Area?

In Chapter 3, we learned that Environmental Defense's Scorecard website (www.scorecard.org) allows you to locate pollution in local communities throughout the United States. It also shows the levels of

Continued

environmental burdens felt by the different racial and income groups in each county in the country.

Specifically, Scorecard profiles the different environmental burdens in every community, identifying groups that experience any of four types of disproportionate burdens:

- toxic chemical releases
- cancer risks from hazardous air pollutants
- cancer risks from proximity to Superfund sites
- polluting facilities emitting smog and particulates

Data on environmental justice impacts are also available from Scorecard in Spanish.

Spend some time investigating the different environmental burdens in your community, state, and region. Do different groups suffer disproportionately from toxic chemical releases or other forms of hazardous air pollution or from living near chemically contaminated sites?

Building the Movement for Environmental Justice

One year after the 1991 summit, organizers of the large Southern Organizing Conference for Social and Economic Justice in New Orleans alluded to the "new definition of the term 'environment'" and invited community activists to "to build a new movement" using the "Principles of Environmental Justice" adopted at the summit (letter, June 2, 1992). Indeed, many community activists and others from national civil rights and social justice groups left the 1991 summit to continue building the communication tools, resources, and networks that would be required to change practices in both their own communities and in government agencies.

Opening the Floodgates

The decade of the 1990s saw clear gains for the growing environmental justice movement. Deehon Ferris (1993) of the Lawyers' Committee for Civil Rights in Washington, D.C., observed that, "as a result of on-the-ground struggles and hell-raising, 'environmental justice' [emerged as] a hot issue; . . . floodgates [opened] in the media" (n.p.). Ferris called the early 1990s "a watershed," and the *National Law Journal* reported that the movement—often led by women—had gained "critical mass" (Lavelle & Coyle, 1992, p. 5). A follow-up to the 1991 summit was held, the Second National People of Color Environmental Leadership Summit, in Washington, D.C., October 23–26, 2002. Highlighting women's roles as leaders in the movement, the second event was even larger, attracting more than 1,400 participants. (For information about this event, see www.ejrc.cau.edu/EJSUMMITwlecome.html.)

The "critical mass" of the movement began to be felt: Achievements since the first summit have included expanded media attention, new coalitions with environmental and civil rights organizations, networks offering training and coordination of the growing number of grassroots and community groups, a presidential Executive Order on Environmental Justice, and the beginnings of awareness by state and federal agencies.

In 1993, the movement convinced the Environmental Protection Agency to establish a **National Environmental Justice Advisory Committee** to ensure a voice for environmental justice networks and other grassroots organizations in the EPA's policymaking. The committee—often referred to simply as NEJAC—was chartered to provide advice from the environmental justice community and recommendations to the EPA administrator on environmental justice. For example, NEJAC has produced advisory reports on the cleanup of "brown fields" (polluted urban areas), mercury contamination of fish, and new guidelines for ensuring participation of low-income and minority residentsin decisions about permits for industries wishing to locate in their communities. (For more information, see www.epa.gov/compliance/environmentaljustice/nejac/.)

Finally, the movement achieved an important political goal when President Clinton issued Executive Order 12898, "Federal Actions to Address Environmental Justice in Minority Populations and Low-Income Populations," in 1994. The **Executive Order on Environmental Justice** instructed each federal agency "to make achieving environmental justice part of its mission by identifying and addressing . . . disproportionately high and adverse human health or environmental effects of its programs, policies, and activities on minority populations and low-income populations in the United States" (Clinton, 1994, p. 7629). We'll return to the Executive Order below when we consider a case study of the barriers to environmental justice in the "Cancer Alley" region of Louisiana.

Building a "Net That Works"

In his remarks at the 1991 summit and in workshops on environmental justice, southwestern organizer Richard Moore called for a new effort to build "a net that works" (Moore & Head, 1994, p. 191). By this, Moore meant that the new movement needed to find ways to bring together the diverse communities that were suffering from similar environmental harms. Indeed, the environmental justice movement arose initially from local struggles in which communities were isolated from one another. To encourage communication among the different communities and groups, environmental justice leaders worked to establish regional networks to provide information, training, and the means for organizing political support for projects and campaigns.

One of the first attempts to unite activists was the Southwest Network for Environmental and Economic Justice. SNEED grew out of a multiracial dialogue begun in 1990 in the region by Latino/a Americans, Asian Americans, African Americans, and Native Americans. Its mission was "to build, along with others, a multiracial movement that addresses toxic contamination issues as part of a broad agenda for social and economic justice, one that is fully inclusive of people of color" (Moore & Head, 1994, p. 193). Other regional networks formed in the 1990s were the Asian Pacific Environmental Network, the Indigenous Environmental Network, the Southern Organizing Committee, and North East Environmental Justice. Today, numerous local and regional groups have been formed to promote environmental justice. Additionally, groups such as Urban Habitat started media to disseminate news and information about environmental justice, including the journal *Race, Poverty, and the Environment* (www.urbanhabitat.org). (See also "FYI: Environmental Justice Bibliography Database.")

Finally, Pezzullo and Sandler (forthcoming) observe that there is today "greater awareness of, and sensitivity to, environmental justice issues by at least some environmental organizations" (n.p.). In some cases, vigorous dialogue between leaders of the mainstream green groups and the environmental justice community has led to collaborations between these groups with poor and minority communities.[10] Among the larger, national environmental groups, Greenpeace, Earth Island Institute, Sierra Club, and Earthjustice (a legal advocacy group) have been particularly active in their attempts to support environmental justice concerns.

FYI: Environmental Justice Bibliography Database

The Environmental Protection Agency's Office of Environmental Justice maintains a searchable database called The Environmental Justice Bibliography Database (EJBib). Its Web page declares,

EJBib is a fully-indexed bibliography of published materials relating to environmental justice as well as such related topics as risk assessment and social justice. Intended as a research tool, the database is a project of the U.S. Environmental Protection Agency's Office of Environmental Justice. One aim of the bibliography is to identify significant references to environmental justice in a wide range of literature.

The database represents an ongoing effort that already contains more than 2600 records documenting the environmental justice dialogue. Currently, materials included in EJBib come from various Internet databases of legal, medical, engineering, urban planning, and science periodical articles and books, as well as materials in non-print formats, such as documentary videos, interactive programs on CD-ROM, and other electronic media.

To search the database, go to EJBib online at http://cfpub.epa.gov/ejbib/.

Toxic Tours and Human Sacrifice Zones

One particularly striking form of communication used more and more by environmental justice groups to connect local communities and wider publics is what grassroots activists call **toxic tours.** Communication scholar Phaedra Pezzullo (2004) defines these as "non-commercial expeditions organized and facilitated by people who reside in areas that are polluted by toxics, places that Bullard (1993) has named 'human sacrifice zones' . . . Residents of these areas guide outsiders, or tourists, through where they [residents] live, work, and play in order to witness their struggle" (p. 236). Like other forms of environmental advocacy tours, toxic tours are intended to provide "an occasion for community members to persuade people . . . to better appreciate the value and, thus, the fate of their environment" (p. 236). Although for the last century environmental advocates have taken reporters and others into natural areas such as Yosemite Valley and the Grand Canyon to build support for their protection, use of toxic tours is more recent.[11]

I had the opportunity to join Dr. Pezzullo and other environmental leaders on a toxic tour in Matamoros, Mexico, just south of the U.S. border near Brownsville, Texas, in 2001. Part of the *maquiladora* zone, or manufacturing area, this area has large numbers of industrial plants that have relocated from the United States under the North American Free Trade

Figure 8.3   Toxic Tours help visitors to appreciate how close some people live
to polluting facilities

(Taylor & Francis [http://www.tandf .co.uk]; photograph taken and caption written by Phaedra C. Pezzullo. From Phaedra C. Pezzullo. (2003).
"Touring 'Cancer Alley,' Louisiana: Performance of Community and
Memory for Environmental Justice." *Text and Performance Quarterly,*
23(3), 226–252.

Agreement (NAFTA). Some of the problems associated with this concentration of largely unregulated plants are severely contaminated air and water,
unsafe drinking water, poor sanitation, and the prevalence of rare illnesses
in the population. (See Chapter 6 for a discussion of the high rate of anencephalic births in the *maquiladora* zone.)

The tour through the crowded, makeshift housing for workers and their
families was organized by the Sierra Club and its Mexican allies to introduce
some of the leaders from U.S. environmental groups to the threats to human
health from pollution in the area. As we walked through the unpaved streets
by the workers' homes, we felt overpowered by the sights, smells, and feel of
an environment under assault. Strong chemical odors filled the air, children
played in polluted creeks by their homes, and young children scavenged in
burning heaps of garbage for material they could sell for a few pesos.

Speaking of such experiences, Pezzullo observes that being in a community harmed by such hazards opens our senses of sight, sound, and smell and that this awareness builds support for the community's struggle: "Odorous fumes cause residents and their visitors' eyes to water and throats to tighten . . . , a reminder of the physical risk toxics pose" (p. 248). She shares one toxic tour guide's observation that toxic tours give visitors "firsthand" evidence of "the environmental insult to residents [of having polluters so close to their homes], as well as the noxious odors that permeate the neighborhood" (p. 248). (For more information and a description of a toxic tour in Louisiana's infamous "Cancer Alley," see Pezzullo, 2003).

As toxic tours testify, the movement for environmental justice continues to confront real-world, on-the-ground challenges to building sustainable, healthy communities. Indeed, the vision of environmental justice has always been more than simply the removal of the disproportionate burden on communities. Beyond this goal, the National Environmental Justice Advisory Council (1996) insists that the environmental justice movement also embodies "a new vision borne of a community-driven process whose essential core is *a transformative public discourse over what are truly healthy, sustainable and vital communities*" (p. 17).

Important to the nurture of such a "transformative discourse" is the democratic inclusion of people and communities in decisions affecting their lives. Yet, as we will see in the next section, some community groups have fewer resources—for example, less education, time, money, expertise, and influence—with which to participate in such decision making and may face subtle barriers to speaking in official forums.

Indecorous Voices and Democratic Inclusion

An important theme emerging from the discourse of the movement for environmental justice is the challenge to norms of official decision making and the right of affected communities to be heard. In Chapter 3, I introduced Senecah's (2004) Trinity of Voices (TOV) model of public participation to describe some of the barriers to the ability of citizens to participate and be heard in matters affecting their communities. One important element of the TOV model was a citizen's interpersonal standing—not standing in the legal sense as a plaintiff in court but "the civic legitimacy, the respect, the esteem, and the consideration that all stakeholders' perspectives should be given" (p. 24). It is this sense that often seems at risk as community members struggle to speak and to be respected in official forums. Environmental scholar

Robert Gottlieb (1993) has summed up this challenge as the need to embrace "an environmentalism that is *democratic and inclusive*," as well as one that respects equity and social justice (p. 320; emphasis added).

This section examines one important barrier to a democratic and inclusive environmentalism that arises when agency officials construct the voices of the poor or residents of minority communities as indecorous or inappropriate when they attempt to speak of their concerns in technical forums.[12] We'll also examine a case study of the barriers that one state placed in the path of a rural community as residents tried to speak of their fears of yet another polluting facility in "Cancer Alley."

"Hysterical Hispanic Housewives": Constructing the Indecorous Voice

Let me begin by illustrating what I mean by "construction of an **indecorous voice**." By this, I simply mean the symbolic framing by some public officials of the voices of members of the public as inappropriate to the norms for speaking in regulatory forums and for the level of knowledge demanded by health and government agencies. Believing, for example, that a resident of a low-income community has violated these norms is a way of dismissing the public as unqualified to speak about technical matters. Rose Marie Augustine's story is typical of such dismissal by public officials.

Rose Marie Augustine's Story

On the south side of Tucson, Arizona, where Latino/a Americans and Native Americans are the main residents, chemicals from several industrial plants had seeped into the groundwater table. This contaminated the wells from which some 47,000 residents drew their drinking water. One of the residents, Rose Marie Augustine, described her own and her neighbors' fears: "We didn't know anything about what had happened to us. . . . We were never informed about what happens to people who become contaminated by drinking contaminated water. . . . We were suffering lots of cancers, and we thought, you know, my God, what's happening?" (Augustine, 1991). Environmental Protection Agency officials later confirmed the severity of the toxic chemicals that had been leaching from nearby Tucson industrial plants into their well water and listed this site as one the nation's priority "Superfund" sites for cleanup (Augustine, 1993, n.p.).

Prior to the EPA's official listing, however, residents from the south side struggled to make local officials listen to their fears and concerns. For example, Augustine (1993) reported that when residents met with local officials in 1985, the officials refused to address questions about the health effects of drinking well water. She said that when residents persisted, one county supervisor told them that, "the people in the south side were obese, lazy, and had poor eating habits, that it was our lifestyle and not the TC [toxic chemicals] in the water that caused our health problems." Augustine said that one official "called us 'hysterical Hispanic housewives' when we appealed to him for help" (n.p.). (Augustine's account is typical of the narratives I described earlier, as community activists experience a heightened political awareness.)

Dismissal by public officials of community residents' complaints about environmental illness has occurred in other cases. For example, Roberts and Toffolon-Weiss (2001) reported that local officials in Louisiana's "Cancer Alley" dismissed complaints about illness from pollution as due to lifestyle or to eating high-fat food (p. 117). Earlier, Hays (1987) found that when community members offered bodily evidence of illness, they were often "belittled as the complaints of 'housewives'" (p. 200). As we saw in Chapter 1, such notions of the public sphere mistakenly assume a rational or technical mode of communication as the only permissible form of discourse in public forums. Therefore, I want to describe here some of the ways in which the complaints of certain peoples and communities are routinely dismissed as inappropriate to public discussions about the environment.

Decorum and the Norms of Public Forums

The Tucson official's dismissal of Rose Marie Augustine's complaints suggests that Augustine had violated a norm or an expectation of appropriateness in speaking with government officials. This may appear strange at first, as it is the official's rudeness that surprises us. But the concerns of poor and minority residents are sometimes treated less seriously due to implicit norms for what counts as appropriate or reasonable in matters of environmental health and regulatory responsibilities. It is precisely this subtle barrier that environmental justice advocates continue to oppose as they work to build more democratic and inclusive communities.

In some ways, the unstated rules that operate in many forums addressing environmental problems pose a challenge to those who speak that reflects something akin to the ancient principle of decorum. **Decorum** was one of the virtues of style in the classical Greek and Latin rhetorical handbooks and is usually translated as "propriety" or "that which is fitting" for the particular audience and occasion. For example, the Roman rhetorician Cicero spoke of the "rare judgment" required for the wise speaker, one who is "able to speak in any way which the case requires" or in ways that are most "appropriate"; following the Greeks, he proposed, "let us call [this quality] *decorum* or 'propriety'" (Cicero, 1962, XX.69).

However, within the context of efforts by members of poor and minority communities to speak about technical matters to public officials, the principle of decorum has taken on a much more constraining, even demeaning, role. The norms for what is and is not appropriate in regulatory forums often construct the lay public's ways of speaking as indecorous or inappropriate to the norms of speaking and the level of knowledge demanded by health and government agencies. Although the members of an environmentally harmed community may speak at public hearings or at meetings with a local official, their standing, or the respect afforded them, may be constrained informally by the rules and expectations of agency procedures and norms for knowledge claims.

At this point, it might be useful to describe some of the informal requirements or expectations for speaking in regulatory and technical forums and the violations that encourage officials to construct an indecorous voice for many members of low-income communities.

Epistemic Standing and the Indecorous Voice

With the threat of exposure to chemical contamination, and with official denial or resistance, affected residents often become frustrated, disillusioned with authority, and angry. Ironically, such responses can be prompted by interaction with the very agencies whose official mandate is to help those who feel themselves to be at risk—for example, state or local health departments, the EPA, or state environmental offices. The individuals who become involved with these agencies often find themselves in a baffling environment of overlapping institutional jurisdictions, technical forums, and a language of risk assessment that speaks of "parts per million" of toxic substances. These are unfamiliar contexts for most of us, not simply for the residents of low-income communities. Environmental sociologist Michael Edelstein (1988) explained, "What is lost [for residents in these communities] is their ability to participate directly in understanding and determining courses of action important to their lives" (p. 118). They are, in a sense "captured by [the] agencies upon which they become dependent for clarification and assistance" (p. 118).

This "capture" is enabled by many agency officials' tendency to frame the participation of the public within restricted parameters of agency procedures and norms. As we saw in Chapter 1, industry and government officials often try to move the grounding of environmental discussions from the public to the technical sphere, which privileges more "rational" forms of argument. This is also journalist William Greider's (1992) argument in his provocative book *Who Will Tell the People?* Greider wrote that technical forums too often exclude the lay public by their assumptions about what constitutes legitimate evidence in debates about environment and community health.

Nowhere is this more evident than in the very framing of the discourse that surrounds the category of acceptable risk discussed in Chapter 6. The idea of acceptable risk often stands at the center of a rhetorical struggle between aggrieved communities and regulatory authorities. Environmental educator Frances Lynn (1990) explained, "Public concerns may have as much to do with issues of equity, justice, and social responsibility as with a 10^{-6} possibility of contracting cancer" (p. 96). As long as authorities construe citizen testimony on matters of risk in the bipolar terms of expertise versus ignorance, they obscure critical differences between the claims of technical disciplines and the cultural rationality (Chapter 6) of residents' knowledge and experience.

The weight of past practices helps to explain why government agencies are sometimes reluctant to open public hearings or technical panels to more voices of aggrieved communities. Rosenblum (1983) reported that officials often use technical criteria to restrict the testimony of lay witnesses so that the agency's decision making will not be hampered by what they regard as "an aroused and possibly ignorant public" (cited in Lynn, 1987, p. 359). Under such norms of decorum, for some citizens to speak is therefore to confront a painful dilemma. On the one hand, to enter discussions about toxicology, epidemiology, or the technical aspects of water quality is tacitly to accept the discursive boundaries within which concerns for family health or a sense of caution are seen as private or emotional matters. On the other hand, for worried parents or others to inject such private concerns into these conversations is to transgress powerful boundaries of technical knowledge, reason, and decorum and thus risk not being heard at all.

Indecorous in Mississippi: "The Evidence Is in My Body!"

Charlotte Keyes transgressed such a boundary. Keyes was a young African American woman in the small town of Columbia in southern Mississippi with whom I had worked in my role as president of the Sierra Club in the mid-1990s. Her story continues to motivate my own work now to document the obstacles to citizen involvement in decisions about their environments. Keyes and her neighbors had been living next to an abandoned chemical plant, owned by Reichhold Chemical, that had exploded years earlier. The explosion and fire spewed toxic fumes throughout the neighborhood. The residents also suspected that some of the barrels of chemicals abandoned by the company had leached into the yards of nearby homes and into tributaries of Columbia's drinking water sources. Many of Keyes's neighbors began to complain of unusual skin rashes and illnesses. Officials from the EPA and the mayor of Columbia initially dismissed the residents' complaints as unsubstantiated. No health assessment was conducted. Reichhold spokesperson Alec Van Ryan later acknowledged to the local media, "I think everyone from the EPA on down will admit the initial communications with the community were nonexistent" (in Pender, 1993, p. 1).

Ultimately, Keyes organized her neighbors to speak at a meeting with officials from the federal Agency for Toxic Substances and Disease Registry (ATSDR), who had traveled to Columbia to propose a health study of residents. However, the ATSDR officials proposed only to sample residents' urine and test it for recent, acute exposure to toxins. The residents objected. They explained that their exposure had occurred years earlier, when the plant exploded, and had lasted over a period of years. Having done their homework, they insisted that the appropriate test was one that sampled blood and fatty tissues for evidence of long-term, or chronic, exposure. Keyes urged the ATSDR officials to adopt this approach because, she said, "The evidence is in my body!" (Charlotte Keyes, personal correspondence, September 12, 1995).

The officials refused this request, citing budgetary constraints. In turn, the Columbia residents felt stymied in their efforts to introduce the important personal evidence of their long-term exposure to chemicals that they believed was evident in their bodies. The meeting degenerated into angry exchanges and ended with an indefinite deferral of the plans to conduct a health study.[13]

Unfortunately, the tension between the ATSDR and the residents of Columbia, Mississippi, is not unusual. Too often, agency officials dismiss the complaints and recommendations of those facing risk of chemical exposure who are from low-income communities, believing that such people are emotional, unreliable, and irrational. This is one of the dangers of the highly popular Sandman model of risk (risk = hazard + outrage) that I described in Chapter 6: the tendency of industry and government officials to dismiss citizen complaints as outrage or simply the emotional or hysterical reactions of untrained residents. For example, in a study of public comments on the EPA's use of environmental impact analysis, political scientist Lynton Caldwell (1988) found that "public input into the EIA document was not regarded by government officials as particularly useful. . . . The public was generally perceived to be poorly informed on the issues and unsophisticated in considering risks and trade-offs. . . . Public participation was accepted as inevitable, but sometimes with great reluctance" (p. 80). I have overheard agency officials complain, after hearing reports of family illness or community members' fears, "This is very emotional, but where's the evidence?" "I've already heard this story," and simply, "This is not helpful."

Dismissing Indecorous Voices as NIMBYs

In such settings, citizens who object to the construction of an environmentally hazardous facility or who attribute ill health effects to a polluting plant are often constructed as **NIMBYs**, or "not in my backyard" critics. The phrase usually is meant as a dismissal of critics who object to the location of an industrial facility. The NIMBY label implies that such critics are concerned only about their own community and are therefore selfish and irresponsible. Edelstein (1988) observed that public officials view the NIMBY syndrome as "something of a social disease, a rabid and irrational rejection of sound technological progress" (p. 171). This view undercuts the moral authority of communities who object to being dumped upon insofar as it creates the impression that they would not stand up against such polluting industries if the chosen site were somewhere else.

The charge of NIMBY first arose in the early 1980s as a pejorative label to describe the efforts of well-to-do suburban homeowners who wished to exclude low- or moderate-income housing from their neighborhoods (Williams & Matheny, 1995). However, some officials began to apply the label NIMBY to the motives of environmental justice activists who opposed the construction of hazardous facilities in poor or minority communities. Often, those officials retorted that, "it has to go somewhere." The charge implies that opponents of such facilities fail to suggest an alternative policy (that is, the facility is just placed somewhere else). In response, some advocacy groups such as the Center for Health, Environment and Justice (formerly called the Citizens' Clearinghouse for Hazardous Wastes) use the term **NIABY**, or "not in anybody's back yard" to describe their approach to environmentally just, sustainable communities.

In short, the construction of an indecorous voice—whether as one who is too emotional or as a NIMBY—functions to dismiss the informal standing of certain citizens and their ability to question the claims of public agencies, industries, or expert consultants. To be clear, I am not suggesting that the indecorous voice is the result of rhetorical incompetence, that is, a failure of marginal groups to find the right words with which to articulate a grievance. Instead, I am suggesting that the arrangements and procedures of power may undermine the rhetorical standing, the respect accorded to such groups, by too narrowly defining the acceptable rhetorical norms of environmental decision making.

The result is that citizens from poor and minority communities sometimes face what environmental sociologist Michael Reich has called **toxic politics** (1991). This is the dismissal of a community's moral and communicative standing, the right of residents to matter within the discursive boundaries in which decisions affecting their fate are deliberated. The phrase refers not only to the politics of locating or cleaning up chemical facilities, but to the "poisonous" nature of such politics on occasions. Perhaps one way to understand what is at stake in toxic politics is to examine the case of citizens in a predominantly rural African American community in "Cancer Alley," Louisiana, who tried to speak against a large chemical company.

Trying to Speak in "Cancer Alley"

Although federal agencies have made strides in implementing environmental justice strategies to enable wider public participation, most interactions about environmental matters occur elsewhere. Typically, states are the level of government most deeply involved in decisions about hazardous chemical facilities. Many state agencies have policies patterned on federal statutes for involvement of the public, also are accountable to the EPA, and must comply with its rules for public participation. Nevertheless, some states have come under fire for failing to facilitate the meaningful involvement of citizens who live near hazardous facilities in decisions about these facilities.

Sacrifice Zones in "Cancer Alley"

The small community of Convent in St. James Parish, Louisiana, serves as an example of the failure of some state programs to include low-income citizens in meaningful ways in environmental decision making. Convent lies within the area called "Cancer Alley" by environmental justice activists, dubbed so because of the large number of petrochemical plants that are located along the Mississippi River between New Orleans and Baton Rouge. Pezzullo (2003) notes, "Just as Louisiana's multicultural history and convenient geographical location for water transportation are inviting to tourists, many argue that these features also are central to attracting polluting industries" (p. 227). By 1997, the predominantly African American community of Convent had been surrounded by 11 major industrial sites and ranked third in total toxic emissions in the state (*Louisiana DEQ*, 36, 1997).

In the early 1990s, the large Tokyo-based Shin-Etsu Chemical Company's subsidiary Shintech announced it intended to build a $700 million polyvinyl chloride (PVC) plastics plant in Convent. Polyvinyl chloride production poses particularly hazardous risks for toxic emissions into the air and water of nearby communities. According to the EPA, vinyl chloride emissions "cause or contribute to air pollution that may reasonably be anticipated to result in an increase in mortality or an increase in serious irreversible, or incapacitating reversible illness. Vinyl chloride is a known human carcinogen which causes a rare cancer of the liver" (EPA, 1998, pp. 23785–23786). Shintech's new plant in Convent would have been one of the world's largest manufacturing facilities for vinyl chloride.

Following a brief but highly contentious period of public comment in 1996, Louisiana's Department of Environmental Quality (DEQ) granted air and water permits to Shintech to begin construction on the proposed site. In May 1997, Tulane University's Environmental Law Clinic (TELC) filed two administrative complaints with the federal EPA over the state's handling of the permits. The first complaint alleged violations of the Clean Air Act; the second alleged violations of Title VI of the 1964 Civil Rights Act. (Title VI prohibits discrimination on the basis of race or national origin in connection with programs and activities receiving federal financial assistance and authorizes the appropriate federal agency to take steps to ensure the aims of this policy are met.) On July 16, 1997, the Law Clinic filed an amended complaint with EPA's Office of Civil Rights that supplemented its original Title VI complaint.

The complaints were filed on behalf of a grassroots citizens' group, the St. James Citizens for Jobs and the Environment, and five other environmental organizations. In addition to technical violations of air quality, the second complaint cited unjust, discriminatory effects in the DEQ's administration of its regulatory program, particularly in the conduct of the public comment and hearing process (TELC, 1997). The complaint cited census data for 1990 showing that 81.6% of the residents in the Convent area surrounding the site were African American and poor (p. 2).

The environmental justice community viewed this dispute as an important test case of the EPA's strategy for implementing the provisions of President Clinton's 1994 Executive Order on Environmental Justice. What, then, happened in Convent, Louisiana, that would prompt this precedent-setting investigation?

Standing and Indecorous Voices in the Shintech Case

In February 1999, I had the chance to visit with some of the leaders of the St. James Citizens for Jobs and the Environment group in Convent and to review the complaints they had filed with the EPA.[14] Although the Louisiana DEQ had a legal obligation to involve citizens at every level of review of the Shintech permits, local residents believed that officials had engaged in systematic manipulation and distortion of the process of public participation in the granting of permits for Shintech. The community's Title VI civil rights complaint alleged that the state DEQ had (1) limited citizens' access to public documents relevant to the community's well-being and safety; (2) restricted the communication between DEQ staff and community members in a way that dismissed residents' concerns; and (3) conducted the principal public hearing on Shintech's permits in a manner that greatly lessened the opportunities for opponents of the plant to be heard. Let me cite a few examples of evidence for these charges.

Limited Public Access

Under the procedures established by the state's Department of Environmental Quality, citizens had 30 days to review thousands of pages of technical proposals for Shintech's air permit. In contrast to this, the DEQ had allowed residents in another community as many as 100 days to review fewer than 100 pages in a simple case of a proposed expansion of sewer lines (TELC, n.d.). The citizens' complaint alleged that the level of resources, education, and constraints on time (including family and job commitments) limited the residents' ability to comment on the extensive Shintech material. It stated, "Complainants did not have the qualifications or resources to adequately review the information in such a short period of time" (TELC, *Amended Complaint,* 1997, p. 5).

Compounding this problem were attempts by state and local officials to withhold documents from the public record and therefore from scrutiny by community members. In their study of the Shintech case, environmental sociologists Timmons Roberts and Melissa Toffolon-Weiss (2001) reported that parish officials "appeared to be going out of their way at times to create roadblocks" (p. 121) for the opponents of the Shintech plant. In particular, the opponents had difficulty obtaining a complete copy of the public record of the case. They complained that when they requested public documents, a St. James Parish official raised the cost of photocopies to 75 cents per page, making it unaffordable (TELC, n.d., p. 4). On another occasion, a parish employee admitted to destroying a document related to the Shintech case (Roberts & Toffolon-Weiss, 2001, p. 121).

Refusal to Talk With the Community

In August 1998, a state judge noted obvious bias in the actions of a DEQ official charged with oversight of the Shintech permit. The official apparently had ordered his staff not to meet with citizens' groups and to regard the citizens as adversaries of the department. No such restrictions were placed on meetings between DEQ and Shintech or its supporters (TELC, n.d., p. 8). The Tulane Environmental Law Clinic uncovered evidence that state agencies actively met with business groups and Shintech itself to "try to push forward the [company's] siting decision" (p. 121).

Restrictions on Public Testimony

By all accounts, the major obstacle in the opponents' path was the "highly charged" public hearing on the plant's air quality permit, which took place the night of December 9, 1996 (Roberts & Toffolon-Weiss, 2001, p. 122). The amended Title VI complaint alleged that the state DEQ conducted the public hearing "in a discriminatory manner, favoring the Shintech proponents and impeding African American residents from fully participating in the hearing process" (TELC, 1997, p. 7). This occurred both in the order in which residents were assigned to speak and in the amount of time different speakers were allowed during the hearing.

The manipulation of the hearing procedure appeared evident even before the hearings began. Pat Melancon, president of the St. James Citizens for Jobs and the Environment, testified that she had "arrived two hours early to an empty meeting to find 45 names of people signed up by Shintech who [weren't] there yet" (TELC, n.d., p. 4). The community's amended complaint explained,

> The [DEQ] has a policy of allowing people to speak in the order in which they arrive and register at the hearing. . . . Before the citizens had an opportunity to reach the site, . . . Shintech submitted a stack of sign-in sheets for many of Shintech's paid employees and contractors that Shintech flew in from [their plant in] Texas for the occasion. These sheets were accepted by . . . the LDEQ's assistant administrator for permits, who then proceeded to transfer all of the names on the sheets to the speaking list. (TELC, 1997, p. 7)

Roberts and Toffolon-Weiss (2001) similarly reported that the company "inquired several weeks before the meeting as to the manner in which the order of speakers would be determined," and then its supporters "showed up early and signed in" (p. 123).

This speaking arrangement resulted in Shintech's officers, employees, and paid consultants being the only ones called to speak for the first hour of the meeting. Roberts and Toffolon-Weiss (2001) reported that, of those speaking in favor of Shintech that night, at least 15 speakers "were paid

employees, many of whom were flown in from [its] Freeport, Texas, plant";
other nonlocal speakers supporting the plant included "thirteen industry
consultants, lobbyists, or employees of contractors of Shintech" (p. 122,
237, note 67). Of the citizens who were signed up to speak in opposition to
the plant, at least 16 were excluded from the hearing. "These people's names
were called after 11:15 and [they] had already left the hearing because of
jobs, family obligations, to eat, etc." (p. 123).

Second, the citizens' complaint alleged that, although the DEQ imposed a
five-minute time limit for all public comments at the hearing, the presiding
officer "selectively enforced this limit" (TELC, 1997, p. 7). The complaint
detailed the sequence of events for the hearing: "The time limit was ignored
for the first hour of the hearing when predominantly Shintech proponents
were speaking. No speaker was interrupted or stopped, despite the fact that
many went over the time limit. The DEQ choose to enforce the five-minute
time limit for the first time on a citizen speaker" (TELC, 1997, p. 7).

Finally, when residents complained about the state's conduct of the hearing, the DEQ refused to grant another opportunity for oral comments,
suggesting instead that Convent residents submit written testimony. The citizens' amended complaint objected that this had the effect of dismissing the
views of those opposed to the plant: "For many of these people, written
comments are not an option. Even those having the ability to write comments often do not feel comfortable expressing themselves that way. The
only opportunity that they had to be heard was during the public hearing"
(TELC, 1997, p. 8).

Such limitations and, in some cases, subversion of rules, reminds us that
the processes for guaranteeing public participation that look good on paper
may be co-opted or manipulated in opposition to citizen interests. This is
the point I made at the end of Chapter 3 and in the beginning of Chapter 4,
and you may wish to review those sections to understand the basis for the
Convent complaint. However, in this case the local group's appeal to the
EPA succeeded. On September 10, 1997, EPA administrator Carol Browner
granted the first petition, citing more than 50 technical deficiencies under the
Clean Air Act, and reopened the public comment and hearing process for the
air permits. Browner directed the Louisiana DEQ to rehear Shintech's
request for permits and ensure fair procedures for including citizens' voices.
The ruling deferred the related allegations of discriminatory behavior in the
public participation process but noted that it was taking the Title VI claims
of discrimination seriously and that the EPA Office of Civil Rights would
investigate further. Although the EPA ruling centered on technical faults in
the air permit, it also indicated that the state agency had to address the concerns of minority and low-income residents in the new permitting process

(Ferstel, 1997). On September 18, 1998, Shintech withdrew its plans for the polyvinyl chloride manufacturing plant at the Convent site. The struggle by citizens that had raged for two years ended abruptly. Although many local residents felt they had won, others found the ending inconclusive: A smaller version of the plant would be built elsewhere,[15] and unfortunately there would be no "landmark precedent-setting decision from the EPA" (Roberts & Toffolon-Weiss, 2001, pp. 130–131). The environmental justice movement's challenge to build democratic and inclusive communities would have to continue in other places.

Conclusion

As the multiracial, community-based environmental justice movement introduces new voices into the public dialogue about environmental policy in the United States, it has begun to challenge traditional views of the environment as a place apart—as wilderness or natural areas. In doing so, it reveals the limit of these views, an antagonism that allows other voices to be heard and other relationships to the environment to be voiced. In particular, the charge that poor and minority communities suffer from environmental racism has focused attention on the disproportionate presence of environmental harms in these communities, from east Los Angeles to the rural parishes of Louisiana. The discourse about the meaning of the environment as including the places where people live, work, play, and learn has nurtured not only a more expansive vision of *environment* but also a demand for environmental justice: (1) a call to recognize and halt the disproportionate burdens imposed on poor and minority communities by environmentally harmful conditions, (2) more inclusive opportunities for those who are most affected to be heard in the decisions made by public agencies and the wider environmental movement, and (3) a vision of environmentally healthy, economically sustainable communities.

Although the EJ movement has seen some successes in forestalling new environmental hazards—for example, Shintech's PVC plant in southern Louisiana—the movement continues to face challenges. Foremost has been the effort to open public agencies and regulatory procedures to include the voices of people in affected communities. Unfortunately, the construction of what we have described as "indecorous voices" is still a feature of some regulatory hearings that privilege technical reason and dismiss the objections of community members as private and uninformed.

Finally, both EJ groups and the traditional environmental movement are beginning to discover ways to work together—a heartening sign. Nevertheless, as Robert Gottlieb (2003) observes, there remains a challenging question for both groups: "Can mainstream and alternative groups find a common language, a shared history, a common conceptual and organizational home?" (p. 254). The challenge is complex as diverse groups explore the implications of redefining *environment* as both human communities and natural spaces. In their book *Environmental Justice and Environmentalism: Contrary or Complimentary?* Pezzullo and Sandler (forthcoming) pose similar questions as the environmental justice movement and national environmental groups go about assessing their relationship: "If and when the commitments of environmental justice and environmentalism conflict, how does one determine which ought to take precedence? Does self-determination trump ecological integrity? . . . If environmentalists were to listen, who has the right to speak for environmental justice communities?" (n.p.).

These are difficult questions for both environmental justice and traditional environmental groups. But even as each addresses these concerns, a more robust meaning of the environment already is emerging in the struggles of rural and urban communities and tribal councils and in the ongoing exchanges among leaders in social justice, labor, indigenous, civil rights, religious, and environmental movements. Indeed, as I write, a new vision of "transformative alliances" (Gelobter, et al., 2005, p. 26) is emerging among these movements. Michel Gelobter, executive director of Redefining Progress, and colleagues from environmental justice and allied movements recently issued a provocative challenge in *The Soul of Environmentalism* to "break the unwritten gag rule about race and class" in revisioning environmentalism and to urge social change groups to work more closely together:

> Environmentalism, like poetry, has a soul deeper and more eternal than the one described by its examiners. It's a soul tied deeply to human rights and social justice, and this tie has been nurtured by the Environmental Justice and Sustainability movements for the past 20 years. We are writing to explore this soul, to break the unwritten gag rule about race and class, and to examine the intermingled roots of social change movements. These roots, these rules and this soul together hold the key to environmentalism's new life. (Gelobter, et al., 2005, p. 6)

In the end, nurturing such transformational alliances may offer the best hope for creating a socially just, ecologically sustainable society.

KEY TERMS

Decorum: One of the virtues of style in the classical Greek and Latin rhetorical handbooks; usually translated as "propriety" or "that which is fitting" for the particular audience and occasion.

Disparate impact: Term used to denote the discrimination resulting from environmental hazards in minority communities; adopted from the 1964 Civil Rights Act, which used it to recognize forms of discrimination that result from the disproportionate burdens experienced by some groups regardless of the conscious intention of others in their decisions or behaviors.

Environmental justice: As used by community activists and scholars studying the environmental justice movement, the term refers to (1) calls to recognize and halt the disproportionate burdens imposed on poor and minority communities by environmentally harmful conditions, (2) more inclusive opportunities for those who are most affected to be heard in the decisions made by public agencies and the wider environmental movement, and (3) a vision of environmentally healthy, economically sustainable communities.

Environmental racism: Term used to denote the persistent pattern of locating toxics in poor and minority neighborhoods; defined by Benjamin Chavis at the 1991 First People of Color National Environmental Leadership Summit as "racial discrimination in environmental policymaking and the enforcement of regulations and laws, the deliberate targeting of people of color communities for toxic waste facilities, the official sanctioning of the life-threatening presence of poisons and pollutants in our communities, and the history of excluding people of color from leadership in the environmental movement" (quoted in Di Chiro, 1996, p. 304). Also refers to the disproportionate impact of environmental harms on communities of color. (See also *disparate impact.*)

Executive Order on Environmental Justice: Issued by President Clinton in 1994, Executive Order 12898, "Federal Actions to Address Environmental Justice in Minority Populations and Low-Income Populations," instructed each federal agency "to make achieving environmental justice part of its mission by identifying and addressing . . . disproportionately high and adverse human health or environmental effects of its programs, policies, and activities on minority populations and low-income populations in the United States" (Clinton, 1994, p. 7629).

First National People of Color Environmental Leadership Summit: A key moment in the new movement for environmental justice when delegates from local communities and national leaders from social justice, religious, environmental, and civil rights groups met in Washington, D.C., in October 1991.

Indecorous voice: The symbolic framing by some public officials of the voices of others as inappropriate to the norms for speaking in regulatory forums and for the level of knowledge demanded by health and government agencies; a way of dismissing the public as unqualified to speak about technical matters.

National Environmental Justice Advisory Council (NEJAC): A federal advisory committee in the Environmental Protection Agency that is intended to provide the EPA administrator with independent advice, consultation, and recommendations related to environmental justice.

NIABY: Acronym for "not in anybody's back yard," a term used to describe the response of environmental justice advocates to the charge of being a NIMBY ("not in my backyard"); used to suggest an alternate approach to environmentally just, or sustainable, communities.

NIMBY: Acronym for "not in my backyard," usually meant to dismiss critics of the location of an industrial facility; implies that critics are concerned only about their own communities and are therefore selfish. (See *NIABY*.)

"Principles of Environmental Justice": Seventeen principles articulating an expansive vision for communities of people of color and the right to participate directly in decisions about their environments, adopted by delegates at the First People of Color National Environmental Summit in 1991.

Sacrifice zones: Term coined by sociologist Robert Bullard (1993) to denote communities that share two characteristics: "(1) They already have more than their share of environmental problems and polluting industries, and (2) they are still attracting new polluters" (p. 12).

Toxic politics: Term introduced by sociologist Michael Reich (1991) that refers to the dismissal of a community's moral and communicative standing in deliberations about chemical pollution.

Toxic tours: "Non-commercial expeditions organized and facilitated by people who reside in areas that are polluted by toxics, places that Bullard (1993) has named 'human sacrifice zones' . . . Residents of these areas guide outsiders, or tourists, through where they [residents] live, work, and play in order to witness their struggle" (Pezzullo, 2004, p. 236). (See *sacrifice zones*.)

DISCUSSION QUESTIONS

1. Does environmental racism exist? What evidence would you regard as compelling proof that it does or does not exist in a particular situation?

2. Should we as a society be willing to accept some dangers, and even deaths, in order to enjoy the benefits of advanced industrial society? Who in society most often accepts these burdens? Who most often enjoys the benefits of industrial society?

3. Gottlieb poses a deeply challenging question: "Can mainstream and alternative groups find a common language, a shared history, a common conceptual and organizational home?" (in Warren, 2003, p. 254). What do you think? How effectively can traditional green groups and activists from poor and minority neighborhoods work together on problems of environmental injustice in the future?

4. Are local opponents to facilities such as hazardous waste incinerators merely NIMBYs who are motivated by a not-in-my-back-yard attitude? If not there,

where would they be located? Should society develop alternatives that go beyond simply burning or burying toxic wastes? What might these alternatives be?

5. Should ordinary citizens be permitted to testify at hearings where a decision pivots on technical expertise? Do members of a local community have experience or knowledge that offers a "local expertise," or should they be asked to defer to those with technical expertise?

6. Where do you feel it's important to maintain rules of decorum? In the classroom? In a courtroom? Have you ever found such norms to be culturally biased or limiting? If so, how? Do we have an obligation in a democracy to listen to a broad spectrum of voices, despite different ways of communicating? Why or why not?

REFERENCES

Alston, D. (1990). *We speak for ourselves: Social justice, race, and environment.* Washington, DC: Panos Institute.

Alston, D. (1991). Remarks in *Proceedings: The First National People of Color Environmental Leadership Summit.* New York: United Church of Christ Commission for Racial Justice.

Anderton, D. L., Anderson, A. B., Oakes, J. M., & Fraser, M. (1994). Environmental equity: The demographics of dumping. *Demography, 31,* 221–240.

Augustine, R. M. (Speaker). (1991). *Documentary highlights of the First National People of Color Environmental Leadership Conference* [Videotape]. Washington, DC: United Church of Christ Commission for Racial Justice.

Augustine, R. M. (Speaker). (1993, October 21–24). *Environmental justice: Continuing the dialogue* [Cassette recording]. Recorded at the Third Annual Meeting of the Society of Environmental Journalists, Durham, NC.

Austin, R., & Schill, M. (1994). Black, brown, red and poisoned. In R. D. Bullard (Ed.), *Unequal protection: Environmental justice and communities of color* (pp. 53–76). San Francisco: Sierra Club Books.

Been, V. (1994). Locally undesirable land uses in minority neighborhoods: Disproportionate siting or market dynamics? *Yale Law Journal, 103,* pp. 1301–1422.

Bullard, R. D. (1993). Introduction. In R. D. Bullard (Ed.), *Confronting environmental racism: Voices from the grassroots* (pp. 7–13). Boston: South End Press.

Bullard, R. D. (Ed.). (1994). *Unequal protection: Environmental justice and communities of color.* San Francisco: Sierra Club Books.

Bullard, R. D., & Wright, B. H. (1987). Environmentalism and the politics of equity: Emergent trends in the black community. *Mid-American Review of Sociology, 12,* 21–37.

Caldwell, L. K. (1988). Environmental impact analysis (EIA): Origins, evolution, and future directions. *Policy Studies Review, 8,* 75–83.

Carson, R. (1962). *Silent spring.* Greenwich, CT: Fawcett Crest.

Chavis, B. F., & Lee, C. (1987). Toxic wastes and race in the United States: A national report on the racial and socio-economic characteristics of communities with hazardous waste sites. New York: Commission for Racial Justice, United Church of Christ.

Cicero, M. T. (1962). *Orator* (Rev. ed.). (H. M. Hubell & G. L. Hendrickson, Trans.). Cambridge: Harvard University Press.

Clinton, W. J. (1994, February 16). Federal actions to address environmental justice in minority populations and low-income populations. Executive Order 12898 of February 14, 1994. *Federal Register, 59,* 7629.

Cole, L. W., & Foster, S. R. (2001). *From the ground up: Environmental racism and the rise of the environmental justice movement.* New York: New York University Press.

Cox, J. R. (2001). Reclaiming the "indecorous" voice: Public participation by low-income communities in environmental decision making. In C. B. Short & D. Hardy-Short (Eds.), *Proceedings of the Fifth Biennial Conference on Communication and Environment* (pp. 21–31). Flagstaff: Northern Arizona University School of Communication.

Di Chiro, G. (1996). Nature as community: The convergence of environment and social justice. In W. Cronon (Ed.), *Uncommon ground: Rethinking the human place in nature* (pp. 298–320). New York: W. W. Norton.

Di Chiro, G. (1998). Environmental justice from the grassroots: Reflections on history, gender, and expertise. In D. Faber (Ed.), *The struggle for ecological democracy: Environmental justice movements in the United States* (pp. 104–136). New York: Guilford Press.

Edelstein, M. R. (1988). *Contaminated communities: The social and psychological impacts of residential toxic exposure.* Boulder, CO: Westview.

Environmental Protection Agency. (1998, April 30). *Federal Register, 63*(83), 23785–23786.

Ferris, D. (Speaker). (1993, October 21–24). *Environmental justice: Continuing the dialogue* [Cassette recording]. Recorded at the Third Annual Meeting of the Society of Environmental Journalists, Durham, NC.

Ferstel, V. (1997, September 11). EPA reopens Shintech permit hearings. *New Orleans Times-Picayune,* p. 1.

Gelobter, M., Dorsey, M., Fields, L., Goldtooth, T., Mendiratta, A., Moore, R., Morello-Frosh, R., Shepard, P., & Torres, G. (2005, May 23). *The soul of environmentalism: Rediscovering transformational politics in the 21st century.* Oakland, CA: Redefining Progress. Retrieved May 26, 2005, from www.soulofenvironmentalism.org

Gibbs, L. M. (1995). *Dying from dioxin: A citizen's guide to reclaiming our health and rebuilding democracy.* Boston, MA: South End Press.

Gottlieb, R. (1993). *Forcing the spring: The transformation of the American environmental movement.* Washington, DC: Island Press.

Gottlieb, R. (2002). *Environmentalism unbound: Exploring new pathways for change.* Cambridge: MIT Press.

Gottlieb, R. (2003). Reconstructing environmentalism: Complex movements, diverse roots. In L. S. Warren (Ed.), *American environmental history* (pp. 245–256). Malden, MA: Blackwell.

Greenpeace. (1990, April). *Ordinary people, doing extraordinary things.* [Videotape]. Public service announcement broadcast on VH-1 Channel.

Greider, W. (1992). *Who will tell the people: The betrayal of American democracy.* New York: Simon & Schuster.

Harvey, D. (1996). *Justice, nature, and the geography of difference.* Malden, MA: Blackwell.

Hays, S. P. (1987). *Beauty, health, and permanence: Environmental politics in the United States, 1955–1985.* Cambridge, UK: Cambridge University Press.

Kazis, R., & Grossman, R. L. (1991). *Fear at work: Job blackmail, labor, and the environment.* Philadelphia: New Society.

Lambert, T., & Boerner, C. (1997). Environmental inequity, economic causes, economic solutions. *Yale Journal on Regulation, 14,* 198–203.

Lavelle, M., & Coyle, M. (1992, September 21). Unequal protection: The racial divide in environmental law. *National Law Journal,* S1, S2.

Louisiana Department of Environmental Quality. (1997, February). *Louisiana toxics release inventory 1995* (8th an. ed.). Baton Rouge, LA: Author.

Lynn, F. M. (1987). Citizen involvement in hazardous waste sites: Two North Carolina access stories. *Environmental Impact Assessment and Review, 7,* 347–361.

Lynn, F. M. (1990, April). Public participation in risk management decisions. *Issues in Health and Safety, 1*(2), 95–101.

Moore, R, & Head, L. (1994). Building a net that works. In Bullard, R. D. (Ed.), *Unequal protection: Environmental justice and communities of color* (pp. 191–206). San Francisco: Sierra Club Books.

National Environmental Justice Advisory Council Subcommittee on Waste and Facility Siting. (1996). *Environmental justice, urban revitalization, and brownfields: The search for authentic signs of hope.* (Report Number EPA 500-R-96–002). Washington, DC: U.S. Environmental Protection Agency.

Pender, G. (1993, June 1). Residents still not satisfied: Plant cleanup fails to ease Columbia fears. *Hattiesburg* [MS] *American,* p. 1.

Pezzullo, P. C. (2001). Performing critical interruptions: Rhetorical invention and narratives of the environmental justice movement. *Western Journal of Communication, 64,* 1–25.

Pezzullo, P. C. (2003). Touring "Cancer Alley," Louisiana: Performances of community and memory for environmental justice. *Text and Performance Quarterly, 23,* 226–252.

Pezzullo, P. C. (2004). Toxic tours: Communicating the "presence" of chemical contamination. In S. P. Depoe, J. W. Delicath, & M.-F. A. Elsenbeer (Eds.), *Communication and public participation in environmental decision making* (pp. 235–254). Albany: State University of New York Press.

Pezzullo, P. C., & Cox, J. R. (2001). *Re-articulating 'environment': Rhetorical invention, subaltern counterpublics, and the movement for environmental justice.* Unpublished manuscript.

Pezzullo, P. C., & Sandler, R. (Eds.). (In press). *Environmental justice and environmentalism: Contrary or complimentary?* Cambridge: MIT Press.

Proceedings: The First People of Color National Environmental Leadership Summit. (1991, October 24–27). Washington, DC: United Church of Christ Commission for Racial Justice.

Pulido, L. (1996). *Environmentalism and economic justice: Two Chicano struggles in the southwest.* Tucson: University of Arizona Press.

Reich, M. R. (1991). *Toxic politics: Responding to chemical disasters.* Ithaca: Cornell University Press.

Roberts, J. T., & Toffolon-Weiss, M. M. (2001). *Chronicles from the environmental justice frontline.* Cambridge, UK: Cambridge University Press.

Rosenblum, W. (1983). The politics of public participation in hazardous waste management. In J. P. Lester & A. O. Bowman (Eds.), *The politics of hazardous waste management.* Durham, NC: Duke University Press.

Schwab, J. (1994.) *Deeper shades of green: The rise of blue-collar and minority environmentalism in America.* San Francisco: Sierra Club Books.

Senecah, S. L. (2004). The trinity of voice: The role of practical theory in planning and evaluating the effectiveness of environmental participatory processes. In S. P. DePoe, J. W. Delicath, & M-F. A. Elsenbeer (Eds.), *Communication and public participation in environmental decision making* (pp.13–33). Albany: State University of New York Press.

SouthWest Organizing Project. (1990, March 16). Letter to the "Group of Ten" national environmental organizations.

Tulane Environmental Law Clinic. (n.d.). *Shintech Controversy Timeline.* Unpublished manuscript.

Tulane Environmental Law Clinic. (1997, July 16). *Amended complaint under Title VI of the Civil Rights Act, before the Administrator, the United States Environmental Protection Agency, Washington, DC.* New Orleans: Tulane University.

U.S. General Accounting Office. (1983). *Siting of hazardous waste landfills and their correlation with racial and economic status of surrounding communities.* Washington, DC: Author.

Warren, L. S. (2003). *American environmental history.* Malden, MA, and Oxford, UK: Blackwell.

White, H. L. (1998). Race, class, and environmental hazards. In D. E. Camacho (Ed.), *Environmental injustices, political struggle: Race, class, and the environment.* Durham, NC: Duke University Press.

Williams, B. A., & Matheny, A. R. (1995). *Democracy, dialogue, and environmental disputes: The contested language of social regulation.* New Haven: Yale University Press.

NOTES

1. I am indebted to Dr. Phaedra Pezzullo of Indiana University for permission to cite material from our unpublished paper, "Re-Articulating 'Environment': Rhetorical Invention, Subaltern Counterpublics, and the Movement for Environmental Justice" (2001).

2. In 1978, residents of Love Canal discovered "that Hooker Chemical Corporation . . . had dumped 200 tons of a toxic, dioxin-laden chemical and 21,600 tons of various other chemicals into Love Canal. . . . In 1953, Hooker had filled in the canal, smoothed out the land, and sold it to the town school board for $1.00. . . . [Motivated by the harmful health effects that developed as a result of these chemicals, local residents, led by Lois Marie Gibbs,] organized and won evacuation . . . in 1980" (Gibbs, 1995, p. xvii). For background on Gibbs's story, see Chapter 1.

3. Hays adapted this phrase from the title of Rachel Carson's first book, *The Sea Around Us* (New York: Oxford University Press, 1950, 1951).

4. Di Chiro (1996) noted, "Eventually, environmental and social justice organizations such as Greenpeace, the National Health Law Program, the Center for Law in the Public Interest, and Citizens for a Better Environment would join [the] Concerned Citizens' campaign to stop [the proposed facility]" (p. 527, note 2).

5. For a chronology of major events in the environmental justice movement, see www.ejrc.cau.edu/summit2/%20EJTimeline.pdf

6. Chavis's claim of having coined the term *environmental racism* has been disputed; some activists in Warren County insist that they used this phrase first.

7. The 10 groups were the Environmental Defense Fund, Friends of the Earth, the Izaak Walton League, the National Audubon Society, the National Parks and Conservation Association, the National Wildlife Federation, the Natural Resources Defense Council, the Sierra Club, the Sierra Club Legal Defense Fund (now Earth Justice), and the Wilderness Society.

8. I was fortunate to have the opportunity to attend and participate in the sessions that included leaders of traditional environmental organizations.

9. The Dickerson video was one of a series of 60-second public service announcements produced by Greenpeace U.S.A. and aired by the VH-1 cable music channel throughout Earth Day 1990. The video ads showcased the stories of individuals of different ages, sex, and ethnicity who had worked to protect their communities and local ecosystems from environmental degradation.

10. For example, see the exchange of views between environmental justice leaders and Sierra Club officials in "A Place at the Table: A Sierra Club Roundtable on Race, Justice, and the Environment," *Sierra* (May/June, 1993), 51–58, 90–91. In the decade following this discussion, the nation's oldest environmental organization would go on to establish a Grassroots Environmental Justice Organizing Program, involving volunteers and a network of environmental justice organizers to work— at the invitation of local communities—with African American, Latino/a, and rural Appalachian communities as well as Native American tribes.

11. Pezzullo (2004) observes that, "though not necessarily called 'toxic tours,' tours have been used as a form of anti-pollution advocacy since at least the late 1960s" (p. 253, note 5).

12. Portions of this section are drawn from a paper that I presented at the Fifth Biennial Conference on Communication and Environment (Cox, 2001).

13. Reichhold Chemical ultimately offered to assist community members by helping to fund a health study and a community advisory panel to assist in decisions about the polluted site.

14. Evidence for the civil rights complaint comes principally from citizens' reports of their experiences with the DEQ process and related state documents. Because my aim has been to describe the community's experiences, I have made no attempt here to summarize responding briefs from Shintech Corporation or the State of Louisiana. For an account of both sides of this controversy, see Roberts & Toffolon-Weiss (2001).

15. Shintech officials subsequently announced plans to build a smaller plant 25 miles up the Mississippi River in Plaquemine, Louisiana, in conjunction with an existing Dow Chemical plant.

PART V

Environmental Discourses
of Science and Industry

9

Science and Symbolic Legitimacy

Human beings and the natural world are on a collision course. Human activities inflict harsh and often irreversible damage on the environment. . . . If not checked, many of our current practices . . . may so alter the living world that it will be unable to sustain life in the manner that we know.

—"World Scientists'
Warning to Humanity" (1992)

The scientific debate is closing [against us] but not yet closed. There is still a window of opportunity to challenge the science.

—Frank Luntz, memo
to Republican Party leaders (2001)

On March 7, 2001, Ian Thomas, a 33-year-old government scientist, posted a map of caribou calving areas in the Arctic National Wildlife Refuge on a U.S. Geological Survey website. At the time, Thomas was working as a cartographer for the agency's Patuxent Wildlife Research Center in Maryland. Using satellite imagery and other data, his website displayed more than 20,000 maps showing bird, mammal, and amphibian habitats

Figure 9.1   Caribou Migrating Across Tangle Lake, April 2002

(Photo courtesy of the U.S. Geological Survey-Biological Resources Division and the Alaska Science Center)

and vegetation land covers. Thomas also had been working on maps for all of the national wildlife refuges and national parks, using the new National Landcover Datasets (Thomas, 2001). Nevertheless, his timing in posting the new map of caribou calving areas landed Thomas in the center of a national controversy. The U.S. Congress had begun to debate a proposal from President George W. Bush's administration to open parts of the Arctic National Wildlife Refuge (ANWR) to oil and gas drilling, and the calving grounds appeared to be directly in the path.

On his first day at work after posting his map, Thomas was fired and his website removed. In an official statement, a public affairs officer for the U.S. Geological Survey stated that Thomas had been "operating outside the scope of [his] contract" and had not had his maps "scientifically reviewed or approved" before posting them on the website (Harlow, 2001). Thomas himself believed that his dismissal was "a high-level political decision to set an example to other federal scientists" who might not support the Bush administration's campaign to open the refuge for oil and gas exploration. "I thought that I was helping further public and scientific understanding and debate of the issues at ANWR by making some clearer maps," Thomas wrote in an e-mail to colleagues (2001). Asked about the USGS's removal of his maps, Thomas told the London *Guardian* newspaper, "You don't have to burn books now. You just press the delete key" (Borger, 2001).

News of Thomas's dismissal spread quickly around the globe via Internet chat rooms and listservs; his case became a cause célèbre and was taken up by environmental groups, debated in science and professional societies, and championed by the Public Employees for Environmental Responsibility (an advocacy group for scientists and other federal employees of environmental agencies). The furor over Thomas's map and his dismissal also raise a number of questions about the discourse of science in public debate over environmental policies:

- What is the proper role for science (and scientists) in deciding policy in a democratic society?
- Who should control the agenda of science and the uses of scientific research?
- How should the public interpret the significance of scientific claims when the research is uncertain (e.g., global warming, exposure to toxic substances, or the effects of logging on forest wildlife)?

In this chapter, I'll explore these questions as a source of knowledge and as a site of conflict over symbolic legitimacy. **Symbolic legitimacy** refers to the perceived correctness, authority, or common sense of a policy or an approach to a problem relative to other competing responses. (For a discussion of symbolic legitimacy boundaries, see Chapter 2.) As a site of conflict, the symbolic legitimacy of science is questioned as environmental groups, industry, and the media seek to influence the public by contesting the boundaries of consensus on the meaning and uses of science in environmental problems.

This chapter is organized into four sections. In the first, I'll trace how science became an important source of symbolic legitimacy in a society beset with complexity and specialized technical knowledge. The second section examines one way in which some propose to manage the problem of uncertainty about environmental dangers: by invoking the **precautionary principle**, an appeal to caution or prudence before taking a step that could prove harmful later. Because some in industry fear that too much caution may delay or restrict new products or increase the costs to industry, the third section, therefore, looks at attempts by industry to challenge the claims of environmental science through what some have called *symbolic legitimacy conflict*, or a challenge to the credibility of science itself. The chapter ends with an examination of recent debates about the role of scientists: Should scientists enter the public sphere or serve as advocates for positions?

Science and Symbolic Legitimacy Boundaries

As I write, the EPA and the U.S. Department of Energy disagree about whether the president's Clear Skies proposal can reduce mercury emissions from coal-fired power plants by almost half by the year 2007. (Mercury pollution has been linked to birth defects and neurological damage in fetuses and young children.) Research on the effects of installing new pollution equipment to reduce sulfur dioxide and nitrogen oxide is divided over whether this same equipment would also reduce mercury emissions as a co-benefit (Pianin & Gugliotta, 2003). Similar problems of complexity in scientific research appear in other, major environmental and public health issues at the start of the 21st century: climate change, genetically modified organisms, the amount of critical habitat needed for endangered species, and the effect on human fertility of synthetic chemicals that mimic natural hormones.

Problems involving human health and industrial products are not new. Therefore, it may be useful to look at an earlier era that faced similar concerns, as well as at the emerging role of science in guiding important decisions about human health and the environment.

John Dewey Redux: Complexity and the Problem of the Public

In the early 20th century, the philosopher John Dewey confronted a similar problem as the American public experienced problems with urban sanitation and industrial safety as well as revolutionary changes in communication technologies. In his book *The Public and Its Problems* (1927), Dewey warned of an "eclipse of the public" that he felt would occur as citizens lacked the expertise to evaluate the increasingly complex issues before them. He wrote that the consequences of the decisions before the public are so large, "the technical matters involved are so specialized . . . that the public cannot for any length of time identify and hold itself [together]" (p. 137). With the growing need for technical expertise in making decisions, Dewey feared the United States was moving from democracy to a form of government that he called **technocracy**, or rule by experts.

The solution favored by the Progressive movement of the 1920s and 1930s was grounded in the reformers' faith in science and technology as a source of legitimacy for state and federal regulation of the new industries. Williams and Matheny (1995) explain that, in regulatory policy, the Progressives wanted to rely on trained experts working within government organizations to discover an objective public interest (p. 12). Legitimacy for political decisions would come from these experts' use of "neutral, scientific criteria for judging public policy" (p. 12).

Although the **Progressive ideal** of neutral, science-based policy would run into difficulty, the legitimacy accorded to science by the public grew steadily stronger. Willis Harman observed that, over the past century, popular culture has given "tremendous prestige and power to our official, publicly validated knowledge system, namely science" (1998, p. 116). For example, when the EPA announced in 2001 that the new Bush administration was abandoning a Clinton-era rule requiring lower levels of arsenic in water, EPA administrator Christine Whitman pledged that a new rule would be based on "sound science and solid analysis" (Jehl, 2001, p. A1). (The EPA later reinstated the strict arsenic rule after a review of scientific studies by the National Academy of Sciences.) President Clinton had used the same phrase earlier when he issued an executive order directing that the EPA's environmental policies "be based on sound science" (Chinni, 2001).

The appeals to "sound science" in environmental policy reflected a keen awareness of the cultural norm that policy should be as free as possible of political bias and grounded in reliable and valid knowledge. To some extent, this awareness evolved during the 20th century and continues to do so, as government agencies have sought to incorporate the counsel and findings of scientists in the EPA, the Department of the Interior, and in agencies such as the U.S. Fish and Wildlife Service. Additionally, scientists from the National Research Council, universities, and independent research centers routinely advise policymakers on the scientific implications of environmental proposals.

Still, the Progressive ideal of neutral, science-based policy falls short of its promise in other ways. Agency budgets, pressures from political constituents, ideology, and other factors limit the extent to which policy decisions flow directly from scientific findings. In some cases, the science itself may result in ambiguous conclusions. A recent dispute over the use of science in implementing the Endangered Species Act illustrates some of the ways in which the Progressive ideal falls short. The dispute results from a memo written by the southwestern regional director of the U.S. Fish and Wildlife Service on January 27, 2005, to his staff about recovery plans for certain species.

In the memo, Dale Hale, the director, "instructed members of his staff to limit their use of the latest scientific studies on the genetics of endangered plants and animals when deciding how best to preserve and recover them" (Barringer, 2005, p. A14). He stated that, in planning for recovery of a species such as the endangered Apache trout, staff must "use only the genetic science in place at the time it was placed on the endangered species list—in some cases the 1970s or earlier—even if there have been scientific advances in understanding the genetic makeup of the species and its subgroups in the ensuing years" (p. A14). A factor in this decision was the cost of recovery efforts, particularly if each genetic subgroup is to survive. For example, U.S. Fish and Wildlife Service officials in Arizona have argued that the $2 million to $3 million spent for the recovery of each subgroup of the Apache trout in the last five years "was misdirected, since the species as a whole was on its way to recovery" (Barringer, 2005, p. A14). An official with the Arizona Game and Fish Department agreed with Hall, saying, "By not having to worry about small genetic pools, we can do these things [recovery efforts] faster and better" (quoted in Barringer, 2005, p. A14). As a result, a species could be removed from the endangered list, making it "easier for officials to approve actions, like . . . logging or commercial fishing—that could reduce a species' number" (p. A14).

Yet, other U.S. Fish and Wildlife Service officials and biologists disagreed with the new directive to limit use of the latest science. Ralph Morgenweck, a regional director for the mountain–prairie office, sharply rebuked his colleague. He explained that knowing whether populations of an endangered species are genetically isolated or exist in separate habitats "can assist us in identifying recovery units that will ensure that a species will persist over time. . . . It can also ensure that unique survival adaptations that may be essential for future survival continue to be maintained in the species" (quoted in Barringer, 2005, p. A14). Morgenweck went on to object that Hall's memo limiting the use of the latest science "could run counter to the purpose of the Endangered Species Act" and contradict the act's directive to use the best available science (p. A14). Whatever the outcome, this case illustrates the ongoing tension in federal agencies over whether science will guide policy or whether other factors will prevail, such as cost, political pressure, or differences in management philosophy.

Questioning Symbolic Legitimacy Boundaries

Even as science has become an important source of symbolic legitimacy in society, science itself is increasingly a site of conflict among disputing parties—industry, public health officials, and environmentalists—as they attempt to influence public perceptions of the scope or severity of problems. For example, environmental historian Samuel Hays (2000) reports that, as the new environmental sciences began to document risks from industrial products in the 1960s and 1970s, affected businesses challenged the science "at every step, questioning both the methods and research designs that were used and the conclusions that were drawn" (p. 222). Regulated industries, such as electric utility companies, oil and gas refineries, chemical manufacturing, and older extractive industries (mining, logging, and ranching), placed tremendous pressure on government agencies to justify the science behind new regulations. Some critics have charged that, in response, agency officials have sometimes ignored or misrepresented scientific findings to placate the criticism from regulated industries (Wilkinson, 1998).

In debates about environmental policies, one source of controversy often is the question of whether there is conclusive proof, something that is often beyond the reach of science (Hays, 2000, p. 149). John Fitzpatrick, director of the Cornell Laboratory of Ornithology, recently observed, "A **paradox for conservation** is that knowledge is always incomplete, yet the scale of human influence on ecosystems demands action without delay" (quoted in Scully, 2005, p. B13). This paradox poses a serious challenge for the public's willingness to support steps to protect the environment. At the same time, it provides the opponents of stronger regulations with an opportunity to contest the scientific claims:

> To the public, the question is usually one of "is there enough proof," an issue that the media takes up in order to bring simplicity out of complexity. . . . This complexity of debate, arising out of the complexity of arguments over proof, generates opportunities for those who wish to slow up application of scientific knowledge and establishes . . . caution on the part of decision makers in public agencies. Their watchword is "insufficient proof." (Hays, 2000, p.151)

The challenge for government agencies becomes even more acute when the science fails to tell officials how to choose between technical and political questions (for example, What is acceptable risk?) or how to decide among competing values, such as the health benefits to be gained versus the costs to comply with a regulation (for example, the requirement that power plants reduce mercury pollution by 46% by 2007).

Two important questions, therefore, arise for the study of environmental communication: What counts as scientific knowledge? Who controls its production, dissemination, and use? To ask (and answer) these questions is to ask about the symbolic legitimacy boundaries of science itself. It also asks about the types of communication that contending parties use as they challenge, reinforce, or reframe these symbolic boundaries. For example, in the remaining sections of this chapter, I'll discuss attempts by some opponents of environmental standards to forestall discussion and debate in the public sphere by removing questions about global warming or endangered species to the technical sphere of scientific journals and laboratories as a method of limiting action. (For discussion of the public, personal, and technical spheres, see Chapter 2.)

In the Ian Thomas case, government officials sought to control the type of information that reached the public about the Arctic National Wildlife Refuge. In fact, an earlier communications directive limited the list of people in the federal government who would be allowed to publish anything related to the ANWR (Thomas, 2001). Similar struggles by industry and environmental groups to mobilize the resources of science, control access to information, or challenge a policy's legitimacy occur in almost every major new story about the environment—proposals to ban logging in the national forests, air pollution standards, and, recently, the EPA's deletion of scientific research on the causes of global warming from its first "report card" on the environment (U.S. Environmental Protection Agency, 2003).

In the latter case, White House officials heavily edited the EPA's *Draft Report on the Environment,* deleting a 1999 study showing that global temperatures had risen sharply in the previous decade. In its place, these officials suggested a study funded by the American Petroleum Institute that questioned the 1999 findings on global temperatures (Seelye & Lee, 2003). In the end, the EPA chose to delete the entire section on global warming, "to avoid criticism that they [were] selectively filtering science to suit administration policy" (p. 28A). (For more information on the controversy over the EPA's report card, see Revkin & Seelye, 2003).

The dispute over the EPA's report card also illustrates the importance of the symbolic legitimacy boundaries associated with government uses of science. Earlier, in Chapter 2, I noted that the outcome of arguments between parties over legitimacy depends only partly on the facts. Equally important are the symbolic associations that politicians, business, and the public attach to a proposal, policy, or person (Schulzke, 2000). Symbolic legitimacy boundaries define a particular policy, idea, or institution as reasonable, appropriate, or acceptable. What is often at stake in the disputes between critics of environmental regulations and their supporters is the public's perception of the validity of scientific claims. To understand conflicts over science and the environment, therefore, we need to examine the ways in which the contending parties in society attempt to deal with scientific uncertainty, as well as the communication used in seeking to move scientific knowledge into the public sphere for discussion and as the basis for actions to protect the environment.

Because the symbolic associations of legitimacy boundaries are discursively constituted, they are also open to question and challenge. As far as environmental conflicts go, the fault line for such symbolic legitimacy conflict in a democratic society occurs most explicitly between supporters of an ethic of caution or prudence and others whose economic interests are affected by such caution and who seek to contest the claims of science. We'll discuss each of these tensions in the following sections.

The Precautionary Principle

Earlier, I noted that knowledge about the effects of human behavior on the environment is always incomplete, yet the scale of our influence on the earth demands that we take action. Stanford University biologists Paul Ehrlich and Anne H. Ehrlich (1996) comment that one of the great ironies in the environmental sciences is that science itself can never provide "absolute certainty or the 'proof' that many who misunderstand science say [that] society needs" (p. 27). Although certainty evokes a powerful pull for social reformers, religious adherents, and popular radio commentators, "it is forever denied to scientists" (p. 27). This is particularly the case in areas like chemical pollution and such large-scale problems as global warming and the loss of biodiversity. The Ehrlichs note with some concern that, in the absence of more precise knowledge of complex environmental systems, "Humanity is running a vast experiment on the biosphere and on itself" (p. 29).

Environmental Science and Uncertainty

The absence of scientific certainty also provides openings for some to call for delays before government takes action. For decades, the opponents of the environmental regulation of industry have used the indeterminacy of environmental sciences as a rationale for objecting to new standards to regulate hazardous chemicals such as lead, DDT, dioxin, and polychlorinated biphenyls (PCBs). A classic case, in 1922, involved the introduction of tetraethyl lead in gasoline for cars. Although public health officials thought lead posed a health risk and should be studied more carefully first, the industry argued that there was no scientific agreement on the danger and pushed ahead to market leaded gasoline for the next 50 years. Peter Montague (1999) of the Environmental Research Foundation writes, "The consequences of that . . . decision [to delay standards for leaded gasoline] are now a matter of record—tens of millions of Americans suffered brain damage, their IQs permanently diminished by exposure to lead dust" (para. 3).

Historically, the procedures for assessing risk have given the benefit of the doubt to new products and chemicals, even though these may prove harmful later. (For a description of methods used in risk assessment, see Chapter 6.) For example, existing government standards require only a tiny fraction of the 70,000 or more chemicals in commercial use in the United States today to be "fully tested for their ability to cause harm to health and the environment" (Shabecoff, 2000, p. 149). By the 1990s, however, a number of scientists, environmentalists, and public health advocates had begun to argue that the burden of proof should be shifted to require use of the precautionary principle.

As early as the 1960s, scientists such as René Dubos, Rachel Carson, Barry Commoner, George Wald, and others had begun to warn of possible ecological disaster and danger to human health from new chemicals appearing in water, air, and soil and in the food chain and mothers' breast milk. Rachel Carson's best-selling book *Silent Spring* (1962) became the most visible public warning about the use of chemical agents such as DDT (dichlorodiphenyltrichloroethane) in agricultural spraying and pesticides. (*Silent Spring's* publication prompted congressional hearings and scientific study of the health effects of massive spraying of chemicals on food crops.) Media stories of nuclear fallout from atmospheric tests and chemical residues on foods also fueled growing public anxieties. And, as I pointed out in Chapters 2 and 8, by the early 1980s, the upstate New York community of Love Canal had awakened the nation's consciousness to the hazards of its chemical culture. The angry response of residents to the discovery that an elementary school had been built on top of toxic chemicals fueled demands for cleanup of other contaminated sites throughout the country. Others warned of specific dangers from the new organochlorines (such as PCBs) that can "reduce sperm counts, disrupt female reproductive cycles . . . cause birth defects, [and] impair the development and function of the brain" (Thornton, 2000, p. 6, in Markowitz & Rosner, 2002, p. 296).

The Precautionary Principle and Its Critics

Eventually, scientists and public health officials began to urge that a new approach to regulation of potential environmental risks be adopted, "one that takes science's uncertainty not as a sign that there is no danger but as a sign that serious danger might well exist" (Markowitz & Rosner, 2002, p. 298). This view emphasized an ethic of caution or prudence in evaluating products that, even with low levels of toxicity, could harm populations in the future. In 1991, the National Research Council offered a compelling rationale for the new precautionary approach: "Until better evidence is developed, prudent public policy demands that a margin of safety be provided regarding potential health risks. . . . We do no less in designing bridges and buildings. . . . We must surely do no less when the health and quality of life of Americans are at stake" (p. 270).

An important step toward defining this principle of precaution was taken in January, 1998, at a historic gathering at the Wingspread Conference Center in Racine, Wisconsin. The Wingspread Conference on the Precautionary Principle was convened by the Science and Environmental Health Network and several foundations that funded scientific research. The 32 participants—scientists, researchers, philosophers, treaty negotiators, environmentalists, and labor leaders from the United States, Europe, and Canada—shared the belief that "compelling evidence that damage to humans and the worldwide environment is of such magnitude and seriousness that new principles for conducting human activities are necessary" (Science and Environmental Health Network, 1998, para. 3).

At the end of the three-day meeting, the participants issued the "Wingspread Statement on the Precautionary Principle," which called for government, corporations, communities, and scientists to implement the precautionary principle in making decisions about environmental and human health (Raffensperger, 1998). The statement provided this expanded definition of the **precautionary principle**: "When an activity raises threats of harm to human health or the environment, precautionary measures should be taken even if some cause and effect relationships are not fully established scientifically. In this context the proponent of an activity, rather than the public, should bear the burden of proof" (SEHN, 1998, para. 5).

The new principle is to be applied when an activity poses a combination of potential harm and scientific uncertainty. It therefore requires (1) an ethic of prudence (avoidance of risk) and (2) an affirmative obligation to act to prevent harm. Importantly, Montague (1999) explains that the principle shifts the burden of proof to the proponents of an activity to show that "their activity will not cause undue harm to human health or the ecosystem." Further, he explains that it requires agencies and corporations to take proactive measures to reduce or eliminate hazards, including "a duty to monitor, understand, investigate, inform, and act" when anything goes wrong (para. 13). (See "FYI: The "Wingspread Statement on the Precautionary Principle.")

FYI: The "Wingspread Statement on the Precautionary Principle"

The release and use of toxic substances, the exploitation of resources, and physical alterations of the environment have had substantial unintended consequences affecting human health and the environment. Some of these concerns are high rates of learning deficiencies, asthma, cancer, birth defects and species extinctions; along with global climate change, stratospheric ozone depletion, and worldwide contamination with toxic substances and nuclear materials.

We believe existing environmental regulations and other decisions, particularly those based on risk assessment, have failed to protect adequately human health and the environment—the larger system of which humans are but a part.

Continued

We believe there is compelling evidence that damage to humans and the worldwide environment is of such magnitude and seriousness that new principles for conducting human activities are necessary.

While we realize that human activities may involve hazards, people must proceed more carefully than has been the case in recent history. Corporations, government entities, organizations, communities, scientists and other individuals must adopt a precautionary approach to all human endeavors.

Therefore, it is necessary to implement the Precautionary Principle: When an activity raises threats of harm to human health or the environment, precautionary measures should be taken even if some cause and effect relationships are not fully established scientifically.

In this context the proponent of an activity, rather than the public, should bear the burden of proof.

The process of applying the Precautionary Principle must be open, informed and democratic and must include potentially affected parties. It must also involve an examination of the full range of alternatives, including no action.

SOURCE: Science and Environmental Health Network, 1998

Not all parties rushed to embrace the precautionary principle, however. Some businesses, conservative policy centers, and politicians are concerned that the consequences of using the principle are at odds with assumptions in the Dominant Social Paradigm (Chapter 2) and object that the principle sometimes errs on the side of too much caution. That is, its use poses unnecessary barriers to economic activity and the operation of the free market. Writing for the libertarian policy center, the Cato Institute, Ronald Bailey (2002) argued that, "the precautionary principle is an anti-science regulatory concept that allows regulators to ban new products on the barest suspicion that they might pose some unknown threat" (p. 5). Bailey cites the case of the European Union's ban on imports of genetically enhanced crops from the United States, or what have been called genetically modified organisms (GMOs). He argues that scientific panels have concluded that genetically modified foods are safe to eat and that "the EU ban is not a safety precaution, but a barrier to trade" (p. 4). In arguing this, Bailey and others therefore have demanded that higher standards of scientific certainty be required before entities like the EU or regulatory agencies can order businesses to take precautionary measures. In other words, judgments about environmental risk are best left to the technical sphere rather than to the added considerations and voices that enter into play in the public sphere of debate over environmental and health policy.

On the other hand, defenders of the precautionary principle have continued to refine the conditions under which it may be relevant and the criteria that are important in guiding environmental safety decisions that involve different levels of uncertainty. These criteria suggest the involvement of both the technical sphere and the public sphere in deliberation. For example, Carolyn Raffensperger and Katherine Barrett (2001) of the Science and Environmental Health Network defended the use of the precautionary principle in the dispute over the European Union's ban on genetically enhanced crops. They argued that the ban is both necessary and justifiable because "our ability to predict, calculate, and control the impacts of technologies such as GM organisms is limited. The novelty and complexity associated with inserting isolated gene constructs into organisms, and releasing those organisms on a global scale demand that we acknowledge uncertainties, accept responsibility, and exercise due caution" (p. 4).

(The dispute over the safety of genetically enhanced food and agricultural products is a continuing debate, one that has placed the precautionary principle squarely at the center of the controversy. For a defense of its use, see Raffensperger & Barrett, 2001; for a skeptical study of the precautionary principle, see Goklany, 2001. A sophisticated attempt to balance the uses of the principle in cases of environmental risk in cases before the WTO and NAFTA may be seen in Crawford-Brown, Pauwelyn, & Smith, 2004).

The controversy over the precautionary principle mirrors a larger conflict between some opponents of the role of science generally in setting environmental policy. It is to this conflict, and the attempt to challenge the symbolic legitimacy of science itself, that we now turn.

Industry, Science, and the Symbolic Legitimacy Conflict

Although science and technology have produced "a cornucopia of material abundance for a substantial portion of the human race" (Shabecoff, 2000, p. 138), scientific knowledge about the environmental impacts of industrial actions has been the site of controversy. In their study of business campaigns to shape the public's perceptions of science, Markowitz and Rosner (2002) observe that, during much of the 20th century, industry has argued that there must be "convincing proof of danger before policymakers had the right to intrude on the private reserve of industry in America" (p. 287). Yet, even as new knowledge emerged, some industries challenged the scientific consensus "at almost every step" when that knowledge might lead to new regulations (Hays, 2000, p. 138). The reason for this is not hard to understand. The possibility that some products and industrial pollutants might be linked to cancers, endocrine disruptors, and other health problems, as well as to changes in the earth's climate, raises not only issues of the financial liability of these companies but also prospects for further regulation of industry itself.

One result has been that the industries at risk of regulation by environmental science—particularly petrochemicals, energy, real estate development, and utilities—have "sought to turn science in their direction and [have] attracted scientists who could help with that objective" (Hays, 2000, p. 138). A look at several of these cases is instructive for understanding the communication used by industry to contest the legitimacy of scientific consensus.

Science and the Trope of Uncertainty

The range of communication used by industry to challenge the symbolic legitimacy of environmental science includes the funding of friendly science, the dissemination of research that counters scientific findings that might justify restrictions on industry, and, most importantly, the use of a rhetorical *trope of uncertainty*. (A *trope* is a "turn" or reframing of a claim that alters its meaning or changes our understanding of a statement.) Let me describe this trope briefly and then illustrate its use and the related modes of communication some industries and trade associations have used to challenge the claims of environmental science in recent years.

When skeptics call for further research into the causes of global climate change or the effect of dams in the Pacific Northwest on runs of salmon, they are drawing on a familiar tool in industry's challenge to the legitimacy of science. This **trope of uncertainty** functions to nurture doubt in the public's perception of scientific claims and thereby to delay calls for action. In rhetorical terms, the trope of uncertainty "turns," or alters, the public's understanding of what is at stake, suggesting there is a danger in acting prematurely, a risk of making the wrong decision. For this reason, Markowitz and Rosner (2002) have observed that "the call for more scientific evidence is often a stalling tactic" (p. 10).

In a sense, the trope of uncertainty is an attempt to reverse the assumptions associated with the precautionary principle. Whereas the precautionary principle stresses the need to err on the side of caution before human or corporate actions harm the environment or human health, an appeal to uncertainty or a call for further research turns this caution against scientific claims themselves. Since environmental science cannot guarantee certainty about many things, the trope urges caution before the government bases any regulatory actions on such science.

A standard reference for the basic strategy for nurturing doubt about the legitimacy boundaries of an issue is public relations expert Philip Lesly's (1992) article, "Coping With Opposition Groups." Lesly advises corporate clients to design their communication to create uncertainty in the minds of the public: "The weight of impressions on the public must be balanced so people *will have doubts and lack motivation to take action.* Accordingly, means are needed to get balancing information into the stream from sources that the public will find credible. There is no need for a clear-cut 'victory.' . . . Nurturing public doubts by demonstrating that this is not a clear-cut situation in support of the opponents usually is all that is necessary" (p. 331; emphasis added).

Feeling uncertain about an issue, the advice goes, the public will be less motivated to demand action, and the political will to solve a problem will lessen. For example, in their study of corporations' uses of public relations strategies opposing government regulation, Sheldon Rampton and John Stauber (2002) observe, "Industry's PR strategy is not aimed at reversing the tide of public opinion, which may in any case be impossible. Its goal is simply to stop people from mobilizing to do anything about the problem, to create sufficient doubt in their minds about the seriousness of global warming that they will remain locked in debate and indecision" (p. 271). They note that the group Friends of the Earth International called such attempts to introduce uncertainty in order to dampen the motive for action as "lobbying for lethargy" (p. 271).

A striking case of the introduction of uncertainty into debates over the environment occurred in the report of an important consultant to a political party over the politically sensitive matter of global warming.

Memo on Global Warming: "Challenge the Science"

Sometimes, the conflict over the legitimacy of scientific consensus in environmental matters may be fought on the terrain of language itself, by engaging in what one political consultant called the "environmental communications battle" (Luntz, 2001, p. 136). In a memo entitled "The Environment: A Cleaner, Safer Healthier America" addressed to leaders of a major political party, consultant Frank Luntz (2001) warned, "*The scientific debate is closing [against us] but not yet closed.*" Nevertheless, he advised, "*There is still a window of opportunity to challenge the science*" (p. 138; emphasis in original). The "window of opportunity" to which Luntz referred was the possibility that skeptics could raise enough doubts about the symbolic legitimacy of scientific claims about climate change that the public's uncertainty would delay governmental action in this area.

Luntz's memo offers a rare look into a behind-the-scenes debate over rhetorical strategy in high-level political circles. It is noteworthy especially for its frank assessment of the public relations dilemma that faced many politicians on the eve of the U.S. congressional elections in 2002. For example, Luntz had found that voters particularly distrusted the Republican Party on the environment. Thus, his memo to the party is revealing for his advice on the rhetorical strategy that he believed Republicans needed in order to challenge the growing consensus—the legitimacy boundaries—for many environmental issues, such as safe drinking water, the protection of natural areas, and especially global warming.

In one section of the memo, Luntz asserts that voters currently believe there is no consensus about global warming in the scientific community. "Should the public come to believe that the scientific issues are settled," he writes, "their views about global warming will change accordingly." Advising party leaders, the memo states, "'Therefore, *you need to continue to make the lack of scientific certainty a primary issue in the debate*" (p. 137; emphasis in original). Among the ways to challenge the science, according to the memo, is to "be even more active in recruiting experts who are sympathetic to your view, and much more active in making them part of your message" because "people are willing to trust scientists" more than politicians (p. 138).

FYI: Luntz's Memo on the "Environmental Communications Battle" (2001)

"While we may have lost the environmental communications battle in the past, the war is not over. . . ." [p. 136].

"We have spent the last seven years examining how best to communicate complicated ideas and controversial subjects. The terminology in the upcoming environmental debate needs refinement, starting with 'global warming' and ending with 'environmentalism.' It's time for us to start talking about 'climate change' instead of global warming and 'conservation' instead of preservation" [p. 142].

"The three words Americans are looking for in an environmental policy; they are 'safer,' 'cleaner,' and 'healthier' [p. 131]."

SOURCE: Luntz Research Companies (2001).

Industry-Sponsored Science and Questioning of Scientists

Other evidence of industry-sponsored science and attacks on scientists have appeared in news accounts and academic studies in recent years. Philip Shabecoff (2000), the founder of the Internet news source *Greenwire*, reported that the largest study ever conducted on the effects of polychlorinated biphenyls (PCBs) on workers' health had been funded by an interested party, General Electric. As we noted in Chapter 4, the large corporation had been fighting for years to avoid cleaning up the PCBs it had discharged into New York's Hudson River. Published in the *Journal of Occupational and Environmental Medicine,* the industry-funded study "found no evidence of 'significant' links to cancer deaths among workers exposed to PCBs on the job" (p. 142). In this and other cases of industry-sponsored science that we'll examine below, the rhetorical effect is to question the legitimacy boundaries that accompany the public's perceptions of a scientific consensus. With consensus or agreement, the rationale for government action appears stronger. Let's take a further look at some examples of this "environmental communication battle" (Luntz, 2001, p. 136).

Perhaps the most dramatic and systematic communications attempt by corporations to influence public perceptions of environmental science was disclosed in a *New York Times* report in 1998. The *Times* reporter, John Cushman (1998), uncovered a proposal by the American Petroleum Institute and other corporations to spend millions of dollars to convince the public that the Kyoto accord on global warming was based on "shaky science" (p. A1). Cushman reported that the proposal included a "campaign to recruit a cadre of scientists who share the industry's views of climate science and to train them in public relations so they can help convince journalists, politicians and the public that the risk of global warming is too uncertain to justify controls on greenhouse gases like carbon dioxide that trap the sun's heat near Earth" (p. A1). Other sources noted that the American Petroleum Institute's proposal included a five-million dollar Global Climate Science Data Center that would provide information to the media, government officials, and the public, grant money for "advocacy on climate science," and a Science Education Task Group to put industry information into school classrooms (National Environmental Trust, 1998). Finally, Beder (1999) wrote that other groups also had formed in this period to oppose measures to regulate the emissions contributing to global warming. (I'll discuss the case of one of these groups, the Global Climate Change Coalition, in Chapter 10.)

The campaigns of industry to influence public perceptions of the science of climate change may not be isolated instances. Independent monitoring groups and news accounts have documented a range of practices used by industry to question the consensus—or legitimacy boundaries—for many environmental topics. These have included

- Corporate-sponsored science symposiums (Rampton & Stauber, 2002)
- Letters to editors and paid message ads in newspapers, including payments to scientists to write letters to influential medical journals that dispute evidence of cigarette smoking as a cause of health problems (Hanners, 1998)
- Funding of "defensive science" or encouragement of research that refutes mainstream science (Hays, 2000)
- Corporate funding of scientists who had published in leading biomedical journals on subjects in which the funders had a financial interest (Krimsky, et al., 1998)
- Distribution of materials containing scientific claims sympathetic to industry to schools, journalists, and public officials (Cushman, 1998)

In other cases, companies have deliberately withheld or suppressed scientific findings that revealed harms to human health from products such as asbestos, leaded gasoline, and the toxic chemical in many plastics, such as vinyl chloride monomer (Markowitz & Rosner, 2002; Castleman, 1996).

A striking example of an attempt by industry to discredit or suppress scientific research occurred a little closer to home for me. In 1999, a respected scientist at the University of North Carolina at Chapel Hill (my university) received threats of a lawsuit and other harassment for his research on the health effects of factory hog farms, called confined animal feeding operations (CAFOs), on residents of rural North Carolina. (Most of these residents were from predominantly African American and low-income communities.) The research of Dr. Steve Wing (2002), an epidemiologist in the School of Public Health, found a correlation between complaints of headaches, excessive coughing, diarrhea, and burning eyes and the close location of residents' homes to the CAFOs.

Shortly after the state's health department released a press statement about Dr. Wing's research, attorneys for the North Carolina Pork Council—the industry's trade association—demanded his research files as well as confidential information on residents who had participated in the study. They also informed Dr. Wing that they were reviewing his research report for defamation. Finally, the attorneys contacted state legislators, officials at the University of North Carolina, and the National Institute of Environmental Health Sciences (NIEHS), which had funded his research. Wing (2002) believed these actions to be "harassment and intimidation," and, in the case of the NIEHS contacts, "an effort of the industry to challenge federal support for our research" (p. 441).

Environmental Science and Public Accountability

Recently, new initiatives have gained momentum to scrutinize corporate funding that might influence scientific claims about cancer, climate change, and other public health and environmental concerns. Such efforts to monitor published attacks on science have been fueled by disclosures such as Cushman's *New York Times* story of the campaign by the American Petroleum Institute to discredit the science of global warming. In other cases, the impetus has been more personal, such as the attacks on a modern-day Rachel Carson.

In *Living Downstream: An Ecologist Looks at Cancer* (1997), biologist Sandra Steingraber chronicles her personal investigation into the possible environmental sources of cancer in the United States. (Steingraber herself had bladder cancer.) Writing as a cancer survivor and a scientist, the author traced correlations between cancer registry data in her native rural Illinois and other communities, and concentrations of agricultural pollutants and other sources of chemicals. Steingraber also surveyed related medical research on the effects of DDT, dioxins, and other endocrine-disrupting chemicals on human health. Although public health officials and cancer victims praised *Living Downstream,* the book quickly came under fire from no less credible a source than the prestigious *New England Journal of Medicine.*

Soon after Steingraber's book appeared, the New England Journal of Medicine published a harshly negative review of *Living Downstream* by Jerry H. Berke (1997), challenging the motive of the author and her scientific credibility. (At the time, the *Journal* identified Berke at only as "MD, MPH.") The review accused Steingraber of "oversights and simplifications," "biased work," and "notoriously poor scholarship." Berke also assured readers that her "focus on environmental pollution and agricultural chemicals to explain human cancer has simply not been fruitful," that Steingraber herself was "obsessed," and "the objective of *Living Downstream* appears ultimately to be controversy" (1997, p. 1562). (The personal criticism of Steingraber is similar to some of the personal attacks on Rachel Carson, in which a federal official accused the *Silent Spring* author of being a spinster and therefore unconcerned about future generations [Budwig, 1992, para. 1]).[1]

Berke's own review, however, would itself eventually come under critical scrutiny. In their study of corporate strategies to influence public perceptions of science, Rampton and Stauber (2002) pointed out that the *New England Journal of Medicine* had failed to disclose that Berke was director of toxicology for W. R. Grace, "one of the world's largest chemical manufacturers and a notorious polluter" (pp. 202–203). (Grace is perhaps best known publicly for its role in the book and film, *A Civil Action,* in the town of Woburn,

Figure 9.2   Biologist Sandra Steingraber, Author of *Living Downstream: An Ecologist Looks at Cancer*

(Photo courtesy of Sandra Steingraber and Copyright Frank DiMeo/Cornell University Photography)

Massachusetts, a working-class community in which cases of childhood leukemia led researchers to identify Grace and other nearby companies as a source of the polluted drinking water.) Rampton and Stauber reported that Grace had been a defendant in several thousand asbestos-related lawsuits and had been prosecuted for false reports to the U.S. Environmental Protection Agency. As controversy arose over the *Journal* for its failure to disclose this possible conflict of interest in one of its reviewers, a spokesperson admitted that it had known Berke's identity but thought that Grace was a hospital or a research institute (Rampton & Stauber, p. 203).

As a result of cases such as these, groups such as the Society of Environmental Journalists and the Center for Science in the Public Interest now provide a database to research potential conflicts of interest when reporters read reports by scientists or interview them on controversial public policy topics. The site, linked to the Center for Science in the Public Interest (2005), offers the Integrity in Science Database of more than a thousand professors and scientists who may have affiliations with chemical, gas, oil, food, drug, and other corporations. The database aims to raise awareness among journalists and policymakers "about the role that corporate funding and other corporate interests play in scientific research, oversight, and publication" (para. 9). The database also lists nonprofit organizations and universities that receive industry funding for scientific research. (See www .cspinet.org/integrity.)

The Center for Science in the Public Interest has emerged as perhaps the leading resource in the United States for scientists, government officials, journalists, and public interest groups seeking to monitor and report corporate funding of scientists and university research projects. Among its goals are these:

- To investigate and publicize conflicts of interest and other potentially destructive influences of industry-sponsored science
- To advocate for full disclosure of funding sources by individuals, governmental and nongovernmental organizations that conduct, regulate, or provide oversight of scientific investigation or promote specific scientific findings
- To encourage journalists to routinely ask scientists and others about their possible conflicts of interests and to provide this information to the public

Although it acknowledges the benefits of corporate funding in areas such as genetics, bioengineering, and other cutting-edge research, the Center's Integrity in Science Project seeks to highlight the dangers of commercialization of science and the growing problem of conflicts of interest. The project addresses an important aspect of the debate over the role of science in environmental affairs—the responsibility of journalists, policymakers, and others to scrutinize the possible conflicts of interests in corporate funding of science and other efforts to influence the public's perception of scientific research.

But what should be the role of scientists themselves? In the final section, I'll explore a growing debate within the ranks of environmental scientists: Should scientists, at any point, serve as advocates for environmental policy or enter debates in the public sphere *as scientists?*

Advocacy and Environmental Science

Biologist Paul Ehrlich (2002) expressed the dilemma felt by a number of environmental scientists: Although there is "little dispute within the knowledgeable scientific community today about the global ecological situation and the . . . well-documented environmental danger," he observed that the majority of the public and public decision makers were still unaware of the seriousness of the problem (p. 31). Similarly, epidemiologist Steve Wing (2002) recognized the natural reluctance of many academic researchers to interact with the news media, particularly when their research may be misinterpreted. Nevertheless, he insisted that public health researchers and epidemiologists who work with at-risk communities have a special responsibility to make their findings public. By doing so, research can help community members "protect themselves, can motivate participation in democratic processes, and can influence public opinion and policy makers" (p. 442).

Dilemmas of Neutrality and Scientists' Credibility

The dilemma that Ehrlich and Wing outline springs from the fact that many environmental scientists find themselves asked to choose between two very different and competing identities. Are they laboratory scientists, whose duty is to remain neutral, disregarding the implications of their research? Or are they environmental physicians of a sort, guided by a medical ethic—the impulse to go beyond the diagnosis of problem to a prescription for its cure? This dilemma was heightened by the new discipline of conservation biology that emerged in the late 1980s and a series of provocative essays by one of its founders. Biologist Michael Soulé (1985) insisted that conservation biology was a **crisis discipline**, that its emergence was necessitated by a rapid ecological perturbation with irreversible effects on species, communities, and ecosystems (p. 727). He believed that scientists cannot remain silent in the face of a "biodiversity crisis that will reach a crescendo in the first half of the twenty-first century" (Soulé, 1987, p. 4); that, indeed, scientists had an ethical duty to offer recommendations to address this worsening situation, even with imperfect knowledge, because "the risks of non-action may be greater than the risks of inappropriate action" (Soulé, 1986, p. 6).

Soulé's challenge and the rise of conservation biology have provoked considerable debate within the environmental sciences. Traditionally, scientists have been viewed as neutral parties who rely on objective procedures to investigate problems or questions, with the resulting, empirical evidence laying the basis for any policy implications (Mason, 1962). Shabecoff (2000) summarized this traditional view when he wrote, "The scientist, free of preconceived values, seeks the truth and follows it wherever it leads. It is assumed that whatever the outcome of the search, it will benefit human welfare" (p. 140). As a result, many scientists fear that to abandon this identity by entering public arenas to advocate responses to environmental problems would violate an ethic of objectivity and risk the credibility of scientists themselves (Wiens, 1997; Slobodkin, 2000).

Other scientists, especially ecologists, have begun to question the ethical appropriateness of scientists' silence outside their laboratories in the face of worsening environmental problems. As early as the 1970s, some scientists believed that objective methodologies by themselves often were unable to take into account the important values in environmental controversies. For example, Robert Socolow (1976) observed that the failure of scientific and technical studies to assist in the resolution of these controversies

is part of a larger pattern of failures of discourse in problems that put major
societal values at stake. Discussion of goals, of visions of the future, are enor-
mously inhibited. Privately, goals will be talked about readily, as one discovers in even the most casual encounter with any of the participants.

But the public debate is cloaked in a formality that excludes a large part
of what people care most about. . . . Disciplined analyses brought to bear on a
current societal dispute hardly ever do justice to the values at stake. (p. 2)

The controversy over scientists' identity and their ethical duty in the face
of ecological and human challenges actually has its roots in earlier controversies, and it may be useful to briefly review this history.

Environmental Scientists as Advocates

The advent of nuclear weapons in 1945 and scientists' pivotal role in
their development prompted one of the first major debates over the ethical
responsibilities of scientists. Along with nuclear scientists, molecular biologists also began to insist on a greater scientific voice in informing the public
and policymakers of the consequences of the new research emerging after
World War II (Berg et al, 1974; Morin, 1993). As a result, scientific associations such as the Federation of American Scientists, along with journals
such as the *Bulletin of the Atomic Scientists,* arose to represent scientists in
the public realm (Kendall, 2000).

By 1969, the Union of Concerned Scientists (UCS) had formed to address
survival problems in the late 20th century, particularly the dangers of nuclear
war. Having since expanded its scope to problems of global warming and
the potential dangers of genetic manipulation, the UCS now includes almost
60,000 scientists and citizens. The organization defines its goals as education
and advocacy, including a continuing critique of public policies as well as
support for universities for educational programs at the frontiers of science
and public affairs (Kendall, 2000, p. 11).

Other groups also began to participate in public debates about the environment. For example, Physicians for Social Responsibility seeks to bring the
knowledge of medical science to environmental and health problems caused
by new technologies and industrial practices. In 1992, more than 1,500
members of the scientific academies of 69 nations, including a majority of
then-Nobel laureates, issued the "World Scientists' Warning to Humanity"
(1992): "Human beings and the natural world are on a collision course.
Human activities inflict harsh and often irreversible damage on the environment. . . . If not checked, many of our current practices . . . may so alter the
living world that it will be unable to sustain life in the manner that we
know" (para. 1).

The Debate Within the Scientific Community

Beyond these groups and their occasional statements, in the last decade a more contentious debate has arisen in many journals of conservation, ecology, and biology about scientists' responsibilities in their own work. Along with Michael Soulé's earlier essays, James Karr's 1993 letter in the journal *Conservation Biology* ignited a new debate over the appropriateness of science advocacy. Stressing the responsibility of scientists to report clearly the ecological consequences of society's actions, Karr equated this duty with the responsibility faced by an engineer who discovers a fatal flaw in a design (p. 8).

Other letters to the journal soon followed. Lorna Salzman (1995), a former official of Friends of the Earth, urged scientists to leave their laboratories as necessary in order to reclaim their identity as citizens in debates about environmental policy. As policy rarely results simply from the outcomes of scientific research, she argued, scientists also have a role in the democratic life of their society by joining in debates that affect their lives and their environmental values. In 1996, the debate flowered into full bloom when *Conservation Biology* published a special section on "the role of advocacy in the science of conservation biology" (Noss, 1996, p. 904). The gauntlet was thrown down in the opening essay: "*Conservation biology is inescapably normative. Advocacy for the preservation of biodiversity is part of the scientific practice of conservation biology. . . . To pretend that acquisition of 'positive knowledge' alone will avert mass extinctions is misguided*" (Barry & Oelschlaeger, 1996, p. 905).

Other scientists took a differing view of the role of environmental science, reflecting the traditional belief that advocacy taints a scientist's credibility. In his review of a recent Ecological Society of America symposium on science, values, and policies, Edward Rykiel (2001) argued that scientists must separate their role as providers of impartial information to the public from the inherently opposite role of advocates, as value-driven campaigners. Other ecologists have agreed, insisting that, although scientists should report their results to the public, they should not recommend outcomes or decisions. Frederick Wagner (1999), for example, pointed to the image problems some ecologists have had with public officials when they advocate specific approaches; in these cases, he warns, the officials "not infrequently discount our scientific message" (para. 12).

More recently, the debate about the scientist as advocate has taken a sharper focus as new voices have spoken up. For example, William Schlesinger (2003), dean of the Nicholas School of the Environment and Earth Sciences at Duke University, has argued that scientists have a responsibility "to speak out against a toxic impact to our environment, just as we would expect a physician to speak against a carcinogenic substance that might contaminate our food" (p. 23A). Stanford's Paul Ehrlich similarly urged ecologists to look to biomedical scientists who "gain prestige by diagnosing public health problems and recommending ameliorative steps—and interestingly, they aren't accused of advocacy" (2002, p. 33). Ehrlich argued that, in the face of "unprecedented, escalating, and well-documented environmental danger," scientists not only *can* be advocates but ethically "they must be advocates. . . . The credibility of ecologists . . . has been enhanced as many of them have tried to diagnose environmental ills and suggest cures" (pp. 31, 33).

An unprecedented move by scientists to debate the uses of science by government officials occurred in 2004. More than 60 prestigious scientists (including 20 Nobel Prize winners) released a report sharply criticizing the misuse and suppression of science by federal agencies in Washington, D.C. The report, released by the Union of Concerned Scientists (2004), charged that officials had engaged in "a well-established pattern of suppression and distortion of scientific findings" (p. 2). Among its findings, the report claimed that these officials had "misrepresented scientific consensus on global warming, censored at least one report on climate change, manipulated scientific findings on the emissions of mercury from power plants and suppressed information on condom use" (Glanz, 2004, p. A21). (For the report's principal conclusions, see "FYI: Scientific Integrity in Policymaking.")

FYI: Scientific Integrity in Policymaking

On February 18, 2004, the Union of Concerned Scientists made public its report, *Scientific Integrity in Policymaking: An Investigation into the Bush Administration's Misuse of Science*. The principal findings of the investigation into charges of misuse of science by government officials were stated in the report's executive summary:

- There is a well-established pattern of suppression and distortion of scientific findings by high-ranking Bush administration political appointees across numerous federal agencies . . .
- There is strong documentation of a wide-ranging effort to manipulate the government's scientific advisory system to prevent the appearance of advice that might run counter to the administration's political agenda. . . .
- There is evidence that the administration often imposes restrictions on what government scientists can say or write about "sensitive" topics. . . . [And]

Continued

- There is significant evidence that the scope and scale of the manipulation, suppression, and misrepresentation of science . . . is unprecedented. (p. 3)

The full report is available from the Union of Concerned Scientists,
Two Brattle Square, Cambridge, MA 02238–9105, or from www
.ucsusa.org.

Importantly, the Union of Concerned Scientists report also defended the
importance of scientists' assuming a role in the public sphere. It called upon
other scientists to "encourage their professional societies and colleagues to
become engaged in this issue, discuss their concerns directly with elected representatives, and communicate the importance of this issue to the public,
both directly and through the media" (p. 3). In response, the director of the
Office of Science and Technology Policy at the White House stated, "I think
there are incidents where people have got their feathers ruffled . . . But
I don't think they add up to a big pattern of disrespect. . . . They are individual actions that are part of the normal processes within the agencies"
(quoted in Glanz, 2004, p. A21).

Science and the Public

Although the report of the Union of Concerned Scientists explicitly
engages in criticism of science policy at the highest levels, other approaches
to the role of scientists are less controversial. One example is the proposal
for **civic science** (Lee, 1993), a blend of science and democratic modes of
public involvement. For example, Silvio Funtowicz and Jerry Ravetz (1991)
suggested that when interested citizens, policymakers, and journalists work
closely with environmental scientists to select priorities and, in some cases,
participate in the design of research, it is possible to achieve a "democrati-
zation of knowledge"; this is so not merely in terms of public education but
in "enhanced participation in decision making for common problems" (p. 14).
Similarly, political scientist Frank Fischer (2000) has described a process for
policymaking that incorporates many of the ideals of public participation
that I described in Chapter 3. His approach elicits information from scientists and citizens alike, who in turn comment publicly about the technological, legal, and financial feasibility of proposals (p. 229).

One example of a successful effort by scientists to bridge the gap
between the technical sphere and the public sphere of interested public and

environmental groups was the recent decommissioning of the dam on the Kennebec River in Maine. In his new book *Dam Politics: Restoring America's Rivers*, William Lowry (2003) describes the efforts of scientists to educate the public about the ecological importance of rivers, teaching values that go beyond the economic uses of rivers for transportation, irrigation, and hydroelectric power. In the Kennebec case, local and federal officials, scientists, and public interest groups not only cooperated in removing the dam but have begun restoration attempts to aid the return of spawning fish native to the area. However, Lowry is also quick to note that other attempts to decommission dams that impede the natural ecological functioning of river systems have met with more resistance, such as the controversy over the effects of dams on the Snake and Columbia Rivers in Idaho and Washington State. In the latter case, powerful economic and political interests have stalled efforts to discuss the removal of dams that may be impeding the successful run of salmon. (For recent court rulings that federal officials have "limited and skewed" the scientific analyses of the environmental impacts of dams on the Snake and Columbia Rivers, see Barringer, 2005.)

There is some evidence that support is growing for proposals to bring together scientists and members of the public. For example, Lach, List, Steel, and Shindler (2003) surveyed the attitudes of scientists, resource managers, and members of the public about their preferred roles for research and the involvement of field ecologists in natural resource management in the Pacific Northwest. The study identified five levels of involvement in public communication and decision making that research scientists might have:

- Reporting scientific results that others use in making decisions on natural resource management issues
- Reporting and then interpreting scientific results for others who are involved in natural resource management decisions
- Working closely with managers and others in integrating scientific results into management decisions
- Actively advocating for specific and preferred natural resource management decisions
- Making decisions about natural resource management policy. (p. 174)

Lach et al. (2003) found that, with the exception of scientists, all the groups surveyed most preferred the role of integrating scientific results into management decisions; that is, they would support means to ensure that management decisions—such as deciding where logging could occur—reflected the findings of science more directly. Scientists preferred the slightly more cautious role of interpreting scientific results for others, though there was some support among scientists for the integrative role as well (p. 174).

In other words, most scientists preferred to limit their roles in the public sphere to reports and explanations of their findings, holding back from more direct involvement in managing natural resources.

Act Locally!

Arrange for a conservation biologist, a toxicologist, an ecologist, or other environmental scientist on your campus to visit your class to discuss the role of environmental science in policymaking or the debate about the role of public advocacy in the public sphere.

Discuss with your guest the five levels of involvement in public communication and decision making that scientists can play: reporting, interpreting, and integrating their research findings, advocating policy, and making decisions. What is their viewpoint? What do you believe is the proper role of scientists in the public sphere?

Finally, the ease of research on the Internet has now placed the results of environmental science more easily within reach of anyone with a computer and online access. In some cases, research in the technical sphere has been made available through sites that are easily engaged by the public. For example, in Chapter 3 I discussed the research that is clearly organized and made public by the EPA's Toxic Release Inventory, showing sources of air and water pollution in communities. (See www.scorecard.org.) In addition, the requirement under NEPA for environmental impact statements provides additional scientific information about the effects of proposed actions on the environment. With the increased availability of science, the quality of debate within the public sphere has grown immeasurably.

Conclusion

In this chapter, we have considered several provocative questions about the discourse of science in public controversies over environmental policy. What is the proper role of science (and scientists) in deciding policy in a democratic society? Who should control the uses of scientific research? How should society interpret the meaning of scientific claims when the research is characterized by uncertainty? In disputes over environmental policy especially, access to and command of technical knowledge is an important source of legitimacy. Equally important to the importance of scientific knowledge are the symbolic associations that public officials, industry, and the public attach to the claims of science, which constitute critical symbolic legitimacy boundaries in the public debate. Because such boundaries influence many decisions about business activity, scientific discourse often becomes a site for public debate and controversy.

In the second section, we looked at one way in which some have urged that we manage the uncertainty of scientific claims about environmental dangers. The precautionary principle states that, when an activity threatens human health or the environment, even if some cause-and-effect relationships are not fully established scientifically, caution should be taken. Thus, when deciding what action to take about unsafe products or business activities, it is industry, rather than the public, who should bear the burden of proving that it is safe.

Although it can safeguard against uncertainty, the appeal to caution or prudence also can restrict new products and increase costs to industry. In the third section, we examined the attempts by some industrial and political interests to challenge the claims of environmental science through a trope of uncertainty and other forms of symbolic legitimacy conflict. By funding a series of challenges to scientific claims of global warming and other environmental dangers, political and corporate groups have suggested that there is danger in taking action prematurely, a risk of making the wrong decision. The goal of such legitimacy challenges is to create doubt in the public's minds, thereby lessening the will to political action, particularly action that might harm business or industrial interests.

Finally, we explored recent and sometimes contentious debates about the appropriate roles of scientists themselves. With growing evidence of deterioration of the world's biodiversity and ecosystems, many ecologists and other scientists believe that they must assume a more public role to educate policymakers and, for some, to advocate specific actions. Other scientists fear that, by venturing outside their laboratories, scientists risk their credibility as objective sources of information. At stake is both the public's perception of the symbolic legitimacy of science and the growing sense of urgency among many that time is running out and that "the risks of non-action may be greater than the risks of inappropriate action" (Soulé 1986, p. 6).

KEY TERMS

Civic science: A blend of science and democratic modes of public involvement.

Crisis discipline: Term used to characterize the new discipline of conservation biology; coined by biologist Michael Soulé (1985) to refer to the duty of scientists, in the face of a looming biodiversity crisis, to offer recommendations to address this worsening situation, even with imperfect knowledge.

Paradox for conservation: Awareness that "knowledge is always incomplete, yet the scale of human influence on ecosystems demands action without delay" (quoted in Scully, 2005, p. B13).

Precautionary principle: As defined by the 1998 Wingspread conference, "When an activity raises threats of harm to human health or the environment, precautionary measures should be taken even if some cause and effect relationships are not fully established scientifically. In this context the proponent of an activity, rather than the public, should bear the burden of proof" (SEHN, 1998, "Wingspread Consensus Statement," para. 5).

Progressive ideal: Put forth by the 1920s and 1930s Progressive movement, the concept of a neutral, science-based policy as the best approach to government regulation of industry.

Symbolic legitimacy: The perceived correctness, authority, or common sense of a policy or approach to a problem relative to other competing responses. (For a definition of symbolic legitimacy boundaries, see Chapter 2.)

Technocracy: John Dewey's term denoting a government ruled by experts.

Trope of uncertainty: An appeal that functions to nurture doubt in the public's perception of scientific claims and thereby to delay calls for action; in rhetorical terms, the trope of uncertainty "turns" or alters the public's understanding of what is at stake, suggesting there is a danger in acting prematurely, a risk of making the wrong decision.

DISCUSSION QUESTIONS

1. What does it mean to appeal to "common sense" or the "public interest" in urging support for environmental protection? How does one decide what is common sense in the disputes over the solution to seasonal wildfires in the national forests?

2. How can ordinary citizens evaluate media reports of apparent disagreement among scientists over whether carbon dioxide (CO_2) from cars and trucks is a source of global climate change? Should the public be cautious of scientific research funded by corporate sources? Why or why not?

3. Is the precautionary principle a clear guide to decision making, or does it leave too much discretion to agency staff or others to determine whether a product is unsafe or should be withdrawn from the market? Should industry carry the burden of demonstrating to the general public that its products or chemical substances are safe before releasing them to the marketplace?

4. Does corporate funding of scientific research taint the credibility or influence the conclusions of scientists' reports?

5. What is the role of the media in disclosing the sources of funding or conflicts of interest for scientific reports when they report an environmental story?

6. Should ecologists and other environmental scientists ever serve as advocates in the public sphere? Where do you draw the line—if at all—in how far scientists should go in entering the public sphere or working with government agencies?

REFERENCES

Bailey, R. (2002, August 14). Starvation a by-product of looming trade war. Washington, DC: Cato Institute. Retrieved May 23, 2005, from www.cato.org/dailys/08–14–02.html

Barringer, F. (2005, May 24). New rule on endangered species in the Southwest: Latest scientific research getting less weight. *New York Times*, p. A14.

Barringer, F. (2005, May 27). Government shirked its duty to wild fish, a judge rules. *New York Times*, p. A14.

Barry, D., & Oelschlaeger, M. (1996). A science for survival: Values and conservation biology. *Conservation Biology, 10*, 905–911.

Beder, S. (1999, April/March). Corporate hijacking of the greenhouse debate. *The Ecologist*, 119–122.

Berg, P., Baltimore, D., Boyer, H. W., Cohen, S. N., & Davis, R. W. (1974). Potential biohazards of recombinant DNA molecules. *Science, 185*, 303.

Berke, J. H. (1997). Living Downstream: An Ecologist Looks at Cancer and the Environment. [Book review]. *New England Journal of Medicine, 337*, 1562.

Borger, J. (2001, April 12). Mapmaking martyr. *Guardian Unlimited*. Retrieved June 17, 2001, from www.guardian.co.uk/Archive/Article/0,4273,4169290,00.html

Budwig, L. (1992, Fall). Breaking nature's silence. *Pennsylvania Heritage, 18*(4). Retrieved May 26, 2005, from www.dep.state.pa.us/dep/PA_Env-Her/rachel.htm

Carson, R. (1962). *Silent spring*. Boston: Houghton Mifflin.

Castleman, B. I. (1996). *Asbestos: Medical and legal aspects* (4th ed.). Englewood Cliffs, NJ: Aspen Law & Business.

Center for Science in the Public Interest. (2005). *Integrity in science*. Retrieved May 26, 2005, from http://cspinet.org/integrity/about.html

Chinni, D. (2001, June 14). Arsenic flap and "sound science." *Christian Science Monitor*. Retrieved June 30, 2003, from http://csmweb2.emcweb.com

Crawford-Brown, D., Pauwelyn, J., & Smith, K. (2004). Environmental risk, precaution, and scientific rationality in the context of WTO/NAFTA trade rules. *Risk Analysis, 24*, 461–469.

Cushman, J. H. (1998, April 26). Industrial group plans to battle climate treaty. *New York Times*, p. A1.

Dewey, J. (1927). *The public and its problems.* New York: Henry Holt.

Ehrlich, P. R. (2002). Human natures, nature conservation, and environmental ethics. *BioScience, 52*(1), 31–43.

Ehrlich, P. R., & Ehrlich, A. H. (1996). *Betrayal of science and reason: How anti-environmental rhetoric threatens our future.* Washington, DC: Island Press/Shearwater Books.

Fischer, F. (2000). *Citizens, experts, and the environment: The politics of local knowledge.* Durham, NC: Duke University Press.

Funtowicz, S. O., & Ravetz, J. R. (1991). A new scientific methodology for global environmental issues. In R. Costanza (Ed.), *Ecological economics: The science and management of sustainability* (pp. 137–152). New York: Columbia University Press.

Glanz, J. (2004, February 19). Scientists says administration distorts facts. *New York Times,* p. A21.

Goklany, I. M. (2001). *The precautionary principle: A critical appraisal of environmental risk assessment.* Washington, DC: Cato Institute.

Hanners, D. (1998, August 4). Scientists were paid to write letters: Tobacco industry sought to discredit EPA report. *St. Paul Pioneer Press.* Retrieved September 9, 2003, from http://junkscience.com/news3/pioneer.htm

Harlow, T. (March 16, 2001). [Message posted on Infoterra listserv]. Retrieved June 17, 2003, from www.peer.org/usgs_position.html

Harman, W. (1998). *Global mind change: The promise of the twenty-first century.* San Francisco: Berrett-Koehler.

Hays, S. P. (1987). *Beauty, health, and permanence: Environmental politics in the United States, 1955–1985.* Cambridge, UK: Cambridge University Press.

Hays, S. P. (2000). *A history of environmental politics since 1945.* Pittsburgh: University of Pittsburgh Press.

Helvarg, D. (2003, June). Gale Norton's new environmentalism. *The Progressive, 67*(6), 25–29.

Jehl, D. (2001, March 21). E.P.A. to abandon new arsenic limits for water supply. *New York Times,* p. A1.

Karr, J. R. (1993). Advocacy and responsibility. *Conservation Biology, 7*(1), 8.

Kendall, H. W. (2000). *A distant light: Scientists and public policy.* New York: Springer-Verlag.

Krimsky, S., et al. (1998, July–October). Scientific journals and their authors' financial interests: A pilot study. *Psychother Psychosom, 67*(4–5), 194–201.

Lach, D., List, P., Steel, B., & Shindler, B. (2003). Advocacy and credibility of ecological scientists in resource decision-making: A regional study. *Bioscience, 53*(2), 170–178.

Lee, K. (1993). *Compass and gyroscope: Integrating science and politics for the environment.* Washington, DC: Island Press.

Lesly, P. (1992). Coping with opposition groups. *Public Relations Review, 18*(4), 325–334.

Limbaugh, R. (1992). *The way things ought to be.* New York: Pocket Books.

Lowry, W. R. (2003). *Dam politics: Restoring America's rivers*. Washington, DC: Georgetown University Press.

Luntz Research Companies. (2001). The environment: A cleaner, safer, healthier America. In *Straight Talk* (pp. 131–146). Retrieved June 12, 2003, from www .ewg.org/briefings/luntzmemo/pdf/LuntzResearch_environment.pdf

Markowitz, G., & Rosner, D. (2002). *Deceit and denial: The deadly politics of industrial pollution*. Berkeley: University of California Press.

Mason, S. F. (1962). *A history of the sciences*. New York: Collier Books.

Montague, P. (1999, July 1). The uses of scientific uncertainty. *Rachel's Environment & Health News, 657*. Retrieved August, 25, 2002, from www.rachel.org/ bulletin/pdf/Rachels_Environment_Health_News_1508.pdf

Morin, A. J. (1993). *Science policy and politics*. Englewood Cliffs, NJ: Prentice-Hall.

National Environmental Trust. (1998). *Monitor 404: Information missing from your daily news*. [Press release]. Retrieved September 2, 2005, from www .monitor.net/monitor/9804b/9804b-404.html.

National Research Council Committee on Environmental Epidemiology. (1991). *Environmental epidemiology: Vol. 1. Public health and hazardous wastes*. Washington, DC: National Academy Press.

Noss, R. F. (1996). Conservation biology, values, and advocacy. *Conservation Biology, 10*, 904.

Pianin, E., & Gugliotta, G. (2003, June 30). Air quality rules at risk. [Raleigh, NC] *News & Observer*, p. A3.

Raffensperger, C. (1998). Editor's note: The, precautionary principle—a fact sheet. The Networker, 3(1), para. 1. Retrieved 25 August 2003, from http://www .sehn.org/Volume 3-1.html#a1

Raffensperger, C., & Barrett, K. (2001, September). In defense of the precautionary principle. *Nature Biotechnology, 19*, 811–812. Retrieved May 23, 2005, from www.biotech-info.net/in_defense.html

Rampton, S., & Stauber, J. (2002). *Trust us, we're experts!* New York: Jeremy P. Tarcher/Putnam.

Revkin, A. C., & Seelye, K. Q. (2003, June 19). Report by the E.P.A. leaves out data on climate change. *New York Times*. Retrieved June 19, 2003, from www.nytimes.com

Rykiel, E. J., Jr. (2001). Scientific objectivity, value systems, and policymaking. *BioScience, 51*, 433–436.

Salzman, L. *(1995)*. Letter [untitled]. Conservation Biology, 9*(4): 709*.

Schlesinger, W. (2003, May 18). Academics have right to speak out. [Raleigh, NC] *News & Observer*, p. A23.

Schulzke, E. C. (2000, March 26). Policy networks and regulatory change in the 104th Congress: Framing the center through symbolic legitimacy conflict. Paper presented at the meeting of the Western Political Science Association, San Jose, CA.

Science and Environmental Health Network. (1998, January 26). Wingspread conference on the precautionary principle. Retrieved 25 August, 2003, from www.sehn.org/wing.html

Scully, M. G. (2005, October 3). Studying ecosystems: the messy intersection between science and politics. *Chronicle of Higher Education*, B13.

Seelye, K. Q., & Lee, J. 8. (2003, June 24). E.P.A. calls the U.S. cleaner and greener than 30 years ago. New York Times (Late Ed.), p. A28.

Shabecoff, P. (2000). *Earth rising: American environmentalism in the 21st century*. Washington, DC: Island Press.

Sheldon, R., & Stauber, J. (2001*). Trust us: We're experts! How industry manipulates science and gambles with your future*. New York: Jeremy P. Tarcher/ Putnam.

Slobodkin, L. B. (2000). Proclaiming a new ecological discipline. *Bulletin of the Ecological Society of America, 81*, 223–226.

Socolow, R. H. (1976). Failures of discourse: Obstacles to the integration of environmental values into natural resource policy. In L. H. Tribe, C. S. Schelling, & J. Voss (Eds.), *When values conflict: Essays on environmental analysis, discourse, and decision* (pp. 1–32). Cambridge, MA: Ballinger [for the American Academy of Arts and Sciences, Pub.].

Soulé, M. E. (Ed.). (1985). What is conservation biology? *BioScience, 35*, 727–734.

Soulé, M. E. (1986). *Conservation biology: the science of scarcity and diversity*. Sunderland, MA: Sinauer Associates.

Soulé, M. E. (1987). History of the Society for Conservation Biology: How and why we got here. *Conservation Biology, 1*, 4–5.

Steingraber, S. (1997). *Living downstream: An ecologist looks at cancer*. Cambridge, MA: Perseus.

Stone, D. (2002). *Policy paradox: The art of political decision making* (Rev. ed.). New York: W. W. Norton.

Thomas, I. (2001, March 16). Web censorship. [Email]. Retrieved June 16, 2003, from http://cartome.org/mapgag.htm

Union of Concerned Scientists. (2004, February). Scientific integrity in policymaking: An investigation into the Bush administration's misuse of science. Cambridge, MA: Author.

U.S. Environmental Protection Agency. (June 23, 2003). EPA announces unprecedented first "draft report on the environment." *EPA Newsroom*. Retrieved June 24, 2003, from www.epa.gov/newsroom/headline_062303.html

Wagner, F. H. (1999). Analysis and/or advocacy: What role(s) for ecologists? *EcoEssay Series No. 3*. Santa Barbara, CA: National Center for Ecological Analysis and Synthesis. Retrieved June 12, 2003, from http://nceas.ucsb.ed/ nceasweb/resources/ecoessay/wagner

White House. (August 22, 2002). *President announces healthy forest initiative*. [Press release]. Office of the Press Secretary. Retrieved June 24, 2003, from www.whitehouse.gov/news/releases/2002/08/20020822–3.html

Wiens, J. A. (1997). Scientific responsibility and responsible ecology. *Conservation Ecology, 1*(1), 16. Retrieved June 12, 2003, from www.consecol.org/v011/iss1/ art16

Wilkinson, T. (1998). *Science under siege: The politicians' war on nature and truth*. Boulder: Johnson Books.

Williams, B. A., & Matheny, A. R. (1995). *Democracy, dialogue, and environmental disputes*. New Haven: Yale University Press.

Wing, S. (2002). Social responsibility and research ethics in community-driven studies of industrialized hog production. *Environmental Health Perspectives*, *110*(5), 437–444.

World Scientists' Warning to Humanity. (1992, November 18). Retrieved July 5, 2003, from http://dieoff.org/page8.htm

NOTE

1. Carson "was belittled as an antihumanitarian crank, a priestess of nature, and a hysterical woman. The director of the New Jersey Department of Agriculture believed she inspired a "vociferous, misinformed group of nature-balancing, organic gardening, bird-loving, unreasonable citizenry." An official of the Federal Pest Control Review Board, ridiculing her concern about genetic mutations caused by the use of pesticides, remarked, "I thought she was a spinster. What's she so worried about genetics for?" (Budwig, 1992, para. 1).

10

Green Marketing and Corporate Campaigns

Imagine a world that creates sustainable growth without harming the environment. That is a sustainable world. . . . Imagine a world filled with intelligent devices—devices that think and share information—making people's lives easier, safer, more productive and more fun. That is an amazing world. Now imagine all of it together. That is the world Motorola is bringing to life.

—Motorola Corporation's environmental report
(as quoted in Feller, 2004, p. 57)

A recent television ad sponsored by Americans for Balanced Energy Choices (2004) praised coal as an environmentally friendly source of energy, despite the fact that coal-fired electric power plants have been a major cause of air pollution in the United States and worldwide. In the ad, a bald eagle struggles to fly in a hazy, polluted sky. The year is 1970. The eagle lands on a rocky outcrop, coughs, and then sputters, "Not a good day for flying!" The ad then cuts to 2004, and the sky is clean. The eagle soars in a bright blue sky above snow-capped mountains. A voice-over declares: "Thanks in part to clean coal technologies, our air quality has been improving. And by 2015, emissions from coal-based power plants will be 75 percent less than they were in 1970." "Very nice," says the eagle. (Americans for Balanced Energy Choices is a non-profit group funded by electric power companies and the coal industry.)

The eagle advertisement is just one of many forms of corporate environmental communication within the public sphere. These range from the familiar "green" advertising of products to corporate lobbying aimed at influencing environmental regulations. Corporate lobbying also relies upon media frames such as "economic growth" and the claim that environmental regulations cost jobs. These frames often appear in public relations campaigns and in print or electronic media that carry a message opposing or supporting legislation or other issues affecting the interests of a company or industry.

In general, environmental communication scholars have identified three major types of corporate communication in the public sphere about the environment: (1) the practice of "green marketing," or the construction of an environmental identity for corporate products, images, and behaviors; (2) industry advocacy campaigns aimed at influencing environmental legislation, agency rules, and public opinion, and (3) tactics to discredit or intimidate environmental critics. In this chapter, I'll discuss examples of each type of communication. Also shown throughout the chapter is a skillful and complex dance of identity in corporate communication: the effort by some businesses to appear "green," often while actively opposing environmental protections.

The first section of this chapter provides background for the study of corporate environmental communication by describing the discourse of the free market that underlies much of this communication. Then, the second section examines the first of three major components of corporate communication— the use of public relations and marketing to construct a green identity. I'll describe not only the advertising of products and corporate images but also the image repair that corporations perform to restore their credibility after environmental accidents such as the spill from the oil tanker *Exxon Valdez* in Alaska. We'll also look briefly at the discourse of *green consumerism*— marketing that encourages the belief that, by buying allegedly environmentally friendly products, consumers can do their part to protect the planet.

In the third section, I'll explore the second major component of corporate environmental communication—the role of corporate advocacy campaigns in the public sphere to influence public opinion and environmental laws. In the final section, I'll describe a third major corporate communication practice, the use of tactics to discredit or intimidate those who criticize industry for harming the environment.

Free Market Discourse and the Environment

As I pointed out in Chapter 1, much of the organized opposition to environmental standards has come from two main sources: (1) older extractive, resource-based industries such as timber, ranching, and mining, and (2) some newer industries such as chemical and electronics manufacturing, transportation, electric utility companies, nuclear power, and large energy companies. In each case, opponents of these regulations have engaged in communications in the public sphere to influence media, opinion leaders, the general public, and public officials. In the case of extractive industries, many timber, mining, and agricultural businesses have expressed resentment of the restrictions on their traditional uses of land—for example, rules that limit commercial logging in the national forests or impose strict limits on arsenic drainage from mines. In addition, so-called Wise Use, or property rights, groups have organized landowners to lobby against restrictions on the use of their property that protect wetlands or habitat for endangered species or that establish buffer zones to prevent cattle from grazing in riparian areas. (**Riparian areas** are the areas along rivers, streams, and other natural watercourses that are often important habitat for wildlife species that use these areas for hunting, breeding, or nesting.)

Second, newer industries also have supported campaigns to persuade the public and Congress to oppose environmental rules that they view as cumbersome or expensive. These rules have included higher fuel efficiency requirements for cars and SUVs, liability of companies under the Superfund law for the cleanup of toxic waste, and curbs on pollutants that contribute to global warming.

Before looking more closely at communication methods, it is important to appreciate the ideological premises and sources of persuasion that underlie much corporate environmental communication. Corporate communication that opposes state or federal restrictions on land use or manufacturing does not occur in a vacuum. Therefore, it is important to understand the influence of the discourse of the free market that profoundly influences corporate communication about the environment and about the role of government.

Adam Smith's "Invisible Hand" and the Environment

Behind much of the rhetorical opposition of business and allied groups to environmental standards is a more fundamental belief in the **free market**, a phrase that is usually meant to refer to the absence of governmental restriction of business and commercial activity. Reflecting a belief in the private marketplace as self-regulating, much criticism of environmental rules takes such forms as, "We need to get 'big government' out of our lives," and "Companies will find the best solutions when left to themselves!" At the core of this rhetoric is the belief held by many corporate leaders that adequate environmental protection can be secured by the operation of the marketplace, through the unrestricted or unregulated buying and selling of products and services. Such faith in the market assumes that "the public interest is discovered in the ability of private markets to transform the individual pursuit of self-interest into an efficient social allocation of resources" (Williams & Matheny, 1995, p. 21). For example, the National Consumer Coalition supports market solutions to reduce global warming and solve other environmental problems. The NCC explains, "A market economy benefits consumers by expanding consumer choice and competition and fostering innovation, which lowers costs and improves consumer health and safety" (2004, para. 1).

The assumption that the market is the preferred means for addressing societal problems derives from the Scottish economist Adam Smith's theory of the **invisible hand** of the market. This metaphor is used to name an invisible or natural force of the private marketplace that determines what society values. In his classic book, *An Inquiry into the Nature and Causes of the Wealth of Nations,* Smith (1776) argued that the sum of individuals' self-interested actions in the marketplace promotes the public's interest, or the common good. He explained that an individual "neither intends to promote the public interest nor knows how much he [sic] is promoting it . . . [H]e intends only his own gain. And he is in this . . . *led by an invisible hand to promote an end which was no part of his intention*" (p. 400, emphasis added). Business advocacy groups such as the National Consumer Coalition implicitly evoke Adam Smith's premise when they argue that free and open competition in the market leads naturally to innovations that will ensure broader social goods such as cleaner air and safer products.

Not surprisingly, many business leaders argue that, although government requirements to reduce pollution may have been necessary once, such **command-and-control** policies are now outdated. The phrase *command and control* is used by opponents of environmental regulations to refer to government restrictions on business operations. Such regulations specify procedures and technologies for reducing pollution, as well as measurable levels of performance that a company must meet. In their study of business compliance with environmental regulations, Neil Gunningham, Robert Kagan, and Dorothy Thorton (2003) report, "Public policy analysts today often call for a 'second generation' of environmental regulation that relies less on government prescription and more on the imagination and innovativeness of corporate environmental management" (p. 1).

Opposition to environmental regulations has been reflected in the rhetoric of many conservative politicians in recent years, as the *New York Times* reported in its 2004 post-election headline, "G.O.P. Plans to Give Environment Rules a Free-Market Tilt" (Barringer & Janofsky, 2004, p. A14). Indeed, since the mid-1990s there has been some evidence of a political shift away from command-and-control approaches. Two developments especially have influenced a turn to a more conservative market policy: (1) a new willingness by the EPA and other federal agencies to allow states, corporations, and local municipalities to experiment with collaboration as a means of negotiating environmental rules, such as those implementing the Safe Drinking Water Act and the cleanup of toxic waste sites; and (2) the use of *pollution trading rights* to leverage market forces to reduce air pollution from factories, oil refineries, and other pollution sources. Since we've discussed the use of collaboration in Chapter 4, we'll now look at pollution trading rights.

Pollution Trading Rights: Does the Free Market Reduce Air Pollution?

One result of the popularity of market incentives for addressing environmental problems is the growing use of **pollution trading rights**, also called **cap and trade**. These are legal mechanisms that use market forces (supply and demand) as leverage to reduce pollutants caused by private industry. Pollution trading rights reflect conservatives' belief that "the free market is usually friendly to the environment if it is allowed to work properly," that is, when businesses pay all of the costs of production, including the costs of reducing pollution (Bliese, 2001, p. 57).

The best-known example of pollution trading rights occurred in efforts to reduce sulfur dioxide (SO_2), the chief cause of acid rain. Under the Clean Air Act Amendments of 1990, the U.S. Congress gave businesses the right to trade or sell pollution credits, which a company gained by reducing its SO_2 emissions. The price of the credits would fluctuate depending on demand for the excess pollution credits. The World Resources Institute (2004) explains how such trading systems actually worked in the case of sulfur dioxide and acid rain:

> The predictions in 1990 were that every ton of reduction of SO_2 would cost from $800 to $1,600. The trading system was set up, and pollution reduction credits are bought and sold on the Chicago Commodity Exchange. Companies who find it inexpensive to reduce the amount of SO_2 that they release can make bigger reductions than needed and sell the excess on the exchange, and companies that find it expensive, can buy the excess. Each company acts in its own economic interest.
>
> The reductions have gone much faster than expected. They have been deeper than expected. And the price of a ton of SO_2 reduction credits on the commodity exchange has hovered around $100 to $112, about one-tenth of what the industry said it would cost them. That experience has raised hopes about using market mechanisms for achieving environmental progress. (WRI, 2004, pp. 1–2)

Another Viewpoint: Emissions Trading Unfair?

Peter Montague (1998), writing for *Rachel's Environmental & Health News,* takes a more skeptical view of pollution trading rights. He writes,

> In actual practice . . . tradeable pollution permits have proven to be a very unfair way to allocate pollution, . . . and there is evidence that they do not always reduce pollution. . . . Here are some obvious problems with pollution trading schemes in actual practice:
>
> - Emissions trading moves pollution from one location to another. In practice, this often means dumping more pollution on the poor and on people of color.
> - Setting the total desired amount of pollution assumes that risk assessors can determine how much pollution is "safe" for humans and for the ecosystem. Risk assessors have a notoriously poor track record of making such estimates. . . .
> - An emissions trading system has no inherent, built-in incentives to reduce pollution. Unless the system requires an annual decrease in the total pollution allowed, emissions trading will simply lock in today's pollution levels. (paras. 17–20, 23)

For Montague's complete essay, see www.rachel.org/bulletin/pdf/ Rachels_Environment_Health_News_1208.pdf.

The apparent success of such market experiments has encouraged many neoliberal economists and globalization supporters who believe that, by opening global markets and encouraging investment abroad, poor nations not only will grow economically but will foster stronger environmental protections. For example, U.S. trade representative Robert Zoellick (2002) testified before the Congress that, "Free trade promotes free markets, economic growth, and higher incomes. And as countries grow wealthier, their citizens demand higher labor and environmental standards" (p. 1). (For a somewhat more skeptical view of market solutions for environmental problems, see the box, "Another Viewpoint.")

In summary, the discourse of the free market provides a rhetorical and philosophical rationale for corporate opposition to government-imposed standards for environmental performance. As we shall see, this discourse underlies a range of corporate communication practices, including the construction of a green identity and a sophisticated program of political influence.

Corporate Green Marketing

In the last 30 years, there have been improvements in the environmental performance of many industries (Gunningham, Kagan, & Thorton, 2003). Perhaps as a result of this, most corporations now have a twofold desire that often influences their environmental communication programs: (1) to link corporate goals and behavior to the increasingly popular values of environmental quality, and (2) to influence—or avoid—additional environmental regulations. In this section, I'll focus on the first interest—the use of corporate public relations and marketing to construct green identities for corporate products, images, and behaviors, as well as the discourse of green consumerism that underlies much corporate advertising. In the next section, I'll discuss the second major corporate interest: influencing environmental legislation.

Green Marketing

Before a corporation organizes an advocacy effort to forestall or shape environmental legislation, it usually has invested heavily in influencing consumers' and the public's perceptions of its identity and business operations. John Stauber and Sheldon Rampton (1995), editors of the quarterly journal *PR Watch,* estimated that American businesses were spending $1 billion a year on environmental public relations (p. 125). **Green marketing** is a term often used to refer to a corporation's attempt to associate its products, services, or identity with environmental values and images. It is generally used for one of three purposes: (1) product promotion (sales), (2) image enhancement, and (3) image repair. More recently, the term's definition has expanded to include communication about a product modification that is environmentally beneficial. For example, after negotiations with the Environmental Defense Fund group in 1990, fast-food chain McDonald's shifted from using its environmentally harmful polyfoam clamshell packaging to its quilt-wrap paper for hamburgers.[1] Green marketing proponent Jacquelyn Ottman (2003) argued that McDonald's shift "catapulted the fast-food giant to the top of the corporate responsibility list" (p. 1).

McDonald's public relations gain from its switch to paper wrapping is also an example of the controversy over green marketing among environmental critics, industry sources, journalists, and students of advertising that I'll address as we explore the general theme of green marketing. For example, in *Losing Ground,* journalist Mark Dowie (1995) called the McDonald's deal a high-level capitulation that "allow[s] companies like McDonald's to look a lot greener than they are" (p. 140). Whatever else green marketing may be, it is also an attempt to influence the perceptions of consumers, media, politicians and the public, and it is this function of communication in the public sphere that I'll describe in this section.

Green Product Advertising

Perhaps the most familiar form of corporate green marketing is the association of a company's products with popular images and slogans that suggest a concern for the environment. Such **green product advertising** is the attempt to market products as having a minimal impact on the environment and also to "project an image of high quality, including environmental sensitivity, relating both to a product's attributes and its manufacturer's track record for environmental compliance" (Ottman, 1993, p. 48; see also Goldman & Papson, 1996).

The list of such "environmentally sensitive" products can be lengthy: Coffee, cars, water filters, clothing, hair sprays, SUVs, magazines, allergy pills, breakfast cereals, lipstick, and children's toys are but a few examples. These may be visually linked to images of mountain peaks, tropical forests, clear water, or blue skies, or come with labels such as organic, nontoxic, ozone friendly, biodegradable, phosphate free, fat-free, cruelty free; they may contain the familiar symbol for recycled content (Giuliano, 1999).

Of course, as with advertising generally, the company's product is often secondary. What is being sold at the same time is an image or identification with the environment: "An advertisement for a car shows the vehicle outdoors, and . . . ads for allergy medications feature flowers and 'weeds'" (Corbett, 2002, p. 142). In green advertising, the environment offers a seemingly limitless range of possibilities. From Jeep ads encouraging urbanites to escape to mountain ridges, to "all natural" or "organic" breakfast foods, green ads rely on evocative appeals to nature as powerful rhetorical frames.

Examples of green product ads may be unlimited, but the underlying frames for such advertising draw on common themes. Environmental communication scholar Stephen DePoe (1991) has suggested that there may be three basic frames for such green product advertising: (1) nature as *backdrop* (Jeep ads), (2) nature as *product* ("all-natural" raisins), and (3) nature as *outcome* (products do not harm and may even improve environmental quality).

Figure 10.1   "Whether it's a streambed or flooded underpass, your Wrangler Unlimited has water-fording capabilities you may never need, but it's nice to know are there" (Jeep advertisement).

(Photo courtesy of www.jeep.com.)

Communication scholar Julia Corbett (2002) observes that "using nature merely as a backdrop—whether in the form of wild animals, mountains vistas, or sparkling rivers—is the most common use of the natural world in advertisements" (p. 142).

A classic illustration of the use of nature as backdrop was General Motors Corporation's full-page, color advertisement on the back cover of the nature magazine *Audubon*. The ad showed a new GM truck in a forest of "old-growth redwoods, with sunlight gently filtering through the trees to the ferns below" (Switzer, 1997, p. 130). A caption accompanying the photo declared, "Our respect for nature goes beyond just giving you an excellent view of it," and noted that GM had made "a sizable contribution to The Nature Conservancy" (quoted in Switzer, 1997, p. 130).

The use of environmentally friendly labels on products is a particularly widespread form of green marketing. Ottman (2003) reports, "Polls show that products and their usage are central to how Americans express their concern for the environment. Americans look for eco-labels at the store . . . Roper's Green Gauge poll shows a growing tendency towards 'pro-cotting' -buying products from companies perceived as having good environmental track records" (para. 4). The term **pro-cotting** is a play on *boycotting,* or the refusal to buy certain products. (For rules on the use of environmental labels on products, see "FYI : Guides for the Use of Environmental Marketing Claims.") I'll return to one of the rhetorical purposes of this type of green consumerism shortly.

FYI : Guides for the Use of Environmental Marketing Claims

What does it mean to purchase a product that is promoted as environmentally friendly or labeled "recycled" or "nontoxic"? Are businesses required to prove such claims? The Federal Trade Commission's "Guides for the Use of Environmental Marketing Claims" (Section 260.7) states,

General environmental benefit claims: It is deceptive to misrepresent, directly or by implication, that a product, package or service offers a general environmental benefit. Unqualified general claims of environmental benefit are difficult to interpret, and depending on their context, may convey a wide range of meanings to consumers. In many cases, such claims may convey that the product, package or service has specific and far-reaching environmental benefits. [However,] every express and material [sic] implied claim that the general assertion conveys to reasonable consumers about an objective quality, feature or attribute of a product or service must be substantiated. Unless this substantiation duty can be met, broad environmental claims should either be avoided or qualified, as necessary, to prevent deception about the specific nature of the environmental benefit being asserted.

However, one critic points out, "Currently, there are no federal laws governing what a seller can say about a product. The U.S. Federal Trade Commission . . . guidelines carry no force of law and compliance is strictly voluntary. Many states have advertising regulations, but enforcement is largely non-reactive. Nothing is done unless someone complains" (Giuliano, 1999, p. 1).

Read the complete Federal Trade Commission's "Guides for the Use of Environmental Marketing Claims" at: www.ftc.gov/bcp/grnrule/guides980427.htm.

Image Enhancement

Along with the green marketing of products, corporate communication relies on **environmental image enhancement,** the use of advertising to improve the image or identity of a corporation, reflecting its environmental concern or performance. As environmental values become increasingly popular in the United States and other countries, in the 1980s and 1990s many corporations began to expand their advertising to link their goals and identities with "images of environmentally responsible corporate citizens" (Schumann, Hathcote, & West, 1991, p. 35). For example, during a period of high gasoline prices in the U.S., ExxonMobil (2005) sponsored a series of full-page ads in the *New York Times* promoting its concern for energy and the environment. In one such ad, the giant oil company declared, "Because we take energy seriously, we take our responsibilities seriously too. In how we look for it. How we retrieve it. . . . And why we're now making the largest ever investment in independent climate and energy research that is specifically designed to look for new breakthrough technologies" (p. A5). (As we'll see below, the theme of responsibility has been particularly relevant for ExxonMobile and other oil companies as a result of highly publicized harmful oil spills.)

The use of image enhancement has not been without its critics. For example, in her study of corporate opposition to environmental regulations, Jacqueline Switzer (1997) notes that such "public relations campaigns—called 'greenwashing' by environmental groups—[are] used by industry to soften the public's perceptions of its activities" (p. xv; see also Corbett, 2002). The *Concise Oxford English Dictionary* defines the term **greenwash** as, "[d]isinformation disseminated by an organization so as to present an environmentally responsible public image. . . . Origin from *green,* on the pattern of *whitewash*" (Pearsall, 1999, p. 624). Environmental groups and other critics routinely use the term to call attention to what they believe is deception by a corporation, that is, an effort to mislead or divert attention from a corporation's poor environmental behavior or products.

Not all environmental marketing is greenwashing, however. Australian management scholar Michael Polonsky (1994) suggests that green marketing is a broader concept than simply the selling of an image. It also "incorporates a broad range of activities, including product modification, changes to the production process, packaging changes, as well as modifying advertising" (p. 5). In the discussion that follows, I'll try to illustrate the range of environmental image advertising as well as the challenge of identifying legitimate image promotion and its deceptive cousin.

One interesting example of corporate image enhancement that draws on the company's change in its production process as well as its desire to nurture an environmentally friendly image is BP Australia's (2004) "Man on the Street" campaign. BP Australia is part of British Petroleum Corporation, one of the world's largest oil companies. In recent years, the corporation has worked to boost its image as a forward-looking company that thinks "beyond petroleum" (BP, 2004, para. 4). For example, its website prominently states that BP was the first oil company to leave the Global Climate Coalition (an industry coalition that opposed the Kyoto global warming treaty) and touts BP's investment in solar energy and its introduction of cleaner-burning gasoline.

The company's "Man on the Street" campaign ran TV ads in Australia and the United States in 2004 and 2005. The ads showed candid interviews with ordinary people who were asked to talk about their cars and the environment. A typical 60-second television commercial featured a conversation between a middle-aged, Caucasian married couple as they sit on a park bench in New York City. It began with an off-camera interviewer asking, "Would you rather have your car or a cleaner environment?" The ad continued with the woman and man in lively conversation:

Woman: A cleaner environment.

Man: You'd rather have a cleaner environment than your car?

Woman: Of course!

Man: Come on, Trish!

Woman: We *are* married [laughing]. It's hard to believe, but we are.

Man: Oh, no. She wouldn't rather have a cleaner environment . . .

Woman: Yes, I would!

Man: . . . than a car.

Woman: Yes, I would.

Man: I don't believe you.

Woman: Sorry, it's true.

Man: How much . . . in what degree would you be willing to . . .

Woman: I wouldn't want to be without a car. I love my car, but, but if I had to choose between that and a clean environment, of course I'd choose . . .

Man: Then, why don't you give up your car?

Woman: Because I haven't been asked to yet. [Pause] We never talk politics any more. (Laughing)

Following each interview, a brief statement appeared on the television screen: "In 1999 we were the first oil company to voluntarily introduce cleaner fuels, five years before E.P.A. mandates. It's like taking 100,000 cars off the road every day. It's a start. BP: actions beyond petroleum" (BP, 2004).

Not surprisingly, BP's "Man on the Street" advertising campaign produced a flurry of online comments, including criticism pointing out BP's continued heavy reliance on petroleum. (Earlier, the company had earned a greenwash-ing award, which I'll discuss shortly.) Nevertheless, the campaign appeared to function as BP desired, to build the image of BP in consumers' minds as a com-pany trying to think differently about the future. In case anyone missed the company's rhetorical purpose, its website explained, the ad "points to a com-pany willing to go beyond traditional thinking . . . It points to a company that does indeed go beyond petroleum" (BP, 2004, paras. 3, 4).

As the BP ad shows, enhancement of a corporation's image is not limited to advertising of its product line. Often, trade associations for an industry troubled by a poor environmental image will launch a special program to signal the industry's commitment to environmental values. For example, in the 1990s—following a decade of negative news stories about toxic waste sites—the Chemical Manufacturers Association unveiled its Responsible Care Initiative, which aimed to assure the public of its care in producing and handling chemical products. In addition, many corporations publish annual reports of their environmental performance. First issued in the early 1990s, these **corporate environmental reports** are documents, distributed to share-holders and investors, that praise a company's environmental performance, actions taken, and commitment to environmental values.

In her study of such corporate reports, environmental communication scholar Wendy Feller (2004) argues that they tend to construct a utopian narrative of a company's environmental progress and values. (A **utopian nar-rative** is a story that depicts an ideal future; in this context, especially in its personal, social, and environmental features.) For example, Motorola Corporation's report for 2001 makes this bold claim:

> Imagine a world that creates sustainable growth without harming the environ-ment. That is a sustainable world. . . . Imagine a world filled with intelligent devices—devices that think and share information—making people's lives eas-ier, safer, more productive and more fun. That is an amazing world. Now imagine all of it together. That is the world Motorola is bringing to life. (as quoted in Feller, 2004, p. 57)

Such reports craft a particular outlook about a company. Apart from documentation of specific actions or achievements, the reports also serve a rhetorical purpose. Feller argues that they "function as narratives that unfold a free-market utopia" in which private corporations are portrayed as protectors of consumers' health and the earth's environment (p. 59). For example, Canon Corporation offered this promise in one of its reports: "In the years to come, we will continue fostering environmental protection activ-ities with the aim of contributing to world prosperity and the happiness of people everywhere" (quoted in Feller, 2004, p. 65).

In some cases, a corporation may achieve a good corporate citizenship image simply by doing the right thing, that is, by reforming its operations and environmental practices. The outdoor clothing company Patagonia has been one of the leading corporations to take this route as part of its mission and appears to be reaping consumer loyalty in return. For example, in 1996, Patagonia (n.d.) converted its entire sportswear line to organic cotton after conducting an audit of the environmental harms from synthetic fertilizers, pesticides, soil additives, and defoliants used in traditional cotton growing. In other cases, image enhancement may be an integral part of a larger campaign to position a company attractively for environmentally sensitive consumers, regardless of its actual performance. (For an analysis of some of the first corporate environmental image ads by Mobile and Exxon, see Crable & Vibbert, 1983, and Porter, 1992.)

How, then, can someone tell if a corporate ad is greenwashing or the report of a legitimate environmental achievement? Most critics point to a basic standard of deception. Has the ad conveyed information or an impression that is countered by factual evidence? Many times, the truthfulness of a claim may be difficult for the ordinary consumer to determine. In other cases, there are groups that monitor the statements and behavior of corporations, providing information about a company's record and its compliance with environmental regulations, and even evaluating specific marketing campaigns. For example, the watchdog group Corporate Watch (1999) gave its Summer Greenwash Award to the BP-Amoco Corporation for its "Plug in the Sun" ads. The company had claimed that "by installing solar powered gas pumps, it allows you to "fill your tank with sunshine'" (para. 1). A Corporate Watch spokesperson noted, "Solar panels notwithstanding, the pumps still fill your car with gasoline, the lifeblood of the oil industry and a leading cause of global warming" (para. 2). In the end, such efforts to evaluate the competing voices in the public sphere may allow us to judge the claims by both businesses and green groups who speak about the environment.

Corporate Image Repairs: Apology or Evasion?

One of the most-studied functions of corporate environmental communication is **image repair,** the use of public relations to restore a company's credibility after an environmental harm or accident. Corporations that engage in wrongdoing often face what communication scholar Keith Michael Hearit (1995) has called a "social legitimacy crisis" (p. 1). In such situations, corporate image repair attempts to minimize the harm and accompanying public perceptions that might otherwise "cause the organization irreparable damage" (Williams & Olaniran, 1994, p. 6). Image repair, also called *crisis management,* is vital to a company's continued operations, but the practice can be

Figure 10.2   A collection of dead, oiled seabirds, found after the *Exxon Valdez* oil spill

(Photo courtesy of Pamela Bergmann and the *Exxon Valdez* Oil Spill Trustee Council)

controversial, especially when a corporation's communication is viewed as insincere. A much-studied case of ineffectual image repair is the 1989 shipwreck of the *Exxon Valdez* oil supertanker in Alaska's Prince William Sound. The tanker hit a reef, spilling almost 11 million gallons of oil that "wreaked havoc on the immediate environment, despoiling almost eleven hundred miles of shoreline" (Hearit, 1995, p. 4). Called "the nation's worst oil spill" ("Oil Slick Spreads," 1989, p. 1), the pollution killed thousands of seabirds, sea otters, and other wildlife, and seriously harmed local fisheries.

Exxon faced a flurry of negative publicity as television, radio, newspapers, and magazines worldwide carried stories of oil-soaked birds and sea lions struggling to move or breathe. One story in the *New York Times* reported,

> On a small pebbled beach on Eleanor Island, what appeared to be a blackened rock turned out to be a seabird befouled with oil. As a helicopter descended, the frightened bird raised its wings to flee but was unable to lift itself into the air. Just off Seal Island, a large group of sea lions swam in a tight knot straining to keep their heads well above the oily surface. (Shabecoff, 1989; quoted in Benoit, 1995, pp. 119–120)

As a result of the tragic accident, Exxon offered to respond with remedial actions—help with the cleanup and cooperation with a federal investigation—and with an extensive image repair campaign. In a full-court press, including publication of a full-page "Open Letter to the Public" from Exxon's chairman in major newspapers, the corporation launched a three-part strategy of image restoration. Communication scholar William Benoit (1995), who has examined Exxon's efforts, noted that it first sought to shift the blame for the accident to the captain of the *Exxon Valdez,* who was discovered to have been drinking before his ship hit the reef. The company also tried to lessen the offensiveness of the oil spill through what Benoit (1995) called "minimization" and "bolstering" (p. 123). That is, Exxon tried to minimize reports of damage and bolster the company's image by announcing that it had "moved swiftly and competently" to lessen the impact of the oil on the environment and wildlife (quoted in Benoit, 1995, p. 126).

In the end, Exxon undoubtedly failed to alleviate public blame and loss of credibility in the immediate aftermath of the *Exxon Valdez* disaster. Although the company sought to portray itself as repairing damage caused by the accident, Benoit (1995) concluded that this strategy was undermined by well-publicized delays in the cleanup of the polluted coastlines. Hearit (1995) reported that, as a result of Exxon's bureaucratic handling of the crisis and failure to reestablish legitimacy, the company's public communication did not end with its letter of apology but continued with "a long-term campaign designed to communicate continued concern for, and assessment of, the effects of the *Valdez* spill" (p. 12).

Overall, Exxon's image repair campaign was not particularly successful. Benoit (1995) observes that the company's promises to correct the damage were vague and were undermined by continued negative publicity in the media. As a result, he concluded that "Exxon's reputation suffered from the *Valdez* oil spill, and its attempts to restore it in the short term appear ineffective" (p. 128).

A more successful case of image enhancement may be the efforts of the well-known banana producer, Chiquita Brands International (previously known as the United Fruit Company). In *Smart Alliance: How a Global Corporation and Environmental Activists Transformed a Tarnished Brand,* Gary Taylor and Patricia Scharlin (2004) tell the story of a corporation that had been criticized for decades for its harmful behavior toward both workers and the environment in Central America. Working with the conservation group Rainforest Alliance, Chiquita agreed "to improve conditions for its workers, to minimize the environmental impact of its farms, and to conserve the rainforest surrounding its plantations" (Corporate Social Responsibility, 2004, para. 3). According to Rainforest Alliance, Chiquita's plants now meet the conditions required for a company to merit the Alliance's "Better Banana" seal of approval, which certifies a company's good environmental and worker efforts. (For more information, see www.rainforest-alliance.org/news/2000/chiquita.html.)

Despite such cases as Chiquita, many environmental critics question the validity of green marketing altogether. Corbett (2002), for example, has argued that "the business of advertising is 'brown'; therefore the idea of advertising being 'green' and capable of supporting environmental values is an oxymoron" (p. 144).

Others have made a similar claim about environmental consumerism— the belief that by buying green, consumers can help the environment. It is this debate that I will consider next.

Green Consumerism:
Illusion or Helping the Environment?

Green marketing and discourses based on the free market raise an important question for scholars of environmental communication: Can consumers minimize damage to, or even improve, the environment by their purchase of certain products? That is, can we reduce air pollution, reduce the clear-cutting of our national forests, or protect the ozone layer by buying recycled, biodegradable, nontoxic, and ozone-free products? Many people appear to think so. As we saw earlier, Roper's Green Gauge poll has reported consumers' tendency towards pro-cotting, or "buying products from companies perceived as having good environmental track records" (Ottman, 2003, para. 4). Irvine (1989) referred to this "use of individual consumer preference to promote less environmentally damaging products and services" (p. 2) as **green consumerism**. As we noted earlier, this is the belief that, by buying allegedly environmentally friendly products, consumers can do their part to protect the planet.

Whether green consumerism actually helps the environment is a matter of some debate. Giuliano (1999) notes that eco-labels are often vague, and federal standards for compliance with the content of such labels are unenforceable. Furthermore, as Canadian social theorist Toby Smith (1998) points out, "Some ecologists insist that only a product that has passed a so-called cradle to grave environmental audit can be said to be authentically eco-friendly" (p. 89). For example, a product may be biodegradable but also toxic, and it can still claim to be environmentally friendly under current standards.

Why, then, is the idea of green consumerism popular? Most of us do not wish to harm the environment and believe that we can consciously choose to lessen our impact on the earth's capacity to sustain life. On the other hand, this belief itself is buttressed by green advertising claims that invite a specific identity through the act of buying. In his provocative book, *The Myth of Green Marketing: Tending Our Goats at the Edge of Apocalypse*, Toby Smith (1998) argues that green consumerism is not simply an act—the purchase of a certain product—but a discourse about the identity of individual consumers. Smith explains that our purchasing does not occur in a social vacuum but is "an act of faith"; that is, "it is based on a belief about the way the world works" (p. 89). Our actions have effects, and among these is the effect of our purchasing on producers of products. In other words, when we buy green, we assume that our buying not only can affect the actions of large corporations such as oil companies but that it also can alter our own relationship to, and impact on, the earth. In short, we act on faith; one takes on a particular identity as purchaser.

Smith argues that green consumerism communicates because the act of purchasing is cloaked in an aura of other, authoritative discourses that buttress our identity as purchasers. Smith claims that our belief that we can do well for the environment by green shopping is underwritten by certain discourses that encode our buying with significance. He suggests that two discourses in particular assign meaning to our purchasing decisions: the discourses of market forces and participatory democracy.

First, green advertising affirms the belief that the market can be an avenue for change; that is, that by doing our bit, we contribute to the free market's invisible hand, and as "all the little bits are counted, the consequence will be a net good" (Smith, 1998, p. 157). Second, the discourse of participatory democracy nurtures the belief that, in a liberal democracy, each of us is entitled to a voice in deciding about issues that matter to us. Thus, The Body Shop's founder, Anita Roddick, declares, "We can use our ultimate power, voting with our feet and wallets"; and another retailer claims, "Customers vote at the cash register" (quoted in Smith, 1998, p. 156). In each case, consumers are encouraged to believe that their purchases exercise a democratic will: "Voting" at the cash register affects retailers directly in determining which products succeed and which are in disfavor, and it affirms the consumer's identity as someone who acts responsibly toward the earth.

The discourse of green consumerism can be an attractive magnet, pulling one toward a persuasive identity as a purchaser. "Green consumerism makes sense," explains Smith (1998). "That is why people are attracted to it; they are not irrational, immoral, or uninformed. Quite the opposite: they are . . . moral in their desire to do their bit" (p. 152). Nevertheless, he believes that green consumerism also poses a danger by co-opting a more skeptical attitude toward the social and environmental impacts of excessive consumption. In a provocative charge, Smith claims that green consumerism serves to deflect serious questioning of a larger **productivist discourse** in our culture, one that supports "an expansionistic, growth-oriented ethic" (p. 10). Indeed, whether green consumerism can be a real force in the marketplace or a subtle diversion from the questioning of our consumer society is a question that invites serious debate in our classes and in research by environmental scholars.

In summary, the practice of green marketing is now widespread. It involves subtly and skillfully associating corporations' products, images, and behaviors with environmentally friendly values. As we saw, this effort to construct a green identity can serve any of three purposes: (1) green advertising or product promotion, (2) corporate image enhancement, and (3) image repair in the aftermath of negative publicity about a company. As we shall see shortly, companies may engage in green marketing even as they oppose stronger environmental protections.

Corporate Advocacy: Three Bites of the Apple

As we saw in Chapter 9, the newer fields of environmental chemistry and toxicology began to document health risks from industrial products as early as the 1960s. As these discoveries led to new requirements for industry, the affected businesses challenged the environmental sciences "at every step, questioning both the methods and research designs that were used and the conclusions that were drawn" (Hays, 2000, p. 222). Regulated industries such as chemical manufacturing, oil and gas refineries, electric utility companies, and older, extractive industries (mining, logging, and ranching) placed tremendous pressure on the agencies to justify the science that supported the new regulations. Many corporations mounted advocacy campaigns to alter or defeat environmental laws and regulations for tougher clean air rules, car fuel standards, and disposal of toxic chemicals. Others have sought ways to discredit the symbolic legitimacy of science or silence their critics through public relations and the courts.

Although environmental groups occasionally have countered, if not matched, corporate lobbying campaigns (Kraft & Wuertz, 1996), their efforts at the federal level have been increasingly stymied in recent years by the larger resources of industry and commercial interests. Therefore, in this section I'll explore two of the most common forms of corporate advocacy: legislative and agency lobbying, and the use of issue ads to frame the terms of public debate. In the next section, I'll look at a more aggressive tactic, the use of the courts.

Corporate Lobbying and the Environment

Most corporations that are affected by environmental regulations invest considerable sums of money to influence the legislative process in both

Washington, D.C., and state legislatures. For example, the coal and electric utility industries' eagle ad (discussed at the beginning of this chapter) aired at a time when Congress was scheduled to consider a new energy policy, including possible requirements that coal-fired power plants curb their mercury emissions.

In the past decade, business groups have grown more influential in shaping environmental policies. "Today, through trade associations and the addition of professional lobbyists to their payrolls, major industry groups can match mainstream environmental groups and even overpower their lobbying efforts, especially when the electoral winds blow more in their favor and a policy window appears to open" (Switzer, 1997, pp. 124–125). Industry groups such as the Business Roundtable devote substantial resources to communication within the public sphere—to legislative lobbying campaigns, press releases, and position papers to oppose environmental policies that would effect their operations or profits. Historians Gerald Markowitz and David Rosner (2002) describe some of these means:

> Organizations such as the Business Roundtable, made up of the CEOs of two hundred of the largest corporations in the country, have intensified their lobbying efforts among government officials and established well-funded and large offices in Washington, D.C. Through political contributions, "message ads," support for pro-industry legislators, and direct contact with members of the executive branch—at the very highest levels—industry attempts to protect its interests. (p. 9)

Corporations' public relations campaigns, political contributions, and direct lobbying serve a number of purposes. Journalist Mark Dowie (1995) has described the communication activities used by many corporations to shape environmental law as the **three-bites-of-the-apple strategy**. He explained, "The first bite is to lobby against any legislation that restricts production; the second is to weaken any legislation that cannot be defeated; and the third, and most commonly applied tactic, is to end run or subvert the implementation of environmental regulations" (p. 86).

Corporate lobbying to affect a law while it is being debated in the legislative arena is the most familiar, but more recently business groups have used their influence inside the bureaucracies of state and federal governments. In this strategy, the "third bite of the apple" is the end run, or targeting of agencies that write the rules implementing an environmental law. Switzer (1997) reported that the reason for this interest by business is that "by removing an environmental issue from the legislative arenas to the less visible and more difficult to track bureaucratic arena, organized interests can better control the debate" (p. 154). For example, Chapter 3 presented an example of the third "bite of the apple," in which lobbyists from the meat industry met secretly with the EPA in an effort to weaken Clean Air Act regulations affecting their industry. The industry-proposed Safe Harbor Agreement exempts many concentrated animal feeding operations (CAFOs) from requirements of the Clean Air Act and the Superfund law (Cook, 2004).

To better understand Dowie's three-bites-of-the-apple strategy, let's look at two examples of corporate advocacy: (1) first, how one industry coalition helped to defeat a key international treaty that dealt with global warming; and (2) industry's successful behind-the-scenes efforts to redefine one word in a coal mining regulation that allowed the destructive practice of mountaintop removal to continue.

The Global Climate Coalition

One of the most effective corporate lobbying efforts against new international standards to curb the emissions that cause global warming has been the Global Climate Coalition (www.globalclimate.org). Established in 1989, the GCC billed itself as "a leading voice for business and industry" (Global Climate Coalition, 2000, para. 1). Its early members included corporations and business associations such as the U.S. Chamber of Commerce, Texaco, Shell Oil, General Motors, and the American Forest and Paper Association. The coalition stated that its role was simply to coordinate the participation of business in policy debates about global warming: "The GCC represents the views of its members to legislative bodies and policymakers. And it reviews and provides comments on proposed legislation and government programs" (para. 1). In reality, the GCC commanded a potent war chest that was used to wage aggressive public relations campaigns to protect its members' interests.

In 1997, the Global Climate Coalition launched a well-funded and extensive advocacy campaign to dispute the science behind the theory of global warming and to influence the terms of a new treaty that the United States and other nations had been negotiating in Kyoto, Japan. The Kyoto Protocol, signed in 1997, set international standards requiring governments to reduce emissions of carbon dioxide (CO_2) and other gases that fuel climate change. The GCC's advocacy campaign included the publication of reports suggesting uncertainty in the science of climate change, "aggressive lobbying at [the] international climate negotiation meetings, and raising concern about unemployment that it [claimed] would result from emissions regulations" (PR Watch, 2004, para. 6).

Although the United States signed the Kyoto Protocol when international negotiators completed it in 1997, President Clinton still had to submit the treaty to the Senate for ratification under the Constitution. As a result, the Global Climate Coalition conducted a separate advertising campaign in the United States, objecting to many of the treaty's requirements. One of the GCC's major criticisms was that the United States would be required to meet stringent timelines for reducing so-called greenhouse emissions, yet many developing countries, along with China, would be exempt.

As a result of the questions raised by the Global Climate Coalition and other critics, the Senate voted 97–0 against the Kyoto Protocol in an advisory vote. As a result, President Clinton ultimately decided not to submit the treaty to the Senate for ratification. As the GCC continued its efforts at the first bite of the apple, its campaign claimed victory when newly elected president George W. Bush formally withdrew the United States from the list of signatories to the treaty in 2001.

In 2002, the GCC disbanded. Its sponsors believed that the lobbying campaign had served its purpose. A prominent statement on its deactivated website announced, "The industry voice on climate change has served its purpose by contributing to a new national approach to global warming. . . . At this point, both Congress and the Administration agree that the U.S. should not accept the mandatory cuts in emissions required by the [Kyoto] protocol" (Global Climate Coalition, 2004). Perhaps another reason for the GCC's deactivation may have been that many corporations no longer accepted one of its main premises, that climate change was not a serious threat. Major companies such as BP-Amoco, DuPont, Ford Motor Company, Daimler-Chrysler, Texaco, and General Motors all had left the GCC within three years of its creation in 1997, many announcing initiatives that promised to develop alternative, cleaner sources of energy.

Weakening Mountaintop Removal Regulations

A dramatic example of the three-bites-of-the-apple strategy is the coal industry's campaign to weaken federal rules regulating mountaintop removal in the Appalachian region of the United States. **Mountaintop removal** is the removal of the tops of mountains to expose the seams of coal that are buried in the mountain. Environmentally, it is a particularly destructive form of mining. "Miners target a green peak, scrape it bare of trees and topsoil, and then blast away layer after layer of rock until the mountaintop is gone" (Warrick, 2004, p. A1). In the past decade, hundreds of mountain peaks have been flattened in West Virginia, eastern Kentucky, and Tennessee. Adding to the damage, the mining operations dump tons of rocky

Figure 10.3   The towering dragline, center, is dwarfed by the size of the
mountaintop removal operation

(Photo by Vivian Stockman, May 30, 2003. Photo courtesy of Vivian
Stockman / www.ohvec.org)

debris from the blasts over the sides of the mountain into the valleys below,
"permanently burying more than 700 miles of mountain streams" (p. A1).

Although the rules implementing the Clean Water Act expressly forbid
the dumping of mine waste into streams, lax enforcement by the Army
Corps of Engineers officials who administered the law had allowed the practice of mountaintop removal to continue for years. However, by 1999 environmental groups had succeeded in challenging this illegal practice, and the
number of permits granted for mountaintop removal started to decrease. It
was at that point that industry decided to take a third bite of the apple by
quietly lobbying federal agencies to change the regulation defining waste, the
dumping of which is forbidden by the Clean Water Act.

In 2001, with a change of presidential administration in Washington,
D.C., the coal industry saw an opportunity. On April 6, 2001, lobbyists
from the National Mining Association met with EPA officials to argue for
"a small wording change" (Warrick, 2004, p. A1) to the regulations that
prohibit dumping of soil and rocks from mountaintops into valley streams.

(The EPA is the federal agency responsible for implementation of these rules.) As a result of this lobbying, officials "simply reclassified the [mining] debris from objectionable 'waste' to legally acceptable 'fill'" (p. A1). This change in the definitions of waste and fill "explicitly allows the dumping of mining debris into streambeds" (p. A6). For its part, administration officials insisted that the rule change merely clarified existing policies.

The Bush administration gave final approval for the so-called fill rule for mountaintop mining operations in May 2002. The new regulation represents both a case study of industry advocacy that employs the three-bites-of-the-apple strategy and also the way that the new administration has attempted to reshape environmental policy. *Washington Post* reporter Joby Warrick (2004) explained, "Rather than proposing broad changes or drafting new legislation, administration officials often have taken existing regulations and made subtle tweaks that carry large consequences" (p. A1).

Corporate Issue Ads: Framing the Terms of Debate

Although the ultimate goal of a corporate campaign may be the defeat or weakening of a particular law, the battle may be fought initially in the media and in the court of public opinion. Often accompanying an advocacy campaign is an extensive public relations effort aimed at persuading key opinion leaders and other members of the public. Business advocates attempt to influence the direction of environmental policy and legislation not only by placing advertisements in print and electronic media but also by feeding press releases and other information to reporters.

One of the most frequently used methods of influencing public perceptions of an environmental issue is the message or issue ad. An **issue ad** is a purchased advertisement in print, visual, or other media that carries a message opposing or supporting particular legislation or other issue affecting a company or industry's interests. Such ads often set the terms of debate by successfully framing an issue in terms of economic growth, jobs, a commitment to sustainability, and so forth. Let's look briefly at the growing use of issue ads and some of the framing devices that help to shape debate about the environment.

Issue Ads

In 1976, in the *Buckley v. Valeo* case, the U.S. Supreme Court distinguished issue ads from election campaign ads. Whereas election campaign ads clearly are intended to influence the election of a candidate, issue ads address a concern, such as the environment, health care, taxes, drunk driving, or education reform. Issue ads, which may be sponsored by corporations, by labor unions or other organizations, or by individuals, cannot endorse candidates for public office.

The Annenberg Public Policy Center at the University of Pennsylvania explains that the purpose of issue ads is "to mobilize constituents, policymakers, or regulators in support of or in opposition to legislation or regulatory policy" (2003a, para. 1). For example, the Global Climate Coalition successfully used issue ads and lobbying to mobilize opinion leaders and key members of Congress in its advocacy campaign to scuttle the Kyoto Protocol on global warming. More recently, the industry-funded group Americans for Balanced Energy Choices ran the eagle ad (an issue ad) on television throughout 2004 to mobilize broad public support for coal as a source of clean energy.

Often the purpose of such ads is to frame the debate over an issue by structuring the discussion in terms favorable to industry. (We discussed the role of media frames in Chapter 5.) According to Australian media scholar Sharon Beder (1998), Mobil Oil Corporation (now ExxonMobil) pioneered the use of issue ads to explain their business concerns without the media's filters. In an early issue ad, Mobil introduced the primary media frame that it would use in the future: A free and unfettered business climate is the American way. The ad explained,

> Business, generally, is a good neighbor . . . From time to time, out of political motivations or for reasons of radical chic, individuals try to chill the business climate. On such occasions we try to set the record straight . . . And the American system, of which business is an integral part, usually adapts . . . So when it comes to the business climate, we're glad that most people recognize there's little need to tinker with the American system. (Mobil Oil ad, quoted in Parenti, 1986, p. 67) (For a detailed study of the rhetoric of the early Mobil issue ads, see Crable & Vibbert, 1983.)

Although corporations use issue ads to address many concerns, the environment is clearly one of the main subjects. Indeed, Schumann, Hathcote, and West (1991) found that the public's concern about the environment had, by the early 1990s, "triggered a flurry of response from corporate America (resulting in numerous corporate advertising campaigns)" (p. 1). By 2002, the amount of money spent on issue ads to influence environmental policy had become enormous. For example, during the debates over the Bush administration's energy policy (including the proposed opening of the Arctic National Wildlife Refuge), the Annenberg Public Policy Center estimated that about $15.4 million was spent on issue ads to influence the energy policy, most supporting the Bush proposals. Annenberg (2003b) reported, "Roughly 94% (about $14.5 million) of this spending was sponsored by energy/business interests, with environmental interests spending the remaining 6%" (para. 7).

The largest spender among industry groups promoting the Bush energy policy was the Alliance for Energy and Economic Growth, a political advocacy group of producers of oil, natural gas, nuclear power, coal, and other energy sources that supported the policy. The group was formed in 2001 specifically to push the new policy, which included tax breaks, the opening of the arctic refuge for oil exploration, subsidies, and other incentives to industry. Annenberg's Public Policy Center reports that, in 2002, the Alliance sponsored 3 print advertisements that ran a total of 55 times in such influential Capitol Hill sources as *Roll Call* and *The Hill*. One of the issue ads was headlined, "President Bush. Democrats and Republicans. 1,350 organizations from across the country all agree: it's time to ensure America's energy security." The ad went on to frame the energy proposal in terms of economic growth and U.S. security needs: "to ensure economic growth and national security, America needs to ensure reliable supplies of domestic energy" (quoted in Annenberg, 2003c, para. 1, 2).

Framing the Terms of Debate

Issue ads are critical to corporate advocacy communication primarily because they help to frame the terms of debate in ways favorable to the sponsoring group. As discussed in Chapter 5, a frame is a cognitive map or pattern of interpretation that people use to organize their understanding of reality. For example, in their support for a national energy policy, some industry groups invoked frames for "national security" and "economic growth." Some corporations have used environmental values themselves to frame their support for or opposition to a particular policy. Indeed, even as some corporations oppose stricter environmental protection, they may frame their message in the vocabulary of "environmental progress," a concern for "nature," or "sustainability," as well as jobs and economic growth. Let's look more closely at two different frames that often appear in corporate issue ads—"sustainability" and "economic growth" (and its related theme of "jobs versus the environment").

The terms *environmental sustainability* and *sustainable development* appeared on the scene initially in the 1980s as concerns grew for the future of the earth's environment and its resources. The phrase *sustainable development* entered popular use when the United Nations' World Commission on Environment and Development (1987) published its report, *Our Common Future*. In a frequently quoted passage, the report defined **sustainable development** as "development that meets the needs of the present without compromising the ability of future generations to meet their own needs" (p. 43). As a metaphor for a new ethic toward the environment, the idea gained "massive public currency" (Peterson, Peterson & Peterson, in press, p. 5). In addition to ecologists, businesses also embraced the term.

Nevertheless, with little agreement over the concrete meaning of the phrase, sustainable development was interpreted in disparate ways by the parties who rushed to embrace the term. Many ecological scientists viewed the term as a roadmap for environmentally sensitive policies that would usher in a new orientation for society. On the other hand, some corporate interests used the term to denote sustainable *economic* growth. Such diverse uses of *sustainability* and *sustainable development* have led inevitably to confusion and a growing skepticism on the part of environmental leaders, scientists, and activists. Ironically, with its inherent ambiguity, the idea of sustainable development "fell from grace among ecologists as rapidly as it had become popular" (Peterson, Peterson, & Peterson, in press, p. 7). (For the history of the phrase *sustainable development* and its multiple uses, see Peterson, 1997.)

Business interests have retained an enthusiasm for the term and have appropriated its rich but ambiguous meaning as a powerful frame in marketing claims and issue ads. A prominent example is the World Business Council for Sustainable Development (WBCSD). Formed from business councils, corporations, and business leaders in 40 countries, the WBCSD describes itself as "a coalition of 170 international companies united by a shared commitment to sustainable development via the three pillars of economic growth, ecological balance and social progress" and claims that, "the WBCSD's activities reflect our belief that *the pursuit of sustainable development is good for business and business is good for sustainable development*" (para. 3, emphasis added).

"Economic growth" is an equally popular frame for issue ads. Since the 1970s, efforts by environmental supporters to reduce acid rain, to raise the miles-per-gallon requirement for cars, and to impose strict safety rules for nuclear plants all have met criticism that such actions would cost jobs, damage the economy, or reduce the United States to "the status of a second-class industrial power" (Bliese, 2001, p. 21). Indeed, no more damaging charge has been brought against environmental progress over the years than the claim that such progress costs American jobs. One example is the charge, prominently made in the early 1990s, that the preservation of the Pacific Northwest's old-growth forests as critical habitat for the endangered spotted owl would cost jobs. Bumper stickers and signs reading "Save a Logger, Eat an Owl" and "This Family Supported by Timber Dollars" (Lange, 1993, p. 251) dotted pickup trucks and storefront windows in logging communities throughout Oregon and Washington State. Environmental communication scholar Jonathan Lange (1993) reported that the timber industry "succeeded in creating an 'owl versus people' scenario in the media" (p. 250) with stories about threatened job losses in *Time,* the *Wall Street Journal,* and other national media.

A more recent example of the "jobs-versus-environment" frame occurred in response to the request of environmental groups that Congress raise the average fuel standard for cars to 40 miles per gallon. Automakers replied that this "would devastate the industry, putting 300,000 auto workers out of their jobs" (Bliese, 2001, p. 21). Was this accurate? Where did the figure 300,000 come from? At least one skeptic has pointed out that the claim of 300,000 jobs was based on a faulty study. Communication scholar John Bliese (2001) explains that what the industry's study did was to "simply add up all of their employees currently making cars that get less than forty miles per gallon and assume that every single one of them would lose his or her job!" In other words, the study assumed that "the industry would not even attempt to build a single new car that met the proposed gas mileage standard" (p. 21).

The popular frame of "jobs versus the environment" rose to prominence in the 1970s as businesses felt the impact of new environmental laws. In their book *Fear at Work: Job Blackmail, Labor, and the Environment,* Richard Kazis and Richard Grossman (1991) have documented industry's charge that environmental rules resulted in lost jobs. They reported that businesses often claimed that the cost of environmental regulations forced them to close factories, lay off workers, and delay or cancel projects, resulting in the "elimination of thousands of proposed new jobs" (p. 7). Kazis and Grossman concluded, "the implication of these employers' claims and threats is clear: our nation cannot afford both *jobs* and *environment.* If the public wants careful resource use and a clean, protected environment, that must come at the expense of working people" (p. 7).

The warning that environmental protection will cost workers their jobs has acquired an almost mythic status in contemporary culture. Although this charge has been rigorously challenged, it persists in the popular imagination. (See "Another Viewpoint: Jobs and the Environment.") Indeed, one reason this frame has been so influential is that it is a conflict-oriented frame and, as such, fits well with typical gatekeeper and media filters. It also taps a reservoir of concern about job security felt by many people. For example, a *Wall Street Journal* poll reported that "a third of all American workers apparently fear losing their jobs because of environmental regulations" (Bliese, 2001, p. 29).

Perhaps because of refutations of the claim that environmental standards cost jobs, by 2000 industry had begun to change its strategy. Rather than threaten to close a factory or claim directly that cleaner air, higher gas mileage, or wilderness protection would cost-jobs, issue ads today tend to be more indirect. In her study, *Green Backlash: The History and Politics of Environmental Opposition in the U.S.*, Switzer (1997) observed that industry had "learned not to challenge environmental laws as directly as they did in the past but, instead, to portray them as too costly, without sufficient environmental benefit, or as impossible to implement" (Switzer, 1997, p. 125). Instead of jobs, corporate issue ads often speak of economic growth, along with the insistence that business is committed to environmental excellence and sustainability.

Another Viewpoint: Jobs and the Environment

In his book, *The Greening of Conservative America,* environmental communication scholar John Bliese (2001) compiled considerable evidence refuting the claim that environmental protection hurts business competitiveness, slows economic growth, and costs American jobs. Writing specifically about the impact of environmental regulations on jobs, Bliese stated:

Many believe that stricter environmental protection causes companies to lay off workers. . . .

According to Robert Repetto [1995], the number of jobs created per dollar of expenditure on pollution control is very similar to the employment created per dollar of sales in American industry in general. Eban Goodstein [1994] finds that the overall employment effect of environmental protection is positive: "When the job creation aspects of pollution control policies are factored in, environmental protection has probably increased net employment in the U.S. economy by a small amount" [p. 4]. The OECD [Organization for Economic Cooperation and Development] review of our environmental performance corroborates Goodstein's conclusion: "Over the period 1970–87, the *net employment effect* of federal environmental programs was calculated to be positive, leading to a reduction in unemployment equivalent to 0.4 per cent of the labor force" [OECD, 1996, p. 136]. "At the national level, as Goodstein concludes, "any claim of a trade-off between jobs and the environment is completely without substance" [1994, p. 4]. In an update of this research, Goodstein reaches the same conclusion: "In reality, at the economy-wide level, there has simply been no trade-off between jobs and the environment" [1999, p. 1] (p. 29).

Environmental Backlash: Corporate Responses to Environmental Critics

At the same time that corporations and industry trade groups engage in green marketing and advocacy campaigns to influence legislation, they have not been shy about responding aggressively to their critics in the environmental movement. In this section, we'll look at an escalating series of communication techniques used by some businesses to deny or divert responsibility for environmental problems, to discredit or blame their critics, and to seek damage awards in court against individuals or environmental groups in SLAPP lawsuits, or Strategic Litigation Against Public Participation.

Toxic Politics: Corporate and Governmental Response to Criticism

In an extensive study of corporate and institutional behavior in the face of chemical contamination of communities, Michael Reich (1991) of Harvard University's School of Public Health described the communication methods that some corporations have used in responding to their public critics. His book, *Toxic Politics: Responding to Chemical Disasters,* details cases of chemical poisoning, such as the accidental feeding of the highly toxic chemical polybrominated biphenyls (PBBs) to dairy cattle in Michigan in the 1970s, "one of the worst chemical disasters in United States history" (p. 58). Reich was interested particularly in the range of communication strategies that some companies and governmental agencies used to deny or divert responsibility for the problem or to discredit their critics.

In his investigation, Reich discovered two stages of corporate response to criticism from health officials, media, and residents of the affected communities. During the first stage, as reports of environmental problems first began to surface, responses were of three kinds:

1. Controlling the *definition of the issue* (for example, portraying the problem as "limited in scope" or "exaggerated by the emotional reactions of victims" (p. 182)

2. Issuing limited administrative responses that provide some form of remedy, and also *symbolically reassuring* the public

3. *Legitimating,* attempting to give legitimacy to the definition of the issue by using specialized legitimators (such as technical experts) to speak in public forums (p. 188)

As the public continued to gain information about the toxic poisoning of the Michigan community, and as the conflicts grew more volatile, Reich observed that corporations and agencies often adopted a second set of communication strategies to respond to criticism. He identified three second-stage strategies: dissociation, confrontation, and diversion. In **dissociation**, a corporation "retreats and avoids public involvement in the conflict," often by avoiding public appearances or by using others to lobby on their behalf (p. 235).

Corporations used the second strategy, **confrontation**, when efforts to avoid association with the problem failed. Although the word *confrontation* suggests the use of coercion or pressure, Reich found that confrontation occurred most often in the symbolic realm—particularly in attempts to discredit opponents. Confrontational tactics "blame the victims, political groups, the public media . . . and public agencies not only for causing the conflict but also for creating the problem" (p. 241). For example, Farm Bureau Services, a company involved in the Michigan PBB contamination case, lashed out at its critics, referring to the "greed of four classes of animals: ambitious politicians, poor man's Woodward-and-Bernstein types [the two *Washington Post* reporters who investigated Watergate in the 1970s], scientists on the make for a grant . . . , and overreaching claimants [the affected individuals seeking redress]" (quoted in Reich, 1991, p. 242). Finally, Reich found that some corporations used the strategy of **diversion** to transfer the responsibility for responding to the crisis to other organizations, "a strategy of passing the buck" (p. 236).

The cases Reich studied largely involved responses to critics in the symbolic realm; however, some corporations have gone further, especially in targeting environmental groups that have been critical of logging companies or those involved in the destruction of rain forests. These corporate responses have included threatening communications directed to a group's financial supporters, efforts to persuade the government to strip a group's tax-exempt status, and strategies to dry up a group's sources of funding. For example, in 2001 the pro-business Frontier Freedom Foundation (FFF)—funded by oil and timber groups—pressured Congress to eliminate the tax-exempt status of the Rainforest Action Network (RAN), a forest protection group. Over the years, RAN has targeted major corporations that destroy rain forests, using tactics such as consumer boycotts and scaling corporations' headquarters buildings to unfurl banners criticizing their activities.

The Frontier Freedom Foundation called the activist group "fundamentally radical, anti-capitalist, and lawless" and complained to the Internal Revenue Service "that RAN routinely engages in non-educational activity, violating the legal requirement that it be 'operated exclusively for educational purposes'" (Hazen, 2001, para. 4). (RAN has denied these charges, arguing that its actions to shine the spotlight of the media on corporate misdeeds were highly educational.) In addition to the FFF's complaints to the IRS, Hazen (2001) reported that the giant logging corporation Boise Cascade had "aggressively targeted RAN's funders with threatening letters, trying to undermine the organization by drying up its cash" (para. 2). Boise Cascade later entered into an agreement with RAN pledging to halt its logging of old-growth forests in the United States as of 2004.

Finally, some corporations have turned to a particularly chilling method of attempting to silence or intimidate critics—a legal action known as the SLAPP lawsuit. Let's look briefly at this final method of corporate response to criticism.

SLAPPs: Strategic Litigation Against Public Participation

When Betty Johnson learned that a developer planned to build a large housing tract on the farmland next to her house in suburban Denver, she grew alarmed. After learning of others in her community who opposed the development, Johnson protested at a city council meeting (Pring & Canan, 1996). Nevertheless, the council voted to grant a building permit for the development. Undeterred, Johnson and several neighbors circulated a petition, gathered signatures, and forced a local election to overturn the city council's action. They succeeded, and the city repealed the building permit.

Unfortunately, others did not view Johnson's and her neighbors' exercise in local democracy favorably. A few days later, the developer sued the citizens for an undetermined amount, charging that their act of petitioning the council "had violated the developers' 'constitutional rights' to develop the land and constituted 'restraint' of their business" (pp. 4–5). Although a judge later threw out the case, the lawsuit exacted an emotional toll by distressing and frightening Johnson and her neighbors.

Betty Johnson's experience is not unusual. University of Denver professors George Pring and Penelope Canan (1996) codirect the university's Political Litigation Project, an effort to document cases similar to Johnson's. They report in their influential study, *SLAPPs: Getting Sued for Speaking Out* (1996), that lawsuits have been brought against citizens and environmental groups for writing letters, speaking at public hearings, publicly protesting, filing complaints, and circulating petitions to government:

> An anthropology professor fought to preserve an ancient Indian village found on his California State University campus before the university buried it in apartment buildings and retail stores. He wrote letters to government officials

complaining . . . and was sued for $570,000 by the university's consulting firm for "negligent interference with contractual relations," "libel," [and] "slander" . . .

In 1992 a North Kingston, Rhode Island, homeowner reported to government authorities her concern that a local landfill was contaminating the area's drinking water. The owners sued her for "defamation" and "contractual interference." . . .

Peaceful demonstrators protested a California nuclear power plant. The county responded with a $2,891,000 lawsuit, demanding that demonstrators repay its costs for arresting and jailing them. (Pring & Canan, 1996, pp. 6–7)

Lawsuits against citizens who communicate with their local governments or the media are called **SLAPP lawsuits,** or Strategic Litigation Against Public Participation. Pring and Canan (1996) defined a SLAPP as a lawsuit involving "communications made to influence a governmental action or outcome, which, secondarily, resulted in (a) a civil complaint [lawsuit] . . . (b) filed against nongovernmental individuals or organizations . . . on (c) a substantive issue of some public interest or social significance" such as the environment (pp. 8–9). Such lawsuits have become common. California's State Environmental Resource Center (2004) reports that every year thousands of people are hit with SLAPP suits.

In the end, most SLAPP lawsuits are dismissed because of First Amendment protections of citizens' rights to speak and petition government. But the mere act of filing a lawsuit that alleges libel, slander, or interference with a business contract can be financially and emotionally crippling to defendants. Pring and Canan (1996) explain that corporations or even government units that file SLAPP suits "seldom win a legal victory—the normal litigation goal—yet often achieve their goals in the real world. . . . Many [of those who are sued] are devastated, drop their political involvement, and swear never again to take part in American political life" (p. 29). Even if the group or citizen wins, he or she most likely "has paid large sums of money to cover court costs and has been thrown into the public eye for months or even years. This unlawful intimidation pushes people into becoming less active and outspoken on issues that matter" (California State Environmental Resource Center, 2004, para. 7).

The purpose of a SLAPP is not necessarily to win the lawsuit but to cause the corporation's critic to spend time, energy, and money defending itself and to discourage others from participating in public life. Yet, some have decided to fight back. (See the case of *Sierra Club v. Butz* in "FYI: The First Environmental SLAPP Lawsuit.') Many states are providing remedies for cases in which a court determines that a lawsuit against an individual is a SLAPP action. That is, some courts may agree quickly to dismiss a lawsuit if it appears to be motivated by the unconstitutional purpose of silencing speech and to require the plaintiffs to pay court costs.

Over the years, two principal sources of defense have arisen in response to SLAPP lawsuits—one based in constitutional guarantees of democratic rights and the other in personal injury law. Pring and Canan (1996) refer to these two sources of defense as the "one-two punch" that has characterized successful defense against SLAPP lawsuits.

The core defense against a SLAPP suit is derived from the basic rights granted to citizens in the First Amendment to the U.S. Constitution, particularly the rights of freedom of speech and the right of the people to petition the government for redress of grievances. Often, a court will grant expedited hearings to dismiss a SLAPP if the citizen's criticism was part of a petition to the government. In such cases, the plaintiff (the party bringing the lawsuit) must show that the citizen's petition is a "sham" in order to proceed with the original lawsuit.

The second part of the defense involves what is known as a **SLAPP-back** suit against the corporation or governmental agency bringing the initial allegations against a citizen. Here, the defendant "SLAPPs back" by filing a countersuit alleging that the plaintiff infringed on the citizen's right to free speech or to petition government. Importantly, a SLAPP-back suit allows for the recovery of attorneys' fees as well as punitive damages for violating constitutional rights and inflicting damage or injury on the defendant (malicious prosecution).

FYI: The First Environmental SLAPP Lawsuit

In their pioneering study, *SLAPPs: Getting Sued for Speaking Out* (1996), University of Denver professors George Pring and Penelope Canan identify the case of *Sierra Club v. Butz* (1972) as the first eco-SLAPP lawsuit in the United States. They state,

> The spectacular wilderness areas of California have been a battleground between the Sierra Club and timber/mining/ranching interests since the nineteenth century. One of the great modern battles triggered what we believe is the first officially reported eco-SLAPP and one of the best reasoned to date—*Sierra Club v. Butz*. In 1965, the U.S. Forest Service opened for logging a virgin 3,500-acre area near what has become the Salmon-Trinity Alps Wilderness in the far northwest corner of California. The contract was awarded to Humboldt Fir. . . . In 1970, the

Sierra Club . . . began objecting to the Forest Service that the proposed logging was "illegal," and requested that the area be kept a wilderness. The government denied the request, and in 1972, the club appealed, filing a federal court challenge to overturn the government's decision.

Three days later, Humboldt Fir filed a counterclaim demanding . . . $750,000 in actual damages, and $1,000,000 in punitive damages [from] the Sierra Club. The club promptly filed a motion to dismiss, plainly worried about the "drastic monetary liability," and objecting strenuously to the violation of its political rights:

[Humboldt's] claim is that the presence of a timber sale contract . . . chokes off [the Sierra Club's] freedom to address the Government with their views as to the best use of the public lands in question. . . . It would be difficult to imagine a cruder attempt to deprive ordinary citizens of their right . . . to communicate with their Government and petition it for redress of grievances.

The Sierra Club's decision to focus on political-constitutional issues . . . was quickly rewarded: the U.S. District Court dismissed Humboldt's counter-claim in a near-record four months. One of the very first federal court opinions to rule SLAPPs unconstitutional, *Sierra Club v. Butz* remains a landmark precedent today. (Pring & Canan, 1996, pp. 85–86)

Environmentalists, labor, individual citizens and others have won monetary awards in fighting SLAPP actions. Pring and Canan (1996) report that awards in SLAPP-backs occasionally have been large—jury verdicts of $5 million to a staggering $86 million were awarded against corporations that brought SLAPP suits in the 1980s and 1990s. Increasingly, developers, polluters, and others have had to weigh the chances of a SLAPP-back before bringing a SLAPP action. Pring and Canan (1996) observed, "Even though SLAPP-backs are not a panacea, this risk of having to defend against them may prove to be the most effective SLAPP deterrent of all" (p. 169).

Conclusion

In this chapter, we identified three major types of corporate environmental communication in the public sphere: (1) Green marketing, or the construction of an environmental identity in corporate products, images, and behaviors;

(2) industry advocacy campaigns aimed at influencing legislation, agency rule-making, and public opinion, and (3) a range of communication strategies used by some corporations to discredit or intimidate their environmental critics. We also observed that a broader discourse of the free market underlies much of corporate communication and helps to explain much opposition to government regulation of business. In the view of its proponents, a free-market discourse offers a powerful ideological rationale for determining the value that a society assigns to environmental protection, as well as the best way to secure that value, including such market mechanisms as pollution trading rights.

Finally, we discussed a range of strategies used by some businesses to deny or divert responsibility for environmental problems, to discredit or blame their critics for the problem, and to seek relief in court. This last action is usually intended to discourage critics through lawsuits for large financial awards in what are known as SLAPP suits.

Despite such aggressive responses by some corporations, many businesses in contemporary U.S. society have come to appreciate the environmental values embraced by the general public, consumers, and the media alike. As a consequence, much of corporate communication illustrates a skillful dance of corporate identity—an effort to appear green while at the same time often opposing stronger environmental protections.

KEY TERMS

Cap and trade: See *pollution trading rights.*

Command and control: Phrase used by opponents of environmental regulations to refer to government requirements that impose restrictions on business operations; these specify procedures and technologies for reducing pollution as well as measurable levels of performance that a company must meet.

Confrontation: As used by Reich (1991), a strategy (in the symbolic realm) used by corporations to discredit opponents, to "blame the victims, political groups, the public media . . . and public agencies not only for causing the conflict but also for creating the problem" (p. 241).

Corporate environmental reports: Documents, distributed to shareholders and investors, that praise a company's environmental performance and actions and its commitment to environmental values.

Dissociation: As used by Reich (1991), a communication strategy used by corporations to respond to criticism; a company "retreats and avoids public involvement in the conflict," often by avoiding public appearances or by using others to lobby in their behalf (p. 235).

Diversion: As used by Reich (1991), a strategy used by corporations to transfer the responsibility for responding to the crisis to other organizations, "a strategy of passing the buck" (p. 236).

Environmental image enhancement: The use of advertising to improve the image or identity of a corporation, reflecting its environmental concern or performance.

Free market: Usually, the absence of governmental restriction on business or commercial activity.

Green consumerism: Marketing that encourages the belief that, by buying allegedly environmentally friendly products, consumers can do their part to protect the planet.

Green marketing: A corporation's attempt to associate its products, services, or identity with environmental values and images; generally used for (1) product promotion (sales), (2) image enhancement, or (3) image repair. Recently defined to include communication about environmentally beneficial product modifications.

Green product advertising: The marketing of products as having a minimal impact on the environment and to "project an image of high quality, including environmental sensitivity, relating both to a product's attributes and its manufacturer's track record for environmental compliance" (Ottman, 1993, p. 48).

Greenwash: "Disinformation disseminated by an organization so as to present an environmentally responsible public image. . . . Origin from *green* on the pattern of *whitewash*" (Pearsall, 1999, p. 624).

Image repair: The use of public relations to restore a company's credibility after an environmental harm or accident.

Invisible hand (of the market): Scottish economist Adam Smith's theory of the working of the market; a metaphor for an invisible or natural force of the private marketplace that determines what society values. In his classic book, *An Inquiry into the Nature and Causes of the Wealth of Nations,* Smith (1776) argued that the sum of individuals' self-interested actions in the marketplace promotes the public's interest, or the common good.

Issue ads: Purchased advertisements in print, visual, or other media that contain a message opposing or supporting particular legislation or other issues affecting a company or industry's interests.

Mountaintop removal: The removal of the tops of mountains in the Appalachians to expose seams of coal buried in the mountain; a particularly destructive form of mining environmentally.

Pollution trading rights: Legal mechanisms that use market forces (supply and demand) as leverage to reduce pollutants caused by private industry; also reflects conservatives' belief that "the free market is usually friendly to the environment if it is allowed to work properly," that is, when businesses pay all of the costs of production, including costs of reducing pollution (Bliese, 2001, p. 57). Also called *cap and trade.*

Pro-cotting: Buying products from companies perceived to have good environmental track records; the opposite of *boycotting*.

Productivist discourse: A discourse in our culture that supports "an expansionistic, growth-oriented ethic" (Smith, 1998, p. 10).

Riparian areas: The areas along rivers, streams, and other natural courses of water; often important habitat for wildlife species that use these areas for hunting, breeding, or nesting.

SLAPP-back: A lawsuit against the corporation or governmental agency bringing the initial SLAPP suit against a citizen. The defendant "SLAPPs back" by filing a countersuit alleging that the plaintiff infringed on the citizen's right to free speech or to petition government; importantly, a SLAPP-back suit allows for the recovery of attorneys' fees as well as punitive damages for violating constitutional rights and/or inflicting damage or injury on the defendant (malicious prosecution).

SLAPP lawsuits: Strategic Litigation Against Public Participation. As defined by Pring and Canan (1996), a SLAPP is a lawsuit involving "communications made to influence a governmental action or outcome, which, secondarily, resulted in (a) a civil complaint [lawsuit] . . . (b) filed against nongovernmental individuals or organizations . . . on (c) a substantive issue of some public interest or social significance" such as the environment (pp. 8–9).

Sustainable development: Defined by the United Nations' World Commission on Environment and Development (1987) in its report, *Our Common Future,* as "development that meets the needs of the present without compromising the ability of future generations to meet their own needs" (p. 43).

Three-bites-of-the apple strategy: Phrase used by journalist Mark Dowie (1995) to describe the communication activities used by many corporations to shape environmental law: "The first bite is to lobby against any legislation that restricts production; the second is to weaken any legislation that cannot be defeated; and the third, and most commonly applied tactic, is to end run or subvert the implementation of environmental regulations" (p. 86).

Utopian narrative: A story depicting an ideal future; in this context, especially in its personal, social, and environmental features.

DISCUSSION QUESTIONS

1. Do advertising labels on products, such as "organic," "biodegradable," or "recycled" affect your purchases? Are these labels always accurate?

2. Do you recycle or buy "green" products? Do you believe that Americans are willing to shift from excessive consumption or a materially driven lifestyle to protect the environment?

3. Do you believe that government should regulate business activities that harm the environment? Or do you side with Adam Smith's theory that there is an "invisible hand" in the activities of the private marketplace that naturally leads to the public good?

4. Can green consumerism help to protect the environment? That is, can we reduce air pollution, lessen the clear-cutting of our national forests, or reduce global warming by buying products that are biodegradable, non-toxic, recyclable, and so forth? Or does green consumerism simply reinforce consumption?

5. Are all corporate marketing claims about their environmental achievements greenwashing or deceptive? How can you tell? Can you give an example of a misleading ad?

6. How accurate are claims such as "owls versus jobs"? Does environmental protection cost jobs or otherwise retard economic health?

7. Are the corporations that file SLAPP lawsuits or use tactics such as blaming the victim merely a few bad apples, or do most corporations continue to resist strong environmental standards?

REFERENCES

Americans for Balanced Energy Choices. (2004). *New ads provide next chapter in electricity from coal's increasingly clean story.* Retrieved October 13, 2004, from www.balancedenergy.org/abec/index.cfm?cid=7577

Annenberg Public Policy Center. (2003a). *About issue advertising.* University of Pennsylvania. Retrieved October 16, 2004, from http://www.annenbergpub licpolicycenter.org/issueads/issues.htm

Annenberg Public Policy Center. (2003b). *Energy/environment.* University of Pennsylvania. Retrieved October 16, 2004, from www.annenbergpublicpolicy center.org/issueads/issues_energy_enviro.htm

Annenberg Public Policy Center. (2003c). *Alliance for Energy and Economic Growth (AEEG).* University of Pennsylvania. Retrieved October 16, 2004, from www .annenbergpublicpolicycenter.org/issueads/organizations/alliance_for_energy_ and_economic_growth.htm.

Barringer, F., & Janofsky, M. (2004, November 8). G.O.P. plans to give environment rules a free-market tilt. *New York Times*, p. A14.

Beder, S. (1998). *Global spin: The corporate assault on environmentalism.* White River Junction, VT: Chelsea Green.

Benoit, W. L. (1995). *Accounts, excuses, and apologies: A theory of image restoration strategies.* Albany: State University of New York Press.

Bliese, J. R. E. (2001). *The greening of conservative America.* Boulder, CO: Westview Press.

BP Australia. (2004). Man on the street campaign. Retrieved October 22, 2004, from www.bp.com.au/environmental_social/man/man_on_street_story.asp? menuid=h

California State Environmental Resource Center. (2004). *"Eco-SLAPPs" are a frequent occurrence.* Retrieved October 31, 2004, from www.serconline.org/SLAPP/faq.html

Campbell, K. K. (1973). The rhetoric of women's liberation: An oxymoron. *Quarterly Journal of Speech, 59,* 73–86.

Cook, C. D. (2004, October 25). Environmental hogwash: The EPA works with factory farms to delay regulation of "extremely hazardous substances." *In These Times, 28*(24), 6–7.

Corbett, J. B. (2002). A faint green sell: Advertising and the natural world. In M. Meister & P. M. Japp (Eds.), *Enviropop: Studies in environmental rhetoric and popular culture* (pp. 141–160). Westport, CT: Praeger.

Corporate Social Responsibility Newswire Service. (2004). A notorious company changes course by choice on the environment and human rights. Retrieved October 17, 2004, from www.csrwire.com/article.cgi/2803.html%20

Corporate Watch. (1999, July 28). *BP-Amoco's deployment of solar powered gas pumps garners greenhouse greenwash award.* [Press release]. Retrieved May 29, 2005, from www.commondreams.org/pressreleases/july99/072899f.htm

Crable, R. E., & Vibbert, S. L. (1983). Mobil's epideictic advocacy: "Observations" of Prometheus-bound. *Communication monographs, 50,* 380–394.

DePoe, S. P. (1991). Good food from the good earth: McDonald's and the commodification of the environment. In D. W. Parson (Ed.), *Argument in controversy: Proceedings from the 7th SCA/AFA Conference on Argumentation,* 334–341. Annandale, VA: Speech Communication Association.

Dowie, M. (1995). *Losing ground: American environmentalism at the close of the twentieth century.* Cambridge: MIT Press.

ExxonMobil. (2005, May 9). Energy and the environment. [Advertisement]. *New York Times,* p. A5.

Federal Trade Commission. (n.d.). Guides for the use of environmental marketing claims. Section 260.7. *Environmental marketing claims.* Retrieved November 25, 2004, from www.ftc.gov/bcp/grnrule/guides980427.htm

Feller, W. V. (2004). Blue skies, green industries: Corporate environmental reports as utopian narratives. In S. L. Senecah (Ed.), *The environmental communication yearbook: Vol. 1* (pp. 57–76). Mahwah, NJ: Erlbaum.

Giuliano, J. (1999). Green advertising claims—to heal or deceive? *Healing our world weekly commentary.* Retrieved October 15, 2004, from: www.spiritualendeavors.org/m-earth/how/green_ads.htm.

Global Climate Coalition. (2000). *About us.* Retrieved October 4, 2004, from www.globalclimate.org/aboutus.htm

Global Climate Coalition. (2004). [Statement]. Downloaded October 30, 2004, from www.globalclimate.org

Goldman, R., & Papson, S. (1996). *Sign wars: The cluttered landscape of advertising.* NY: Guilford.

Goodstein, E. (1999). *The trade-off myth: Fact and fiction about jobs and the environment.* Washington, DC: Island Press.

Goodstein, E. B. (1994). *Jobs and the environment: The myth of a national trade-off.* Washington, DC: Economic Policy Institute.

Gunningham, N., Kagan, R. A., & Thorton, D. (2003). *Shades of green: business, regulation, and environment.* Stanford, CA: Stanford University Press.

Hays, S. P. (2000). *A history of environmental politics since 1945.* Pittsburgh, PA: University of Pittsburgh Press.

Hazen, D. (2001, June 26). *Green group comes under right-wing attack.* Retrieved June 14, 2003, from www.alternet.org/story.html?StoryID=11102

Hearit, K. M. (1995). "Mistakes were made": Organizations, apologia, and crisis of social legitimacy. *Communication Studies, 46,* 1–17.

Irvine, S. (1989). *Beyond green consumerism.* London: Friends of the Earth.

Kazis, R., & Grossman, R. L. (1991). *Fear at work: Job blackmail, labor, and the environment* (New ed.). Philadelphia: New Society Publishers.

Kraft, M. E., & Wuertz, D. (1996). Environmental advocacy in the corridors of government. In J. G. Cantrill & C. L. Oravec (Eds.), *The symbolic earth: Discourse and our creation of the environment* (pp. 95–122). Lexington: University of Kentucky Press.

Lancaster, J. (1991, May 16). Western industries fuel grass-roots drive for "wise use" of resources. *Washington Post,* p. A3.

Lange, J. I. (1993). The logic of competing information campaigns: Conflict over old growth and the spotted owl. *Communication Monographs, 60,* 239–257.

Markowitz, G., & Rosner, D. (2002). *Deceit and denial: The deadly politics of industrial pollution.* Berkeley: University of California Press.

Montague, P. (1998, December 9). Sustainable development–Part 5: Emissions trading. *Rachel's Environmental & Health News, 628.* Annapolis, MD: Environmental Research Foundation. Retrieved from www.rachel.org/bulletin/pdf/Rachels_Environment_Health_News_1208.pdf

National Consumer Coalition. (2004). *Proclamation of the NCC.* Retrieved November 15, 2004, from www.consumeralert.org/ncc/proclaim.htm

Oil slick spreads toward coast: FBI begins probe. (1989, April 2). *Los Angeles Times,* Sec. 1, p. 1.

Organization for Economic Cooperation and Development (OECD). (1996). *Environmental performance reviews: United States.* Paris: Author.

Ottman, J. A. (1993). *Green marketing: Challenges and opportunities for the new marketing age.* Lincolnwood, IL: NTC Business.

Ottman, J. A. (2003). *Hey, corporate America, it's time to think about products.* Retrieved October 14, 2004, from www.greenmarketing.com/articles/IB_Sept_03.html

Parenti, M. (1986). *Inventing reality: The politics of the mass media.* New York: St. Martin's Press.

Patagonia. (n.d.). *Louder than words.* [Pamphlet]. Ventura, CA: Author.

Pearsall, J. (Ed.) (1999). *Concise Oxford English dictionary* (10th ed.). Oxford, UK: Oxford University Press.

Peterson, N. M., Peterson, M. J., & Peterson, T. R. (in press). Conservation and the myth of consensus. *Conservation Biology.*

Peterson, T. R. (1997). *Sharing the earth: The rhetoric of sustainable development.* Columbia: University of South Carolina Press.

Polonsky, M. J. (1994, November). An introduction to green marketing. *Electronic Green Journal, 1*(2), retrieved May 28, 2005, from http://egj.lib.uidaho.edu/egj02/polon01.html

Porter, W. M. (1992). The environment of the oil company: A semiotic analysis of Chevron's "People Do" commercials. In E. L. Toth & R. L. Health (Eds.), *Rhetorical and critical approaches to public relations* (pp. 279–300). Hillsdale, NJ: Erlbaum.

Pring, G. W., & Canan, P. (1996). *SLAPPs: Getting sued for speaking out.* Philadelphia: Temple University Press.

PR Watch. (2004). *Global climate coalition.* Retrieved October 4, 2004, from www.prwatch.org/improp/gcc.html

Reich, M. R. (1991). *Toxic politics: Responding to chemical disasters.* Ithaca, NY: Cornell University Press.

Repetto, R. (1995). *Jobs, competitiveness, and environmental regulation. What are the real issues?* Washington, DC: World Resources Institute.

Schumann, D. W., Hathcote, J. M., & West, S. (1991). Corporate advertising in America: A review of published studies on use, measurement, and effectiveness. *Journal of Advertising, 20* (3), 35–56.

Shabecoff, P. (1989, March 31). Captain of tanker had been drinking, blood tests show. *New York Times,* pp. A1, A12.

Smith, A. (1910). *An inquiry into the nature and causes of the wealth of nations: Vol. 1.* London: J. M. Dent & Sons. (Original work published 1776.)

Smith, T. M. (1998). *The myth of green marketing: Tending our goats at the edge of apocalypse.* Toronto: University of Toronto Press.

Stauber, J., & Rampton, S. (1995). *Toxic sludge is good for you: Lies, damn lies and the public relations industry.* Monroe, ME: Common Courage Press.

Switzer, J. V. (1997). *Green backlash: The history and politics of environmental opposition in the U.S.* Boulder, CO: Lynne Rienner.

Taylor, J. G., & Scharlin, P. J. (2004). *Smart alliance: How a global corporation and environmental activists transformed a tarnished brand.* New Haven: Yale University Press.

Warrick, J. (2004, August 17). Appalachia is paying the price for White House rule change. *Washington Post,* pp. A1, 6–7.

Williams, B. A., & Matheny, A. R. (1995). *Democracy, dialogue, and environmental disputes.* New Haven: Yale University Press.

Williams, D. E., & Olaniran, B. A. (1994). Exxon's decision-making flaws: The hypervigilant response to the *Valdez* grounding. *Public Relations Review, 20,* 5–18.

World Business Council for Sustainable Development. (2004, December 19). *About the WBCSD.* Retrieved from www.wbcsd.ch/templates/TemplateWBCSD5/layout.asp?type=p&MenuId=NjA&doOpen=1&ClickMenu=LeftMenu

World Commission on Environment and Development. (1987). *Our common future.* Oxford, UK: Oxford University Press.

World Resources Institute. (2004). Will pollution trading schemes remain in vogue? Retrieved October 17, 2004, from http://jlash.wri.org/letters.cfm?ContentID=2417

Zoellick, R. B. (2002, February 6). *Statement of U.S. trade representative before the Committee on Finance of the U.S. Senate.* Washington, DC: Office of the U.S. Trade Representative.

NOTE

1. Environmental critics had charged that the manufacture of the polyfoam package resulted in the release of chlorofluorocarbons (CFCs), which affected the ozone layer, and took up more space in landfills.

Epilogue

Imagining a Different World

The world will not evolve past its current state of crisis by using the same thinking that created the situation.

—Albert Einstein, scientist

Glance at the sun.
See the moon and the stars.
Gaze at the beauty of earth's greenings.
Now, think.

—Hildegard von Bingen, poet
(both quoted in McDonough & Braungart, 2002)

In April 2001, I joined tens of thousands of people from the United States, Canada, and other nations in Quebec's old city, known for its cobblestone lanes and fortress walls. We were questioning a Free Trade Area of the Americas treaty being negotiated by officials from 34 nations of the Western Hemisphere. Protesting in the streets below the old citadel where the officials met, we worried that the treaty would threaten workers, environmental quality, human rights, and even civil society itself. We believed that the treaty would constrain the ability, particularly of third-world countries, to regulate working conditions and environmental protections. Challenging these officials, some of the activists unfurled a large banner that stated,

"Imagine a different world!" It would be a world that respected workers' rights and safety, that ensured families' access to unpolluted water, that offered health care and schools for their children—a world both ecologically and economically sustainable. It was an ambitious, even an audacious, vision. Yet, the banner's most stirring message was simply, "Imagine!"

William McDonough and Michael Braungart (2002) issued a similar call at the start of their inspiring book *Cradle to Cradle: Remaking the Way We Make Things*. Quoting Albert Einstein and the 12th-century poet Hildegard von Bingen (this chapter's opening quotes), they invited readers to *think*—to imagine new ways to confront the challenges facing us today. Their call has never been timelier. In some ways, the task of environmental communication in the years surrounding Earth Day 1970 was more straightforward than the task facing us today. The challenges then had "tangible, local, and immediate consequences for the public. Lake Erie was dying under the boats of fishermen, the Cuyahoga River could be seen to burn by Clevelanders . . . and children in Los Angeles could not go out and play hundreds of days of a year" (Pope, 2004, p. 7). In response, scientists, environmentalists, editorial writers, students, and others sounded an alarm and rallied individuals to protect not only the nation's rivers and air but also the places where people lived, attended school, and worked. State and federal officials responded with laws to clean up rivers, reduce air pollution, and regulate the disposal of toxic waste.

By contrast, the challenges that alarm scientists, environmentalists, and some government leaders today are intangible, delayed in their effects, and global in scale. As one environmental leader put it, "Global warming, habitat fragmentation, and the loading of global ecosystems with persistent but toxic and disruptive industrial chemicals are simply harder for an opportunistic, reactive primate species [us] to understand as threats" (Pope, 2004, p. 7). Gradual heating of the earth's climate, invisible chemicals, the disappearance of biological diversity, loss of tropical forests—the earth's "lungs"— require more from us than business as usual and more than environmental communication as usual. They require us not only to imagine a different world but to compose a compelling way of speaking to each other and to broader publics about our planet's possible futures.

In this book, I have surveyed many different forms of environmental communication: advocacy campaigns, news stories, risk reports from EPA officials, and the courageous testimony of the residents of "Cancer Alley," among others. Building on these, some environmental leaders are now calling for a language of aspiration—that is, an ethically compelling narrative, grounded in core values, to address these new global challenges (Werbach, 2004). Such a language would speak more urgently of our values and the vision we hold for the future, an urgent, convincing appeal that addresses both planetary warming and what some ecologists warn could be the "sixth great extinction," "an extinction of plant and animal species that matches the catastrophe of the dinosaurs 65 [million] years ago" (Radford, 2001, para. 1).

In ancient Greece, communication that addressed a community's values was called **epideictic rhetoric,** speech that celebrated the accomplishments and values of a community as well as the character of its citizens and leaders. Orators praised the achievements of Athenian athletes, warriors, and others, as well as the virtues of Athens and other city-states. But they also condemned shortcomings, criticizing leaders for failure in governance or the community itself for selfishness or lack of courage. Most importantly, epideictic orators encouraged citizens to step back from everyday routines and the press of business to reflect, recall the norms and behaviors that bound them together, and consider their actions within a longer arch of history. They asked, What mattered to them as a community? What was essential to their survival? Were they, as a people, behaving in ways that ensured their safety, honor, and prosperity? What did their future hold? Some Native American cultures had a related tradition. Before taking an important action, tribal leaders would deliberate and ask what the effects would be "unto the seventh generation," a reminder that their choices would have lasting consequences for many generations after their own.

Similarly, I suggest that you and I, as well as public officials, scientists, business leaders, and environmentalists, explore more urgently an epideictic rhetoric for today, and where one might be found. What would constitute a compelling, ethical narrative about our future, one that would mobilize public concern about the intangible and long-term consequences of our fossil fuel economy and our consumption of the earth's biological heritage and future? Are there stirrings of such rhetorics today? In what forums are they occurring, and what are they saying?

To begin, such a rhetoric would undoubtedly build upon credible and accurate assessments of threats to our global environment: the decline of fresh water sources, evidence of the melting of permafrost in northern Canada, rapid deforestation, new evidence of warming temperatures in the lower to middle troposphere as well as on the surface of the earth, and so forth. Public discussion, debate, and warnings would be based on the best science and understanding of the dangers before us. In fact, we see such assessments now, not only in the technical sphere of scientific reporting but also in public forums: books, TV shows, commercial and documentary films, websites, and community alerts. For example, PBS's (2001) documentary, *Earth on Edge,* looked at the early, sobering results of a four-year study of the deterioration of Earth's ecosystems called the Millennium Ecosystem Assessment. Books such as James Speth's (2004) *Red Sky at Morning: America and the Crisis of the Global Environment* describe the chilling decline of Earth's ability to sustain life. More recently, Commander Eileen Collins told reporters that she had seen "widespread environmental damage on Earth" as she looked at our planet from the orbiting space shuttle *Discovery* (Frank, 2005, para. 1).

But warnings of danger, dire as they may be, are not enough, for the simple reason that danger can paralyze as well as motivate. If we believe that nothing can be done, we are more likely to turn aside or divert ourselves with daily cares and work. Instead, what is needed is the ability to imagine a different future and the values and principles that can help us design pathways to it, the ability to envision other, possible ways of living and doing business. Many believe that this requires new cognitive maps, new ways of thinking. For example, business entrepreneur and environmentalist Paul Hawken thinks that the prevailing mental model of human behavior toward the environment—the assumption that the natural world of rivers, plants, animals, and air are there simply for our use or abuse— should be abandoned. This model, Hawken believes, "usurps language and meaning, nullifying vision, reason, and perception" (quoted in Lertzman, 2002, p. 193). Even doing "less bad"—more recycling, buying green—is not enough. Hawken argues that we need to change our mental models in order to locate where we might intervene in the systems of modern life to produce the greatest change: "Downstream is obviously the least effective" (p. 193); that is, clearing up after the damage has been done will not get us out of our current situation, nor will it prevent things from worsening.

Indeed, a trend is growing in some quarters to begin thinking in precisely this direction—new voices, ideas, and proposals for designing a more sustainable world. At recent meetings of the mayors of the world's major cities, in the work of innovative research centers such as Amory and Hunter Lovins's Rocky Mountain Institute (www.rmi.org), at community festivals for sustainable agriculture and workshops at the World Social Forum (2004) (www.wsfindia.org), and in publications of environmental, human rights, and new "sustainability" groups, these voices are beginning to alter the mental maps of our generation.

Let's take the case of global warming. Whereas many U.S. political leaders have been hesitant to deal with the growing evidence of climate change, some cities have started to act on their own. For example, Portland, Oregon, recently achieved "stunning reductions in carbon emissions," an important cause of the warming of Earth's atmosphere (Kristof, 2005, p. 11). By offering public transportation, building bikeways, reducing sprawl, and conserving energy, the city reduced its carbon emissions to below 1990 levels, the goal of the Kyoto Protocol (see Chapter 10). The steps actually brought Portland many benefits: "less tax money spent on energy, more convenient transportation, [and] a greener city" (p. 11). Indeed, local initiatives to address global warming may be growing. At the United Nation's 2005 World Environment Day conference, the mayors of Zurich, Istanbul, San Francisco, Melbourne, Seattle, and other cities around the world agreed to pursue 21 steps to make their cities greener. Among the steps is greater use of renewable energy, a move that will allow cities to meet 10% of their electrical needs from this source alone by the year 2012 (Norton, 2005). (For more information, see www.wed2005.org.)

Accompanying these initiatives is a robust, epideictic rhetoric that identifies certain values or principles that underlie the commitment to ecological sustainability and social justice. For example, The Natural Step (www.naturalstep.org), a nonprofit group working with businesses, governments, and communities, outlines four "principles of sustainability" that should guide our efforts to create "new ways to live and prosper while ensuring an equitable, healthy future for all people and the planet" (The Natural Step, n.d., para. 1). These principles are stated this way: "In a sustainable society, nature is NOT subject to systematically increasing

1. concentrations of substances extracted from earth's crust [e.g., oil and other forms of carbon]

2. concentrations of substances produced by society [e.g., toxic chemicals]

3. degradation by physical means [e.g., deforestation, pollution of air and rivers], and in that society

4. human needs are met worldwide" (para. 9).

Elsewhere, ecologists, advocates of sustainability, and others are speaking of similar values. Collectively, these principles are beginning to constitute a vocabulary of aspiration, or an epideictic discourse, one that is appropriate to the global challenges before us. Among the values put forth to guide new approaches are these basic principles:

1. Preservation of the earth's biodiversity

2. Ecological, social, and economic sustainability

3. Social and environmental justice

4. Use of the precautionary principle in human behavior ("the seventh generation")

5. A nonpolluting energy economy (e.g., use of renewal sources, energy efficiency, conservation, and other forms of "decarbonizing" the economy)

As these values appear more widely in the public sphere in news stories, films, Web blogs, and conversations, there is emerging a holistic vision of a nonexploitative, nonpolluting, environmentally just, sustainable society—a world that respects both the biological heritage of a living Earth and the aspiration of its peoples for social justice and humane, prosperous lives.

Nor is such a vision a fantasy. We are seeing actions that build upon these values today, from the return of local, sustainable farming to the prospects of a thin film that captures the sun's rays. In some cases, these are first, halting steps; in others, scientists and entrepreneurs are acting boldly to realize a different world. For example, on my campus the North Carolina Botanical Garden is building a **LEED** Platinum Conservation Garden and Visitor Education Center. Platinum is the highest rating of the LEED (Leadership in Energy and Environmental Design) system for energy-efficient buildings. The building itself "employs a geothermal-supported energy system, photovoltaics to generate electricity, day-lighting, and many other 'green' features. Cisterns will collect roof water that will be used to grow a diverse and colorful botanical garden based only on water that falls directly on the site" (NC Botanical Garden, 2004, para. 23). The director of the Botanical Garden, Dr. Peter White, explains that the entire project will be an educational exhibit:

> [W]e have pledged that construction materials will come from within a 500-mile radius—to reduce the generation of carbon dioxide through transportation and to support local economies—and we will use only wood from certified sustainable sources. We plan to develop recycling programs for construction waste and do everything we can to support pedestrian, bike, and public transportation access to our new Center. (para. 24)

Although LEED buildings and recycling can contribute to a sustainable society, obviously a wider, systemic approach is also needed. That is why many thoughtful scientists and environmentalists are urging the leaders of the United States and other nations to seriously rethink their energy policies. A move away from the widespread use of fossil fuels (such as oil, gas, and coal) to renewable sources of energy may be the single biggest step we can take to lessen the stress we place on the earth's ecosystems. And it is here that a discourse that celebrates the values of a nonexploitive and sustainable society can play a critical role. For example, The Natural Step founders have expressed their hope that its four principles of sustainability will provide not only "a practical set of design criteria used to direct social, environmental and economic actions," but will also "transform debate into constructive discussion" (para.10).

Such debates now are appearing in unlikely places in the public sphere. For example, the *Wall Street Journal* carried a story about a study conducted by the Rocky Mountain Institute, "Winning the Oil Endgame," which lays out a strategy for ending U.S. dependence on oil. The article explains, "The U.S. can drastically slash its oil consumption by shifting its auto fleet to vehicles built with carbon composites—materials that are lighter than steel and yet, Mr. Lovins [the institute's director] argues, even stronger in a crash" (Ball, 2005, para. 5). Such lighter-weight vehicles would achieve greatly enhanced miles-per-gallon gasoline consumption and thus energy savings. Since the study appeared, "It has been touted in places not known for out-of-the-box thinking: Wall Street and Capitol Hill" (para. 7).

Some go even further. In their book *Cradle to Cradle: Remaking the Way We Make Things,* McDonough and Braungart (2002) want us to reinvent the idea of the automobile. Instead of designing a car, they urge automakers to design a "nutrivehicle" (p. 179). They explain, "Instead of aiming to create cars with minimal or zero negative emissions, imagine cars designed to release positive emissions and generate other nutritious effects on the environment" (pp. 179; emphasis in original). But don't stop there. "Push the design assignment further: 'Design a new transportation infrastructure.' In other words, don't just reinvent the recipe, rethink the menu" (p. 179). As authors, McDonough and Braungart appear to take their own advice; their book *Cradle to Cradle* consumed no trees to create the pages and cover for the book; instead, the authors explain, these consist entirely of "plastic resins and inorganic fillers" (p. 5).

If nutrivehicles seem farfetched, other visionary ideas may be much closer. In a recent forum, Inventing Tomorrow, *Sierra* magazine reported that researchers now think it is possible to use quantum dots—particles that are only a few nanometers (billionths of a meter) in size—to capture the sun's energy that comes from the infrared spectrum (Slater, 2005, p. 39). This is significant because half of the sun's energy reaching the earth exists in this spectrum. Unfortunately, even the best solar cells now available, capture only 6% of this energy. According to University of Toronto professor of computer engineering Ted Sargent, it now may be possible to tap this source of solar energy. The secret is the use of quantum dots, which, stacked together, can capture a full spectrum of light, including the infrared. The implications of this are huge. The quantum particles "are so tiny that they can be dispersed in a solvent and then painted onto something else—a house, a car, even a sweater [and] . . . could be used to charge cell phones and laptops, solar building materials that could provide all the electricity needed in the home, and electric cars powered by a solar cell on the roof" (p. 39). The practical applications are years away, and public support will be necessary to ensure that researchers have the resources to continue. However, once developed for the market, the light, flexible cells could be easily produced and installed for less money than the cumbersome solar panels now available (Slater, 2005).

In the end, however, the prospects for such ideas will depend on more than the breakthrough discoveries in the lab or the inspiration of books such as *Cradle to Cradle*. No imagined future is possible without an informed and mobilized public that is willing to demand it and work to achieve it. As the Sierra Club's executive director Carl Pope (2004) put it, without such popular demand, "decision makers have not been forced to confront the need for fundamental changes in the way our society uses carbon (and other greenhouse gases)" (para. 3).

Educating the public and building popular demand for fundamental changes will require all of us to become involved—in public conversations, Web blogs, documentary filmmaking and reviewing, public hearings, public education campaigns, and other forums of the public sphere that I've described in this book. Yet, Paul Hawken says, "This is heartening because it means that farmers, teachers, mechanics, parents, architects, and people in every other vocation have a role to play" (Lertzman, 2002, pp. 191–192). That also includes you and me. What will be our role? The conversation about the future of our cities, about our forests, water, air, and wildlife, and about the life of our planet itself has started. The debate is under way. Will you join this already-in-progress conversation and help imagine a different world "unto the seventh generation"?

KEY TERMS

Epideictic rhetoric: In classical Greece, speech that celebrated the accomplishments and values of a community as well as the character of its citizens and leaders.

LEED: Leadership in Energy and Environmental Design, a system for rating energy-efficient buildings.

REFERENCES

Ball, J. (2005, July 25). Tilting at energy windmills. *The Wall Street Journal On-Line*. Retrieved August 19, 2005, from http://online.wsj.com/article/0,,SB112187456076990937,00.html

Frank, J. (2005, August 5). Shuttle commander sees wide environmental damage. *Environmental News Network*. Retrieved August 14, 2005, from www.enn.com/today.html?id=8443

Kristof, N. D. (2005, July 3). A livable shade of green. *New York Times, Weekend*, p. 11.

Lertzman, R. (2002). Down to business: Paul Hawken on reshaping the economy. In A. H. Badiner (Ed.), *Mindfulness in the marketplace: Compassionate responses to consumerism* (pp. 185–200). Berkeley, CA: Parallax Press.

McDonough, W., & Braungart, M. (2002). *Cradle to cradle: Remaking the way we make things*. New York: North Point Press.

The Natural Step. (n.d.). Understanding sustainability. Retrieved August 16, 2005, from www.naturalstep.org/learn/understand_sust.php

North Carolina Botanical Garden. (2004, August 28). *North Carolina Botanical Garden receives 2004 sustainability award*. Retrieved August 18, 2005, from www.ncbg.unc.edu/Media.htm

Norton, J. M. (2005, June 6). Mayors sign urban environmental accords. *Maui News* [Hawaii], p. A5.

PBS. (2001, June 19). *Bill Moyers Reports: Earth on edge*. Retrieved August 3, 2005, from www.pbs.org/earthonedge

Pope, C. (2004, December). *Carl Pope response to "the death of environmentalism": There is something different about global warming*. Retrieved July 7, 2005, from www.sierraclub.org/pressroom/messages/2004december_pope.asp

Radford, T. (2001, November 29). Scientist warns of sixth great extinction of wildlife. *The Guardian* [United Kingdom]. Retrieved August 26, 2005, from www.guardian.co.uk/uk_news/story/0,3604,608510,00.html

Rocky Mountain Institute. (n.d.). Available at www.rmi.org

Slater, D. (2005, July/August). Earth's innovators. *Sierra*, pp. 36–41, 71.

Speth, J. G. (2004). *Red sky at morning: America and the crisis of the global environment*. New Haven & London: Yale University Press.

Werbach, A. (2004, December 19). *Is environmentalism dead?* Speech presented to the Commonwealth Club of San Francisco. Retrieved August 4, 2005, from www.3nov.com

World Social Forum 2004. (n.d.). Available at www.wsfindia.org

Index

Yaffee, S. L., 133
Yellowstone National Park
    Ulysses S. Grant and, 79*n. 2*
    gray wolf in, 14–15, 17*fig.*
    visual rhetorical depiction of, 63
Yosemite National Park, 42, 43
Yosemite Valley
    indigenous inhabitants removal
        from, 63
    John Muir and, 42, 253
    visual rhetorical depiction of, 63

Zoellick, Robert, 372
Zuni Salt Lake, New Mexico
    coal mining environmental advocacy
        campaign, 243, 257, 265–274,
        272*fig.*
Zuni Salt Lake Coalition.
    See Environmental advocacy
    campaigns: Zuni Salt Lake, New
    Mexico case

About the Author

J. Robert Cox (Ph.D. and M.A., University of Pittsburgh; B.A., University of Richmond) is Professor of Communication Studies and the Ecology Curriculum at the University of North Carolina at Chapel Hill. His principal research and teaching foci are rhetorical theory, environmental communication, and critical study of the discourse of change agents and social movements. Considered one of the nation's leading scholars in environmental communication, he has been President of the Sierra Club twice (2000–2001 and 1994–1996) and has served on the Sierra Club's Board of Directors for 12 years. His published work includes critical studies of the rhetoric of civil rights, antiwar protest, labor, and the environmental movement. Cox has served as Associate Editor for the *Quarterly Journal of Speech* and advises environmental groups on strategy in their advocacy campaigns. In addition to his teaching activities, he is called upon regularly to participate in and comment on numerous national initiatives concerning the environment. While serving as Sierra Club President in 2000, he campaigned with former Vice President Al Gore in the U.S. presidential election.